IN THE WORLD

**FREDRIC
JAMESON**

editors

**ROBERTO
DAINOTTO**

GRAMSCI

in the world

DUKE UNIVERSITY PRESS

DURHAM
AND LONDON
2020

© 2020 DUKE UNIVERSITY PRESS
All rights reserved
Designed by Drew Sisk and Aimee C. Harrison
Typeset in Portrait Text by Westchester Publishing Services

Library of Congress Cataloging-in-Publication Data
Names: Dainotto, Roberto M. (Roberto Maria), [date] editor. | Jameson,
    Fredric, editor.
Title: Gramsci in the world / Roberto Dainotto and Fredric Jameson,
    editors.
Description: Durham : Duke University Press, 2020. | Includes
    bibliographical references and index.
Identifiers: LCCN 2019047953 (print)
LCCN 2019047954 (ebook)
ISBN 9781478007999 (hardcover)
ISBN 9781478008491 (paperback)
ISBN 9781478012146 (ebook)
Subjects: LCSH: Gramsci, Antonio, 1891–1937—Political and social
    views. | Marxian historiography. | Communism—Italy—History. |
    Philosophy, Marxist.
Classification: LCC HX288 .G698 2020 (print)
LCC HX288 (ebook)
DDC 335.4092—dc23
LC record available at https://lccn.loc.gov/2019047953
LC ebook record available at https://lccn.loc.gov/2019047954

Cover art: Thomas Hirschhorn, *Gramsci Monument*, 2013. Forest
Houses, Bronx, New York. Copyright Thomas Hirschhorn. Courtesy
of the artist and Gladstone Gallery, New York and Brussels. Photo by
Andrew Russeth.

To the memory of Joe Buttigieg
and Frank Rosengarten

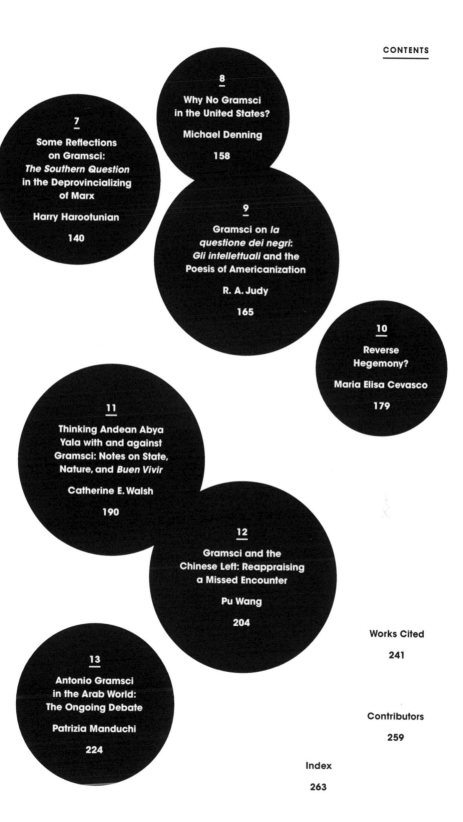

All translations from texts in any language other than English are the author's own, unless otherwise indicated. References to the Italian critical edition of Gramsci's *Prison Notebooks*—Antonio Gramsci, *Quaderni del carcere*, ed. Valentino Gerratana (Turin: Einaudi, 1975)—follow the internationally established standard of notebook number (Q), note number (§), and page reference. Whenever available, English translations from the *Prison Notebooks* are provided from one of the following editions:

Antonio Gramsci, *Selections from the Prison Notebooks*, ed. Quintin Hoare and
  Geoffrey Nowell Smith (London: Lawrence and Wishart, 1971).
Antonio Gramsci, *Selections from Cultural Writings*, ed. David Forgacs and
  Geoffrey Nowell-Smith (Cambridge, MA: Harvard University Press, 1985).
Antonio Gramsci, *Further Selections from the Prison Notebooks*, ed. Derek Booth-
  man (Minneapolis: University of Minnesota Press, 1995).
Antonio Gramsci, *Prison Notebooks*, 3 vols., trans. Joseph A. Buttigieg
  (New York: Columbia University Press, 1992–2007).

Gramsci in the World

FREDRIC JAMESON

Much of Gramsci's fascination lies in the ambiguities of his thought, attributable not least to the character of that "open work" that the *Prison Notebooks* shares with other monumental yet incomplete and indeed perhaps ultimately unrealizable projects such as Pascal's *Pensées*, Benjamin's *Arcades*, or even Lacan's *Seminars*. But this also marks out his unique status within the Marxist traditions: we can indeed argue about the meaning of *Capital*, or that of Lenin's works, or of Lukács or Althusser; but that there exists in them a central and fundamental purport, an intention and a strategy, would be far easier to sustain. With Gramsci, the conditions of composition in a Fascist prison camp can always be appealed to as a justification for reading unorthodox terms as translations and disguises of more familiar, more recognizable, and thus suspect ones (philosophy of praxis = Marxism), thereby revising unconventional ideas back into acceptable positions. But even this external situation need not preclude a more complex internal and subjective one, which might have led Gramsci himself, in the course of seeking alternative phrasing, into wholly new paths and new problems, if not, indeed, solutions altogether new and distinctive. Meanwhile, the uniquely central position of culture in these fragments, as the well-nigh indispensable mediator between the "objective historical situation" and some ultimately political class consciousness and class mobilization, certainly marks Gramsci off from the more purely economic or strategic Marxist thinkers named above and lends it increasing relevance in an information age in which even the existence of social classes has become the object of doubt and the topic of polemic. Meanwhile, the eruption of digitality and computerization at the very heart of this presumed informationalization of social life then adds yet another productive uncertainty to Gramsci's legacy, by way of the question of how to adapt (or once again, translate) his analyses into political diagnoses of the internet and its mentalities and possibilities of action.

My own position is that it is precisely the ambiguity of Gramsci's analyses of this or that issue or topic that makes for the richness of his work and its urgent relevance for us today. Whatever the arguments about Gramsci's own positions on these matters, and however necessary it is to pursue them, it is the dispute itself that produces problems and is thereby of enormous value in its own right. It renews old problems in new ways, it restructures the historical contexts against which political and cultural positions are to be read, and last but not least, it makes Gramsci's texts available for parts of the world in which, once unknown or only representative of a single, univocal position, they have now come to have their own history no less complex and interesting than that internal to the West and its various national components.

The disputes themselves are well known and quickly resumed. They turn at least in part on the relations between the party and the masses (or the militant workers), and even more hotly on the well-known distinction between wars of movement and wars of position, which would seem to make a place for a now-defunct social democracy alongside the now equally defunct yet once central Communist Party.[1] It is a debate whose stakes also turn on the legitimacy of armed struggle against parliamentary participation, and which does or does not allow for a "historic compromise," an alliance politics in which class-based institutions might function in cooperation with nonclass formations such as ethnic, gender, or racial movements. But this question then returns us to an alliance absolutely fundamental to Gramsci historically—namely, the alliance between workers and peasants, between north and south, and the resultant investigation of "subaltern groups" as well as the interrogation of the structure of "revolutions from above," of transformations without mass participation, and ultimately of fascism itself. Two related issues then impose themselves throughout Gramsci's work as well as any sustained interrogation of it: namely, the role of intellectuals and in particular the continuing value of the concept of the "organic intellectual"; and the nature of the state itself, whose promotion Gramsci's contemporary critics denounce on the basis of his party affiliation insofar as they have come to view the Communist Party as an essentially statist institution, whether in opposition in the West or in power in the East.

But what flows back over the question of Gramsci's conception of the role of the state in a now and future revolutionary politics is his far more decisive emphasis on the nation, or rather the national, in the revolutionary pedagogy of his own time. In a world in which the value of "national autonomy" has led to a proliferation of ever-smaller state units claiming sovereignty on the basis of secessionary ethnic nationalities, the association of a pedagogy of the national culture with that of a revolutionary proletarian consciousness may no longer seem as persuasive and exciting as it once was, thereby producing the problem of national and ethnic autonomy in new and more desperate forms. But it was precisely to produce such new problems, or to sharpen and intensify older ones by their juxtaposition with situations Gramsci himself would never have foreseen, that makes for the freshness and adaptability of his thinking, its suggestiveness as a resource for contemporary theory, if not as some model or party line that he never offered in the first place.

Gramsci in the world: such is the working program of the present collection, whose richness will perhaps surprise even the most fervent Gramscian. The philosopher of the "Southern Question," the theorist of "subaltern groups," the factory organizer of the north of Italy, who always carries Sardinia and Sicily, Naples, and the world of the peasants and great landlords in his mind, turns out to be perfectly at home everywhere in the world today, from India to the Andes, from China and Brazil to the Caribbean and the American South and its pan-African emanations. Gramsci proves relevant there where the peasant still exists as well as where he has become extinct, from the old Third World to the postmodern West.

These big concepts—war of position versus war of maneuver, subalterns, revolution from above, the "organic intellectual," the southern question, even the strategic debate with Bordiga—these then inform left political thinking around the world and are still very much the object of discussion, contestation, and revision by international scholars, as the present collection demonstrates. What is less often prone to pass through the filters of abstraction, interposed between national situations and languages with their individual traditions, are Gramsci's extraordinary fine-grained analyses of cultural dynamics and the way in which the institutions as well as the texts of both literary and mass-cultural production play their subtle and complex roles in what are essentially local political and social dynamics. Not only does Gramsci here set an example of a conception of "cultural studies" that spans the whole range from the most ambitious philosophical treatises to the *fait divers* of the newspapers or the serialization of novels and the popular consumption of entertainment; he conceives of their individual autonomies as the participation in a never-ending stream of distinct political and historical situations, which are not to be separated from the contradictions of the larger society or nation or region as a whole.

He thereby sets an example for intellectuals, not only of an unequaled and incomparable intelligence and flair, but of a view of social life and historical dynamics that transcends sterile distinctions between base and superstructure and damaging specializations in which economics is dealt with by specialists in one department and ideological productions in another, with ignorance, contempt, and indifference reigning on both sides, even among Marxists. This was not Marx's own practice (nor Lenin's either), but only Gramsci has given us a vibrant and fully realized picture of the work and sensibilities of a genuine left intellectual and the responses and analyses demanded by an ever-more complex postcontemporary "current situation."

NOTE

1   Perry Anderson's newly reissued *Antimonies of Antonio Gramsci* (Verso, 2017) vividly describes the impact of this final opposition on the very editing and publication of Gramsci's text.

Introduction

ROBERTO DAINOTTO

Writing for a monographic issue of *Rinascita* devoted to Gramsci, Eric Hobsbawm once commented on the "250 Most-Cited Authors in the Arts and Humanities Citation Index, 1976–1983" with the now-famous words: "In this list, there is neither Vico nor Machiavelli, but there is Antonio Gramsci" (Hobsbawm 1987, p. 15). It was Hobsbawm again, a few decades later, who pointed out that Antonio Gramsci, still the most-cited Italian Marxist ever, and even "per-

> *"Importuning the texts."* In other words, when out of zealous attachment to a thesis, one makes texts say more than they really do. This error of philological method occurs also outside of philology proper, in studies and analyses of all aspects of life.
>
> —Antonio Gramsci, *Quaderni del carcere*, Q6§198

haps the most well-known and influential Italian thinker of the century," owed his bibliometric fortunes to a rather unfortunate event: "Among the most distinguished intellectuals of the twentieth century, perhaps no other left his own body of work upon his death in a less accessible form than Antonio Gramsci" (Hobsbawm 2010, p. 7).

Because of incarceration, censorship, bad health, and premature death, Gramsci was unable to bring to publishable order the over two thousand presumably preparatory notes he had written in jail. Instead, he left posterity an unwieldy mass of thirty-three notebooks filled with over two thousand annotations, fragments, aphorisms, reflections, allusions, translations, and bibliographic references that could be coaxed into saying, well beyond what they actually did say, a great number of things, in a number of worldly contexts, and for a number of goals.

Reformism and the United Front

The fate of the "not-yet-book" (Baratta 1993, p. 410) was sealed even before the public could know of its very existence. It was barely the end of World War II when the needs of reconstruction, the first signs of an imminent Cold War, and the military presence of the U.S. Army in Italy convinced some in the Italian Communist Party (PCI), advised in this by the Soviet Union itself,[1] that—in the West at least—the armed struggle for the cause of Communism had to be prudently suspended and postponed till better times. After all, communism in Italy was by 1944 a political force of barely a few thousand militants who had managed to survive executions and arrests by joining the Resistance or fleeing the country altogether (Vacca 1990, p. 9). During the twenty years of Mussolini's regime, their leaders had been persecuted, their headquarters shut, and their printing presses burned down. Even after the war, their situation was not that promising: the U.S. liberation army showed little intention of leaving such a strategic geolocation, smack in the middle of the Mediterranean, open to the influence of Moscow, and liberal democracies around the world were already at work to keep Italy under the orbit of a nascent Atlantic alliance. The communists' massive (and for many, deadly) participation in the anti-fascist struggle had certainly conferred on its members some sort of moral leadership in postwar Italy; but to gain a more concrete political one, the party needed to elaborate specific strategies for survival and growth in a largely hostile national and international environment.

The so-called Salerno turn, announced by Gramsci's longtime collaborator and now party leader Palmiro Togliatti on April 11, 1944, marked the beginning of the strategy for the formation of a "new party" that, surrendering all revolutionary ambitions, aimed now at becoming the institutional leader of a large coalition of national unity that would include all the anti-fascist forces in Italy, left to center. The PCI, in short, was to become a parliamentary force, even if this meant, for the specter that had once haunted Europe, its mutation into a reformist and social-democratic party of sorts. Togliatti's strategy, in fairness, had had some precedents. Way back in 1895, in the introduction to Marx's *The Class Struggles in France 1848–1850*, Friedrich Engels himself had proposed that after the defeat of the Paris Commune *manu militari*, proletarian tactics had better change from armed insurrection to parliamentarianism: "The irony of World history turns everything upside down. We, the 'revolutionists,' the 'overthrowers'—we are thriving far better on legal methods than on illegal methods and overthrow. The parties of Order, as they call themselves, are perishing under the legal conditions created by themselves" (Marx and Engels 1976, vol.

22, p. 525). Ironically indeed, it was not Engels whom Togliatti invoked to promote a turn that many in the party considered a reckless surrender (Mordenti 2011, pp. 112–115), but rather the *auctoritas* of Italy's own "hero and martyr" (Togliatti 2014, p. 1063), whose prison notebooks the same Togliatti was already considering to "use" before making them public (Daniele 2005, pp. 61–64). Speaking next to the ashes of Gramsci at the Cimitero Acattolico in Rome on April 27, 1945, Togliatti moved that it was the party's moral responsibility to realize Gramsci's own dream of "the unity of all democratic, antifascist, and progressive forces" (Togliatti 2014, p. 1045). Again, on April 29 at a second Gramscian commemoration at the Teatro San Carlo in Naples, Togliatti insisted that

> the central idea of Gramsci's political action was that of unity: unity of workers' parties in the struggle for the defense of democratic institutions and for the overthrow of fascism; unity of the workers' parties with the democratic forces that then began to organize themselves particularly in southern Italy; unity of the socialist working masses with the Catholic working masses of the cities and the countryside, unity of workers, unity of workers and peasants, unity of workers and intellectuals—for the creation of a great bloc of national forces, on the basis of which it could be possible to impede the further advance of fascism and save . . . our country. (Togliatti 2014, p. 1064)

Of course, when Gramsci had mentioned an anti-fascist unity in the early 1930s, while Mussolini was firmly in power, the historical conditions were radically different than after the war (Spriano 1977, p. 73); of course, Gramsci meant unity as a transitional phase before a future return to properly communist tactics and strategies (Liguori 2006, p. 129); of course, Togliatti's was a blatant "instrumentalization of [Gramsci's] thought for official purposes, as defence and illustration of the political line of the PCI" (Anderson 2016, p. 72); and of course, Togliatti's ex post reinterpretation of Gramsci as patron saint of the "Salerno turn" ended up creating more problems than solutions, both for the party and for any understanding of Gramsci's texts themselves (Canfora 2012, p. 169). Yet, while philologically arguable, Togliatti's use of Gramsci's "central idea" well beyond its intended scope might have had some bearing on the growth of the PCI as the largest communist party in the whole of Western Europe—even if this had meant establishing for years to come the modus operandi of a permanent methodological confusion between Gramsci's actual words and some particular interpretations of them (Luperini 1971, p. xxviii).

This modus operandi, and this very methodology, from early on became the editorial canon for the very first publications of Gramsci's *Prison Notebooks*.

Soon after Gramsci's death on April 17, 1937, the notebooks were moved to the Soviet embassy in Rome and from there to Moscow by Gramsci's friend Piero Sraffa, professor of economics at Cambridge University and future awardee of the Söderströmska Gold Medal by the Swedish Academy. Still exiled in Moscow, Palmiro Togliatti was already considering (according to a May 20, 1938, letter to Sraffa) "the possible publication, and in any case the study and utilization, of [Gramsci's] writings" (cited in Spriano, Ricchini, and Melograni 1988, pp. 165–166). His problem was that Tania Schucht, Gramsci's sister-in-law and confidant, was in no way willing, as she had written to Sraffa on May 12, to let Gramsci's works be published "in a distorted form, which means to say, with someone usurping the right to complete what Antonio never finished" (cited in Vacca 1990, p. 333). That the "someone" in question could have been Togliatti is a plausible hypothesis. The fact remains that it was none other than Togliatti whom the Comintern chose in 1940 to manage the literary estate of the deceased Gramsci.

Togliatti's editorial policy was established in a letter to Georgi Dimitrov in April 1941: "Gramsci's *Notebooks*, which I have already studied carefully almost in their entirety, contain materials that can be used only after careful processing [*elaborazione*]. Without this treatment, the material cannot be used, and indeed some parts, if used in the form they are currently in, may not be useful to the party. This is why I believe it is necessary for this material to remain in our archive and be processed there" (cited in Pons 2004, pp. 130–131). "Processed" and carefully "treated," Gramsci's notes were kept hidden from curious eyes until they were published by Einaudi in six "thematic editions," edited by Felice Platone and supervised by Togliatti himself, from 1948 to 1951.[2] It was nothing else than the *mise en livre* (Chartier 1997, p. 272) of what a book was not, the sequencing of "what Antonio never finished" into the seeming coherence of a completed book's "bookhood" (Couturier 1991, p. 52).

By rearranging notes scattered in different notebooks and jotted down by Gramsci at different times, in different contexts, and for different purposes, Togliatti seemed quite aware that, as in Kuleshov's experiment, one could produce "a totally different meaning through montage" (Kuleshov 1974, p. 192). That the first volume of the Platone-Togliatti thematic edition was *Il materialismo storico e la filosofia di Benedetto Croce* (Historical materialism and the philosophy of Benedetto Croce) was certainly not by chance: the national and international stature of Croce had made of his philosophy *the* philosophy of anti-fascism par excellence. To make things more urgent, with the fall of the regime, Croce had returned to the Italian political scene as leader of the Liberal Party, becoming minister without portfolio of the governments chaired by Pietro Badoglio (from April 24 to June 18,1944) and Ivanoe Bonomi (from

June 18 to December 22, 1944). In those months, he had elaborated a theory of fascism as a "parenthesis of History" (Croce 1963, vol. 1, p. 370)—"History" being, it goes without saying, the unstoppable history of liberalism. In such a context, Gramsci's "Points for an Essay on Croce" would become timely and useful: "Is it possible that Croce's approach has something to do with the present time? A new 'liberalism' under modern conditions—wouldn't that be, precisely, 'fascism'?" (Q8§236, pp. 1088-1089; trans. Gramsci 1992-2007, vol. 3, p. 378). Togliatti, writing for *Rinascita* in June 1947, could then but echo Gramsci's point that Croce's liberalism "is roughly the same as the one that was used in massive quantities by the so-called ideologues and the loose propagandists of fascism" (Togliatti 2014, p. 1081). Gramsci's *Notebooks*, in short, were to become "an *Anti-Croce* that in today's cultural climate could have the same significance that *Anti-Dühring* had for the pre-war generation"(Q10i§11, p. 1234; trans. Gramsci 1995a, p. 356); against Croce's interpretation of fascism as a "parenthesis" in the history of Italy, the Platone-Togliatti edition offered an alternative reading of fascism as a continuity in Italy's liberal history—a continuity that Croce's Liberal Party was still unwilling to question.

Gramsci's own anti-fascism, moreover, represented the possibility of attracting—"molecularly," as Gramsci would have said[3]—those anti-fascists who still gravitated around Croce, and to whom the new and "Gramscian" PCI of Togliatti could now offer a home (Liguori 1991, p. 676). In addition, by denying the Crocean autonomy of philosophy from "politico-economic" life, Gramsci's Anti-Croce had the indubitable advantage of assigning a clear and indispensable role to intellectuals in the reconstruction of the new Italy, at a time when the historical complicity of culture in the establishment of fascism, and the needs for "cultural reconstruction," were perhaps the most debated issues of all (Hewitt and Wasserman 1989, pp. 3-4).

Togliatti's philological manipulation of Gramsci's notes into an Anti-Croce, and into a parallel strategy for the post-fascist united front led by the PCI, paid some dividends: even self-professed "bourgeois" began to see in "the frail figure of Antonio Gramsci . . . a key to proceed further" (Bandinelli 1962, p. 242). As for the electoral dividends, however, the elections of 1948 were not kind to the Popular Democratic Front headed by the PCI. The electoral failure of the "Salerno turn" meant that the Gramsci of the United Front needed now to make room for a new, more "culturalist" Gramsci, announced by the release in 1949 of a second volume of the Platone-Togliatti—*Gli intellettuali e l'organizzazione della cultura* (Intellectuals and the organization of culture). The PCI was to reorganize and rebuild itself from the (cultural) ground up, and Gramsci, yet again, was to pave its way.

Gramsci, repeatedly recalling (and translating) Marx's "Preface to the *Critique of Political Economy*" in his notebooks, had insisted that "humans become conscious of their tasks on the ideological terrain of the superstructures" (Q4§15, p. 437; trans. Gramsci 1992-2007, vol. 2, p. 157). If so, then culture—"the superstructures"—had a much more central role to play in social and political life than the canonical interpretations of Marxism canonized by the Third International had understood. But what did this centrality of culture really mean? Any number of Gramsci's notes, including several from the already-published thematic edition on Benedetto Croce, would have made it abundantly clear that by this, Gramsci did not mean any autonomy of the cultural from the structural level, or even less, the primacy of the former over the latter. If vulgar materialism erred in presuming culture to be mechanistically determined by economy, any claim of culture's autonomy from economics was, for Gramsci, a fall into "the opposite error" (Q4§43, p. 469; trans. Gramsci 1992-2007, vol. 2, pp. 192-193). More likely, what Gramsci had to offer on the topic was the perhaps trivial observation that structure and superstructure coexist in a dialectical relation—and that, therefore, "one might perhaps prepare [a] funeral oration" for the whole question of what determines what, or of what is relevant and what is irrelevant for political action (Q11§12, p. 1395, trans. Gramsci 1971, p. 342; on this, see also Cospito 2011a, pp. 19-76).

As the PCI was to shift its strategy from parliamentary alliances to "a great cultural and philosophical, progressive battle"—as Togliatti put it in a preface to Voltaire in 1949 (Togliatti 2014, p. 2091)—the publication of a "book" by Gramsci on intellectuals and the organization of culture could not but force Gramsci into a debate that had been fundamentally extraneous to his elaborations: it was Gramsci, once more, who legitimated the strategy of the centrality of a cultural over any other kind of battle for the strategic plans of the PCI. In this alleged predilection for a cultural battlefront, was Gramsci then but a closet idealist who really thought that intellectuals and ideas can change the world by the sheer power of thinking? The first ever monographic study devoted to Gramsci—Nicola Matteucci's *Antonio Gramsci e la filosofia della prassi* (1951)—did not help to dispel the confusion. By insisting (correctly so) on Gramsci's "Leninism," Matteucci ran the risk of flattening such Leninism into an antideterministic reevaluation of subjectivity over the objectivity of the structural conditions (Matteucci 1951, pp. 156-159). To no avail was at this point the warning that Gramsci's critique of mechanistic interpretations of materialism did not intend to replace materialism with "Crocean or any other kind of idealism" (Aloisi 1950, p. 109). Kicked out the door, Croce was coming back in through the window. Gramsci, *qua* culturalist, was an idealist—and a Crocean one at that!

The global (mis-)fortunes of this culturalist Gramsci are undoubtedly tied to the name of Norberto Bobbio. On several occasions, Bobbio insisted on the idea that "Gramsci expounds a frankly idealistic interpretation of Marxism" (Bobbio 1968, p. xlii). It was in his paper "Gramsci and the Conception of Civil Society," delivered at the International Symposium of Gramscian Studies (Cagliari, April 23-27, 1967), that the idea of a Gramscian "autonomy" from Marxism began to acquire impetus. According to Bobbio, for Gramsci, history is determined not by the economic structure, but rather by the cultural—idealistic—superstructures. Civil society, the world of culture and ideas, is the true theater of history. Gramsci thus became for Bobbio, as Jacques Texier bemoaned, but the "theoretician of superstructures" (Texier 2014) where all historical changes happen: "In Marx this active and positive moment [in history] is a structural moment, while in Gramsci it is a superstructural one" (Bobbio 2014, p. 31).

It was with Bobbio, in short, that one of the most polysemic and misinterpreted concepts of Gramsci (Boothman 2008)—hegemony—was supposed "to lead to a profitable result only if we understand that the concept of hegemony . . . includes the moment of cultural leadership. And it is also necessary to recognise that by 'cultural leadership' Gramsci means the introduction of a 'reform,' in the strong meaning which this term has when it refers to a transformation of customs and culture" (Bobbio 2014, p. 39). No matter that Gramsci had insisted that civil society was always an integral part of the state apparatuses—its "'private' fabric" (Q1§47, p. 56; trans. Gramsci 1992-2007, vol. 1, p. 153), as it were; and no matter that the notebooks had made it explicit that (cultural) hegemony was always dialectically implicated with the force of state apparatuses, "in the sense, one might say, that state = political society + civil society, that is, hegemony protected by the armor of coercion" (Q6§88, pp. 763-764; trans. Gramsci 1992-2007, vol. 3, p. 75). By erasing altogether any armored and "'military' [*poliziesco*] aspect of hegemony" (Antonini 2016, pp. 181-84), Bobbio was fitting Gramsci into the "liberal absurdity" (Guha 1997a, p. 23)—Benedetto Croce's *in primis*—of an "ideal" and cultural moment autonomous both from the material one and from the coercive force of the state (Liguori 2006, p. 31). Moreover, in stressing the determining importance of the cultural moment over all others, Bobbio was transforming Gramsci into a theorist, not only of superstructures, but also of some sort of reformism that Gramsci might have called "war of position": if the superstructure is the determining locus for social change, the attainment of power can no longer consist in a frontal attack on the state (a "war of maneuver"), but will be the result of a long and gradual cultural warfare for the accumulation of hegemonic power (understood merely as cultural power) on the part of civil institutions. If the October Revolution, in sum, had marked the success of a war of maneuver in the East, then for "Western Marxism"—to use Maurice Merleau-Ponty's (unfortunate) moniker (Merleau-Ponty 1955, pp. 43–80)—it was a matter of engaging in a long, protracted war of position fought in the "formidable complex of trenches and fortifications" (Q3§49, p. 333; trans. Gramsci 1992–2007, vol. 1, p. 53) of civil society itself—"a great cultural and philosophical, progressive battle" indeed!

When Gramsci's *Notebooks* began circulating in the world, it was most often through the filter of Bobbio's interpretation. A new, culturalist, Crocean and idealist Gramsci had taken the place of the earlier Anti-Croce (Riechers 1970); it was the Gramsci of "discursive or hegemonic formations" (Laclau 2005, p. 111), and the trite question of structures and superstructures, which the *Notebooks* wanted to bury with a "funeral oration," could result only in unresolved antinomies (Anderson 1976). As Paolo Capuzzo and Sandro Mezzadra summarize:

> Norberto Bobbio, who emphasized the "super-structural" elements of Gramsci's concept of civil society . . . made this concept itself an important political battlefield. Bobbio's reading was rooted in the liberal reading of Gramsci that had its antecedents in Benedetto Croce and Piero Gobetti. But it resulted, on the one hand, in making Gramsci even more distant from the intellectual references of the diverse spectrum of the radical left, and, on the other, it attracted severe criticism from intellectuals tied to the Communist Party. One could even say that Bobbio's insistence on the cultural fabric of civil society anticipated some terms of later Gramscian revivals. (Capuzzo and Mezzadra 2012, p. 47)

In the Vast and Terrible World

The world is truly vast and terrible!
—Gramsci, Letter to Tania Schucht, March 12, 1927 (Gramsci 1994, p. 80)

To be sure, the Gramsci of the United Front and the culturalist one trapped in the local skirmishes of the Italian Left were certainly not the only ones circulating in the world. Gramsci did not circulate much in continental Europe until at least the mid-1970s, since his work, compromised by Togliatti's "treatments," was presumed to be nothing more than a betrayal of communism and remained largely untranslated and unpublished (Paris 1979; Soriano 1993; Wenzel 1995; Lussana 1997). Somewhat different was the reception of Gramsci in the Anglophone world, where he appeared, albeit often still informed by Togliatti's editions and manipulations, in several different guises: as the theoretician of the party—and by implication, of the Communist Party of Britain?—with the publication of Louis Marks's *The Modern Prince and Other Writings* (1957), gestated in the milieu of the Historians' Group of the British Communist Party; as the expression of the "open Marxism" of the New Left antagonistic to the party, in *The Open Marxism of Antonio Gramsci* (1957b) or in Quintin Hoare and Geoffrey Nowell-Smith's *Selections from the Prison Notebooks* (1971); and, last but not least, as the historian of that "sort of 'pre-historic' stage of social agitation" (Hobsbawm 1959, p. 10) that Gramsci had identified as typical of the subaltern groups "at the margins of history,"[4] and which, in the 1980s, would open new paths to the historiography of colonial India (Guha 1997b).

The Althusserian critique of Gramsci, notwithstanding its comparable understanding of ideology and state apparatuses as organic parts of the same social being (Moe 2011, p. 131), did not much improve Gramsci's standing with the European Left (Haug 1999, pp. 108–111). Inaugurating a split between Hegelian and Spinozean Marxism (Macherey 2011), Althusser's *Reading Capital* in 1965 pitted "the form of scientificity" of *Capital*, which cannot be "itself historicized" (Althusser et al. 2015, pp. 131–132), against the "absolute historicism" (Q15§61, p. 1826; trans. Gramsci 1971, p. 417) of Gramsci—which is so absolute, in fact, as to deny any epistemic break from the structures of immanence to Marx himself: "How could Marx have thought that superstructures are appearance and illusion? Even his theories are a superstructure" (Q4§15, pp. 436–437; trans. Gramsci 1992–2007, vol. 2, p. 157).

For the European new movements on the left, already wary of an image of Gramsci tailored by Togliatti, Althusser's refusal of a relativist conception of knowledge meant also a refusal of the PCI's realpolitik of "historicist" contingencies. If "Togliatti would present as the central theme of Gramsci's reflection his historicism, making it in turn the specific character of the PCI" (Santucci 2001, p. 85), it was then against the traditional communist parties that the new Western movements of the Left would declare "a break with the 'historicist' front" (Frosini 2014, p. 353) and with Gramsci altogether. As Roberto Finelli writes:

> The constitutive character of the new cultures of emancipation had to be the rejection of all the fundamental theoretical categories that had shaped 20th-century Marxism, such as those primarily of dialectics and totality,

historicism and historical materialism. . . . To this very end, the interpretation of Louis Althusser gave its fruits, by moving the basis of Marxism from Hegelian historicism to structuralism—that is, with a radical overturning, from a science of history to a science of language. Many of the intellectual members of the Left became Althusserian, and then, through that gap he had opened, became exposed to the whole French culture of desire, of difference and rhizomes, of the microphysics of power. (Finelli 2014, pp. 14–15)

Or, for those less inclined toward differences and rhizomes, the Italian workerist tradition offered forms of autonomy other than "the historicist reformism trademarked by Togliatti" (Gatto 2016, pp. 115–116), yet still, and despite the potential attraction that Notebook 22 on Americanism and Fordism could have represented for that tradition, under the sign of a "difficult" relationship with Antonio Gramsci (Tronti 1976, p. 71).

Rather than in Europe, it was in Europe's ex-colonies that a different Gramsci was being considered and acted on politically. Before the Gramsci "useful" for the analytics of *Orientalism* (Said 1979, p. 6) and the Gramsci of "the decolonizing struggles for national independence in developing, post-colonial societies" (Hall 1986, p. 16), it was most notably in South America that Gramsci started to appear—almost as early, in fact, as he did in Italy. Filtered by the racialized dimension of a colonial reality (Mariátegui 1971), Gramsci's "Southern Question"—"the Mezzogiorno was reduced to the status of a semi-colonial market" (Q19§26, p. 2038; trans. Gramsci 1971, p. 94)—presented a few parallelisms to the Latin American question. From jail, Gramsci had tried his best to follow Latin American events,[5] especially vis à vis a growing "hegemony of the United States" that he was quick to notice (Q2§16, p. 172; trans. Gramsci 1992–2007, vol. 1, p. 265). In 1953, Héctor Agosti returned the attention: writing the preface to the proceedings of a conference organized around Palmiro Togliatti's paper "El antifascismo de Antonio Gramsci," Agosti attempted an Argentinian variation on the theme of the Salerno turn. The Latin American proletariat, he argued, could not engage at the same time in fights against both the national bourgeoisie and international imperialism. Since the second of these constituted, in the years of the Cold War, a more immediate and present danger, an albeit temporary alliance of the proletariat with the "national bourgeoisie"—a United Front—was indispensable (see Massardo 1999, pp. 329–341).

Whether or not the strategy was yet one more Togliattian "importuning" of Gramsci's texts, what is certain is that Agosti put the *Notebooks* at the very center of Argentinian and Latin American militant and intellectual life. In

1958, José Aricó would begin the first translation ever of the *Notebooks* in any foreign language. What mattered for Aricó in the political contingency of the late 1950s, however, were not only the notes on the southern question, those on Latin America, and the several ones on colonialism, but also, and perhaps against Agosti's politics of the United Front, those on the Italian process of national construction.

What had Italy to offer, besides its still unresolved southern question, for the analysis of Latin American matters, in which the conflicts between the creole elites from the city and the indigenous peoples in the country-side plausibly echoed the Italian conflict between north and south? For one thing, Gramsci had compared the Italian nation-state, born in the 1860s, to its original model—the revolutionary French republic of 1789. The Italian copy, Gramsci famously wrote, had been the by-product of a "revolution without revolution [or, in Cuoco's words . . . a passive revolution]" (Q1§44, p. 41; trans. Gramsci 1992–2007, vol. 1, p. 137), in which the old royal order of the Savoys, all but vanquished, had triumphed by making a "nation" out of a territory until then shared among the papacy, the Bourbons, the Hapsburgs, and the Savoys themselves. In addition to the royal and semifeudal order of the Savoys, a semi-feudal economic and political apparatus had remained in Italy, unaltered by the epochal event of the French bourgeois revolution: a parasitical economy of rent, a nonproductive oligarchy, and a ruling class utterly detached from the nation-people. When this order was threatened in the "red years," 1919 to 1920, the passive revolution turned dictatorial—into Mussolini's fascism, that is.

Gramsci's analysis of Italy's national formation as a passive revolution seemed to acquire new meanings after the *Revolución Libertadora* of 1955: the Latin American national bourgeoisie, which Agosti had tried to enlist in a struggle against imperialism in 1953, now seemed to be precisely in the business of passive revolutions. It had created nations in Latin America—but only to thrive in a parasitical extractive economy of rent. Its nonproductive oligarchy began to display its most dictatorial tendencies, resisting anything that would attempt to bridge the gap between "the people" and the (creole) liberal elite (Agosti 1959).

Between 1975 and 1981, as the continent was being ravaged by the alliance of national bourgeoisies and the imperial politics of regime change—and while in Europe the name of a reformist and social-democratic Gramsci was "more widely and insistently invoked than any other for the new perspectives of 'Eurocommunism'" (Anderson 1976, p. 6)—it was in Latin America that the idea of a revolutionary, communist Gramsci was being revived. From the *Pasado y Presente* group in their Mexican exile to the *Teología de la liberación* (1971) of Gustavo Gutiérrez; from Carlos Nelson Coutinho's *Gramsci* (1981) to *La revolución pasiva: Una lectura de los Cuadernos de la cárcel* (1985) by Dora Kanoussi and Javier Mena—Gramsci *Notebooks*, in Aricó's translation or in the popular *Antologia* (1974) of Manuel Sacristán, became in Latin America "a model for arming" (Aricó 2005, p. 129) the resistance to fascism:

> [Gramsci's fascism], *mutatis mutandis* . . . has nothing that distinguishes it in an essential way from what we know in the region. [His] thought comes to maturity in a prison, even though Gramsci's prison is not too different from those that still exist on our continent today. Perhaps, *cum grano salis*, Gramsci is, to a certain extent, Latin American: because he was born in that extension of internal colonialism that is Sardinia, which we can easily imagine as a gateway to Latin America; because he was born in a place that, even without capitalist relations of production, suffered the removal of any surplus through mechanisms of concentration and centralization of capital; or simply because, in the final analysis, this Gramsci that we can read so familiarly, this Gramsci that . . . inspires us in such a natural way, only reminds us that revolutionary politics is made, today as yesterday, with human beings who struggle; with human beings who, even in these times of "globalization," feel "on the skin" the brutality and the absurdity of the society that currently exists. (Massardo 1999, pp. 345–346)

Central in this Latin American recuperation of a revolutionary Gramsci was Juan Carlos Portantiero, who wrote a series of essays later collected as *Los usos de Gramsci*. As he put it, a "use of Gramsci" was politically much needed in South America, as "stimulus for a concrete revolutionary task. Our proposal implies seeing his work as the ideological and political testimony of a long-range strategy for the conquest of power" (Portantiero 1981, p. 68). The problem, as it had always been, was how to use a text long "misused" (Diggins 1988), to the point that the bizarre idea had gelled of a "Gramsci precursor of Togliattism" (Portantiero 1981, p. 67):

> "Voluntarist," "Leninist," announcer of the "broad popular front," Gramsci has always been suspected of "social democracy" in Latin America. The marginal, almost surreptitious way in which the "liberal wing" of the Argentine communist party introduced him into Spanish has undoubtedly contributed to this. It was a depoliticized Gramsci, with a biography that did not go through the internal tensions of the communist movement of his time; an exemplary antifascist Gramsci (to the point of sacrificing his life), but also "cultured," broad in his horizons to judge literature and aesthetics; a contender, at his same stature, of Benedetto Croce. Locked in

those narrow limits, never used for a political development of their premises, seen as the work of a "humanist," Gramsci's notebooks left little trace in the Latin American political debate. (Portantiero 1981, pp. 69–70)

In this, Portantiero dramatizes the very point of the book that is being introduced here.

The point of this collection of essays, *Gramsci in the World*, is not to chronicle the many epiphanies of Gramsci in different historical and geographical contexts—an impossible feat, after all, for a most-cited author in the arts and humanities, as Hobsbawm would have it. At any rate, excellent books on the afterlife of Gramsci in Italy (Liguori 2012) and in the world (Filippini 2016) have been published already. Moreover, the Fondazione Istituto Gramsci in Rome, coordinated by Maria Luisa Righi, regularly updates a Gramsci bibliography, along with an entire book series, Studi gramsciani nel mondo (Gramscian studies in the world), regularly published by il Mulino of Bologna. The goal of this collection, rather, is to present some "differential pragmatics" (Holub 1992, p. 21) through which Gramsci is approached—to be accepted or rejected, it matters little here—by eminent scholars working on different geographies and from different disciplinary perspectives, always keeping in mind that any presence of Gramsci in the world, any political use of Gramsci, is in fact mediated by the ways his words have been "introduced."

In other words, our assumption is that the philological question, as Togliatti well knew, *is* a political question: the order of the notes, their appearance on the page, the layout, the commentary, the annotation and paratexts, the prefaces, postfaces, and critical assessments are all a matter of political choices, as they are the different contexts in which these texts are to acquire meaning. This much, Togliatti knew; so did Valentino Gerratana, who in 1975, as if to respond to Portantiero's invitation, finally archived Togliatti's thematic edition—the party's Gramsci—and replaced it with a new, philological one, introduced by this citation from Gramsci: "*Questions of Method*. If one wishes to study the birth of a conception of the world which has never been systematically expounded by its founder . . . some preliminary detailed philological work has to be done. This has to be carried out with the most scrupulous accuracy scientific honesty and intellectual loyalty and without any preconceptions, apriorism or *parti pris*" (Q16§2, p. 1840; trans. Gramsci 1971, p. 382). A clarification of what Gramsci actually said, without "importuning the texts," is certainly an unfinished endeavor (Francioni 1984)—especially so in the Anglophone world, where a critical edition based on Gerratana's is, as of this writing, yet incomplete. Absent such an attempt, Gramsci, "locked in . . . narrow limits," as Portantiero put it, can certainly be dismissed as "dead" (Day 2005), or as a name associated with some theory that "no longer holds" (Beasley-Murray 2010, p. xi). With that, however, the risk is that what Portantiero saw as a "stimulus for a concrete revolutionary task" will thus be buried or discarded prematurely.

At the same time, as Gramsci's reflections are effectively and concretely deployed from South America (Coben 2005), through India (Zene 2013), to Africa (De Smet 2016), it might be preferable simply to ward off the ongoing appropriations and manipulations of Gramsci to transform his thought into some kind of liberal anti-Marxism (on this, see Davidson 2008). Our goal, in short, is not to affirm some kind of "purist" version of Gramsci, or to pit "philology" against "political use," but rather to return to his texts in order to bring into relief possibilities and limits of Gramscian thought in cultural politics and political culture within a global context.

The structure of *Gramsci in the World* follows such an objective. While the first four contributions go after the textual traces of four of the central concepts of Gramsci—the "modern Prince," the "theory of history," the "organic intellectual," and the "vitalism" of what Gramsci called "philosophy of praxis"—the last ten look at historical limits and possibilities for a use of Gramsci in (following their order) Italy, India, Japan, the United States, Black America, Brazil, the Andes, China, and the Middle East. Because Gramsci, Hobsbawm's "most well-known and influential Italian thinker of the century," is an "Italian thinker" only to the extent that one could not think of nation-states if not from an international (a word we prefer to as "global") perspective, "the concrete life of states," as Gramsci wrote, "is fundamentally international life" (Q1§138, p. 126; trans. Gramsci 1992–2007, vol. 1, p. 223).

NOTES

1   "Characteristically cautious, and in any case still maintaining working relations with the Western powers, Stalin thus initially pursued a tactic already familiar from the Popular Front years of the 1930s and from Communist practice during the Spanish Civil War: favouring the formation of 'Front' governments, coalitions of Communists, Socialists and other 'anti-Fascist' parties, which would exclude and punish the old regime and its supporters but would be cautious and 'democratic,' reformist rather than revolutionary" (Judt 2005, pp. 130–131).

2   *Il materialismo storico e la filosofia di Benedetto Croce* (1948); *Gli intellettuali e l'organizzazione della cultura* (1949); *Il Risorgimento* (1949); *Note sul Machiavelli, sulla*

politica, e sullo Stato moderno (1949); *Letteratura e vita nazionale* (1950); *Passato e presente* (1951).

3 "Molecular" attraction is the capacity of a political force to attract individuals (rather than masses) from competing parties toward its own political program. It is one of the mechanics of the sort of "transformism" that operated in Italy in the years of national unification, when the democratic Action Party hemorrhaged members to the royalist Moderate Party: "From 1860 to 1900, 'molecular' transformism; that is, individual political figures molded by the democratic opposition parties were incorporated one by one into the conservative-moderate 'political class'" (Q8§36, p. 962; trans. Gramsci 1992–2007, p. 257).

4 "Ai margini della storia (Storia dei gruppi sociali subalterni)" [At the margins of history: History of subaltern social groups] is the title of Notebook 25, which begins with an analysis of Lazzaretti's millenarist movement, also analyzed in *Primitive Rebels* (Hobsbawm 1959, pp. 57–73).

5 See, for instance, Q2§135, Q3§5, Q3§124, Q4§49, Q6§190.

1

Toward the
Modern Prince

PETER D. THOMAS

In early 1932,[1] over two years after beginning his carceral writing project, Gramsci wrote what were to become some of the most famous lines of the *Prison Notebooks*. "The modern Prince," he argued, "the myth-Prince, cannot be a real person, a concrete individual. It can be only an organism, a social component in which a collective will—one that is recognized and, to some extent, has asserted itself in action—has already begun to take shape. Historical development has already produced this organism, and it is the political party—the modern formation that contains the partial collective wills with a propensity to become universal and total" (Q8§21, pp. 951–953; trans. Gramsci 1992–2007, vol. 3, p. 247). It is on the basis of citations such as this that it has often been argued, from the early years of the reception of the *Prison Notebooks* until today, that the metaphor of the modern Prince should be understood as merely a "codeword" for a Communist Party, conceived either in continuation with a supposedly "Leninist," democratic-centralist conception of the party or as a "Western Marxist" alternative to it, depending on particular interpreters' predispositions.[2] The modern Prince has also sometimes been "deciphered" in a more expansive sense, as a generic description of the modern political party as such, representing a distinctive synthesis of the normative, motivational, and executive sources of the democratic ethos that underwrites modern mass societies.[3] More recently, and increasingly, it has been suggested that the modern Prince should be understood as representing a paradigmatic embodiment of the novel conception of political power that was consolidated in the early twentieth century: namely, the notion of political power as self-foundational, rather than legitimated by (moral or institutional) tradition or (subjective) consent.[4] It is a notion that runs from Weber's theorization of charismatic domination to its formalization in the Schmittian notion of the self-referential decision, right down to the various reproposals of an "autonomy of the political," which continue strongly to mark our "post-'68" theoretical conjuncture. The *Prison Notebooks*, according to this reading, are properly understood as a hitherto neglected moment in this paradigmatically modernist tradition. In the juvescence of the year arrives not Eliot's Christ the Tiger, but Gramsci's modern Prince: a proletarian kairos.[5]

It was obvious to the first readers of the *Prison Notebooks* that they do indeed contain extensive notes on the political party as a necessary protagonist of modern political life—unsurprisingly, given that they were written by the leader of a revolutionary political party. At an advanced stage of his imprisonment, in February 1933, Gramsci develops a novel tripartite theory of the "fundamental elements" required for the existence of a political party: "a mass element"; a "principal cohesive element"; and "an intermediate element, which articulates the first [mass] element with the second [cohesive element] and maintains contact between them, not only physically but also morally and intellectually" (Q14§70, p. 1733; trans. Gramsci 1971, p. 153).[6] He distinguishes between democratic and bureaucratic centralism, in a polemic against not only the anti-Stalinist Bordiga's "programmism" (Q13§36, pp. 1632–1635; trans. Gramsci 1971, pp. 186–190) but also the consolidating Stalinist orthodoxy itself.[7] He also argues for the specific nature of the type of leadership that should characterize a communist party, progressively reducing the distance between leaders and the led, in a relation of "dialectical pedagogy." It is in this dynamic that we find the distinctiveness of Gramsci's theory of hegemony translated into the terms of a theory of political organization.

Such is the richness of Gramsci's reflections on political organization that there is a great temptation to synthesize Gramsci's disparate notes on the art and science of politics scattered throughout the *Prison Notebooks* into a systematic presentation of the figure of the modern Prince as a mythological euphemism for the political party. This is precisely what was done by Gramsci's first editors, Felice Platone and Palmiro Togliatti, when they assembled a special volume out of some of Gramsci's writings on Machiavelli and politics in the postwar thematic edition of the *Prison Notebooks*. Published in 1949, as the fourth volume of Gramsci's notes to be made available to a wider audience, it was titled *Note sul Machiavelli, sulla politica e sullo stato moderno* (*Notes on Machiavelli, Politics and the Modern State*). The editorial preface established an explicit equation between "the problems of the political party of the working class and of the foundation of a socialist state'" and "the problems of the 'modern Prince.'"[8] Furthermore, the particular emphasis of the organization of the notes in this volume, and perhaps even more so, its exclusions, established the coordinates for Gramsci's early reception in Italy and abroad, and in the Anglophone world in particular. *The Modern Prince and Other Essays* was the title of the first presentation of Gramsci's carceral writings in English in 1957 (see Gramsci 1957a). Platone and Togliatti's selection and organization of these notes also formed the basis for the section dedicated to "the modern Prince" in *Selections from the Prison Notebooks* (Gramsci 1971, pp. 123-204), the publication more responsible than any other for the international diffusion of Gramsci's thought. Thus was created the image of a "political" Gramsci, related to but distinct from the many other images of Gramsci that have been derived by different disciplinary interests: a Crocean "philosophical" Gramsci and a Desanctian "literary" Gramsci, alongside "cultural," "sociological," and "historical" Gramscis. These early thematic presentations also played a role in establishing an image of that which Gramsci was not. The exclusion from *Selections from the Prison Notebooks* of many of Gramsci's reflections on economic history and theory, for instance, gave credence to the hoary old myth that Gramsci, supposedly a "Western Marxist," had never concerned himself with this central dimension of the Marxist *Weltanschauung*—an unsubstantiated claim that was writ so large and wide that a growing body of scholarship has only recently been able to partially dislodge it from the image of the Gramsci that "everybody already knows."[9]

Gramsci himself seems to propose a project of systematization of his political reflections, in Q4§10 (written in the summer of 1930), when he projects a "book that extracts from Marxist thought an orderly system of actual politics along the lines of the *Prince*. The topic would be the political part, in its relations with the classes and with the state—not the party as a sociological category but the party that wants to establish the State" (Q4§10, p. 432; trans. Gramsci 1992-2007, vol. 2, p. 152).[10] Immediately, however, he specifies that the distinctive feature of Machiavelli's *The Prince*, which any modern rewriting of it must also embody, is its dramatic form. "In short, the point is not to compile an organic repertory of political maxims but rather to write a book that is, in a certain sense, 'dramatic,' an unfolding historical drama in which political maxims are presented as a specific necessity and not as scientific principles" (Q4§10, p. 432; trans. Gramsci 1992-2007, vol. 3, p. 152). Gramsci, the theorist of a "living philology" (*filologia vivente*), later argues in the spring of 1932 that "the basic thing about *The Prince* is that it is not a systematic treatment, but a 'live' work, in which political ideology and political science are fused in the dramatic form of a 'myth'" (Q13§1, p. 1555; trans. Gramsci 1971, p. 125).[11] Or again, in the same note, he argues that Machiavelli did not have recourse to "pedantic classifications of principles and criteria for a method of action." Instead, he represented this process in terms of the "qualities, characteristics, duties and requirements of a concrete individual" (Q13 §1, p. 1555; trans. Gramsci 1971, p. 125).

Again and again, the former theater critic and professional revolutionary Gramsci emphasizes the dramatic form of the playwright and politician Machiavelli's *Darstellungsweise*.[12] This in fact seems to Gramsci to have been Machiavelli's fundamental innovation, of much greater importance than the identification of an "autonomy" or "specificity" of the "political."[13] Machiavelli, according to Gramsci, literally created the modern "political manifesto" in the dramatic epilogue of *The Prince*, where the Prince, that "concrete phantasy," merges with the people whose dispersed and pulverized lives it has organized into a collective will (Q13§1, p. 1556). Machiavelli's "new Prince," for Gramsci, is not the prophet who has created his own people, according to a decisionistic reading of Machiavelli's thought already current in Fascist readings in the 1920s, and which has only grown stronger as the "long twentieth century" continues to entrap the early decades of the twenty-first in its shadows.[14] Rather, according to Gramsci's reading, the "new Prince," that delicately embodied balance between *virtù* and *fortuna*, suddenly emerges as an "impassioned, urgent cry" in the wilderness of an enslaved Italy at the end of Machiavelli's dramatic enactment of the "qualities, characteristics, duties and needs" of the people itself, a "fever" or even "fanaticism of action" that retrospectively reorganizes the entire preceding narrative sequences (Q13§1, p. 1555 [May 1932]).

I would like to suggest that Gramsci's Machiavellian metaphor of the modern Prince needs to be understood in a similar sense; namely, not as a systematic presentation, codified in a series of directly political maxims or organizational proposals, which were or even could be contained within one special notebook, and which could then be presented as a merely mythical—in an illusory sense—euphemism for the concept of the political party. Gramsci's was no "Menardian" project of quixotically attempting to "repeat" his predecessor's Renaissance text in the changed conditions of the full-blown crisis of political modernity represented by Fascism, with the Communist Party replacing the figure of the Prince. He was not trying, that is, to rewrite *The Prince* according to the interpretation of a still influential tradition that has read it as a cumulative linear narrative exhibiting various component parts of an already known figure or given political form (a reading which, in effect, reduces Machiavelli's "little book" to the *specula principum* genre that preceded it). Rather, Gramsci's project consisted in the more difficult (and perhaps even more profoundly "Menardian") project of "re-inhabiting" the dynamic that he comes to see as the distinctive feature that makes of Machiavelli's text a qualitatively new genre of political writing. For this reason, Gramsci's "modern Prince" should be understood not simply as one distinctive "figure" alongside the many others that emerge within the overall architecture of the *Prison Notebooks* (the "organic intellectual," the factory worker subject to Fordist discipline, the "subaltern," and so forth). Rather, the transition from Machiavelli's "new Prince" to Gramsci's "modern Prince" gives rise to a dramatic development that unfolds throughout "the discourse itself" of Gramsci's carceral writings, alchemically transforming the dispersed and pulverized lives of the subaltern social groups into a new principle and practice of social organization (Q13§1, p. 1561 [May 1932]).

The distance between Gramsci's two suggested projects—between the initial plan for a treatise of an ordered doctrine and the later aim to present the unfolding development of a "dramatic" or "living" book, an "historical drama in action"—marks a fundamental change of terrain of the research project of the *Prison Notebooks*. From a bestiary of the bizarre forms of bourgeois domination in the early notebooks, the later notebooks become a laboratory for experimentation in a new principle and practice of sociopolitical organization. The modern Prince is the name of this new research project, within which Gramsci expands his conception of the political party to signify not simply an institution, form, or subject, but a process of totalizing moral and intellectual reform, or a "politics of another type."[15] In order to understand the terms and the significance of this development, we need consider the role of Machiavelli in Gramsci's overall project, both before prison and during the different phases of development of the *Prison Notebooks*.

Gramsci's interest in Machiavelli was notable already during his university years, if not before; as Leonardo Paggi notes, Machiavelli was not a "metaphor or exterior analogy, but a concrete point of reference for [Gramsci's] entire political evolution" (Paggi 1969, p. 834). While a functionary of the Comintern traveling through Berlin in 1922, he encountered his old professor, Umberto Cosmo, who urged Gramsci to write the book on Machiavelli that Cosmo had long awaited from him.[16] Mussolini was soon to write his own "Prelude" to *The Prince* (published in the Fascist journal *Gerarchia* in April 1924), as would Lev Kamenev a decade later, an editorial "indiscretion" used against him by the Stalinist prosecution at his show trial in 1936.[17] Before his imprisonment

Gramsci took a keen interest in the debate then underway in Italy and the rest of Europe between liberal and Fascist interpretations of the Florentine Secretary, including contributions from Chabod, Mosca, Ercole, Russo, Croce, and Gobetti, among many others.[18] He even undertook a detailed survey of studies that emerged in the wake of the commemorations of the fourth century of Machiavelli's death in June 1927, as he recalled later that year in a letter to his sister-in-law Tania.[19]

It is therefore notable that Machiavelli is absent from Gramsci's first work plans, in his letters and at the beginning of his first notebook.[20] When Machiavelli does appear in the first notebooks, in 1929 to 1930, it is largely as a historically important figure in early European modernity and Italian state formation.[21] This focus has led some readers—Lefort and Althusser among them—to view Gramsci's interpretation of Machiavelli as effectively a continuation of Risorgimento myths of national unification.[22] Gramsci's reason for this emphasis, however, was that the debate on Machiavelli in the 1920s had made him well aware of the risks of a decontextualized reading of a Machiavelli as a "man for all seasons": it was precisely to domesticate him to contemporary ideological currents, rather than comprehending the explosive and "untimely" historical force of his thought by considering it in the specific conjuncture of the crisis of the Renaissance. It is on this basis of this "contextualization" that Gramsci then steadily but surely begins to emphasize Machiavelli's importance for a genealogy of the philosophy of praxis, in Notebooks 4 and 5, in 1930 to 1931.[23] By the time of the beginning of Notebook 8 in 1932, however, these still largely historical interests begin to solidify into a distinctively new theoretical research project.

Gramsci provides this new research project with its name in the title of the decisive note Q8§21, written in January to February 1932: "the modern Prince." "Under this title can be gathered all those ideas of political science that can be assembled into a work of political science that would be conceived and organized along the lines of Machiavelli's *Prince*" (Q8§21, p. 951 [January–February 1932]). He specifies that

> Machiavelli's *Prince* could be studied as a historical exemplification of the Sorelian "myth," that is, of a political ideology that is not presented as a cold utopia or as a rationalized doctrine but as a concrete "fantasy" that works on a dispersed and pulverized people to arouse and organize its collective will. The utopian character of the *Prince* comes from the fact that the "prince" did not really exist historically and did not appear before the Italian people in a historically immediate form, but was himself a "doctrinaire abstraction," the symbol of the generic leader, of the "ideal

condottiere." One can study how Sorel never advanced from the conception of "myth" to the conception of the political party. (Q8§21, p. 951 (January–February 1932)

Here, in early 1932, the notion of the "political party" appears to Gramsci as the immediate way of making *The Prince* comprehensible to a contemporary audience and, thus, the figure by means of which it could be "updated" or "actualized" in the vocabulary of the present.

This situation is fundamentally transformed only a few months later, in May 1932. In the intervening period, Gramsci has begun his so-called special notebooks, in which he transcribes, sometimes with significant amendments, notes previously written in earlier notebooks, alongside new notes.[24] He has also read and deeply meditated on Luigi Russo's *Prolegomeni a Machiavelli*, a remarkable instance of (post-)Crocean aesthetics that is both a not-so-coded critique of the fascist appropriation of Machiavelli and a profound renovation of the tradition of interpretation deriving from the Risorgimento.[25] Notebook 13, titled "Notes on the Politics of Machiavelli," opens with a note that substantially reproduces the argument outlined only a few months earlier in Q8§21, though the continuous text of the earlier note is here broken up into ten ordered paragraphs.[26] He repeats that "the utopian character of the *Prince* comes from the fact that the 'prince' did not really exist historically and did not appear before the Italian people in a historically immediate form, but was a pure doctrinaire abstraction, the symbol of the leader, of the ideal *condottiere*." In a significant development of the interpretation proposed only a few months earlier, Gramsci now attempts to specify the precise sense in which *The Prince* constitutes a "a concrete 'fantasy.'" In February 1932, Gramsci had defined *The Prince* as a "living" book because it "anthropomorphically" represented the process of formation of a "collective will" in a "concrete personality," arousing passion through the use of "artistic fantasy" (Q8§21, p. 951 [January–February 1932]). In May 1932, however, he emphasizes not merely the representative power of *The Prince*'s content, but also the power of retrospective reconfiguration that lies in its distinctively dramatic form:

> With a dramatic movement of great effect, the mythical, passional elements contained in the entire little volume are drawn together and become alive in the conclusion, in the invocation of a prince who "really exists." Throughout the book, Machiavelli discusses what the Prince must be like if he is to lead a people to found a new State; the argument is developed with rigorous logic, with scientific detachment. In the conclusion, Machiavelli merges with the people, becomes the people, but not with

some "generic" people, but the people whom he, Machiavelli, has convinced by the preceding argument, the people of whom he becomes and feels himself to be the conscience and expression, with whom he feels himself to be one [*si sente medesimezza*].[27] It now seems that the entire "logical" argument is nothing other than a self-reflection of the people, an inner reasoning worked out in the popular conscience, which has its conclusion in an impassioned, urgent cry. Passion, reasoning on itself, becomes once again "affect," fever, fanaticism of action. This is why the epilogue of *The Prince* is not something extrinsic, "tacked on" from the outside, rhetorical, but has to be understood as a necessary element of the work—indeed, the element that projects its true light [*riverbera la sua vera luce*] onto the entire work and makes it a kind of "political manifesto."[28]

Herein lies Gramsci's "little discovery" in Machiavellian scholarship, comparable to his earlier modest contribution to the study of Dante.[29] In his reading of canto 10 of the *Inferno*, Gramsci had polemicized against Croce's distinction between "poetry" and "structure" in his aesthetics in general and his criticism of Dante in particular ("structure" for Croce being understood not simply in an "architectural" or formal sense, but above all as the "nonpoetical," or those formal and doctrinal features in the *Divine Comedy* that were not products of pure, unified intuition).[30] While many critics of canto 10 had focused on the proud Farinata, Gramsci argued that instead it is Cavalcante who constitutes the true emotional focus of the canto, despite his all too brief appearance. When Cavalcante, interpreting Dante's use of the past tense to mean that his son Guido is dead, falls back into his tomb, the reader sees "*in action [in atto]* the torment of the damned" (Q4§78, p. 517 [May 1930]). Dante does not, Gramsci argues, "represent this drama," but "suggests it to the reader; he gives to the reader the elements for reconstructing the drama, and these elements are given by the structure." "The structural passage," Gramsci therefore concludes, "is not only structure, . . . it is also poetry, it is a necessary element of the drama that has occurred" (Q4§78, p. 518 [May 1930]).

It is not simply the dramatic "suggestion" of action, however, that constitutes the dialectic between poetry and structure in this canto. As Gramsci argues nine months later, the true meaning of Cavalcante's torment for the "poetry" of the canto is not immediately apparent with the description of his action, but only becomes fully clear to the reader retrospectively. It is only when the "magnanimous" Farinata explains to Dante the nature of the torments of the heretics in this circle, condemned to see the past and future but deprived of knowledge of the present, that the full extent of Cavalcante's anguish can be understood. "Farinata is reduced to the structural function of 'explicator' in order to make the reader penetrate into the drama of Cavalcante" (Q4§83, p. 524 [March 1931]). Farinata's discourse in an important sense reorganizes the proceeding narrative sequence; it is only after he has spoken that the reader can "relive" the drama "in action" of Cavalcante's slump into silence and grasp its significance, as the unrepresentable anguish of the moment in which Cavalcante confronts concretely the death of his son, in a present that he cannot know.

Just as Gramsci focuses on the dramatic dimensions of Dante's "indirect representation" of Cavalcante, so too does his reading of *The Prince* emphasize the significance of its "structure" for comprehending its "poetry." The conclusion of *The Prince* in fact "incompletes" it, because the entire book needs to be read again in the light of what those stirring final pages reveal. Viewed in this light, *The Prince* constitutes a "concrete fantasy" because Machiavelli's impassioned advocacy in the epilogue that the time has come for Italy's redemption from enslavement, oppression, and scattering reacts back on the entire preceding argument (Machiavelli 1961, pp. 80–81). The figures of the Prince that Machiavelli has explored through the text—Moses, Cyrus, Romulus, Theseus, Savonarola, and Valentino—are revealed as having been nothing more than the self-reflection of the "people" on its own limitations and, crucially, potential capacities.

This is an almost Brechtian inversion of the Aristotelian sequence in which *anagnórisis* should give rise to *peripéteia*. For Aristotle, it is knowledge that constitutes the condition of possibility for the reversal of the tragic narrative, a reconfiguration of both its temporal flow and internal organization that relies on a recognition of that which was not known before.[31] In Gramsci's suggestive reading of Machiavelli, it is instead a type of "reversal" (of perspective) that enables a startling "re-cognition," in the etymological sense of the word, a rethinking of all that was previously taken for granted in its apparent obviousness. In the epilogue, the "people" crafted by Machiavelli's discourse suddenly realizes that all along throughout the book it has only been observing itself—that is, the dramatic staging of its own "qualities, characteristics, duties and needs." Only now, at the moment of the narrative's almost *auto-détournement*, can the people recognize, or rethink, those capacities as its own. The epilogue of *The Prince* thus makes the book a kind of "political manifesto" because it performs—in a strong, "structural" sense—the very process of liberation that the protagonist of the book has been called on to enact. The people thereby discover that *The Prince* has been no mere "utopian" or "doctrinaire" description, but the "concrete fantasy" of its own really existing capacities, above all, for self-liberation and self-governance.

From May 1932 onward, the "modern Prince" becomes something more than a rubric under which are gathered Gramsci's reflections on politics, and the reference to Machiavelli something more than one topic among others.[32] Above all, the notion of an impassioned urgent cry retrospectively reorganizing a preceding "logical" sequence, of reason become "affect," will be fundamental to both the content and the form of Gramsci's later notes. Though Notebook 13 (which Gramsci will continue to write until late 1933 or early 1934) has often seemed to readers as the notebook in which Gramsci comes closest to his plan for a systematic book on political theory, this attempted reorganization of his research into something resembling monographic form soon spills over into a significant number of entirely new notes on Machiavellian themes in other notebooks (particularly in Q14, 15, 17).[33] From his marginal status in earlier notebooks, Machiavelli becomes an ether that pervades almost all of Gramsci's notes, arguably present even in his absence, in the most unexpected ways. In early spring 1932, for instance, he asks Sraffa, with whom he discussed economic theory regularly throughout his imprisonment, questions about Machiavelli's possible relationship to the physiocrats.[34]

Why this turn to Machiavelli, which exceeds its own boundaries? At least two reasons seem to me to be decisive: the first, a reason that is "internal" to the development of the text of the *Prison Notebooks* project and in fact decisive for its "refoundation" in this period; the second, a reason that is equally "internal" to the dynamic of Gramsci's text, even if its presence can only be reconstructed "symptomatically," as the questions to which Gramsci was attempting to respond: namely, the political context that overdetermines his project in all of its stages.

On the one hand, Gramsci's deepening engagement with Machiavelli occurs at a moment when his previous organizing perspectives have reached an impasse. In the early phases of the *Prison Notebooks*, when Machiavelli played a predominantly historical rather than theoretical or "dramatic" role, Gramsci had primarily been concerned to analyze the emergence of the forms of bourgeois political modernity.[35] This line of research is encapsulated in his distinctive notion of "passive revolution," a concept that has sometimes been thought to undergo a process of "over-extension" or "stretching" in three distinct stages, but that is instead defined by the consistent development of a fundamental orientation.[36] It is this development that gives rise to the "modern Prince" and its afterlives, as passive revolution's theoretical and practical antidote.[37]

In his first notebook, in early 1930, Gramsci appears to appropriate the concept of passive revolution from Vincenzo Cuoco, the historian of the failed Neapolitan revolution of 1799, "extending" it beyond the Napoleonic period in order to provide an analysis of the distinctive features of the Italian Risorgimento (Q1§44, pp. 40–54 [February–March 1930]).[38] In actual fact, however, this "first" appearance of passive revolution in the *Prison Notebooks* is a later, retrospective addition to a note that begins by discussing the Risorgimento, but which tellingly concludes with reflections on the "Jacobin" slogan of the "Revolution in Permanence" (Q1§44, p. 41 [February–March 1930]).[39] In this context, the term *passive revolution* was used to describe what Gramsci later calls in early 1932 the "historical fact of the absence of popular initiative in the development of Italian history" (Q8§25, p. 957). In particular, this note highlights the role of the moderates in the Risorgimento in actively preventing popular initiative in an organized political form, or the lack of the radical-popular "Jacobin moment" that had distinguished the experience of the French Revolution. The formation of the modern Italian nation-state, according to Gramsci, had been a "revolution without revolution," or in other terms, a "royal conquest" and not popular movement (Q1§44, pp. 40, 53).[40] It was a transformation of political forms undertaken by elites, sometimes garbed in the rhetoric of previous revolutionary movements, but without the extensive involvement of subaltern classes that had led to the placing in question of social and economic relations in earlier transformations.

The chronologically first note in which Gramsci refers to passive revolution, however, had already used it in a more expansive sense. From the outset, Gramsci questions whether the concept could have a more general significance as a criterion of historical research into periods and countries that lacked an impetus to modernity "from below" (Q4§57, p. 504). In this sense, passive revolution describes the not-so-exceptional *Sonderweg* to modernity taken by other European nation-states with experiences similar to those of Italy, characterized by transformations of the political forms of a society that nevertheless failed to place in question their economic contents.[41]

In early 1932, Gramsci draws the logical conclusion of this line of research: if passive revolution is not confined to the peculiarities of an "Italian *misère*" but instead might have a more general, pan-European if not even global validity, it can be used to analyze an entire historical period: roughly, a period he characterized as the "Restoration" that followed on the exhaustion of the energies that had driven the French Revolution, beginning in 1848 with the defeat or "deformation" of the Europe-wide revolts but intensifying after the defeat of the Paris Commune and extending to his own day in the form of Fascism (Q8§236, p. 1089 [April 1932]; Q10i§9, p. 1228 [April–May 1932]). In this version, passive revolution comes to signify the pacifying and incorporating nature assumed by bourgeois hegemony in the epoch of imperialism, particularly in its Western European heartlands but with determinant effects on the colonial periphery. "Revolution" here still refers to the capacity of the ruling class still to deliver substantive and real historical gains, producing real social transformations that could be comprehended, formally at least, as progressive; "passive" continues to denote the attempt to produce these transformations without the extensive involvement of subaltern classes as classes, but by means of molecular absorption of their leading elements into an already established hegemonic project (a process Gramsci describes as "transformism").[42] However, "passive revolution," as a concept, seems to have taken on a more general significance, as a "logic" of a particular type of "modernization from above." In a certain sense, the concept has almost become synonymous with modernity as such, which is now viewed as a melancholy tale in which the mass of humanity is reduced to mere spectators of a history that "progresses" without its active involvement; a rationalized and bureaucratic Weberian "iron cage."

Readings that stop here fail to note that it is precisely at this moment in early 1932 when Gramsci is reflecting most critically on passive revolution's presuppositions that he turns most intensely to the Florentine Secretary. Revealingly, it is in a series of notes titled "Machiavelli" that Gramsci explores the "limits" of passive revolution, as an historical process and theoretical concept.[43] Thus, in early 1933 he argues that the concept of passive revolution needs to be "cleansed of every trace of fatalism" (Q15§17, pp. 1774–1775 [April–May 1933]).[44] The concept of passive revolution can have a concrete political sense only if it "assumes, or postulates as necessary, a vigorous antithesis," which autonomously and intransigently sets all its forces in motion (Q15§62, p. 1827 (June–July 1933). The exploration of the conditions of development of such a "vigorous antithesis" constitutes the focus of Gramsci's work for the remainder of the *Prison Notebooks*, throughout the "special notebooks" in particular. It is the "modern Prince" that provides Gramsci with a name for this new project, constituting a synthetic form into which his previous research flows and within which it is transformed.

The second reason for the irruption of this "Machiavellian moment" in the *Prison Notebooks* coincides with the deepening of Gramsci's call for a *costituente* of anti-fascist forces. This had already been a significant theme in his thought since at least the famous carceral colloquia with other party inmates in 1930; it remains, in my view, the central political perspective throughout and beyond the *Prison Notebooks*.[45] This was not simply a reproposal of the republican assembly of 1924 to 1926, or a suggestion of the possibility of a post-fascist constituent assembly, as later occurred in the preconstitutional phase of what became the postwar Italian republic. Both gatherings of anti-fascist forces, in the 1920s and 1940s alike, remained focused on a strategy of transition, in a periodizing conception of stages of political development. In the 1930s, Gramsci was instead arguing for a deeper process of unification of the anti-fascist forces already within and against the Fascist regime, as an immediate form of political struggle. Fundamentally, in the face of the sectarian madness and suicidal politics of the "Third Period," it was an argument for the reactivation of the politics of the United Front, founded on an active memory of the decisive debates in which Gramsci had participated in Moscow 1922 to 1923, the attempted implementation of which had marked his own tenure as head of the Italian Communist Party. "More enslaved than the Hebrews, more oppressed than the Persians, more widely scattered than the Athenians; leaderless, lawless, crushed, despoiled, torn, overrun" (Machiavelli 1961, p. 81): only a thoroughgoing constituent process, and not the arrival of any singular redeemer, could liberate the Italians from the barbaric fascist yoke. What could be the forms of such a constituent process of political struggle?

My thesis is that the development of the figure of the modern Prince was a decisive phase in Gramsci's ongoing attempt to respond to this challenge. But this response is elaborated not only in the figure of the modern Prince, or only in the notes that explicitly cite Machiavelli, or even in those notes in which Gramsci discusses the political party or political organization. Rather, as a "living book," it is developed, above all, in a practical form, in the twenty-one notebooks (that is, the majority of the twenty-nine *Prison Notebooks*) that Gramsci compiles from spring 1932 onward, including notebooks of both revised texts and new departures.[46] In particular, the "special notebooks" (Q10–13, 16, 18–29) are the true "creation of a concrete phantasy," or the modern Prince "in action." The form of these later notebooks has often struck even the most attentive readers as a sign of Gramsci's exhaustion, elevating his normal "incompletions" into a structuring principle, as he attempts to shore up fragments against his impending ruin.[47] It may indeed seem that they often do not speak of political organization at all, but rather cultural, socioeconomic or historical themes (e.g., culture, Risorgimento, Catholic Action, popular literature, literary criticism, journalism, folklore, Fordism, the development of subaltern social groups, and historical linguistics). However, far from an effective retreat from politics, these special notebooks need to be understood as a process of working out the possible forms of a proletarian hegemonic apparatus— that is, of undertaking the rigorous reconnaissance of the intertwining of the national and international terrains that Lenin had recommended to Western Communists in the debates over the United Front in the early 1920s.

Taken together, I would argue that these special notebooks constitute an articulated "cognitive map" of the many different "terrains" of the modern

Prince. Out of the diversity and richness of the themes in these notebooks, Gramsci slowly composes a sketch, or many sketches, of the forms of popular practice and organization that could constitute a politics "of another type," an antidote to the politics of passive revolution. Just as the conclusion of Machiavelli's text retrospectively redefines the logical sequence that has led to it, so too does the architecture of the *Prison Notebooks* fold back on itself, as lines of research in earlier notebooks are "restaged" in the context of this refoundation of Gramsci's politico-theoretical project. No mere "transcriptions," Gramsci's reorganization of his previous notes in the special notebooks fundamentally transforms their meaning, even and especially when, in a Menardian fashion, their outward form may seem simply "to repeat," with greater or smaller revisions, the content of earlier notes. The light of the modern Prince "reverberates" back throughout them, as the forms of abject subalternity induced by the bourgeois hegemonic project that were analyzed in the earlier notebooks are redimensioned into the passionate forms of potential self-liberation of the subaltern social groups. This is the dramatic discourse that concludes—or rather, "incompletes"—the *Prison Notebooks*: "an impassioned, urgent cry."

This phase of research "beyond the modern Prince" also gives rise to an expansion of Gramsci's concept of the political party, or more precisely, of the type of party-form that would be capable of defeating the passive revolution of bourgeois political modernity itself.[48] The movement from the formulation of the figure of the modern Prince in 1932 to the theorization of the political party in 1933, that is, represents not simply the continuation of Gramsci's advocacy prior to his imprisonment of "democratic centralism" as an organic link between leaders and followers. Rather, it signals an extension of Gramsci's conception of the political party from being a singular instance of "political condensation" amid a multiplicity of social interests to becoming a totalizing political, social, and ultimately ethical process that progressively annuls any hierarchical distinctions between them. The party-form that Gramsci attempts to delineate in these later notes thus cannot be limited to any of the usual figures by means of which modern political thought has traditionally conceived such a "composite political body," whether as institution, form, or subject. The modern Prince elaborated into a new party-form does not represent a type of nascent state-organization confined within the paradigm of constitutionalism, according to which the party functions as a discrete "political" instance of an organization besieged on all sides by the anarchy of the associative "social." Rather, "the modern Prince, as it develops, revolutionizes the whole system of intellectual and moral relations . . . the Prince takes the place of the divinity or the categorical imperative, and becomes the basis for a modern laicism and for a complete laicization of all aspects of life and of all customary relationships" (Q13§1, p. 1561 [May 1932]).

No mere institutional apparatus, the modern Prince is conceived much more as a totalizing process of civilization reformation and refoundation. Similarly, this party "of another type" is not a given and fixed form, but must constitutively overflow itself in order to be itself. This is to say that the modern Prince, conceived as party-form, represents only the tip of the iceberg of a broader process of collective political activation of the popular classes throughout the society, in all of its instances of deliberation and decision making. For this reason, the proposal of the modern Prince cannot be reduced to the type of political formalism that has dominated political modernity, from Hobbes to Rousseau and beyond, in which a given political form arrives "from outside" to dominate its (now) subaltern social content. Rather, the modern Prince is a form that is merely the expression of a content that constitutively exceeds it.

Finally, the consolidation of this process in a party of a new type cannot be understood as the formation of a "political subject," as a unified center of intention and initiative, or as an "instrument" or "machine," in Weber's famous phrase from *Politics as Vocation* (Weber 1994, p. 339). The modern Prince, that is, is not a Communist Leviathan, or a Marxist *volonté générale*. It does not signify an organizational form in which unity and stability dominate over difference and conflict, which can then only appear as un- or pre-political, as the social chaos that (state) politics must organize, in a transcendental fashion. Rather, it is an always provisional condensation of relations of force that continuously modify the composition of the modern Prince as a collective organism, and as an expansive revolutionary process in movement. No unity closed within itself, the modern Prince is conceived instead as a "terrain," or even as a "categorical imperative," the "organiser [of a popular-national collective will] and simultaneously active and effective expression" of the same (Q13§1, p. 1561 [May 1932]).

The modern Prince as political party, the collective organism that merges with its "people," thus represents the simultaneous point of departure and summation of that process of the "unprecedented concentration of hegemony" that Gramsci had indicated as the goal of an offensive war of position against the logic of the passive revolution (Q6§138, p. 802 [August 1931]). It represents an active organizational synthesis of various levels and instances of the struggles of subaltern social groups, in Gramsci's creative formulation, or the working classes in the broadest sense (that is, all those excluded from the current distribution of power—the sufferers of injustice and the oppressed, in Lenin's terminology, or what Rancière calls the "part of no part"). The modern Prince was a proposal for the political recomposition of the decimated Italian subaltern classes within and by means of what we could call, using the vocabulary of the early Italian workerist tradition, a "compositional party," which integrates the moments of the mass party, as representative or expressive of the class, with the vanguardist emphasis on leadership, as the necessary result of and potential solution to the unevenness and contradictoriness of the capitalist stratification of the subaltern social groups. As an institutional embodiment of the specificity of hegemony or leadership of what Badaloni has felicitously called a method of "political work" (see Badaloni 1972), the modern Prince represents a constituent process of the politically overdetermined recomposition of the subaltern classes. In this sense, the modern Prince should be properly situated in the tradition of the "Revolution in Permanence" invoked by Marx after 1848 as the foundation for an autonomous working-class politics, and continually recalled by Gramsci as the original formulation of hegemonic politics; or, to use the terms of Marx's later reflections on the Paris Commune, the expansive political form finally found in which to work out the emancipation of the subaltern social groups.[49]

The development of the figure of the modern Prince and its organizational consequences was Gramsci's final recommendations for the forging of a new United Front in his own time. I would suggest that this Machiavellian metaphor, and particularly the method of its dramatic development, could be redeployed today as a prefigurative vocabulary for understanding and contributing to the movements of our own time. For after reason's slumber in the long epoch of the neoliberal counterrevolution, the uprisings and revolutions of the early twenty-first century have posed a fundamentally Gramscian question: how is it possible to coordinate the diversity of interests of our pluralized, pulverized, and dispersed peoples into a hegemonic force capable not simply of resisting the current order, but of initiating a constituent process, a construction of a socialist order in the forms of struggle already underway? One of the ways of searching for an answer to this theoretical and practical challenge may be to experiment with Gramsci's Machiavellian technique of the dramatic enactment of the "qualities, characteristics, duties and needs" of the peoples themselves, in which Prince and peoples, form and content, knowing and feeling, merge into no form or decision except that of their own collective totalizing expansion.

NOTES

1   Dates of individual notes are given according to the chronology established in Francioni 1984, and the revisions contained in the appendix to Cospito 2011b.

2 Althusser, for instance, argued that "Gramsci's Modern Prince is the Marxist-Leninist proletarian party" (Althusser 1999, p. 13), effectively reproducing verbatim the "allegorical" interpretation of the notion of the modern Prince (and of the *Prison Notebooks* in general) employed by Gramsci's early, postwar readers, who were sometimes bewildered by the seemingly novel, if not even heretical, vocabulary he employed in his carceral writings. On the (often much exaggerated) "codeword thesis" in general, and the obstacle it poses for full engagement with the dynamic quality of the *Prison Notebooks* as a distinctive type of (non-)"text," see Haug 2000 and Thomas 2009b.

3 For a recent argument in this direction, see White and Ypi 2010.

4 On the distinctiveness of this notion of political power and the novelty it represents in relation to the tradition of modern political theory, see Mommsen 1989, particularly pp. 20–21, and Farris 2013, particularly pp. 197–201.

5 For representative readings that tend in this direction, see Kalyvas 2000 and Morfino 2009, particularly p. 99. Negri's belated encounter with Gramsci has been entirely dominated by this figure: "What a formidable image [of the modern Prince] this is—the image of a new subjectivity that is born from the nothingness of any determination or preconstituted destiny and that preconstitutes collectively each determination and destiny!" (Negri 1999, p. 320).

6 On Gramsci's theory of the party, see Sassoon 1987, pp. 150–179.

7 The development of Gramsci's concept of centralism has been extensively studied by Cospito 2011a, pp. 228–244.

8 See the editorial preface to Gramsci 1949, p. xix.

9 Anderson 1976 in particular was influential in diffusing this judgement. For a salutary corrective, see Krätke 2011. *Further Selections from the Prison Notebooks*, edited by Derek Boothman, made a wider range of economic notes available to Anglophone readers.

10 Gramsci repeats the identification of "the notion of the 'Prince,'" "translated into modern political language," with the political party in Q5§127, pp. 661–662 (November–December 1930), where he also specifies that the foundation of such a "new type of state" occurs not on the basis of "constitutional Right, of a traditional type," but according to a "system of principles that affirm the end of the State as its own end, its own vanishing, that is, the re-absorption of political society in civil society."

11 For the corresponding A text, see Q8§21, p. 951 (January–February 1932). On the notion of "living philology," also developed in relation to the political party as collectivity, see Q7§6, p. 857 (November 1930); Q11§25, p. 1430 (July–August 1932).

12 The importance of the theater in Gramsci's cultural and political formation is often forgotten. Yet in a decisive period of his development, he acted as the theater critic for *Avanti!* from 1915 to 1920, and later claimed to have discovered and helped to popularize Pirandello, whose theater in fact constituted the third topic in Gramsci's first plan of work in prison, in a letter to Tania of March 19, 1927

(Gramsci 1996, p. 56). Gramsci's theater criticism from this period has been collected in a substantial volume of 489 pages (Gramsci 2010). Similarly, the importance of drama in Machiavelli's work in general, and not only in his innovative comedies, is all too often overlooked—remarkably, even in such a clearly dramatic work as *The Prince*.

13 For Gramsci's critical consideration of the Crocean thesis of an autonomy of the political in Machiavelli, cf. Q4§4, p. 425 (May 1930); Q4§8, pp. 430-431 (May 1930).

14 While articulated in an older moral vocabulary linked to notions of a "civil religion," "moral renewal," and even a surprisingly Crocean conception of a "religion of liberty," Viroli's emphasis today on Machiavelli's (and Gramsci's) Prince as a "redeemer" cannot but effectively situate itself in this tradition. On the "religion of liberty," see Viroli 2010, p. 286, and Viroli 2014, p. 141.

15 The reference is to Lenin's characterization of the Soviets as representing a form of political "power of a completely different type," in comparison to constitutional parliamentary democracy. See Lenin 1964, vol. 24, p. 38.

16 The encounter is recorded in Gramsci's letter to Tania of February 23, 1931; see Gramsci 1996, p. 399.

17 See Mussolini 1979 and Kamenev 1962. Gramsci refers to Mussolini's "Prelude' in Q3§34, p. 312.

18 For a survey of the Italian debate on Machiavelli in the 1920s, see Paggi 1969, 1970, and 1984, p. 404 et seq., and Fiorillo 2008 (which provides details of the interventions in the pages of Gobetti's *La rivoluzione liberale*).

19 Gramsci 1996, pp. 132-133 (letter to Tania of November 14, 1927).

20 See the letter to Tania on March 19, 1927, in Gramsci 1996, pp. 54-57 and themes noted at the beginning of the first notebook on February 8, 1929, QI, p. 5.

21 See, e.g., QI§44, pp. 43-44 (February-March 1930); QI§150, p. 133 (late May 1930); Q2§41, pp. 196-197 (early June 1930); Q2§60, p. 216 (August-September 1930); Q2§116, pp. 257-258 (October-November 1930).

22 Elements of such a reading are present in Lefort 1972 (p. 242 in particular), which may have led Althusser also to sometimes overestimate Gramsci's indebtedness to this tradition (Althusser's *Machiavelli and Us* in fact opens with a homage to Lefort's study; see Althusser 1999, p. 3). Althusser's emphasis elsewhere on Machiavelli's "solitude," and particularly the notion of "primitive political accumulation," however, displays a deeper appreciation of the novelty of Gramsci's historical analysis (1999, pp. 10-11, 121). For critical surveys of interpretations of Machiavelli that emerged from the Risorgimento, see Sartorello 2009 and Bianchi and Mussi 2013. For a study of Althusser's reading of Machiavelli, see Lahtinen 2009.

23 See, e.g., Q4§8, pp. 430-431 (May 1930); Q5§127, p. 657 (November-December 1930). For an exploration of the elective affinities of Machiavelli and Gramsci, see Fontana 1993.

24 On the different phases of Gramsci's work, and their reorganization in "special" notebooks, see Francioni 2009 and 2016.

25 The reference to Russo occurs on the first page of Q13§1 (p. 1555). Frosini 2013a reconstructs in detail the decisive impact of Gramsci's reading of Russo's *Prolegomeni a Machiavelli* on the development of the notion of the modern Prince, particularly Russo's suggestive argument regarding the poetic architecture of *The Prince*, and the integral role played by the epilogue in it, which Gramsci extends and radicalizes (see Russo 1931, p. 32). Frosini's study also includes a fundamental rereading of Gramsci's notion of "myth" and in particular, the features that make it irreducible to either a purely Sorelian matrix or its Schmittian continuation.

26 Compare the manuscripts of both notes in Gramsci 2009, vol. 13, pp. 45–49 and vol. 14, pp. 165–168. Significantly, Q13§1 begins directly by discussing the fundamental character of *The Prince* as a "living" book, thus dispensing with the opening line of Q8§21 that had continued to project a "work of political science" conceived and organized like Machiavelli's work, but with the title of "The Modern Prince." It is also notable that in the manuscript version Q13§1, unlike Q8§21, is not preceded by the usual note number or paragraph sign that Gramsci habitually used to indicate discrete topics. It could thus be interpreted as an introduction to the notebook as a whole or synthesis of its main themes and order of treatment.

27 Frosini 2013a draws attention to the strategic use of the rare term *medesimezza*, one of only a handful of occurrences in all of Gramsci's writings (and one of only two in all of his carceral production).

28 The translation offered of this passage in Gramsci 1971 (p. 127)—"the element which gives the entire work its true colour"—fails to capture the specificity of the rare verb *riverberare*. It thereby ascribes the *vera luce* to the entire work itself (a "true colour" previously hidden but finally revealed by the epilogue), rather than specifically to the epilogue (which projects its own "true light" back onto the work). Earlier in the same note, Gramsci had written that "this passionate invocation reflects [*si riflette*] on the whole book" (Q13§1, p. 1555). The manuscript seems to indicate that Gramsci hesitated in his choice of verbs for the concluding phrase to this paragraph; see Gramsci 2009, vol. 14, p. 165. The slight change of verbs may reveal a significant conceptual precision that is crucial for grasping the implications of Gramsci's reading of the conclusion of *The Prince*: while reflection implies a direct and passive linear relation of subject-object, reverberation suggests a more diffuse and active process, as the epilogue "reverberates" back across or even "projects" its true light on the entire work—not simply revealing something that was already there, but actively transforming it.

29 Gramsci refers to his new reading of canto 10 of the *Inferno* as a "little discovery" in a letter to Tania of August 26, 1929 (Gramsci 1996, p. 280). His reading of the drama of Farinata and Cavalcante is elaborated in Q4§78–§87, pp. 516–530, written intermittently between May 1930 and August 1932. Interestingly, Luigi Russo's criticism also played a role in the development of this interpretation. See Rosengarten 1986. Angelo Rossi and Giuseppe Vacca (2007, particularly pp. 38–46) advance the hypothesis that Gramsci's correspondence with Tania, Sraffa, and

his old professor Cosmo was also, in part, a form of "coded" communication with Togliatti regarding Gramsci's reaction to the Comintern politics of the "Third Period."

30 See Croce 1921, particularly pp. 53–72.

31 "The finest form of discovery (*anagnorisis*) is one attended by reversal (*peripeteia*), like that which goes with the discovery in *Oedipus*" (*Poetics* 1452a, 31–33).

32 The "modern Prince" in fact appears only in six notes throughout the *Prison Notebooks* (Q8§21, pp. 951–93; Q8§37, pp. 964–965; Q8§48, p. 970; Q8§52, pp. 972–973; Q8§56, pp. 974–975; Q13§1, pp. 1555–1561). All were written in 1932, and Q13§1 is the term's last appearance, despite the fact that Gramsci continues to write until 1935.

33 See, for instance, Q14§33, p. 1690 (January 1933); Q17§27, p. 1928 (late 1933). Cospito and Francioni 2009, p. 154 provide an overview of the dissemination of Machiavelli throughout the "special" and later "miscellaneous" notebooks.

34 Gramsci 1996, pp. 548–549 (March 14, 1932); see Q8§78, p. 985 (March 1932). For an important study of Machiavelli's thought in relation to Florentine economic history, which sets out from Gramscian insights, see Barthas 2011.

35 For an extensive reading of Gramsci as a theorist of political modernity, see Burgio 2002.

36 Formulated first in November 1930 (Q4§57, p. 504), the phrase "passive revolution" is then at a later date inserted in the margins of chronologically prior notes: Q1§44, p. 41 (from February–March 1930) and Q1§150, p. 133 (from late May 1930).

37 Alex Callinicos (2010) has argued that a tendency to "over-extension" (or, following Lakatos, "concept-stretching") of passive revolution, both in Gramsci's own writings and in those of later scholars who have attempted to develop it for the analysis of contemporary political processes, leads it to lose analytic precision. This notion of a progressive expansion of Gramsci's concepts, and subsequent loss of analytic clarity, is closely modelled on Perry Anderson's influential (for Anglophone Marxism) interpretation of transformations in the concept of hegemony and Gramsci's "antinomies"; for a refutation of the philological errors on which Anderson's reading was based, see Francioni 1984. While Callinicos notes Gramsci's retrospective insertion of the term *passive revolution* in his first notebook (2010, p. 493), his genealogy of the concept nevertheless ignores the extent to which passive revolution was conceived by Gramsci in an "expanded" sense from the outset, and thus was not subject to any "stretching" throughout the development of the *Prison Notebooks*.

38 See Cuoco 1998, particularly pp. 325–326.

39 See also Q1§150, p. 133 (late May 1930). Both Gerratana and Francioni note that "passive revolution" is inserted in the margins in these notes at a later date, after the concept's "first" appearance in Notebook 4 in November 1930. See Gramsci 1975, p. 2479 (critical apparatus) and Gramsci 2009, vol. 1, p. 4. A more precise dating of this marginalia does not seem possible, though it is interesting to note that the

phrase "passive revolution" is not used again in other notes until early 1932, in Q8§25, p. 957, in which Gramsci relates Cuoco's formula to both Quinet and Gioberti.

40 "Revolution without revolution" was Gramsci's original formulation in Q1§44, subsequently equated with "passive revolution."

41 "The concept of passive revolution seems to me to be precise not only for Italy, but also for other countries that modernize the state by means of a series of reforms of national wars, without going through a political revolution of the radical-Jacobin type" (Q4§57, p. 504). As Pasquale Voza argues, the "concept of passive revolution, born as a radical re-elaboration of the expression of Cuoco, is always posited, even when it is referred to the Risorgimento, as a concept valid for connoting and interpreting the mode of formation of modern states in nineteenth century continental Europe" (Voza 2004, p. 195).

42 See Q8§36, p. 962 (February 1932).

43 See in particular the following notes, all titled "Machiavelli": Q15§11, p. 1766 (March–April 1933); Q15§15, p. 1772 (April–May 1933); Q15§17, p. 1774 (April–May 1933); Q15§25, p. 178 (May 1933).

44 Significantly, this argument is directly linked to Gramsci's novel interpretation of Marx's 1859 "Preface," a text often thought to authorize a strongly deterministic understanding of the relation of base and superstructure.

45 For a famous firsthand account of those discussions, see Lisa 1973. Vacca 2012 both critically interrogates the traditional historiography on this topic and provides a synthesis of the most recent archival and documentary research.

46 On the dates of composition of the special notebooks, see Cospito 2011b.

47 On the constitutive and productive "incompletion" of the *Prison Notebooks*, see Gerratana 1997.

48 The central note in this development is the already cited Q14§70, p. 1733 (February 1933).

49 On the notion of the "actualization" of the "Revolution in Permanence" in the concept of hegemony, see Q10i§12, p. 1235 (April–May 1932) and Q13§7, p. 1566 (May 1932–November 1933).

2

Gramsci, Historian of Modernity

ALBERTO BURGIO
(TRANSLATED BY ELIZABETH TREMMEL)

The years 1870 to 1871—Labriola would call it a "sociological date" (Labriola 1973, p. 850)—marked the beginning for Gramsci of an organic crisis of bourgeois society, accompanied by a series of processes that a few decades later "formed a 'mound'" and produced the "historical break" of World War I (Q15§59, p. 1824; trans. Gramsci 1971, p. 106). The completion of the French revolutionary process, of Italian unification, and of the Reich of Wilhelm I, all propelled by a growing nationalism; the escalation of conflicts among the most powerful colonial empires; the growing influence of monopolistic and financial capital at a global level—all these coeval processes fuel a war-inducing dynamic that, on the one hand, shows a regression in the progressive potentiality of modern society and, on the other, evokes the transformation of the politico-historical conflict between capital and labor into new "totalitarian" forms (Q6§136, p. 800; trans. Gramsci 1992–2007, vol. 3, p. 108).

By pointing out 1870 to 1871 as the start of an organic crisis of capitalistic society, Gramsci was not arguing anything new. By agreeing with what Lenin had already stated in *Imperialism: The Highest Stage of Capitalism*,[1] the *Prison Notebooks* but repeat the typical historical timeline proposed in the analyses of the Comintern. However, it is still worth asking ourselves the reasons why it is the tragic end of the Paris Commune that becomes, for Gramsci, the very symbol of the historical crisis of bourgeois modernity tout court. Beyond the importance given to the tragic events by Marx himself, the real question, for Gramsci, regards the ambivalent if emblematic role played by the bourgeoisie in the "French civil war" of May 1871. The real question, in other words, concerns the dialectical nature of capitalistic modernization, which Gramsci frames against the background of the theory of historical transitions sketched by Marx in the "Preface to *A Contribution to the Critique of Political Economy*" (1859).

For Gramsci, as for Marx, the bourgeoisie had emerged as a progressive class against the old aristocratic society because its "expansion never ceases" (Q6§98, p. 774; trans. Gramsci 1992-2007, vol. 3, p. 84)—it has a propensity, that is to say, to build cohesive and dynamic social structures. If the societies of the ancien régime remained divided into ranks allowing for no social mobility, in the bourgeoisie, disposition to progressive expansion lay instead the dynamic nature of capital, in its constitutional need to grow and expand by involving in its process of accumulation every other social class. The most evident progressive result of such "expansivity" was the promotion of sectors of the subaltern classes to managerial positions and, more generally, the gradual betterment of the living conditions of the social groups incorporated in the development of capitalism.

However, the bourgeois potential for inclusiveness was certainly not infinite; it could not expand endlessly, lest the very foundation of its mode of production—private property—would self-destruct. The assimilation of the working class to the productive process could not, in other words, entail the emancipation of the entire collectivity from its subordination to capital, since such an event would mean the end, the material impossibility, of valorization. This is why the effective historical development of a dynamic that Gramsci calls expansion must be followed by a "standstill" (Q8§2, p. 937; trans. Gramsci 1992-2007, vol. 3, p. 234) of the progressive phase: bourgeois universalism turns now into a mere ideological mask, barely disguising the effective supremacy of one class over another.[2] In sum, "in 1870-71, with the attempt of the Commune, that all seeds that sprouted in 1789 were historically exhausted: that is, when the new class struggling for power defeated not only the representatives of the old society that refused to admit it had been definitively superseded but also the representatives of the latter-day groups who maintained that the new structure created by the 1789 revolution was itself superseded; thus the new class demonstrated its vitality in contrast to both the old and the very new" (Q4§38, p. 456; trans. Gramsci 1992-2007, vol. 2, p. 178). In this evocation of the double offensive of the dominant bourgeoisie against the residue of the "old society" on the one hand and against the proletariat that carries an "even-newer" social order on the other, the key word is *superseded*. The bourgeoisie wins the dual struggle (or, even better, it wins the same war on two fronts) not only because the old regime is effectively "superseded," but also because, in contrast to what its "very new" enemies claim, the "new structure" that came to light in 1789 *is not yet* superseded: because it is, on the contrary, still "vital" (able to stand the test of time), in spite of the elements of organic crisis that already undercut its development and impede further progressive transformations.

In the background of this evocation, a theory of the margins of development becomes visible. Gramsci elaborates it on the basis of the two "rules of historical methodology" (Q4§38, p. 455; trans. Gramsci 1992–2007, vol. 2, p. 177) formulated in Marx's "Preface," whose complementarity *Prison Notebooks* elaborate. "No social formation—the first 'rule' would have—is ever destroyed before all the productive forces for which it is sufficient have been developed, and new superior relations of production never replace older ones before the material conditions for their existence have matured within the framework of the old society" (Marx and Engels 1976, vol. 29, p. 263). Also, Marx's second "rule" qualified, "Mankind thus inevitably sets itself only such tasks as it is able to solve, since closer examination will always show that the problem itself arises only when the material conditions for its solution are already present or at least in the course of formation" (Marx and Engels 1976, vol. 29, p. 263). Gramsci realizes that these two theses constitute a single blueprint, which he then combines and uses in his own historical analysis.

Gramsci decided to adopt the principle of "super-cession" to explain the outcome of the social and political conflict that culminated in the definitive elimination of feudal society and the clash with the revolutionary proletariat.[3] This shows, in fact, that in his view, the historically significant results of the class struggle (then, ultimately, historical periodization itself) derive, *in the last instance*, from the objective fact constituted by the (persistent or exhausted) evolutionary potential of the existing social structure.[4] To this framework, inferred in toto from Marx, Gramsci adds some new elements of theoretical originality— the first of which is the dialectics of epoch/duration (see Burgio 2014, pp. 112–116).

There is no doubt that a social system, if unable to develop, is somehow "destined" to decline. It is also at least probable that the exhaustion of its "margins of development" corresponds to a phase of organic struggle that we could define, as does Marx, as a "social revolution" (Marx and Engels 1976, vol. 29, p. 263; on this, see Burgio 2018, pp. 418–493). This organic struggle is then probable, insofar as a dialectic connection exists between conflictuality and the evolutionary potentiality of the social formation. What Gramsci underlines, however, is the nonmechanistic nature of the relationship between organic crisis and historical transition; or, better still, *the multiple possible configurations* of the processes of transition.

A society that finds itself in an organic crisis can still defend itself from the pressure of the "very new" (a "very new," namely, that reveals itself as not yet mature) over a long period of time. It can "last" a long time, even centuries (for Gramsci, this is the case with capitalistic society). This explains why, going back to the symbolic meaning of the repression of the Paris Commune, the victory of the French bourgeoisie over all its enemies coincides with the end of "its" historical epoch. It seems a paradox—but not for Gramsci, aware of the fact that an epoch can "last" and endure, beyond its organic ending, against "very new" processes that do not necessarily eliminate the "viscous forces" of a social system (Q14§76, p. 1744; trans. Gramsci 1971, p. 256) or necessarily impede its long survival.

From this, the opportunity arises to distinguish between two arguably antithetical understandings of the idea of development implicated in this reflection. The polarity epoch/duration suggests that a type of controlled development is possible, *internal to the epoch and corresponding to its duration*, that allows the social formation to react to the threats that undermine its existence. This controlled development is not simply different from but, in fact, is in opposition to the progressive development (evolutionary in its strongest sense) *that triggers the historical transition* (epochal). These two forms of development exclude each other on a logical level (conceptual); although they can evidently coexist, in actuality, they usually coexist in the final phases of every organic crisis—that is, throughout every historical transition. This makes it even more important to distinguish between the two and characterize them correctly.

It is easy to show how, in the "Preface" of 1859, Marx employs both meanings *without distinguishing* between them. When he writes that the economic structure of society is constituted by the totality of the relations of production corresponding "to a given stage in the development of their material forces of production" (Marx and Engels 1976, vol. 29, p. 263), he refers to development in its strongest sense—as that which determines, at a macro-historical level, what he calls "epochs marking progress in the economic development of society" (Marx and Engels 1976, vol. 29, p. 263). However, when he says that development of the forces of production carried out by social formation is the prerequisite for the very existence of that social formation, he is clearly referring to controlled development—a development, in short, that is not "epochs marking progress," but that rather allows an epoch to perdure beyond its end.

That these two forms of development are not distinguished in Marx's "Preface" bears powerfully on the understanding of the mechanics of "social revolution." In the "Preface," a social revolution takes place when "the material productive forces of society come into conflict with the existing relations of production." That happens, Marx writes, "at a certain stage of development." What type of development? It is clear that Marx is referring here to a putatively normal development—one that has accompanied the entire life of the existing social formation. But insofar as it puts the transition into motion, this development is also, *at the same time*, a *qualitatively different* development: an evolutionary dynamic that—growing "in the womb" of the existing society but "creat[ing] also the material conditions for a solution of this antagonism" (Marx and Engels 1976, vol. 29, p. 264)—begins a *genetic mutation* of the social formation, its *incipient metamorphosis* into a new society.

While working inside Marx's framework, Gramsci fine-tunes it, using the distinction between the two forms of temporality and two possibilities of development. This allows Gramsci to understand fully the complex historical meaning of an event (the bloodshed of the Paris Commune) in which bourgeois society successfully proves its own strength in the same moment in which its evolutionary capacity dissolves. It also allows him to reflect on the causes of the organic crisis—a reflection that generates, in turn, two other thematic considerations (one implicit, the other clearly stated). It is worth dwelling on these briefly.

Let's start with the first. For Gramsci, the bourgeoisie is different from the previous dominant classes due to the elasticity of its social composition and its ability to assimilate the subaltern classes. From this perspective, the *Prison Notebooks'* focus is on considering *social mobility* as a typical aspect of modern society. But this is, evidently, only one side of modernity—its progressive face. There is, as we have seen, an opposing and equally important face of modernity, which impedes social mobility after a certain point. Let's be more precise.

The structure of capitalistic social relationship prevents the mechanism of expansion from functioning forever. Despite the fact that the bourgeoisie "posits itself as an organism in continuous movement" Q8§2, p. 937; trans. Gramsci 1992-2007, vol. 3, p. 234) capable of eradicating the hierarchic structure of society by totally assimilating it, and, therefore, achieving the objective of democratic self-government; despite the fact that its ideology revolves around a universal interpretation of the principles of 1789 and promises a society (actually a world) of universal freedom and equality—despite all this, the bourgeoisie is not actually able to achieve such an ambitious revolutionary program.

On the contrary, an inevitable gap exists between the ideological self-representation of the bourgeoisie (according to which the bourgeoisie considers itself able to absorb society in its entirety, *denying* itself as the dominant class) and the material historical forms of its domination. In reality, the expansion of the bourgeoisie *must* stop. It *must* reverse itself; it *must* negate itself and turn its emancipatory process into the "dis-integration" of the dominant class from the subordinate ones, and into the "dis-assimilation" of some parts of itself (the demotion from middle to working class) from the structure of bourgeois society: "The bourgeois class is 'saturated': it not only does not expand—it starts to disintegrate; it not only does not assimilate new elements—it loses part of itself (or at least its losses are enormously more numerous than the assimilations)" (Q13§17, p. 937; trans. Gramsci 1971, p. 260). The bourgeoisie *must*, at a certain point in its own development, exclude—that is, maintain in a subordinate condition—large social sectors, negating, in practice, rights asserted in principle.

There is more. This description seems to represent a diachronic sequence between expansive phases and dis-aggregative phases. In reality (and Gramsci attaches great relevance to this point), the expansive dynamics are always accompanied by, inextricably linked with, movements of disintegration. Why does this happen?

Far from being random, the continuous oscillation between liberal and repressive moments, the continuous alternating between "enlargement and restrictions" (Q13§37, p. 1637) shows the essential aspect of capitalistic development—that is, its characteristically contradictory nature, rooted in the antagonistic nature of a hierarchically structured social relationship, which survives thanks to the "free" cooperation of the subaltern classes. As every expansive dynamic implies crises, conflicts arise for the (antagonistic) reallocation of material and symbolic conflicts and for redefining positions, roles, and identities of each group.

This is what Marx's *On the Jewish Question* (which Gramsci had at his disposal while incarcerated) already points out, thematizing the separation between legal equality and social inequality, whose functional basis, on the level of the mechanism of material reproduction, is investigated in the *Critique of Political Economy* (see Burgio 2018, pp. 114–133). The means of capitalistic production imposes an insurmountable (objective) limit on the expansivity of the dominant class. The bourgeoisie makes the social body more dynamic, but *it cannot* abolish its hierarchical structure since it cannot expel the antagonistic (coercive) heart of a social relationship whose engine is, in the last instance, the relationship between capital and labor. This relationship is necessarily asymmetrical—with no dominion over living labor, no extraction of surplus value, and no possible appreciation or accumulation of capital.

However, in Marx this analysis risks being obscured by the emphasis on the importance of the "compulsion of economic relations" (Marx 1977, p. 899) as a distinctive aspect of the modern structure of society. In a rushed reading, this element can make us believe that Marx deduces that the disappearance of military violence in modern society and, therefore, its pacification, depends on the centrality of the market. Gramsci's arguments help prevent such errors in judgment. With direct experience of the violent reaction of the bourgeoisie against its own crisis (a violence of which Marx saw only a few signs), Gramsci insists on the coercive dimension of bourgeois modernity. His focus on the theme of expansivity is what allows him to highlight the entire range of its dialectical structure. The "modern" appears to the reader of the *Prison Notebooks* as the location of an inextricable web between expansion and violence, between assimilation and discrimination. Or, if preferred, between innovation and archaism. The reading of Gramsci's notes makes it extremely clear that there is never, in bourgeois society, one without the other; and that the magnitude, the effect, and the function of the archaic in the womb of modernity concretely define, time and again, the salient aspects of the politico-historical situation.

Two quick examples should suffice. On the structural level, Gramsci defines the capitalistic market as the place where "a given commodity (labour) is, first of all, undervalued, then placed in a condition of competitive inferiority, and finally made to shoulder the cost for the whole of the given system" (Q10ii§20, p. 1258; trans. Gramsci 1995a, p. 183). Gramsci writes here against naively naturalistic representations of the market as a pure state of nature, but also insists on that market always being a "determinate market" (Q10ii§20, p. 1258; trans. Gramsci 1995a, p. 183)—determined, that is to say, by class logic, and stimulated by the coercion, *also military*, of bourgeois dominance. The second example, on the superstructural level, is constituted by the affirmation, somehow Machiavellian, of the constant operative interconnection of "two major superstructural 'levels'" (Q12§1, p. 1518; trans. Gramsci 1971, p. 12) of direction and of command (i.e., hegemony and coercion), where military (extra-economic) violence is not only an always available option, but also a *constantly active* component in the normal exercise of bourgeois power. Therefore, while in "moments of crisis of command and direction when spontaneous consent has failed" the "apparatus of State coercive power" is mobilized against "the whole society," during those phases when it is instead easier to control social dynamics, the dominating class merely "'legally' enforces discipline on those groups who do not 'consent' either actively or passively" (Q12§1, p. 1519; trans. Gramsci 1971, p. 12). Why is this clarification—a clarification that doesn't modify the Marxian depiction, but reformulates it in a more balanced and lucid way—important? Because it seems to us that against every naïve progressivism, this clarification effectively counters the recurrent illusion that a fully emancipative capitalism is possible.

The awareness of a persistent archaic core present in the heart of modernity informs also the last integration of the Marxist theory of historical transitions into the *Notebooks*. In Q8§2, Gramsci explains in the most organic and clear way the idea that expansivity characterizes bourgeois dominance by differentiating this dominance from the one exercised by previous social formations. Gramsci defines as "conception of a closed caste" the attitude that informed power relationships in premodern societies: "In former times, the dominant classes were essentially conservative in the sense that they did not seek to enable other classes to pass organically into theirs; in other words, they did not seek to enlarge, either 'technically' or ideologically, the scope of their class—they conceived of themselves as an exclusive caste" (Q8§2, p. 937; trans. Gramsci 1992–2007, vol. 3, p. 234). As mentioned already, for Gramsci, while premodern societies are constituted by dis-organic sets of separate groups, modern society is characterized by cohesion and internal mobility. We now understand that such a differentiation can be summarized by the caste/class polarity.

The caste structure is typical of previous societies: it is static, it is crystallized, it is made rigid, indeed, by the reciprocal closing-off of its components, starting with each dominant group (castes, indeed)[5] being protective of its own superiority. Instead, the expansivity of the dominant bourgeoisie, its propensity to assimilate, to integrate, to include, to transform society into one homogenous block, a block that is entirely bourgeois (and therefore coextensive with the market), is the main characteristic of modern society.

Class *versus* caste. It could be said that through this polarity the *Notebooks* reformulate from a sociohistorical perspective a scheme typical of juridical historiography that refers to the passage from feudal-aristocratic society based on bloodlines to modern "contractual" society, based on the functions and the dynamics of the market.[6] But the transition to modernity does not extinguish, according to Gramsci, the characteristic aspect of premodern societies (for instance, the extra-economical use of military violence): the passage from the logic of the caste to the dialectics between classes is, then, similarly partial and revocable.

In effect, it is evident that Gramsci thinks that in the context of capitalistic modernity, the transition to class consciousness (considered here for its progressive element, e.g., fluidification of caste structures) is neither fully nor definitively achieved. Just as an archaic core rooted in the hierarchical structure of the means of production persists in the heart of modernity (a core that informs the command structures during the phases of hegemonic crisis), so does an irreducible (premodern) core of caste structure endure in the capitalistic social relationship, a core that has the chance to take over after the depletion of the expansive dynamic. In this sense, Gramsci says that when the process of assimilation of subaltern subjects "comes to a halt," when the "bourgeois class is 'saturated,'" then "the conception of the State as pure force is returned to" (Q13§17, p. 937; trans. Gramsci 1971, p. 260).

To point out in detail the development of this reflection in all its complexity would be impossible here. Let's limit ourselves to the essentials, which in our opinion focus precisely on the *reversibility* of the progressive movement (of the passage, namely, from a caste structure to the organization of society into classes). As we have seen, caste, in the language of the *Prison Notebooks*, is synonymous with a closed static system based on the hereditary preservation and transmission of privilege. From here derives the strong esprit de corps that usually connotes castes and their "natural" inclination toward the "'patrimonial' conception of the State" (Q8§187, p. 1054; trans. Gramsci 1992–2007, vol. 3, p. 343). We must also add here a caste's loyalty to a rigid and crystallized doctrinal body (and to a linguistic field), and, above all, *detachment from the people*. This is, in Gramsci's eyes, the essential characteristic of caste itself, which makes it a place of blind resistance to modernization understood as the creation of homogenous social bodies.

This consideration allows us to intuit which social sectors are under the right conditions to become modern "castes." These sectors are the clergy and high-ranking military; the bureaucracy; and the intellectuals—in the strictest sense of the word—with particular reference to the world of the academy and universities (see Dainotto 2013). An "anti-democratic" attitude relentlessly persists in these worlds, a fixed "opposition to any form of national-popular movement," which is "determined by the economic-corporate caste spirit." Such a spirit is certainly "of medieval and feudal origin," but connotes, to this day, in the peak of modernity, large parts of society (Q23§8, p. 2198; trans. Gramsci 1985, p. 216).

That the phenomenon of castes is not a remnant from the past but a persistent element—and in many cases, a product of modernization itself, dictated by its contradictory structure—emerges with particular clarity from the analysis of the processes of passive revolution. Just as the Restoration was a result of the transformation of the old feudal classes "demoted from their dominant position to a 'governing' one" and their consequent reconversion from class to caste (Q10ii§61, p. 1358; trans. Gramsci 1971, p. 115), so was modernization between the nineteenth and twentieth centuries a result of the same dynamic, as is particularly evident from the study of the situation in Germany.

Also in Germany "the old feudal classes remained as the governing stratum of the political State, with wide corporate privileges in the army, the administration and on the land" (Q19§24, p. 2032; trans. Gramsci 1971, p. 83); in fact, the old class preserved a kind of "political monopoly" and a considerable "politico-intellectual supremacy" (Q12§1, p. 1526; trans. Gramsci 1971, p. 19). In this conservative metamorphosis, the Prussian Junkers "exercised a national function, became the 'intellectuals' of the bourgeoisie" (Q19§24, p. 2032; trans. Gramsci 1971, p. 83); this makes them "resemble a priestly-military caste," but one endowed with an "economic base of its own" and enjoying "a virtual monopoly of directive-organisational functions in political society" (Q12§1, p. 1526; trans. Gramsci 1971, p. 19).

Europe, with its remnants of the ancien régime, is not the only location where the caste system operates tenaciously, if it is true that—as Gramsci thinks—in the United States of Fordist innovations, too, the growing separation between "upper classes" and "working masses" is "determining a psychological split and accelerating the crystallisation and satura tion of the various social groups, thereby making evident the way that these groups are being transformed into castes just as they have been in Europe" (Q22§11, p. 2169; trans. Gramsci 1971, p. 306).

It is noteworthy that already in Notebook 1, Gramsci had asked whether "an organic study of the clergy as a 'class-caste'" could be done in this perspective. Such a study seemed "indispensable as a beginning and as a condition for the whole study that remains to be done on the function of religion in the historical and intellectual development of humanity" (Q1§154, p. 137; trans. Gramsci 1992–2007, vol. 1, p. 234). This idea will not be expanded on explicitly, but, as we have seen, it anchors the entire discussion that we have begun to explore here. Arguably, this idea adds an important piece to the puzzle regarding the reflection on the constitutive characteristics of capitalistic modernity: its fundamental dialectic, its two faces, its torn look, in which innovation and progressive drive are inevitably intertwined with persistent reactionary impulses.

It can easily be seen that from Gramsci's complex reflection on the expansivity of the bourgeoisie emerges the *utopic* nature of modernity—its unattainability—and the insurmountable distance between principles, ideological representations, and concrete historic reality. Retraced from the sociohistoric perspective we have taken here, the historic experience of the decades following 1889 shows the impossibility of giving life to a society totally controlled by class logic. This impossibility exists both under bourgeois dominance (keeping in mind the perpetuation of an irreducible core of caste logic) as well as after its decline (since division into classes is "destined" to disappear in the "new" communist "society" due to the fact that the political implications of the social division of labor will be left behind, since class division will be considered simply a technicality).

The *Prison Notebooks* do not fail to highlight, albeit briefly, the hypothesis of the absorption of "the whole of society" inside the dominant class—of the latter's theoretical capacity of "assimilating it to its cultural and economic level" (Q8§2, p. 937; trans. Gramsci 1992–2007, vol. 3, p. 234). In fact, it is not inconceivable that, in addition to "posit[ing] itself . . . as capable of absorbing the whole of society," a dominating class "would take this notion of the state and of the law to such a level of perfection" as to conceive the state as "educator" (Q8§2, p. 937; trans. Gramsci 1992–2007, vol. 3, p. 234), devoid, by definition, of coercive functions because its "aim is to put an end to the internal divisions of the ruled etc., and to create a technically and morally unitary social organism" (Q8§179, p. 1050; trans. Gramsci 1992–2007, vol. 3, p. 338). But such a hypothesis, hinting at those classes whose "expansion never ceases, until the whole of society is entirely absorbed" (Q6§98, p. 774; trans. Gramsci 1992–2007, vol. 3, p. 84), implies, by definition, the superseding of the historic context of bourgeois modernity and the transition to a new epoch characterized by the beginning of a new modes of production that will no longer be based on exploitation.

This is clearly the place where the fundamental reflection regarding the hypothesis of the "regulated society" present in the *Notebooks* inserts itself (Q6§12, p. 693; trans. Gramsci 1992–2007, vol. 3, p. 11). In the *Notebooks*, the radically democratic rewriting of the relationship of management and government (a relationship that, in the context of the historic transition to a post-capitalistic social structure, engages the entire social body) embraces head-on the relationship between the two dimensions of the sociopolitical bond: "civil society" and "political society." In this new politico-historical context, the expansion of the new ruling class that progressively assimilates the masses (transforming them into an operative part of society, that rules itself, that is the subject of self-government) promotes the disappearance of the authoritarian aspect of the bourgeois state (that is, its typical dimension of coercion and control) to the improvement of the social relationship.

In such a context, the Leninist point of view on the extinction of the state as an "coercive organization" is explained as the result of the gradual reduction of its "authoritarian and coercive interventions" (Q6§88, p. 764; trans. Gramsci 1992–2007, vol. 3, p. 75). More precisely, this process implies, at the sociopolitical level, the transformation of the functions of government and management as regards their technical functions, and tends to create, together with new forms of representation besides the parliamentary ones (Q9§69, p. 1140–1141), the collective self-government of a community where everybody is effectively both manager and ruler of oneself. On an economic (structural) level, this evidently evokes the superseding of the capitalistic mode of production and, therefore, of the relationship of domination and exploitation.

In this situation, the working class can, in principle, "expand" until it envelops the entire society (and, therefore, puts an end to class division), since the power of the worker is antithetical to any relationship of power and any dynamic of exploitation. Along this line of reasoning, Gramsci appears to be fully in sync with the tradition of revolutionary Marxism. In his eyes, a true democracy is the one in which the social body realizes *self-governance*, a result that assumes the radical transformation of the social structure through the socialization of the means of production.

This scenario, however, concerns only the future. The present is still "pre-history" (Marx and Engels 1976, vol. 29, p. 264). For the time being, we can, at this point, address the last—and perhaps most relevant—moment in Gramsci's complex sequence of arguments. The idea of *relative expansivity*, as we have seen, immediately implies the idea of the *limit* of possible expansion. It thus involves a double question, of which Gramsci is fully aware. Through which apparatus and based on which criteria is the uncrossable boundary regarding the "assimilation" of subaltern classes established? And what actually happens inside capitalistic society when the dialectics between classes approaches that boundary, almost threatening it?

It appears to us that these questions push Gramsci to reflect on modernity even further, thus elaborating his most original theories. In looking for answers, Gramsci gives shape to a *general theory of crises* that refers primarily—but not only—to modern (bourgeois, capitalistic) history.[7] This is a theory that introduces new elements with respect to the Marxian overture from which it takes inspiration.

Why a general theory of crises? If what we have discussed thus far is on point, crisis itself is the essence of modern history; it is its natural environment. Given the centrality of the expansive dynamic, social mobility is the defining characteristic of modernity. As every expansive dynamic implies crises, conflicts arise for the (antagonistic) reallocation of material and symbolic conflicts, and for redefining positions, roles, and identities of each group. In this sense, modern society actually lives in "a continuous process of formation and superseding of unstable equilibria" (Q13§17, p. 1584; trans. Gramsci 1971, p. 182).

Evidently *these* crises are, by their nature, different from the one triggered when the conflict that arises from the process of assimilation compromises the existence of the social structure itself. Different types of development fuel different crises. Because of this, Gramsci has the opportunity to develop a typology that allows us to distinguish between the different dynamics and forms of crises and their respective consequences.

We want to remind briefly our readers about the dialectic framework of Marx's theory of transitions as formulated in the "Preface" of 1859. Here, Marx considers the conflict between the forces of production and the relations of production as a key factor, due to its dialectical structure. During the phases of development of the social formation, the adequate context to deploy the energy available to society is found inside the historic social system: the relations of production function, in these phases, as "form[s] for the development of society's productive power" (Marx and Engels 1976, vol. 29, p. 38). However, this development of the forces of production, until now *promoted* by the existing relations of production (that is, by the complete set of structural and superstructural relationships—economical, juridical, political, cultural—that organize the process of production and social reproduction), generates now a "contradiction." Some productive forces that have gone beyond a "given stage of development" find, in these relations of production, an *unsurmountable obstacle* to their further development: *fetters*. From here, according to Marx, a new epoch of social revolution begins—a new phase of transition toward a different social formation.

As we have seen, Gramsci does not simply borrow this theory; he clarifies it, inspired in particular by the historic experience of the last decades (the half-century of organic crisis that is already behind him). The history of modernity teaches that not all the phases of social conflict, not *even those of a structural nature*, are systemic crises—they cannot trigger epochal transitions. On the contrary, labor and social conflict (in the language of Marx, the contradiction between the forces of production inside the given relations of production) are contained and normalized as ordinary crises. As long as conflicts are produced by expansive dynamics that are compatible with the stability of a given social formation (in the actual case of modern society, with the accumulation of capital and with the social organization controlled by the bourgeoisie), those conflicts primarily constitute *random physiological events*, internal to the evolution of the social formation and functional to its stabilization. When Gramsci speaks of an uninterrupted sequence of "molecular changes which in fact progressively modify the pre-existing composition of forces, and hence become the matrix of new changes," and summarizes its consequences, he is actually referring to the aforementioned conflicts (Q15§11, p. 1767; trans. Gramsci 1971, p. 109).

Obviously, not all crises fit this typology. The fact that (at least in the Marxian theory borrowed by Gramsci) the very existence of social formations implicates their decline means that, at a certain phase in the development of the forces of production, crises *make a qualitative leap*. Such a leap opens—this is still Marx's hypothesis—a revolutionary process. Gramsci seems fully aware of this difference and, as already seen with his theorization on the idea of development, he also highlights the need to make the appropriate distinctions regarding his theorization on the processes of crises.

A note on the "relations of forces"—a crucial text in the economy of the theoretical-political discourse of the *Notebooks*—actually starts with this reflection, the practical relevance of which is also emphasized by Gramsci. After quoting the entire passage of the "Preface" of 1859, Gramsci writes: "In studying a structure, it is necessary to distinguish organic movements (relatively permanent) from movements which may be termed 'conjunctural' (and which appear as occasional, immediate, almost accidental). Conjunctural phenomena too depend on organic movements to be sure, but they do not have any very far-reaching historical significance. . . . When an historical period comes to be studied, the great importance of this distinction becomes clear" (Q13§17, p. 1579; trans. Gramsci 1971, pp. 177-178). Soon after this passage, Gramsci explains why it is necessary to make a clear distinction between conjunctures and structural dynamics, and why such a distinction must *always* be made. It is important to clarify that what is at stake here is not only the interpretation of the past, but also—and more concretely—the making of an "art of politics": carrying out an "objective and impartial analysis" aimed at finding "the correct relation between what is organic and what is conjunctural" becomes as essential as silencing "one's own baser and more immediate desires and passions" in that art that is construction of "present" and "future" (Q13§17, pp. 1579-1581; trans. Gramsci 1971, pp. 178-179).

It is important at this point to examine what Gramsci thinks about the specific causes that engender a critical "movement"—what can their consequences be, and what their predictable developments? First, we note that Gramsci connects organic crises to the systemic accumulation of the effects of long-term conflicts. When Gramsci reflects on the conditions and the objectives of hegemonic relations, he highlights their ambivalence. In one sense, "hegemony presupposes that account be taken of the interests and the tendencies of the groups over which hegemony is to be exercised"—that is to say, the dominant group has to recognize the interests of the subaltern ones. In this sense, hegemony lies on a "compromise equilibrium" and requires concessions on the part of the ruling class. At the same time, concessions must remain within a precise and unsurmountable limit, and "cannot touch the essential"—namely, "the decisive function exercised by the leading group in the decisive nucleus of economic activity." In short, the "sacrifices" and concessions made by the dominant class can only be "of an economic-corporative kind. But there is also no doubt that such sacrifices and such a compromise cannot touch the essential" (Q13§8, p. 1591; trans. Gramsci 1971, p. 161).

In his analysis, Gramsci gives us a clear image of the dynamics of organic crises, implying a mutual relationship of the latter with occasional crises. If the "essential" is threatened, if the development of the conflict permanently and critically calls into question that "dominant function"—namely, "individual and group appropriation of profit" on the part of capital (Q10i§9, p. 1228; trans. Gramsci 1971, p. 120)—it can then be said that the crisis has become organic, and will effectively endanger the survival of the social formation. As long as this risk is forestalled, as long as social conflict—no matter how harsh—is compatible with the existence (or "duration") of the social formation, the crisis is included by definition inside the normal dialectic, a dialectic that is functional to the development of the social formation itself. If this is true, then it can be deduced that the first consequence relates, once again, to the event that Gramsci considers emblematic of the conclusion of the French revolutionary dynamic and of the beginning of the organic crisis of modernity. There is no doubt that with the defeat of the Paris Commune, the French bourgeoisie celebrates its triumph, showing at the same time the vitality of the middle class and the immaturity of the historical-political aspirations of the proletariat. Not by chance, in the note on the "relations of forces," Gramsci points out: "Forces of opposition . . . seek to demonstrate that the necessary and sufficient conditions already exist to make possible, and hence imperative, the accomplishment of certain historical tasks (imperative, because any falling short before an historical duty increases the necessary disorder, and prepares more serious catastrophes). (The demonstration in the last analysis only succeeds and is 'true' if it becomes a new reality, if the forces of opposition triumph . . .)" (Q13§17, p. 1580; trans. Gramsci 1971, p. 178). Nonetheless, the fact that the followers of the Paris Commune were defeated remains a contingent event; at a fundamentally (organic) historical level, their rebellion effectively puts into question the "essential" of bourgeois dominance, as demonstrated by the fact that the bloodshed of the Commune coincides with the beginning of the organic crisis of modern society. This will be confirmed in the next few decades, with the explosion of the "phenomenon of trade unionism" (Q15§47, p. 1808)—a "phenomenon" under which Gramsci subsumes an entire set of processes ("parliamentarianism, industrial organizations, democracy, liberalism, etc.") that are all consequences of the establishment of the "new social force" of the labor movement, which "has a weight which can no longer be ignored" (Q15§59, p. 1824; trans. Gramsci 1971, p. 106; on this, see Burgio 2003, pp. 164–167).

The organic crisis is the result, accordingly, of "incurable structural contradictions" (Q13§17, p. 1580; trans. Gramsci 1971, p. 178) that prove the *non-reversability* of the long-term effects of conflictuality developed through the entire life of the social formation. In particular, the nonresolvability of the contradictions that is present under the systemic conflict that generates the organic crisis brings with it two immediate consequences that are connected to each other—or, better, one double consequence. On the one hand, it brings a crisis that is "'structural' and not just due to the conjuncture, and that it cannot be overcome except by creating a new structure that will take account of the tendencies built into the old structure and dominate these through the new premises it is based on" (Q14§57, p. 1716; trans. Gramsci 1995a, p. 224). On the other hand, because of this, the nonresolvability of the organic or structural crisis makes all the responses given by the dominant class, challenged by the crisis, purely defensive countermeasures—the vain attempt to contain a macro-historic dynamic that it can no longer coerce. Having said that, it is natural that "no social formation will ever admit that it has been superseded" and will therefore try "within certain limits . . . to overcome" the structural contradictions that, at this point, will remain unresolvable. The impossibility of resolving such conflicts any longer will relegate the "incessant and persevering efforts" of the until now dominant class, and that class itself, to the "the terrain of the 'conjunctural'" (Q13§17, p. 1580; trans. Gramsci 1971, pp. 177–185).

Fascism in Europe and Fordism in the United States are fully situated, for Gramsci, inside this general theory—they represent defensive responses. They are, no doubt, significant responses, as they are based on real needs. Even fascism "is a function of present historical necessities" (Q14§74, p. 1743; trans. Gramsci 1971, p. 255), such as the adoption of measures of economic planning (as discussed in Q10i§8; trans. Gramsci 1995a, pp. 346–348). Yet, to the extent that their responses attempt to solve what is at this point unresolvable, they are doomed to remain contingent: they are events in the mere "duration" of bourgeois modernity, but they are not "epoch making."

To turn now to the crucial question, the fact that the bourgeoisie is destined to eventually disappear does not compromise in any way the length of the crisis, or the rhythm of the processes of transition. While the note on "relations of forces" talks about the "exceptional duration" of the crisis, it also mentions that the crisis may unfold over a relatively brief temporal arch—"sometimes lasting for decades" (Q13§17, p. 1579; trans. Gramsci 1971, p. 178); similarly, Notebook 22, considering an acceleration of the "transformations of the material bases of European civilization" as a "repercussion of American super-power [*prepotenza*]," highlights the fact that "in the contemporary period everything happens much faster than in the past ages" (Q22§15, p. 2179; trans. Gramsci 1971, p. 317). However, it must be remembered that Gramsci portrays the "medieval crisis" that brought feudalism in Europe to its decline as a process that "lasted for several centuries, until the French Revolution" (Q6§10, p. 691; trans. Gramsci 1992-2007, vol. 3, p. 9). Moreover, one should never underestimate the "often unsuspected" power of resistance—the already mentioned "viscous forces"—of social formations: "With respect to this, it should be noted that the fact of 'not constituting an epoch' is too often confused with brief 'temporal' duration: it is possible to 'last' a long time, relatively, and yet not 'constitute an epoch'" (Q14§76, p. 1744; trans. Gramsci 1971, p. 256). Accordingly, when celebrating the incommensurable greatness of Marx—"Marx . . . has produced an original and integral conception of the world"—Gramsci states that his work "initiates intellectually a historical era that will probably last for centuries, that is, until the demise of political Society and the advent of regulated society" (Q7§33, p. 882; trans. Gramsci 1992-2007, vol. 3, p. 183). This unequivocally puts out of play any impatient revolutionary impulse, born from incorrect readings of the historic phase, of the nature of ongoing conflicts, and of the macro-historic aspect of the crises. A naïve impatience always needs to be reminded that every "social form 'always' has marginal possibilities for further development" (Q13§27, p. 1622; trans. Gramsci 1971, p. 222).

This affirmation of the (presumably) long duration of the crisis is not a change in diagnosis—almost as if predicting the slow development of the organic crisis would be equal to affirming the intact vitality of bourgeois society. Gramsci takes very seriously the idea that the crisis of modernity has reached a point of no return. This was proven, to Gramsci, by the essential aspects of class conflict that emerged in the Western world in the aftermath of World War I—namely, the emergence of a "totalitarian policy" (Q6§136, p. 1622; trans. Gramsci 1992-2007, vol. 3, p. 108).

Gramsci's general theory of crises that we have outlined here, and that takes a consistent shape in Q13§17, which we have often quoted, is the result of the revision of note Q4§38 that Gramsci writes during the same period of time (fall 1930) in which he begins to draft Notebook 6. It is precisely in this last notebook that we encounter three short notes (§§136-138) that, taking up the themes discussed in Q13§17, give detailed and particularly important descriptions of the current "politico-historical" scenario: a picture of the configuration of the "balance of political power relations [*rapporto delle forze politiche*]" (Q2§114, p. 257; trans. Gramsci 1992-2007, vol. 1, p. 342) in the aftermath of World War I.

From a parallel reading of these quick annotations, a very organic and coherent picture emerges. Gramsci starts by defining the "transition from the war of maneuver (and from frontal attack) to the war of position—in the politi-cal field as well" as "the most important postwar problem of political theory; it is also the most difficult problem to solve correctly" (Q6§138, p. 801; trans. Gramsci 1992–2007, vol. 3, p. 109). In part, we already know why he thinks this: the question goes back to the already quoted need "to distinguish organic movements (relatively permanent) from movements which may be termed 'conjunctural' (and which appear as occasional, immediate, almost accidental)" (Q13§17, p. 1579; trans. Gramsci 1971, pp. 177–178), which had emerged already in the earlier draft of Q4§38. Serious consequences could result from potential errors and from mistaking the permanent for the contingent, or vice versa.

Reading now Q6§138 gives us further insight. The description of the "politico-historical situation" generated from the change in the forms of con-flict (from war of maneuver to trench warfare) offers, first of all, an extremely dramatic scenario that Gramsci calls "totalitarian policy." What character-izes the current phase is the attempt (put into place by the dominant class) to reduce drastically the structural and organizational pluralism that previously characterized the social sphere by giving the "intellectual and moral" power to a single political party: "A totalitarian policy in fact attempts: 1) to ensure that the members of a particular party find in that one party all the satisfactions that had previously found in a multiplicity of organizations, that is, to sever all the ties these members have with extraneous cultural organizations; 2) to destroy all other organizations or to incorporate them into a system solely reg-ulated by the party" (Q6§136, p. 800; trans. Gramsci 1992–2007, vol. 3, p. 108). The goal of regimenting the entire social sphere under the unique control of "big, 'totalitarian' types of parties" (Q7§93, p. 922; trans. Gramsci 1992–2007, vol. 3, p. 219) is a qualitative leap in the exercise of power of the dominant class—a class that has by now "lost consensus . . . it no longer 'leads,' but only 'rules'" (Q3§34, p. 311; trans. Gramsci 1992–2007, vol. 2, p. 32). Its new offensive occurs simultaneously at both the hegemonic level (with the goal of rebuilding and organizing consensus) and the level of public order.

In this sense, we read that in a "war of position," "an unprecedented con-centration of hegemony is required and hence a more 'interventionist' kind of government that will engage more openly in the offensive against the oppo-nents and ensure, once and for all, the 'impossibility' of internal disintegration by putting in place controls of all kinds—political, administrative, etc., rein-forcement of the hegemonic positions of the dominant group, etc." (Q6§138, p. 802; trans. Gramsci 1992–2007, vol. 3, p. 109). This is precisely the reason why, in Q6§137, Gramsci criticizes those (in this case, Daniel Halévy of *Décadence de la liberté*) who continue to understand the state in a restrictively traditionalist way—a state limited to the "representative apparatus" of parliamentarianism, and to the "political organisms generated by universal suffrage"—and who do not see that the modern state also includes "the 'private' apparatus of hegemony or civil society" (Q6§137, p. 801; trans. Gramsci 1992–2007, vol. 3, p. 108). The state must now be understood "organically and more broadly" (Q6§87, p. 763; trans. Gramsci 1992–2007, vol. 3, p. 74).

In order to understand society and modern types of conflict "in the post-1870 period" (Q10i§13, p. 1238; trans. Gramsci 1995a, p. 360), the fundamental categories of the political lexicon must be revised. If not, the attempt made by "modern dictatorship"—putting "the centralization of the whole life of the nation in the hands of the ruling class" (Q3§18, p. 303; trans. Gramsci 1992–2007, vol. 2, p. 25)—can never be understood. Such understanding—which reveals pronounced analogies with the phenomenon of Caesarism analyzed in Q9—hinges primarily on the *ambivalence* of "totalitarian policy," an ambivalence that corresponds in full to the duplicity of Caesarism itself. We have seen that totalitarianism of the dominant class tries to suppress associative and ideological pluralism, submitting the entire society to the control of its own "hegemonic apparatus." Gramsci now warns that such a phenomenon can derive from a regressive movement, as when "the party in question wants to prevent another force, bearer of a new culture, from becoming itself 'totalitarian'"; but it can also derive from a progressive drive, as "when the party in question is the bearer of a new culture" (Q6§136, p. 800; trans. Gramsci 1992–2007, vol. 3, p. 108).

The analogy between totalitarian politics and Caesarism then deserves our full attention. In Q9§133 (rewritten in Q13§27), Gramsci highlights the causative aspect around which his entire analysis of the phenomena of Caesarism rotates. These phenomena, Gramsci writes, "express a situation in which the struggling forces are in a catastrophic equilibrium; that is, they are balanced so that the continuation of the struggle can only be concluded with their mutual destruction" (Q9§133, p. 1194). Let's put aside the last sentence, echoing the incipit of Marx's *Manifesto*, and focus on the first one. When Gramsci talks about catastrophic balance, it evokes an idea of a full *symmetry* of the powers involved. Gramsci has already mentioned this element, in some way, in Q3§34, dedicated to an analysis of the "crisis of authority" (that is, of hegemony) that became more radical in the postwar period. In that note, having pointed out that the "reduction to economy and to politics" is the most important aspect of the crisis, Gramsci notes that the "reduction of the highest superstructures to what is closest to the structure" proves a "possibility [and necessity] of creating a new culture" (Q3§34, p. 312; trans. Gramsci 1992–2007, vol. 2, p. 33).

But now, in Notebook 6, this diagnosis takes a qualitative leap. After having elucidated an abstract *formal* aspect of the dialectical relation, Gramsci moves now to a *concrete* assertion of the symmetry of powers. This is precisely the aspect—a crucial one—that Gramsci refers to when he analyzes the trench warfare that characterizes the postwar scenario—one in which, we read, "the siege is reciprocal" (Q6§138, p. 802; trans. Gramsci 1992–2007, vol. 3, p. 109). This *reciprocity* shows nothing other than the equivalence of the forces in the field—their equilibrium.

This theme increasingly attracts Gramsci's attention, as he finds in it the key to deciphering the characteristics of the ongoing crisis and to foreseeing its development. The theme of the totalitarian conflict is analyzed in Q25§§4–5, where a sequence of materials that were originally dispersed in Q3§18 and Q3§90 are merged. In particular, here we find two extremely important notes where Gramsci connects two opposing dynamics: the "totalitarian" centralization put into place by "contemporary dictatorships" (Q25§4, p. 2287; trans. Gramsci 1971, p. 54) and the intensification of the "spirit of cleavage" in the subaltern groups (Q25§5, p. 2288; trans. Gramsci 1971, p. 52), which prepares for the construction of an equally strong antagonistic force.

The symmetry of these forces is a crucial element. This is particularly the case if we think back to the considerations about the structural origins of the processes of organic crisis; we easily realize what it means to affirm, as Grasmci does here, that a profound difference exists between how things appear (in this case, the clear supremacy of the dominant class) and how things are in reality—the reciprocal siege of equivalent forces.

Since we are analyzing the political scenario created by World War I through a macro-historic lens, affirming that, *in reality*, the dominant class (the bourgeoisie) is up against another class (the proletariat) equipped with the same power means claiming that during the first phase of the "modern crisis" (1870–1918), the proletariat has been accumulating a counterpower big enough to compete with the currently dominant bourgeoisie for control of society, just as the bourgeoisie, throughout the medieval crisis (the centuries preceding the French Revolution), was able to accumulate the power necessary to dethrone the feudal powers. Totalitarian policy grows against the background of an absolute life-or-death conflict inside the culminating phase of a crisis that, in Gramsci's eyes, is becoming increasingly clearer. It grows against the background of a tragic conflict that has as its goal the creation of completely different projects for society, and against the background of a total clash that for the first time in history has at stake both the control of the entire society and the power to determine its configuration and development in any situation.

The reason for this is that finally, the fundamental struggle includes a power that, at its core, is interested in the total transformation of society; a power that has *the need* to complete the bourgeois political revolution (the building of cohesive and homogenous social bodies); a power that is *aware* of its historic function and of its own potentiality; a power that is *able* to fulfill this task, which is to "put an end to class divisions" (Q14§70, p. 1732; trans. Gramsci 1971, p. 152), because it has an unlimited "expansivity," capable as it is to "absorb society in its completeness" (Q6§98, p. 774). The proletariat, in short, possesses a "historically necessary" power (Q14§70, p. 1733; trans. Gramsci 1971, p. 152). That is why Gramsci not only writes that understanding the passage to trench warfare is "the most important question of political theory," but also affirms that "we have entered a culminating phase of the politico-historical situation." The struggle is symmetrical; "all the resources for the hegemony of the State" are put into the struggle; the conquest of "decisive positions" is essential. All this means that the outcome of this struggle will decide the fate of an epoch: "once the 'war of position' is won, it is definitively decisive" (Q6§138, p. 802; trans. Gramsci 1992–2007, vol. 3, p. 109). For this reason, a mistake in the analysis of the characteristics of an historic phase and, in particular, of the nature of the processes of the ongoing crisis, would determine devastating consequences. Mistaking an occasional crisis for an organic one would waste an enormous amount of resources against a powerful adversary still standing strong on its own structural basis. On the contrary, interpreting an organic crisis as an occasional crisis would mean misunderstanding both the target of the conflict and its unwritten rules, its concrete forms.

Gramsci's concern is revealed by a revision on the note on the "relations of forces" that, as we have seen, runs parallel to the entire reflection on the logic of crises and transitions. In Q13§17, Gramsci adds that, as a consequence of the events that occurred between 1870 and 1871, "the body of principles of political strategy and tactics engendered in practice in 1789, and developed ideologically around '48, lost their efficacy" (Q13§17, p. 1582; trans. Gramsci 1971, p. 179). The defeat of the Paris Commune may itself be due to the misunderstanding of this historical shift. What remains is a fact: with the Commune, and climaxing in World War I, the final phases of bourgeois modernity has begun. Which is to say that its (rather long) pure and simple *duration* began. In this duration, a decisive mutual siege, whose outcome is impossible to foresee, also began. This siege is decisive not because modernity—capitalism—might overcome an organic crisis that by definition can be resolved only by "creating a new structure" (Q14§57, p. 1716; trans. Gramsci 1995a, p. 224), but because it cannot be excluded that the epochal struggle between capital and labor ends with their reciprocal destruction.

1 "The development of premonopoly capitalism, of capitalism in which free competition was predominant, reached its limit in the 1860s and 1870s. We now see that
  it is precisely after that period that the tremendous 'boom' in colonial conquests
  begins, and that the struggle for the territorial division of the world becomes
  extraordinarily sharp. It is beyond doubt, therefore, that capitalism's transition to
  the stage of monopoly capitalism, to finance capital, is connected with the intensification of the struggle for the partitioning of the world" (Lenin 2010, p. 83).

2 We can point out here the similarities with the scheme proposed in Marx's
  "Preface": "At a certain stage of development, the material productive forces
  of society come into conflict with the existing relations of production or—this
  merely expresses the same thing in legal terms—with the property relations within
  the framework of which they have operated hitherto. From forms of development
  of the productive forces these relations turn into their fetters" (Marx and Engels
  1976, vol. 29, p. 263).

3 This is a process that, for Gramsci, happened *everywhere in Europe*. For this reason,
  he maintains that the "the theory of the passive revolution" is a "necessary critical
  corollary" of Marxian canons (Q15§62, p. 1827; trans. Gramsci 1971, p. 114).

4 It is the "refractory reality [that] nobody can alter" (Q13§17, p. 1583; trans. Gramsci
  1971, p. 181).

5 Note from the translator: in Italian, *casta* comes from the Latin *castus*, meaning
  "cut off" or "separated," so here, Burgio reminds us that the quality of separation
  present inside this social formation is implied in the name itself.

6 See Maine [1861] 1986, p. 141.

7 As always happens in the *Notebooks*, Gramsci disseminates this theory, by necessity,
  through different notes that the reader must put together in an organic sequence.

3

Adam Smith

A Bourgeois Organic Intellectual?

KATE CREHAN

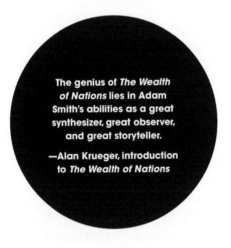

The genius of *The Wealth of Nations* lies in Adam Smith's abilities as a great synthesizer, great observer, and great storyteller.

—Alan Krueger, introduction to *The Wealth of Nations*

The question of the shifting nature and role of intellectuals over time and across space runs through the prison notebooks. As Joseph Buttigieg writes, "Gramsci never doubted the centrality of the study on the intellectuals to almost everything else he wanted to do" (Buttigieg 1992, p. 29). Gramsci's primary concern is not individual intellectuals, however, but the process by which societies produce and distribute "knowledge." When he discusses individual intellectuals he tends to focus on their links to their historical moment. Socially significant knowledge, for him, emerges out of a collective endeavor. This collective endeavor does not merely involve intellectuals, it encompasses the ceaseless dialogue inherent in social life itself, which takes many different forms.

One of the tasks Mussolini's prisoner set for himself was to trace out the different forms knowledge production takes under different regimes of economic and political power. Central to his argument is a distinction he makes between traditional and organic intellectuals—a distinction that has given rise to much debate, since the notebooks do not provide us with precise definitions of either category. To understand this apparent lack of clarity, it is helpful to remember Gramsci's concern with process: traditionality and organicity are not characteristics possessed by individual intellectuals; they refer rather to the nature of the relationship between the work intellectuals do as intellectuals and the wider world in which that intellectual activity is embedded.

To think through Gramsci's concept of organic intellectuals, this chapter takes the example of Adam Smith, a thinker who lived and wrote in the dawn of modern capitalism. From a conventional perspective, this eighteenth-century intellectual, later to be enshrined as something like the patron saint of laissez-faire capitalism, who lived his professional life within the academic institutions of his time, might seem a quintessentially traditional intellectual. But viewed through the prism of the organic intellectual, Smith assumes a rather different form, one that can both shed light on what makes intellectuals organic and suggest the potential usefulness of Gramsci's concept for contemporary analysts interested in other times and places.

The Organic Intellectual in the *Notebooks*

Gramsci may not give us a precise definition of organic intellectuals, but in a number of notes he tells us what organic intellectuals do. Two helpful notes are "The Formation of the Intellectuals" and a note left untitled in the notebooks, to which the English editor gives the title "Liberty as the Identity of History and Mind and as Ideology" (Q10i§10). This latter is one of a series of notes critiquing Benedetto Croce.

In "The Formation of the Intellectuals" (Q12§1), Gramsci writes, "Every social group, coming into existence on the original terrain of an essential function in the world of economic production, creates together with itself, *organically*, one or more strata of intellectuals which give it homogeneity and an awareness of its own function not only in the economic but also in the social and political fields" (Gramsci 1971, p. 5, my emphasis). Note that it is the creation of intellectuals that is organic.

The kind of social group Gramsci has in mind would seem to be a class, as in this passage from "Liberty as the Identity of History and Mind and as Ideology" (Q10i§10) in which he talks explicitly of a particular class's creation of a particular narrative: "[Croce] thinks he is writing a history from which every element of class has been exorcised and he is, instead, producing a highly accurate and praiseworthy description of the political masterpiece whereby a particular class manages to present and have the conditions for its existence and development as a class accepted as a universal principle, as a world view, as a religion" (Gramsci 1995a, p. 353).

Central to the process by which a new class is brought into being is the creation of new kinds of intellectuals organically linked to "the conditions for [that class's] existence and development as a class." The process by which a class generates a coherent narrative of the world as seen from its vantage point, and is able to get this narrative "accepted as a universal principle," is a key focus for Gramsci as he traces out the shifting nature and role of intellectuals in history. Crucially, as in Q4§49, intellectuals are not defined by their possession of specific skills:

> Can one find a unitary criterion to characterise equally all the diverse and disparate activities of intellectuals and to distinguish these at the same time and in an essential way from the activities of other social groupings? *The most widespread error of method seems to me that of having looked for this criterion of distinction in the intrinsic nature of intellectual activities, rather than in the ensemble of the system of relations in which these activities (and therefore the intellectual groups who personify them) have their place within the general complex of social relations.* Indeed the worker or proletarian, for example, is not specifically characterised by his manual or instrumental work, but by performing this work in specific conditions and in specific social relations. (Gramsci 1971, p. 8, my emphasis)

Despite Gramsci's clarity here, many readers of the notebooks apparently miss the radical nature of Gramsci's refusal of traditional understandings of what defines intellectuals and his insistence that we direct our attention to the "complex of social relations" within which intellectuals are embedded rather than focusing on individual intellectuals. Part of the problem here is that the definition of the intellectual as a particular kind of thinker is so taken for granted that questioning it seems to go against obvious common sense. If we want to grasp Gramsci's concept of the organic intellectual, however, we need to relinquish our commonsense assumptions and shift our focus to the *process* by which a social group or a class "creates together with itself, organically, one or more strata of intellectuals."

What might this process look like in practice? It is here that the example of Smith is useful. However traditional a scholar he might appear, as an intellectual Smith was the product of the historical moment that gave birth to those we might see as the initial bourgeois organic intellectuals. These were the intellectuals who would provide the class rising to dominance within a nascent industrial capitalism with "homogeneity and an awareness of its own function," the intellectuals who furnished the building blocks for a narrative that both laid out "the necessary conditions of existence" for industrial capitalism and explained why such a system would be in the interests of society as a whole.

I should preface my account of Smith, and the world of the Scottish Enlightenment to which he belonged, with a disclaimer: I am an anthropologist, not a historian, and certainly not a specialist of eighteenth-century Scotland. I approach the cultural world of the Scottish Enlightenment as a disciplinary outsider; my account of Smith and his world is based on secondary sources. Essentially, what I have done is to take a number of arguments from a wide range of scholars and assemble them in a perhaps novel way. I realize that some of these scholars might object to how I have used their work. In an effort not to distort their arguments, I have tried as far as possible to use their own words.

A Scottish Intellectual

In a review of Nicholas Phillipson's 2010 biography of Smith, Colin Kidd notes that nowadays Smith is "popularly identified as the founder of economics, an apostle of capitalism and honoured prophet of the new right" (Kidd 2010, p. 21). Phillipson and other Smith scholars, however, reject this characterization as not merely a gross simplification, but a fundamental misreading. To understand Smith's argument in his canonical *An Inquiry into the Nature and Causes of the Wealth of Nations* and his intellectual project as a whole, they argue, we need to situate him in the historical context of eighteenth-century Scotland. He was formed as a thinker by what has come to be called the Scottish Enlightenment, that extraordinary flowering of scholarship that included philosophers, theologians, scientists (although the term *scientist* was not coined until the nineteenth century), inventors, and engineers. The Scottish Enlightenment was part of the larger Europe-wide Enlightenment, but also specifically Scottish. Three major factors Scottish historians point to as contributing to Scotland's intellectual flowering are the economic and political realities of early eighteenth-century Scotland; its universities and learned societies and the character of its intellectual life; and, particularly relevant in the context of this essay, Scottish intellectuals' awareness of their country's recent loss of political autonomy and their sense of being looked down on by the English.

First, there is Scotland's poverty. The country had long been poor, with few natural geographical advantages and relatively little cultivable land. By the late seventeenth century many Scots had already recognized that, as one historian writes, "if the country was to prosper, men would need to be trained, the economy improved and science brought to bear on problems" (Emerson

2003, p. 11). The project of national development, or in the language of the day, "improvement," provides an important context for much of what Scottish intellectuals would achieve in the eighteenth century.

Poverty, however, was not the whole story; Scotland had a number of prosperous cities. Particularly important for Smith were Edinburgh, Scotland's capital city, and Glasgow. Both were lively, stimulating places that were growing rapidly during Smith's lifetime. Much of Glasgow's vibrancy derived from an economic prosperity based largely on the slave trade. While Glasgow merchants were seldom slave traders themselves, they grew rich from the trade in slave-produced crops—first sugar and tobacco, and later cotton. In Smith's day the city was primarily a merchants' town, but industry too was developing, spurred on by the needs of local agriculture, the opportunities for processing the imported goods of the Atlantic trade, and the demand for manufactured goods that could be sent back across the Atlantic and sold to buy yet more plantation crops.

The major political reality of early eighteenth-century Scotland was what is usually referred to as the 1707 Act of Union, although technically it was a Treaty of Union, not an act of Parliament. Ruled by a single monarch for the previous century, England and Scotland had nonetheless remained independent kingdoms, each with its own parliament; now there was a single state, the United Kingdom of Great Britain. And while the Act of Union allowed Scotland to retain its own independent legal system, it abolished the Scottish Parliament, replacing it with a limited number of Scottish representatives in the English Parliament. The loss of its own, independent political institutions, Phillipson argues, was traumatic for the Scottish political community. "One way of looking at the Scots inquiry into the Science of Man," he writes,

> is to think of it as a critique of the classic language of civic morality under-
> taken by a group of men living in a sophisticated but provincial commu-
> nity which had been stripped of its political institutions at the time of
> the Act of Union in 1707 and still hankered after an understanding of the
> principles of virtue which would make sense of their present provincial
> condition. . . . The Scots' concern with the principles of virtue can be
> related to the traumatic effect of the Act of Union on the Scottish politi-
> cal community. . . . In a long, sophisticated debate about the political and
> economic crisis in which the country was engulfed in the early years of
> the century, the Scots discovered that the language of contemporary poli-
> tics was not well suited to making sense of their present predicament. In
> the three decades which followed the Union philosophers, politicians and
> men of letters set out to fashion an alternative language of civic morality.

By the 1760s the process was complete, and a new language of civic morality had been created which provided the Scots with a new understanding of civic virtue. (Phillipson 1981, p. 22)

It would be this new "language of civic morality" that Smith would use in his writings—language and a view of the world that originated from the vantage point of the dominated rather than the dominant, or those who are, to use Gramsci's terminology, subaltern. It is important to note that the term *subalterns* in the notebooks is not, as is sometimes claimed, simply a codeword or euphemism for proletarians and their particular forms of oppression and subordination. Rather, as Buttigieg (2013) and Marcus Green (2011a, 2011b) show, it is a general term that encompasses the many different forms power can assume. At different points in the notebooks "slaves, peasants, religious groups, women, different races, and the proletariat" are all identified as subaltern social groups (Green 2011a, p. 69). It is possible to define the meaning of subalternity more precisely only when we are talking about a specific subaltern group at a specific moment in history. In line with this, the general term *subalternity* appears only once in the notebooks. Subalternity is nonetheless a useful concept precisely because it directs our attention to relations of power while leaving open the question of the specifics of those relations. Characterizing the condition of the intellectuals of the Scottish Enlightenment as one of subalternity can help us trace the multifaceted nature of "the traumatic effect of the Act of Union."

Eighteenth-century Scotland may have been poor, but it had exceptional knowledge-producing institutions and a dynamic intellectual life. The universities of Edinburgh, Glasgow, and Aberdeen were all radically reorganized in the late seventeenth and early eighteenth centuries. From being, as Phillipson describes the universities of Edinburgh and Glasgow, "little more than seminaries, designed to prepare young men of relatively humble background for the kirk and to give the sons of the gentry a smattering of classics and philosophy" (Phillipson 1981, p. 28), Scotland's universities became centers of the most advanced secular scholarship of the day. Their transformation included the introduction of new, more effective teaching methods and the establishment of chairs in new subjects such as humanity, history, mathematics, oriental languages, law, botany, medicine, and chemistry. In part, Phillipson argues, these changes were a response to a demand for a more relevant education by "a civic-minded gentry and professional class" (Phillipson 1981, p. 28). Using a Gramscian perspective, we might say that the reformers had implicitly recognized that the economic and political realities of the day demanded new forms of education capable of producing new kinds of intellectuals.

The universities, however, were not the only places in Scotland where new Enlightenment knowledge was produced. There were also the many learned societies and clubs "devoted to the improvement of manners, economic efficiency, learning and letters" (Phillipson 1981, 27). Not that the creation of learned societies was a phenomenon peculiar to Scotland; the eighteenth century saw the establishment of a profusion of such societies and clubs throughout Europe and the New World. These learned societies and clubs were intended not only as spaces where members could exchange knowledge, but also as a means to disseminate that knowledge to the wider society. A related concern, particularly strong perhaps in the case of the Scottish societies, was that knowledge should be useful. We need to bear in mind, however, that "in the Enlightenment, the concept of 'usefulness' encompassed both practical, economic benefit and a sense of utility related to the moral or intellectual improvement of the individual" (Wood 2003, p. 103). In general, these clubs and societies were equally interested in what we today tend to see as the distinct fields of "pure" and "applied" knowledge—a distinction that was far less marked in the eighteenth century.

The intellectuals of the Scottish Enlightenment, very conscious of the "backwardness" of their homeland, were committed to the dissemination of knowledge in a form accessible to nonspecialists, which their "progressive" compatriots, such as "improving" farmers, could use in practical ways. Theory and practice were for them closely linked. In the notebooks, a unity between theory and practice is a hallmark of genuinely organic intellectuals. Gramsci saw the Italian "Popular Universities" of his day as failures precisely because they were not based on this kind of unity between intellectuals and the popular masses. These attempts at popular education would only have been successful, we read in Q11§12, "if the intellectuals had been organically the intellectuals of those masses, and if they had worked out and made coherent the principles and the problems raised by the masses in their practical activity, thus constituting a cultural and social bloc" (Gramsci 1971, p. 330). Transposing Gramsci's formulation to an earlier historical period when the emerging class was the bourgeoisie, we might see Scotland's clubs and learned societies as very much concerned with working out and making coherent the principles and the problems raised in the practical activity not of "the masses," in this case, but of an emerging capitalist class.

In the process of their formation, emerging classes produce new types of intellectuals. So, in Q12§1, "the capitalist entrepreneur creates alongside himself the industrial technician, the specialist in political economy, the organisers of a new culture, of a new legal system, etc." (Gramsci 1971, p. 5). The economist is one of these new forms of intellectual who emerges together with the rise of the bourgeoisie. Smith demonstrates this newness. In his lifetime, neither "economics" nor "economist" existed as recognized categories. He himself was a professor, first of logic and metaphysics and then of moral philosophy; neither he nor his contemporaries ever referred to him as an economist. Indeed, the earliest citation in the OED for "economist," used in the modern sense of a specialist in matters having to do with the understanding and management of a society's financial and other resources, is 1804. "Economics" and "economist" are a branch of knowledge and a type of expert that, as Gramsci puts it, "the capitalist entrepreneur creates alongside himself."

"We Are Slaves to the Language We Write"

Viewed from the twenty-first century, the intellectual achievements of eighteenth-century giants such as David Hume, Smith, and all the other Scottish virtuosi represent one of the high points of modern European thought. But this was not always so clear to those men themselves. These eighteenth-century Scottish intellectuals could not think of themselves as part of a distinct Scottish Enlightenment; the term *Scottish Enlightenment* was coined only in 1900 (Broadie 2003, p. 3). And while the Scottish literati were highly cosmopolitan and well aware that they could more than hold their own in Europe's Republic of Letters, they were also aware that they were citizens of an impoverished and economically backward nation that had surrendered its political independence. Looming over Scottish intellectual life was the giant shadow of England; English disdain for the Scots and Scotland was often palpable. The relationship of the Scottish literati to their southern neighbor was, we might say, distinctly subaltern.

A revealing dimension of this subalternity is the embarrassment felt by so many Scottish intellectuals for what they saw as the deficiencies of their language. Except in the Highlands, few Scots had any knowledge of Gaelic or much interest in the Gaelic tradition; the language of the educated Scot was English and the model, the language spoken in polite English society. But this was not the language of most Scots. In addition to the distinct Scottish accent, the English written and spoken by the Scots differed in its grammar, syntax, vocabulary, and idioms from that of the educated English man or woman. Smith was fortunate in that, thanks to six years of study at Oxford during his late teens and early twenties, he was fluent in the spoken and written English of England. Hume's English, by contrast, was always that of a Scotsman, and he never lost his strong Scottish accent. He might be acknowledged across

Europe as one of the intellectual titans of the age, but throughout his life, he remained anxious about "Scotticisms" creeping into his writings, relying on English friends to check his manuscripts before publication so that any such blemishes could be removed. His spoken language he regarded as beyond hope of anglicization, writing in one letter in the 1750s, when he was already well established as a European scholar, "I am still jealous of my Pen. As to my Tongue, you have seen that I regard it as totally desperate and Irreclaimable" (quoted in Mossner 1980, p. 370). While he had no doubts about Scottish literary achievement, Hume also had no doubts as to the inferiority of Scots English, as he makes clear in another letter in which he marvels that "at a time when we have lost our princes, our Parliaments, our independent Government, even the Presence of our chief Nobility, *are unhappy in our Accent & Pronunciation, speak a very corrupt Dialect of the Tongue which we make use of*; is it not strange I say, that, in these Circumstances, we should really be the People most distinguish'd for Literature in Europe?" (quoted in Mossner 1980, p. 370, my emphasis). Note also Hume's acknowledgment of England's political hegemony over Scotland. We can see the unquestioned acceptance of linguistic inferiority by eighteenth-century Scottish intellectuals as one of the effects of this very real hegemony.

As the Hume biographer Ernest Campbell Mossner explains, the Union made Scots English newly problematic for those anxious to participate in public life beyond the confines of their native land. Instead of its own parliament, Scotland now had representatives in the English Parliament, and those Scottish representatives were often incomprehensible to the English members. As one prominent Scot despairingly reported of a Scottish peer who had addressed the House of Lords, "Deil *ae* word, from beginning to end, did the English understand of his speech." Another Scots peer, whose witty anecdote fell flat at a dinner with English lawyers, appealed to a fellow Scot at the table, "My story is not understood, Adam; for God's sake translate for me, as I can utter no sound like an Englishman but sneezing" (Mossner 1980, p. 371, emphasis in original). This failure of communication was seen by Scots and English alike as the Scots' problem; if they wanted to participate in English political and cultural life, they would have to learn to speak an English understandable by those south of the border.

The problem was that the educated English of England was not an English with which most Scots felt at home. Noting that the first chair in English in Britain was established by Edinburgh University in the mid-eighteenth century, Mossner comments, "Perhaps for the very reason that English was still, in Scottish ears, almost a foreign language" (Mossner 1980, p. 371). In the later eighteenth century the Scottish philosopher James Beattie wrote a revealing letter to an Englishman detailing the problems faced by those who may know a language well, yet lack a sense of ownership of it. The letter vividly delineates a characteristic subaltern anxiety:

> We who live in Scotland are obliged to study English from books, like a dead language. Accordingly, when we write, we write it like a dead language, which we understand but cannot speak; avoiding perhaps all ungrammatical expressions and even the barbarisms of our country, but at the same time without communicating that neatness, ease, and softness of phrase, which appears so conspicuously in Addison, Lord Lyttleton, and other elegant English authors. Our style is stately and unwieldy, and clogs the tongue in pronunciation, and smells of the lamp. We are slaves to the language we write, and are continually afraid of committing *gross* blunders; and, when an easy familiar, idiomatic phrase occurs, dare not adopt it, if we recollect no authority, for fear of Scotticisms. In a word, *we* handle English as a person who cannot fence handles a sword; continually afraid of hurting ourselves with it, or letting it fall, or making some awkward motion that shall betray our ignorance. An English author of learning is the master, not the slave of his language, and wields it gracefully, because he wields it with ease, and with full assurance that he has the command of it. (Quoted in Mossner 1980, p. 374; emphasis in original)

The anxiety captured here runs like a thread through the Scottish Enlightenment as a whole. An awareness of their subalternity as Scots was a persistent sore that never healed, but it was also an irritant that helped produce the proverbial pearl. As Phillipson argues, one way of approaching "the Scots inquiry into the Science of Man" is precisely as a response to the trauma of 1707, which brought home to the Scots the undeniable reality of their subalternity. The towering achievement of Smith's *Wealth of Nations* can be seen in part as a product of that subalternity.

"It Is but Equity"

In the two centuries since Smith's death, *Wealth of Nations* has come to be seen as one of the urtexts of capitalism, but as often happens to such sanctified texts, it is treated as a revered monument more to be admired from afar than to be read. In the popular imagination, its five books and close to a thousand pages of thoughtful argument have shrunk to a single soundbite: all that is required for a society's economic well-being is that market forces are allowed to operate freely; the market itself will do the rest with its all-powerful "invisible hand." Given this caricature, it is instructive to look at some of the strands of Smith's argument that have been airbrushed out of the popular image of Smith. Emma Rothschild's *Economic Sentiments: Adam Smith, Condorcet, and the Enlightenment* provides an invaluable guide to these often ignored strands. What follows draws heavily on her account.

The first point to note is that for Smith himself, *Wealth of Nations* was just one element of a far broader intellectual project concerned with developing a new Science of Man. As Phillipson writes, Smith believed that "it was now [that is, in the light of recent philosophical advances] possible to develop a genuine Science of Man based on the observation of human nature and human history; a science which would not only explain the principles of social and political organization to be found in different types of human society, but would explain the principles of government and legislation that ought to be followed by enlightened rulers who wanted to extend the liberty and happiness of their subjects and the wealth and power of their dominions" (Phillipson 2010, p. 2). In the event, his earlier exploration of the emergence of morality out of the experiences of everyday life, *The Theory of Moral Sentiments*, would be the only other volume he completed.

It is worth stressing that, contrary to the caricature, Smith very much believed in an active role for governments and legislators. He also had strong views on what is just and what is not. Today Smith may be remembered as a passionate advocate of free trade, but his denunciations of injustice and inequity in *Wealth of Nations* are just as passionate. Take, for instance, the following passage where, after noting that "servants, labourers and workmen of different kinds, make up the far greater part of every great political society," he makes this plea for their right to a decent life: "No society can surely be flourishing and happy, of which the far greater part of the members are poor and miserable. *It is but equity*, besides, that they who feed, cloath and lodge the whole body of the people, should have such a share of the produce of their own labour as to be themselves tolerably well fed, cloathed and lodged" (Smith 1976, p. 96, my emphasis). Smith's argument here is far from simply economic efficiency—although he certainly believes that an equitable system would be more efficient. It is a question of a basic and undeniable right, "it is but equity."

Smith, like other Enlightenment thinkers, assumed that human history was progressive. As R. H. Campbell and A. S. Skinner put it in their introduction to the authoritative 1976 edition of *Wealth of Nations*: "The belief in the natural progress of opulence, almost its inevitability, is so strong throughout the WN that, when dealing with a contemporary problem, Smith's main objective

Kate Crehan

is to isolate those barriers which lay in the path of natural progress as he saw it, and to advocate their speedy removal" (Campbell and Skinner 1976, p. 59). In line with this progressivist vision, *Wealth of Nations* can be seen as having two faces: one that looks to the past, focused on the fetters of residual feudal restrictions and encumbrances; and one that looks to the future, in which an economy freed from the restrictive encumbrances of the past will lead to increased prosperity across society. The magic mechanism here is the division of labor, which Smith sees as stemming from what he famously termed the uniquely human "propensity to truck, barter, and exchange one thing for another" (Smith 1976, p. 25).

One particularly pernicious residue of the past, in his view, was the apprenticeship system. Apprenticeship was both inefficient and oppressive. It was inefficient because, as a form of monopoly, it tended to keep both profits and wages artificially high. It was oppressive because it gave employers unreasonable power over apprentices. It might surprise those familiar only with his popular image that Smith was "much more disturbed by high profits than by high wages" (Rothschild 2001, p. 93), seeing workers as having far less power to combine to raise wages than employers had to raise prices. "We have," he observes, "no acts of parliament against combining to lower the price of work; but many against combining to raise it," and goes on to note, "Masters are always and every where in a sort of tacit, but constant and uniform combination, not to raise the wages of labour above their actual rate" (Smith 1976, p. 84). It was the duty of an enlightened government to reign in the rapacity of masters: "the mean rapacity, the monopolizing spirit of merchants and manufacturers, who neither are, nor ought to be, the rulers of mankind, though it cannot perhaps be corrected, may very easily be prevented from disturbing the tranquillity of anybody but themselves" (Smith 1976, p. 493). It is notable that Smith, writing before the French Revolution and the development of large-scale industrial, factory-based production, displays none of the fear of the poor and dispossessed that haunts the writings of so many later commentators.

Smith is chiefly remembered nowadays for his celebration of free trade and the magic of the market mechanism once freed from unnecessary encumbrances. It is certainly true that "freedom" was important to Smith. Indeed, Rothschild argues that "the idea of freedom is central to everything that Smith wrote" (Rothschild 2001, p. 70). Today, those who invoke him usually assume that the "freedom" he championed was the freedom from interference by states and government. Often overlooked in our more secular times is Smith's concern with another kind of freedom: freedom from the need for divine guidance. The story told by *Wealth of Nations* is a resolutely secular one. Deriving from the uniquely human "propensity to truck, barter, and exchange one thing for another," and given the inherent tendency of societies to progress, a new, "free" economic system will develop naturally without the need for divine intervention. After his death, while Smith's assumption of progress would remain central to his popular image, its close association with his rejection of religious authority would be forgotten.

Smith himself was always very circumspect as regards his religious convictions, and his own religious beliefs remain unclear. His caution is understandable at a time when even the suspicion of religious skepticism could be dangerous. As late as 1697, the Scottish teenager Thomas Aikenhead was hanged after he merely "orally ridiculed some passages in the Old Testament" (Mossner 1980, p. 354). But whatever Smith's own religious beliefs may have been, "the break with the tradition of Christian authority [in *Wealth of Nations*] is obvious" (Campbell and Skinner 1976, p. 51). Whether or not Smith was a believer, the economic mechanism he lays out in *Wealth of Nations*, like the moral system he elaborates in *The Theory of Moral Sentiments*, has no need for a divine presence. But while we may not need God in order to arrive at an economically efficient and morally just world, we do need wise legislators. Smith's celebration of the market is often taken to mean that he was opposed to government regulation, but nothing could be further from the truth.

The Organicity of Adam Smith

Earlier I quoted Gramsci's comment that despite Croce's insistence that he is providing a disinterested account of history, in reality he was describing "the political masterpiece" that transformed an account of the world as seen from the vantage point of a specific class into "a universal principle" (Gramsci 1995a, p. 353). Smith's *Wealth of Nations* can be seen as helping to provide a rising bourgeois class with just such a narrative, a narrative of laissez-faire that "manages to present and have the conditions for its existence and development as a class accepted as a universal principle, as a world view, as a religion." This is not to say that this was Smith's intention; it took time for his complex and nuanced text to be refashioned as a simple, persuasive story of an all-powerful market mechanism. Missing from this story is Smith's insistence on the right of "they who feed, cloath and lodge the whole body of the people" to a decent life, and the importance of government intervention to reign in self-interested merchants and manufacturers.

Given the wide divergence between the historical Smith and the market fetishist the name Adam Smith would come to evoke, can he be termed an organic bourgeois intellectual? In what sense is he part of those "strata of intellectuals" (Gramsci 1971, p. 5) that a rising bourgeois class, like "every social group, coming into existence on the original terrain of an essential function in the world of economic production, creates together with itself, organically" (Gramsci 1971, p. 5)? We need to remember here Gramsci's insistence that understanding the role and nature of intellectuals requires that we focus not on individual intellectuals and their "intrinsic" qualities, but on the *process* by which knowledge is produced. As I began by arguing, the definition of intellectuals as traditional or organic ultimately depends on the relationship of their intellectual work to the wider world. Is that work part of the process by which a class achieves "homogeneity and an awareness of its own function"? If the answer is yes, then those intellectuals can be considered organic to that class. In other words, organic intellectuals are those whose work as intellectuals provides to a class emerging from subalternity the particular forms of knowledge its conditions of existence require. It is important to stress here that such intellectuals may well not be aware that this is what they are doing. Like Croce in Q10i§10, they may see themselves as engaged in intellectual inquiry "from which every element of class has been exorcised" (Gramsci 1995a, p. 353). Intellectuals' tendency to see themselves as disinterested seekers of "truth" is why Gramsci insists in Q11§12 that "the starting-point of critical elaboration" is an understanding of oneself "as a product of the historical process to date which has deposited in you an infinity of traces, without leaving an inventory" (Gramsci 1971, p. 324). All responsible intellectuals must begin by making such an inventory.

Smith's intellectual formation, like that of the other intellectuals of the Scottish Enlightenment, occurred at a moment of historical transition, a moment when a new dominant class, the bourgeoisie, was beginning to stir. In Scotland this formation was overshadowed by the trauma of the Act of Union; Scottish intellectuals viewed the world from a subaltern vantage point. In Smith's eyes, *Wealth of Nations* is a polemic written against the existing economic order. In a famous letter he described it as "the very violent attack I had made upon the whole commercial system of Great Britain" (quoted in Phillipson 2010, p. 247). By "commercial system," Smith means the full panoply of outmoded feudal institutions and practices that he saw as holding back the "natural" progress of economic life to ever greater "opulence."

From this perspective, *Wealth of Nations*, with its plea for the facilitation of natural economic progress beneficial to all, can be seen as a key building block for the emergent-hegemonic narrative of a rising bourgeois class. The close-knit fraternity of Scottish virtuosi to which Smith belonged was especially well placed to articulate the viewpoint of an emerging bourgeoisie. It included not only academics but also progressive-minded merchants, landowners, and other "practical men," all searching for solutions to the many problems facing post-Union Scotland. Academics and "practical men" came together in the learned societies and clubs, where "improvement"—what it entailed and how it might be achieved—was a frequent theme of discussion. The perspective from which Scotland's predicament was seen was very much that of Scotland's progressive landowners, merchants, and other men of business. Smith was a regular attendee of such clubs and societies in both Edinburgh and Glasgow; for all his criticisms of self-interested "masters" heedless of the needs of their workers, part of what he does in *Wealth of Nations* is to turn the experience of Scotland's practical men of business—their common sense, if you will—into a coherent narrative. As Broadie puts it, "Smith's *Wealth of Nations* was a product of many things, amongst which was Smith's close contact with the merchant class of Glasgow" (Broadie 2003, p. 5).

Prior to its publication, a number of Smith's friends feared that its intellectual sophistication would prevent *Wealth of Nations* from finding a wide readership. What his friends seemed to have missed was that Smith was doing far more than providing an account of a theoretical system. "There was," as its modern editors explain, "another side to the WN, a more pragmatic, down to earth side, which gave the work a practical relevance in the eyes of many to whom the intellectual system was perhaps a mystery or merely irrelevant." Smith "commanded respect because the practical conclusions which followed from the chief elements of his system were evidently related to the economic problems of the middle of the eighteenth century" (Campbell and Skinner 1976, pp. 42–43).

Crucially, Smith observed those economic problems as a Scot. The country that produced the intellectual ferment in which he would flourish was one whose intellectuals saw themselves as having, in the words of Hume in his letter quoted above, "lost our princes, our Parliaments, our independent Government, even the Presence of our chief Nobility." These were intellectuals struggling to make sense of Scotland's subaltern condition within the United Kingdom of Great Britain. Part of what Smith does in *Wealth of Nations* is to provide a coherent narrative of the world as seen from the vantage point of progressive merchants and landowners who, while they may have been dominant within Scotland, felt themselves to be subaltern within the British state. Turning the complex and nuanced historical Smith into the apostle of laissez-faire, and his "very violent attack" on the existing economic order into bourgeois common sense, required considerable work, however.

Smith died in 1790, a year after the storming of the Bastille. As the turbulent events in France unfolded, there were many to whom his perceived sympathy for the poor, his championing of free trade, a more equitable tax system, and freedom of the press began to seem dangerously radical. In this climate of mounting fear that revolution would spread across the channel, Dugald Stewart, who had known Smith, published a memoir of him. This memoir, published in 1793, was destined to become "by far the most important biographical work about Smith, and an early source of Smith's conservative renown" (Rothschild 2001, p. 56). Stewart's aim was to correct the view that his fellow Scot was a liberal; his Smith is that quintessentially modern form of the intellectual, the apolitical expert. Yes, he argues for economic freedom in *Wealth of Nations*, but not political liberty. As long as a country's laws are just, Stewart's Smith contends, that country's people "would have little reason to complain, that they were not immediately instrumental in their enactment" (Stewart [1794] 1980, p. 310). "Stewart's defence of Smith," Rothschild explains, "was part of a far more extensive discussion, in the mid-1790s, about the distinction between politics and political economy, and about the definition of freedom. His object, in the memoir, seems to have been to show that political economy was an innocuous, technical sort of subject. Smith was a retiring, innocuous sort of person, quite unconcerned to influence public opinion, and interested only in offering hints on policy to 'actual legislators'" (Rothschild 2001, p. 58). Thanks in part to Stewart's memoir, this conservative reading of Smith would become the dominant one. By 1800 the liberal and potentially seditious Smith had been eclipsed; he had become "the modern hero of commerce" (Rothschild 2001, p. 64). And the process continued: academics and popularizers picked up certain arguments in *Wealth of Nations* while discarding others, until the reflection in the mirror held up to the world by this Scottish intellectual provided an image satisfactory to the bourgeois spectator. In the process, Smith's complex argument was reduced to bourgeois common sense. The "truth" of *Wealth of Nations* would become, in the words of James Buchan, author of *The Authentic Adam Smith*, "that, like Fra Pacioli's treatise on double-entry bookkeeping in 1494, it reproduces commercial knowledge and practice in the vernacular, and like that great work provides them with respectability" (Buchan 1995, p. 13).

Even more than respectability, I would argue, the transmuted Smith turned that "commercial knowledge and practice" into an authoritative account of how the world works, one that only deluded idealists or the hopelessly ignorant could question. And that account would prove a central plank in the larger bourgeois class narrative that gave that class "homogeneity and an awareness of its own function not only in the economic but also in the social and political fields" (Gramsci 1971, p. 5). Insofar as Smith, however unwittingly, helped give a coherent voice to "the monopolizing spirit of merchants and manufacturers"—people whom he thought "neither are, nor ought to be, the rulers of mankind" (Smith 1976, p. 493)—he can surely be considered a bourgeois organic intellectual.

NOTE

A longer version of this chapter is included in Kate Crehan, *Gramsci's Common Sense: Inequality and Its Narratives* (Durham, NC: Duke University Press, 2016).

4

Gramsci's Bergson

CESARE CASARINO

> Only passion sharpens the intellect and cooperates with it in making intuition clearer.
>
> —Antonio Gramsci, *Quaderni del carcere*, Q15§50 (my translation)
>
> ———
>
> Intelligent idealism is closer to intelligent materialism than is stupid materialism.
>
> —Vladimir Ilyich Lenin, *Collected Works*

If I invoke Lenin's dictum from his 1915 "Conspectus of Hegel's *Lectures on the History of Philosophy*," that is because few have gone further in re-elaborating it and deploying it as a veritable theoretical-methodological principle than Antonio Gramsci in his *Quaderni del carcere*. I am not referring merely to Gramsci's complementary engagements with, for example, the idealism of Benedetto Croce and the materialism of Nikolai Ivanovic Bukharin. I am referring also to the fact that such a theoretical-methodological principle was thematized and investigated explicitly on several occasions in the *Quaderni*.

Take, for example, Q4§3, titled "Two Aspects of Marxism" and later revised in Q16§9 as "Some Questions for the Study of the Development of the Philosophy of Praxis." Here, Gramsci in effect identifies the historical conditions of possibility for the insight expressed by Lenin. Gramsci replies to Lenin something along these lines: intelligent idealism is closer to intelligent materialism because it finds it necessary to assimilate certain aspects of intelligent materialism so as to compete with the latter, whereas stupid materialism diverges from intelligent materialism to the extent to which it does not recognize the latter as philosophy in its own right, in our modernity. In Q4§3, Gramsci writes:

Marxism has been a moment of modern culture and to a certain extent has determined and fertilized some of its currents. . . . Marxism has undergone a double revision . . . it has given rise to a double combination. On the one hand, some of its elements have been explicitly or implicitly absorbed by certain idealist currents (Croce, Sorel, Bergson, etc., the pragmatists, etc.); on the other hand, the "official" Marxists, anxious to find a philosophy that would encompass Marxism, have found it in the modern derivations of vulgar philosophical materialism or even in idealist currents like Kantianism (Max Adler). (Q4§3, pp. 421–422; trans. Gramsci 1992–2007, vol. 2, p. 140; trans. modified)

Later, in Q16§9—where "Marxism" has now turned into "philosophy of praxis"— Gramsci adds:

The currents which have attempted combinations of the philosophy of praxis with idealist tendencies consist of the most part of "pure" intellectuals, . . . [who] as elaborators of the most wide-ranging ideologies of the dominant classes and as *leaders* of the intellectual groups of their own countries, could not fail to make use of at least some elements of the philosophy of praxis, to strengthen their conceptions and moderate the excessive speculative philosophism with the historicist realism of the new theory and to provide new arms for the arsenal of the social groups to which they were tied. (Q16§9, p. 1855; trans. Gramsci 1971, pp. 389–390; trans. modified)[1]

Importantly, in both versions of this note Gramsci singles out Antonio Labriola—arguably the first Marxist academic philosopher—as the one thinker who does not belong to either of these idealist or materialist camps and whose position hence needs to be reevaluated, inasmuch as he "affirms that the philosophy of praxis is an independent and original philosophy which contains in itself the elements of a further development, so as to become, from an interpretation of history, a general philosophy" (Q16§9, p. 1855; trans. Gramsci 1971, p. 390; trans. modified). I will return to Labriola.[2]

In many ways, these two notes anticipate Louis Althusser's arguments in his essay "Lenin before Hegel" regarding the agon between idealism and materialism in philosophy as a form of class struggle in its own right. Gramsci's preoccupation, however, is rather different in the end, as these pages lead him to the inevitable question, "Why has the philosophy of praxis had this fate of having served to form combinations between its principal elements and either idealism or philosophical materialism?" (Q16§9, p. 1856; trans. Gramsci 1971, p. 390; trans. modified). To answer this "complex and delicate" question, he adds, "means no more and no less than writing the history of modern culture since the activity of the founders of the philosophy of praxis" (Q16§9, p. 1856; trans. Gramsci 1971, pp. 390–391; trans. modified).

My question in this essay will be less ambitious: why does Henri Bergson play a crucial role in the formulation of Gramsci's own question, namely, in Gramsci's attempt to investigate the "double revision" and "double combination" "undergone" by the philosophy of praxis? After all the passages quoted above—in which Bergson is mentioned alongside Croce and Sorel—Gramsci, in his typical fashion, proceeds to outline a research program. When it comes to inquiring into the ways in which philosophical idealism has absorbed aspects of the philosophy of praxis, in both versions of this note the emphasis falls finally and decidedly on Bergson: "But the most important study, it seems to me, should be that of Bergsonian philosophy and of pragmatism, in order to find out to what extent certain of their positions would be inconceivable without the historical link of the philosophy of praxis" (Q16§9, p. 1856; trans. Gramsci 1971, p. 391). Leaving pragmatism aside—since, among other things, it is not entirely clear whom exactly Gramsci has in mind here, though there are occasional references to William James in the *Quaderni*—I want to ask: why Bergson?

Undoubtedly, Gramsci must have seen in Bergson an ally of sorts in his struggle against the mechanistic outlook, scientism, and positivism of the philosophical cultures of the day, including the tendencies toward economic determinism of both the Second and the Third Internationals. This is clear already as early as Q1§78—titled "Bergson, Positivistic Materialism, Pragmatism"—in which Gramsci summarizes an article on Bergson, published in occasion of his Nobel Prize for literature in 1927. Gramsci's summary focuses on Bergson's critique of positivism and is termed in ways that are rather similar to Gramsci's own antipositivist positions later in the *Quaderni*. But already here, in this first reference to Bergson in the *Quaderni*, we are faced immediately with a conundrum that we will encounter each and every time Bergson is mentioned throughout the rest of this work. In effect, we are faced with an exact inversion of the research program outlined in both Q4§3 and Q16§9: rather than investigating what crucial insights Bergson absorbed from the philosophy of praxis, and hence rather than investigating how exactly Bergson would have been "inconceivable" without the philosophy of praxis—which Gramsci indicates is the most important part of this research program—Gramsci instead appeals to Bergson as a potentially kindred spirit, does not disdain on occasion to re-elaborate concepts from his philosophy, and never subjects him to any type of criticism.[3] Rather than showing how the philosophy of praxis constituted a condition of possibility for Bergson, Gramsci shows in effect what Bergson can do for the philosophy of praxis. In short, such a discrepancy between, on the one hand, the role that Gramsci declares Bergson ought to play in his research, and, on the other hand, the role that Bergson actually plays in his research, signals that Bergson may constitute a symptomatic aporia in the *Quaderni*. The question, thus, needs to be reformulated: what is the problematic that constitutes the absent presence—namely, the determinate and determining absence—indexed by the Bergsonian symptom in the *Quaderni*?

The answer to this question lies only partly in the most obvious place— namely, in the heated political debates between "spontaneism" and "voluntarism" to which Gramsci devotes numerous pages throughout the *Quaderni*.[4] From a philosophical standpoint, the debates between "spontaneism" and "voluntarism" revolved around the contested concept of the will—a concept that is certainly central to Bergson and that is certainly troubling for Gramsci's understanding of the political. But if the problem of the will is the answer to the question of why Bergson marks a peculiar aporia in the *Quaderni*, that is so only to the extent to which the will constitutes a screen behind which there hides another and far more troubling problem for Gramscian politics—namely, the dialectical intertwining of (class) interest and desire. I will return to this Gordian knot. For the moment, I think it is more expedient to approach the question via a more circuitous route, and to seek the answer elsewhere first.

In Q5§127—one of the many notes simply titled "Machiavelli"—Gramsci discusses a 1929 essay on "The Politics, Science, and Art of the State" by a "certain . . . M. Azzalini" (Q5§127, p. 656; my translation). After having criticized the essay's treatment of Niccolò Machiavelli as confused and nonsensical, Gramsci does nonetheless linger on Azzalini's contention that there is such a thing as an art of politics, which is distinct from a science of politics and which is characterized by intuition. It is at this point that Gramsci turns to the Bergson of *Creative Evolution*. I need to quote at length:

> It is necessary to disentangle . . . what "intuition" might mean in politics from the expression "art" of politics, etc.—Remember also some points made by Bergson: "Of life (reality in movement), intelligence offers us only a translation in terms of inertia. It circles around, taking the greatest possible number of external views of the object, which it draws toward itself rather than penetrating it. But what will lead us into the very interior of life is intuition." . . . "Our eye perceives the traits of the living being, but juxtaposed to each other rather than organically related. The purpose of life, the simple movement which runs through the lineaments, which links them together and gives them a meaning, escapes it; and it is this purpose

that the artist tends to capture, situating himself within the object by a kind of sympathy, breaking down by an effort of intuition the barrier which space places him between him and his model. It is true, however, that aesthetic intuition only captures that which is individual." . . . First of all, separation of political intuition from aesthetic, lyric, or artistic intuition; only by metaphor does one speak of art of politics. Political intuition does not express itself in the artist but in the "leader," and "intuition" must be understood not as "knowledge of that which is individual" but as swiftness in connecting seemingly unrelated facts [and in conceiving the means adequate to the end which is discovering the interests involved and] rousing the passions of men and directing men to a determinate action. The "expression" of the "leader" is "action." . . . However, the "leader in politics" can be an individual but also a more or less numerous political body. (Q5§127, pp. 660-661; trans. Gramsci 1971, pp. 381-382; trans. modified)[5]

With this final comment, Gramsci has cleared the way for elaborating, in the rest of this note, one of the earliest versions of his famous argument regarding how Machiavelli's "notion of 'Prince' . . . can be translated in modern terms as 'political party'" (Q5§127, p. 662; trans. Gramsci 1971, p. 382; trans. modified).

For Gramsci, if the expression "art of politics" can only be a "metaphor," "political intuition," on the other hand, is a type of knowledge that is rooted in metonymy and that turns passions into actions. Political intuition, in fact, involves a fast two-step process. The first step involves two simultaneous, distinct yet indiscernible operations—namely, relating apparently unrelated phenomena and conceiving means adequate to the end. The second step consists in precisely this end and hence is part and parcel of the first step. The second step constituting the end of the first step itself involves three other operations at one and the same time: revealing the interests immanent in such relations among unrelated phenomena, eliciting the passions attendant and constitutive of such interests, and directing such passions toward determinate actions. Given that this entire tripartite second step is internal to the first step, we may infer further that for Gramsci, truly producing relations among unrelated phenomena is tantamount to at once realizing our interests, generating our passions, and moving us to actions. If the steps and substeps of this process seem all to fold back into one aneach other, that is because, strictly speaking, political intuition does not consist of any of these operations at all; it consists, rather, of the "swiftness" with which these operations unfold and are conducted. I repeat: "'Intuition' must be understood . . . as swiftness in connecting seemingly unrelated facts [and in conceiving the means adequate to the end which is discovering the interests involved and] rousing the passions of men and directing men to a determinate action" (Q5§127, p. 661; trans. Gramsci 1971, p. 381; trans. modified). Such is political intuition: a swiftness, a rapidity, a clinamen begetting new worlds, a sudden and radically transformative shift in gaze. Who is the political subject of this gaze?

Before turning to this crucial question, let us retrace our steps back to Bergson. Gramsci, as you recall, on the one hand dismisses Azzalini's definition of an art of politics characterized by intuition, and on the other hand wants to disentangle intuition from the art of politics. Far from falling into contradiction here, Gramsci evidently is interested in showing that, even though there is no such a thing as an art of politics per se, there is indeed such a thing as political intuition (whose relation to a science of politics is yet to be determined). Gramsci turns to Bergson's discussion of intuition in the attempt both to define political intuition and to determine its relation to a science of politics. Though it is precisely Bergson's discussion of aesthetic and artistic intuition that Gramsci invokes here, even as he declares that political intuition has nothing to do with aesthetic intuition, Bergson has definitively left his mark: the explicit insight that Gramsci retains from Bergson, in fact, is that intuition constitutes a dynamic and relational knowledge—that is, a production of relations among unrelated, moving, shifting elements. Recall how Bergson tells us: "Our eye perceives the traits of the living being, but juxtaposed to each other rather than organically related. The purpose of life, the simple movement which runs through the lineaments, which links them together and gives them a meaning, escapes it; and it is this purpose that the artist tends to capture, situating himself within the object by a kind of sympathy, breaking down by an effort of intuition the barrier which space places him between him and his model" (Q5§127, p. 661; trans. Gramsci 1971, p. 381).[6] Gramsci places the "'leader'"—whether individual or collective—in a position homologous to that of this artist, who relates otherwise disconnected aspects of the object, who gives meaning and purpose to the life of the object by producing such relations, who deploys the passion of sympathy with the object so as to perform the action of breaking barriers and situating himself within the life of the object, and who does all that "by an effort of intuition." Gramsci's protestations to the contrary notwithstanding, I believe we are dealing with more than a metaphor here and perhaps even with a structural homology (between Bergson's aesthetic intuition and Gramsci's political intuition).

We can now return to the question—namely, who or what is the political subject of that radically transformative gaze which is intuition?—and answer it: the leader—whether individual or collective—and, in Gramsci's specific case, the party. This turns out to be, however, a peculiar kind of subject. To begin with, political subject and grammatical subject do not coincide. Gramsci writes: "Political intuition does not express itself in the artist but in the 'leader'" (Q5§127, p. 661; trans. Gramsci 1971, p. 381). The grammatical subject is "political intuition," the political subject is the leader—and the real subject, as it were, lies in the gap at once dividing and linking the two. Nowhere in the passage quoted above, in other words, does Gramsci tell us that the leader has an intuition; on the contrary, it is intuition that expresses itself in and as the leader, it is intuition that has a leader. In short, it is intuition that makes the leader, not the other way around—which is another way of saying that it is the gaze that produces and that has a subject rather than it is the subject who produces or who has a gaze. Moreover, Gramsci writes also: "The 'expression' of the 'leader' is 'action'" (Q5§127, p. 661; trans. Gramsci 1971, p. 381). According to this political grammar, then, intuition expresses itself, the leader is the expression, and action is that which is expressed. Intuition-leader-action: in this triadic structure, the leader is the medium of expression, it is the process of mediation between intuition and action as well as immanent in both, it is the translator and convertor of this entire political proposition, it is the pivotal axis around which hinges revolution. Under the gaze of intuition, the leader, the party, is neither subject nor object: it is the process of situating within and penetrating life so as to give rise to radically transformed subjects and objects and so as to produce meaning, purpose, end.

Still, what could it mean to say that the party is the process of mediation joining political intuition and revolutionary action? In Q5§127, Gramsci's investigation into the question of political intuition emerges from a reflection on the relations between science of politics and art of politics. Whether or not one understands art of politics as metaphor only, and whether or not one sees a clear distinction between art of politics and science of politics, political intuition seems to constitute here something in excess of political rationality, a surplus with respect to political reason. What need would there be for Gramsci, after all, to elaborate a concept of political intuition if the political rationality operative in the science of politics would suffice in and of itself— that is, it would be adequate to the historical conjuncture? Isn't the disastrous experience of fascism, among other things, the proof for Gramsci that such a political rationality—especially in its mechanistic and positivistic forms—is woefully inadequate to the historical conjuncture? Isn't Gramsci's attempt to produce a concept of political intuition precisely an attempt to reconceptualize political reason altogether? Didn't Bergson tell us, in fact, that intuition can take us there where intelligence fears to tread—namely, within life itself?

And does this plunge into Bergsonism constitute a regrettable lapse of reason into irrationalist vitalism on Gramsci's part? I would argue that there is nothing either irrationalist or vitalist about Gramsci's attempt to reconceptualize political reason in the wake of Bergsonian intuition.

Let me turn to a moment in the *Quaderni* in which Bergson is all the more implicitly present and ubiquitous for being explicitly absent. Q7§6—titled "The *Popular Manual* and Sociology" and revised in Q11§25 as "Reduction of the Philosophy of Praxis to a Sociology"—is one of the many notes in which Gramsci at once critiques Bukharin and deploys such a critique so as to produce his own new and original concepts. The new concept in question here is "philology," specifically a method that would "expand the sphere of philology as it is intended traditionally" and that would assert "the importance of ascertaining and specifying particular facts in their unique 'individuality'" (Q11§25, p. 1429; my translation). For Gramsci, "this method is challenged by another one, namely, the method of 'large numbers,' or 'statistics,' that is borrowed from the natural sciences, or at least from some of them" (Q7§6, p. 856; trans. Gramsci 1971, p. 159; trans. modified). In Q7§6, Gramsci writes:

> But not enough attention has been paid to the fact that the law of "large numbers" can be applied to history and politics only as long as the great masses of the population remain passive or are assumed to remain passive with regard to the issues that interest the historian and the politician. This extension of the law of large numbers from the natural sciences to . . . the science and art of politics . . . can lead to catastrophes so devastating as to be irreparable. In the science and art of politics, the elevation of the law of large numbers to the status of an essential law is not just a scientific error; it is a political error in action: it induces mental laziness and superficial political programs, it is an aprioristic affirmation of the "unknowability" of the real. . . . Political action has a tendency, precisely, to bestir the great multitudes out of passivity, that is, to destroy the "law" of large numbers. How, then, could this be taken to be a "law"? Within this context too one can see what turmoil is brought about in the art of politics by placing the collective organism in the leadership role rather than the single individual, the individual leader. The "single individual" knows the standardized sentiments of the great masses as expression of the law of large numbers (that is, rationally, intellectually), and, if he is a great leader, he translates them into ideas-as-force, into words-as-force. By contrast, the collective organism knows the sentiments of the great masses through "coparticipation," through "compassionality," and, if the collective organism is vitally

embedded within the masses, it knows their sentiments through experience of immediate particulars, by a system of living "philology," so to speak. (Q7§6, pp. 856–857; trans. Gramsci 1971, p. 159; trans. modified)

To this, Gramsci adds in Q11§25: "In this way, a tight bond is formed among great mass, party, and leadership group, and hence the entire complex is well articulated and can move as a 'collective-man'" (Q11§25, p. 1430; my translation).

In this passage—in which, notably, "science of politics" and "art of politics" are deployed together rather than being separated and differentiated, and in which the expression "art of politics" does not seem to carry metaphorical connotations—language strains to capture thought, as Gramsci gropes for words and struggles to produce a name for a most elusive concept that has no name (hence the coinage of neologisms like *coparticipation*" and *compassionality* as well as the high metaphoricity of expressions such as "a system of living 'philology,' so to speak"). And yet, had Gramsci not found a name for this elusive form of knowledge already in Q5§127? There is at least a close affinity between, on the one hand, this method of "'living philology'" that enables the party as collectivity to embed itself vitally within the masses and to know their sentiments through "'coparticipation'" and "'compassionality,'" and, on the other hand, what Gramsci earlier had called "political intuition." In both cases, we are dealing with a political epistemology that enables one to know that which cannot be comprehended within the limits of political reason alone. In both cases, we are confronted with a form of knowledge that situates us within that which is to be known and hence that operates in a zone of indistinction between subject of knowledge and object of knowledge and that problematizes any type of subject-object distinction whatsoever. In both cases, what is at stake is a dynamic process by which at one and the same time passions turn into actions and the party becomes enmeshed with and virtually indistinguishable from the masses—namely, the process that gives rise to a revolutionary machinic assemblage or revolutionary war machine. It would take me farther afield to argue that such a process cannot be reduced to either "spontaneism" or "voluntarism."[7] Moreover, it would take me farther afield to show not only that Gramsci had had a tantalizing yet crucially formative taste of such a process in his early Turin years and especially in 1919 and 1920 with the struggles surrounding the factory councils, but also how it is precisely such struggles that now, more than a decade later, he is attempting to recapture in theory and to conceptualize as "'living philology'" or "political intuition." It would take me farther afield also to show how the attempt to recapture and translate those struggles into theory takes place according to a fundamental historical-materialist principle that is stated several times in the *Quaderni*. This is the principle according to which it is theory understood as a moment immanent in political praxis that must adapt itself to the nonschematizable complexities of what Gramsci calls "the real" rather than the other way around; that is, rather than "the real" and its complexities having to be purified and reduced by the schematisms of a theory that hence makes itself transcendent to the world of political praxis.[8] All that aside, I want to stress that the congruities and correspondences between living philology and political intuition have the effect of clarifying and emphasizing that the latter is a question of method—namely, that political intuition indeed constitutes immanent method rather than transcendent epiphany or immediate and quasi-mystical knowledge. It is precisely when elaborating such a method, among other things, that Gramsci proves himself to be the true inheritor of Labriola, for whom the historical-materialist conception of politics and, indeed, the philosophy of praxis is a "philosophy immanent to the things on which it philosophizes" (Labriola 1902, p. 216; my translation).

I will return to the apparent paradox of intuition as method. Here, I want to conclude my analysis of all these passages in the *Quaderni* by putting forth the following hypothesis: if—as Peter Thomas has argued compellingly in his remarkable study *The Gramscian Moment*—Gramsci re-elaborates the concept of hegemony so as to produce in effect a Marxist theory of the constitution of the political (Thomas 2009b, pp. 194–195), in enlisting Bergson for the elaboration of the concept of political intuition Gramsci is struggling to produce a strictly complementary historical-materialist theory of revolutionary becoming—which, as we know from Gilles Deleuze and Félix Guattari, among others—is indissoluble from the question of desire. Put differently, I want to argue that it is the very question of desire—or, more precisely, the question of the nexus between (class) interest and desire understood as an ineludible political question—that constitutes the problem to which Gramsci attempts to offer political intuition as the solution. Desire as an eminently political category is the problematic indexed by the Bergsonian symptom in the *Quaderni*.

Ultimately, however, Gramsci's Bergson is nowhere to be found in the *Quaderni*. What we do find there is a series of appropriations and re-elaborations of Bergsonian concepts put in the service of the philosophy of praxis, so as to extend its reach into those nether regions of the life of the political for which it was as yet ill-equipped and inadequate, or, put differently, so as to potentiate and radicalize its explanatory, mobilizing, and transformative powers. What we do not find, however, is the ensemble of elements that Bergson purportedly appropriated and re-elaborated from the philosophy of praxis; what we are not shown is precisely what—as I indicated at the beginning of this essay—

Gramsci insists is the most important aspect of any attempt to historicize the philosophy of praxis as the prime motor of modern culture from the middle of the nineteenth century to his own present day—namely, "to ascertain to what extent certain positions of" Bergson's "would be inconceivable without the historical link of the philosophy of praxis" (Q16§9, p. 1856; trans. Gramsci 1971, p. 391). Is Gramsci's Bergson destined to remain, thus, the proverbial riddle wrapped in a mystery inside an enigma? No, not entirely.

One of the many other thinkers who, arguably, "would be inconceivable without the historical link of the philosophy of praxis" is Deleuze, who, unlike Bergson, is well aware of the immense debt all philosophers—including himself—owe to the philosophy of praxis from the mid-nineteenth century onward. It is perhaps because of such acute awareness of the impossibility to think philosophy at all today without the philosophy of praxis that it is Deleuze who provides some clues as to what Gramsci's Bergson might have looked like. The entire first chapter of Deleuze's *Bergsonism* aims to demonstrate how for Bergson intuition constitutes a precise and rigorous philosophical method. Deleuze writes:

> The most general methodological question is this: How is intuition—which denotes an immediate knowledge [*connaissance*]—capable of forming a method, once it is accepted that the method essentially involves one or several mediations? Bergson often presents intuition as a simple act. But, in his view, simplicity does not exclude a qualitative . . . multiplicity . . . in which it comes to be actualized. . . . Bergson distinguishes essentially three distinct sorts of acts that in turn determine the rules of the method: The first concerns the stating and creating of problems; the second, the discovery of genuine differences in kind; the third, the apprehension of real time. It is by showing how we move from one meaning to another . . . that we are able to rediscover the simplicity of intuition as lived act, and thus answer the general methodological question. (Deleuze 1991, pp. 14–15)

Though arguably all three of these acts constituting and determining intuition as method may be shown to owe specific debts to the philosophy of praxis, it is the first one that Deleuze explicitly singles out. Deleuze quotes from Bergson's *The Creative Mind* (1946):

> In philosophy and even elsewhere it is a question of *finding* the problem and consequently of *positing* it, even more than of solving it. For a speculative problem is solved as soon as it is properly stated. By that I mean that its solution exists then, although it may remain hidden and, so to speak, covered up: The only thing left to do is to *un*cover it. But stating the problem

is not simply uncovering, it is inventing. Discovery, or uncovering, has to do with what already exists, actually or virtually: it was therefore certain to happen sooner or later. Invention gives being to what did not exist; it might never have happened. Already in mathematics . . . the effort of invention consists most often in raising the problem, in creating the terms in which it will be stated. The stating and solving of the problem are here very close to being equivalent: The truly great problems are set forth only when they are solved. (Deleuze 1991, pp. 15–16, italics in original)

Deleuze comments thus on this passage:

It is not just the whole history of mathematics that supports Bergson. We might compare [this passage] with Marx's formulation "Humanity only sets itself problems that it is capable of solving." In neither example is it a case of saying that problems are like the shadow of pre-existing solutions. . . . Nor is it a case of saying that only the problems count. On the contrary, it is the solution that counts, but the problem always has the solution it deserves, in terms of the way in which it is stated (i.e., the conditions under which it is determined as a problem), and of the means and terms at our disposal for stating it. The history of man, from the theoretical as much as from the practical point of view is that of the construction of problems. It is here that humanity makes its own history, and the becoming conscious of that activity is like the conquest of freedom. (Deleuze 1991, p. 15)

It is not at all far-fetched to state that the Bergsonian method of intuition would have been precisely "inconceivable" without Marx's discovery of the mutual immanence of problems and solutions, as articulated in his 1859 "Preface to *A Contribution to the Critique of Political Economy*"—which Deleuze quotes from here, and which is a text that Gramsci translated from the German into Italian while in prison (Marx and Engels 1978, p. 5). Marx's discovery, moreover, is turned by Gramsci into a fundamental methodological principle, as he cites, paraphrases, and modifies this very sentence Deleuze quotes from Marx numerous times throughout the *Quaderni*.[9] It turns out, in the end, that Gramsci's Bergson is implicit in Gramsci's re-elaborations of Bergson: in producing the concept of political intuition in the wake of Bergson, Gramsci is also re-appropriating Marx through Bergson, is also pointing to the enabling historical-materialist element in Bergson, is also putting the complex dialectic between intelligent idealism and intelligent materialism into motion as well as turning such a dialectic into a problem for philosophy and for politics alike.

And—as Deleuze reminds us—it is only in constructing such problems that humankind at once makes its own history and posits it as history of freedom.

Let me return now to the first epigraph of this essay, so as to end with a provocation. In Q15§50—another one of the many notes titled "Machiavelli"— Gramsci writes: "Solo la passione aguzza l'intelletto e coopera a rendere più chiara l'intuizione" (Only passion sharpens the intellect and cooperates with it in making intuition clearer) (Q15§50, pp. 1810-1811; my translation). Baruch Spinoza knew two or three things about intuition. In fact, he knew exactly three. I am referring to Spinoza's tripartite epistemology, with its three distinct kinds of knowledge—namely, imagination, reason, and intuition. This is not the place to examine the complex relations between Spinoza's and Bergson's conceptions of intuition—conceptions that Deleuze has shown to be intricately similar. This is also not the place to pursue the potentially very fruitful investigation of the surprising ways in which Spinoza and Gramsci are brought together by their profound affinity for and substantive engagements with Machiavelli, who, importantly, is the topic of Q15§50.[10] And neither is this the place to show precisely how this passage in Q15, written in 1933, constitutes for Gramsci a reflection on and a re-elaboration of his own early political experiences with the Turin factory councils approximately fifteen years earlier. Here, I want simply to draw attention to the fact that Gramsci's triangulation of passion, intellect, and intuition does not merely uncannily resonate with Spinoza's tripartite epistemology but also constitutes a specifically historical-materialist rendition of Spinoza's theory of knowledge.

In Spinoza's *Ethics*, the first kind of knowledge—or, imagination—is described as inherently inadequate representational knowledge based solely on sensory perceptions and semiotic systems: this is the realm of images, affects, affections, passions, and of their vagaries—a turbulent realm that for Spinoza is at once imaginary, specular, deceitful, and yet never absolutely false, never fully erasable or destructible, and even indispensable and necessary. The second kind of knowledge—or, reason—is inherently adequate conceptual knowledge based on common notions: this is the realm of the intellect and of the generalizable and universalizable knowledge of that which modes of substance, beings in the world, share in common. Finally, the third kind of knowledge— or, intuition—is inherently adequate intuitive knowledge; for Spinoza, this is the highest kind of knowledge—an eminently relational knowledge that reveals and explains the essence of modes, the essence of things, by at the same time linking such essence to the eternal essence of substance, the eternal essence of God (that immanent God that Spinoza at one point in the *Ethics* refs to as *concatenatio rerum*, the concatenation of all things).[11] (It is crucial to keep in mind that essences for Spinoza cannot be shared in common, that each and every mode, each and every thing, has its own different essence, that modal essences are different from substantial essence; that is, the essences of things are different from the essence of God, and that essence, thus, is always a singularity.) Genevieve Lloyd has encapsulated the interlocking assemblage of the three kinds of knowledge in an admirably succinct and clear manner: "The first way of knowing is focused on singular things, but is inherently inadequate. The second is inherently adequate, but unable to grasp the essence of singular things. The third and highest kind of knowledge is inherently adequate and able to understand singular things" (Lloyd 1996, p. 67). Lloyd implies that the reason why intuitive knowledge is indispensable, even though conceptual knowledge is just as adequate and truthful in and of itself (see *Ethics* 2, P41, P42), is that these two kinds of knowledge have radically different aims or ends: whereas conceptual knowledge is concerned with that which things actually have in common, intuitive knowledge is concerned with the essence of things—namely, with that which makes things singular and which, thus, cannot be had or shared in common by definition. Lloyd also suggests that in effect, the first kind of knowledge and the third kind of knowledge, imagination and intuition, share in a secret affinity: their aim is the same—to understand the essence of things—and whereas the first fails in achieving this understanding, the third succeeds. Further, it is crucial to emphasize that for Spinoza, these three kinds of knowledge are cumulative and, under propitious circumstances, cooperate with one another: one cannot achieve reason without the imagination, and one cannot achieve intuition without building on and going through imagination and reason in the first place. Under the right conditions, one passes swiftly from imagination to reason all the way to intuition.

Are Gramsci's living philology and political intuition forms of intuition in the Spinozean sense? Perhaps. What is certain is that both Gramsci and Spinoza are dealing with "a swiftness in connecting seemingly unrelated facts," with a form of knowledge that produces relations among otherwise disconnected phenomena and modes of being, with a form of knowledge that produces such relations by zeroing in on essence as singularity (remember, for example, Gramsci's description of living philology as asserting "the importance of ascertaining and specifying particular facts in their unique 'individuality'") (Q11§25, p. 1429; my translation). Moreover, in both cases we are dealing with an eminently passionate knowledge that leads us to action; as far as Spinoza is concerned, we need to keep in mind that the path leading to intuition begins in the imagination, that the imagination and intuition share in common ends and goals, that the passions of the imagination are precisely transformed into actions in and by intuition. And as far as Gramsci is concerned, let me repeat his definition of political intuition: a "swiftness in connecting seemingly unrelated facts [and in conceiving the means adequate to the end which is discovering the interests involved and] rousing the passions of men and directing men to a determinate action" (Q5§127, pp. 660–661; trans. Gramsci 1971, pp. 381–382; trans. modified). Or, as I stated earlier, for Gramsci, truly producing relations among unrelated phenomena is tantamount to at once realizing our interests, generating our passions, and moving us to actions. Most importantly, perhaps, Gramsci's statement that "only passion sharpens the intellect and cooperates with it in making intuition clearer" constitutes an explicit politicization of Spinoza's third kind of knowledge (Q15§50, pp. 1810–1811; my translation). And it is at this point that we have definitively left Gramsci's Bergson behind and we are wandering down a well-trodden, familiar path, yet in a different, oblique, unfamiliar way. There are many who have shed light on the path that led Gramsci back to Machiavelli; nobody yet, however, has gone down the path that leads from Gramsci to Machiavelli's political intuitions via Spinoza.

NOTES

I want to thank Stanley Aronowitz, Roberto Dainotto, Ida Dominijanni, Marcus Green, Michael Hardt, Fredric Jameson, Karen Pinkus, Emanuel Rota, Henry Schwarz, Eleonora Stoppino, Peter Thomas, and, above all, the students in my seminar on Gramsci in 2013, for their incisive questions and comments on earlier versions of this essay.

1   As Quentin Hoare and Geoffrey Nowell Smith note, the term *leaders* is in English in the original, which is presumably why they italicize it; it is not italicized in the original (Gramsci 1971, p. 390).

2   I am very grateful to Roberto Dainotto for having pointed out Labriola's importance for the arguments of my essay, as well as for having taken important steps toward the long overdue reevaluation of this major thinker in his admirably lucid and insightful essay "Historical Materialism as New Humanism: Antonio Labriola's 'In Memoria del Manifesto dei comunisti'" (1895).

3   The only exception occurs in Q10i§6.

4   Incidentally, it is important to note that Gramsci's occasional criticisms of the purported voluntarism of Bergsonian philosophy are directed at politically tendentious misreadings of Bergson rather than at Bergson himself—see, for example, Q3§42 (trans. Gramsci 1992–2007, vol. 2, p. 41).

5   As Joseph Buttigieg notes, Gramsci does not quote directly from Bergson but from an essay by L. Gessi, who does quote directly from Bergson's *L'Évolution créatrice*. In quoting from Bergson, Buttigieg uses Bergson, *Creative Evolution*, trans. Arthur Mitchell (New York: Modern Library, 1944). (For full bibliographical reference, see Gramsci 1992–2007, vol. 2, p. 689n9.)

6   For full bibliographical reference (i.e., Bergson's citation), see preceding note.

7   At the very least, this argument would entail a detailed analysis of Q3§48, titled "Past and Present: Spontaneity and Conscious Leadership" (Q3§48, vol. 1, pp. 328–332; trans. Gramsci 1992–2007, vol. 1, pp. 48–52).

8   See, for example, the conclusions drawn in the last paragraph of Q3§48. (Q3§48, vol. 1, p. 332; trans. Gramsci 1992–2007, vol. 2, p. 52). On this point, see also Thomas (2009b, p. 363).

9   See, for example, Q15§17 and Q7§4 (Q15§17, vol. 3, p. 1774; Q7§4, vol. 2, p. 855; trans. Gramsci 1992–2007, vol. 3, p. 158). On this matter, see also Thomas (2009b, p. 156).

10 Spinoza writes about Machiavelli in his *Political Treatise*—which is a rare occurrence, in the sense that Spinoza seldom names and discusses explicitly other thinkers in his works (Spinoza 1951, p. 315). Explicit reference aside, Spinoza's engagement with Machiavelli is also implicit at other points in his works. In the growing literature on Spinoza and Machiavelli, two remarkable works stand out, namely, Vittorio Morfino's *Il tempo e l'occasione: L'incontro Spinoza-Machiavelli* and Filippo Del Lucchese's *Tumulti e indignatio: Conflito, diritto e moltitudine in Machiavelli e Spinoza*.

11 The first instance of definition and discussion of all three kinds of knowledge occurs in *Ethics* 2, P40S2 (Spinoza 2000, pp. 148–149). Spinoza discusses in more detail his theory of knowledge in *Ethics* 2 (especially from P13 onward) as well as in *Ethics* 5 (which is primarily devoted to the third kind of knowledge). I have discussed Spinoza's epistemology—including the special position that intuition occupies in it, as well as the importance of a definition of God as *concatenatio rerum* for it—in an essay that was on my mind at all times while thinking and writing about Gramsci's encounter with Bergson. See Casarino, "Marx before Spinoza: Notes toward an Investigation" (2011).

5

Scattered Ashes

The Reception of the Gramscian Legacy
in Postwar Italy

ANDREA SCAPOLO

Lo scandalo del contraddirmi, dell'essere
con te e contro te; con te nel core
in luce, contro te nelle buie viscere

—Pier Paolo Pasolini,
"Le ceneri di Gramsci"

In his poem "Le ceneri di Gramsci," written in 1954 and published in 1957 as part of a collection with the same title, Pier Paolo Pasolini pays tribute to the tomb of Gramsci in the Non-Catholic Cemetery in Rome.[1] The poet imagines Gramsci as a "humble brother" ("non padre ma umile/ fratello")[2] still in his youth proposing a path toward a possible, better, and more just future, a path that seemed to be lost forever in postwar Italy. Confronting this image, the poet cannot help but experience a painful contradiction within himself—"lo scandalo del contraddirmi"—between on the one hand, his ideological allegiance to Gramsci, and on the other, his "visceral" nostalgia for a preindustrial world from which he seeks no redemption or liberation and to which instead he can only give poetic expression ("mi so ad esso attaccato nel calore / degli istinti, dell'estetica passione; / attratto da una vita proletaria / a te anteriore").[3] Writing at a time he sees as the dawn of a radical "anthropological mutation" of Italian society, Pasolini, in fact, laments the assimilation of cultural and social norms imported from the United States and the consumeristic homogenization of all social and regional differences (see Pasolini 1999, pp. 307–312). The poet's deep connection to this preindustrial world, the marginality of which mirrors his own personal isolation from the mainstream Italian intelligentsia of the time, cannot be reconciled with his rational acceptance of the Marxist ideology, and thus at the end of the poem, Pasolini is left with no other option than to leave Gramsci's tomb ("me ne vado, ti lascio nella sera"), skeptically contemplating the possibility of any action now that he knows that "our history is over" ("la nostra storia è finita").

The very same contradiction tearing apart Pasolini's conscience and exposing the "scandal" of his conflicted relationship with Gramsci was also tarnishing Italian society. Away from the civilized urban peace of Rome's Non-Catholic Cemetery, only occasionally disturbed by the distant sounds coming from the proletarian world ("E, sbiadito, solo ti giunge qualche colpo d'incudine dalle officine di Testaccio"), and in the living body of a country that was entering a phase of rapid economic expansion and deep social transformation, Gramsci's ashes were less and less a memento of the "dream of a thing" that could have been; rather, they represented one betrayed and forgotten.[4] Even the Italian Communist Party, the putative guardian of the Gramscian legacy, seemed, very much like the poet, doomed to inertia and silence. How did Italy come to this? How did the economic and social changes that were transforming postwar Italy affect the interpretations of Gramsci's thought? How do we make sense of the many contradictions surrounding Gramsci's legacy? This chapter attempts to answer some of these questions by focusing on the reception of Gramsci's thought in Italy during a key period in the long history of the debate on Gramsci: the 1960s and 1970s. What makes this period particularly interesting is the fact that it is the first moment when a systematic attempt to reinterpret Gramsci against Togliatti's orthodoxy concerned both the radical Left and the reformist Right.

In fact, even outside of Italy, the years in question were crucial in establishing a robust tradition of alternative readings of Gramsci. In France, as illustrated by André Tosel and Paolo Pulina, the decade 1965 to 1975 was marked by a real "Gramsci Renaissance" (see Tosel 1995), a period of rediscovery and intense debate over Gramsci's Marxism ushered in and, at the same time, contrasted by the emergence of the "Althusserian moment."[5] In Great Britain "Gramsci was . . . conveyed into the culture of the Left on the tide of the post-1956 thaw, destalinization and the formation of the first new Left" (Forgacs 1989, p. 73). It was only in the early 1960s, however, that the real "brokerage came in thanks to the work on culture and class produced by intellectuals such

as Raymond Williams and Edward Thompson and . . . the theoretically innovative writings on the British state and the labour movement by Perry Anderson and Tom Nairn which appeared in New Left Review in 1963-64" (Forgacs
1989, p. 74). In Germany, while the peak of the "Gramsci Renaissance" corresponds with Riecher's anthology of Gramsci's works, *Philosophie der Praxis*,
published in 1967, throughout that decade the influence of Gramsci's thought
reverberated in many fields, from history to the social sciences, and in many
research directions, from the interpretation of Fascism to the Italian southern
question (see Brissa 1970, pp. 393-395). Meanwhile, in the larger world outside
of Europe, the history of Gramsci's influence in Latin America, which is particularly long and eventful, witnessed a major turning point with the first translations into Spanish of the Sardinian thinker's works published in Argentina. These
translations will not only have a long-lasting impact on the reception of Gramsci
on the continent, but they will also serve as a springboard for the diffusion of his
work in Spain, where direct access to and translation of his texts were heavily
limited by the censorship imposed by Franco's regime (see Bollettino 2010).
Finally, this brief overview must include at least a mention of the 1967 publication of John Cammett's *Antonio Gramsci and the Origin of Italian Communism*
in the United States, which sparked an ever-increasing interest among North
American scholars in Gramsci's political thought and historicism.[6] It was in
Italy, however, where the specter of Gramsci haunted the public discourse for
decades, imposing itself as a constant reference point in intellectual debate,
defining the boundaries of the political lexicography, and occupying, even in
its absence, center stage of the political arena.

In what follows, I first present a brief account of the sketching of a "hegemonic" portrait of Gramsci by the leadership of the Italian Communist Party
in the newly liberated and democratic Italy. I then focus on the reception of
the Gramscian legacy, especially the challenges to the hegemonic reading of
Gramsci carried out by the Italian New Left and the response to these challenges by the Communist Party. Finally, I consider the significance that this
particular phase in the long history of the debate on Gramsci has for us today.

Before delving into the analysis of the different interpretations of Gramsci,
however, it is important to clarify my analytical approach. The very question
of the significance of Gramsci could be, in fact, a deceptive one, as it presupposes a general consensus on the meaning of the term *Gramsci*, on the identity
and equivalence of signified and signifier. Indeed, even before trying to address
the question of Gramsci's significance, we should ask ourselves which Gramsci
we are referring to: which one, that is, among the many different images that
have been offered over the years. It is not by chance, for example, that in his

"Antonio Gramsci: the Message and the Images," Attilio Monasta suggests that "the [true] challenge [of any genuine critical approach to Gramsci] is not how much we will know of [his] heritage, but rather to compare the different images of his work, [and of his persona] which have been diffused" (Monasta 2002, p. 68; see also Burgio 2014, pp. 105–112). Certainly, despite the lack of a comprehensive study examining these different images,[7] the sheer "frequency with which Gramsci is cited suggests that he has attained the status of a classic" (Buttigieg 2009, p. 20). However, as Roberto Dainotto points out, "Like all classics, Gramsci [has] started telling us so many new things at every reading, that in the end his very name [has become] a formula, an empty signifier, good to decorate arguments on virtually anything, from hegemony and subalternity, to the most reactionary of right-wing causes" (Dainotto 2009b, p. 50).

In order to avoid the pitfalls of yet another misappropriation of the Gramscian legacy, it is therefore crucial to reconnect Gramsci's intellectual trajectory to the sociopolitical context of his time. As Gramsci was, in fact, deeply absorbed in the very real and present political struggle of his time period, using a historical approach in analyzing his work is of value. Even when navigating a complex work such as his *Notebooks*—a work in which Gramsci was sowing the seeds of a more farsighted analysis (*für ewig*)—the best compass is, as Peter Thomas has masterfully shown in *The Gramscian Moment*, the thread of that very *living philology* that the Sardinian thinker adopted in the study of the Marxian opus (Thomas 2009b, pp. 127–131). Historicizing is key in addressing the reception of the Gramscian legacy, which does not happen in the vacuum of any celebrated "ends of history," but instead populates the crowded and messy space of its constant making. It is, more specifically, only in the context of the emergence of a new form of capitalism that we can fully understand the contrasting appropriations of the Gramscian legacy in the 1960s and 1970s, and it is only by historicizing that debate that we can, in turn, put to better use Gramsci's thought in the context of today's world. However, it is worth reiterating that historicizing the debate on Gramsci does not mean adopting a relativistic perspective; nor does it imply the need to confine the Gramscian legacy to a dusty page of a history book. Instead, by using this approach we are able to single out the general trends that survived the referenced political and cultural disputes.[8]

In the long history of the debate on Gramsci, these trends have often taken the form of competing narratives about the life and character of the Sardinian thinker, or of critiques, parodies, or deconstructions of those narratives and, in particular, of the "hegemonic" narrative of Gramsci concocted by the leadership of the Italian Communist Party (PCI) (see Liguori 2012). Even before his death, Gramsci's legendary status imposed an image that conformed more to the canons of heroic narratives than to reality. This is the reason why, for instance, after Gramsci's arrest, his fellow inmates could hardly believe that the weak, deformed body in front of them belonged to the already mythical persona of the revolutionary leader, since, as one of them said, "Antonio Gramsci must be a giant."[9] This episode, narrated by Gramsci himself in his letters, is emblematic of a tendency to create an idealized representation of Gramsci, a tendency that the tragic circumstances of his imprisonment and death only reaffirmed and multiplied.

In 1937, the very year of Gramsci's death, Togliatti published in *Lo Stato Operaio* a testament to the Sardinian thinker's contribution to the history of the Italian workers' movement (Togliatti 1967, pp. 7-36). In this article, titled "Il capo della classe operaia italiana," Togliatti offers a questionable interpretation of the relationship between Gramsci and Stalin. Of course, it comes as no surprise that an article written in the heyday of Stalinism avoided any overt reference to the critical stance adopted by Gramsci toward the controversy over Lenin's succession or the impact that fight was having on the Italian Communist Party's internal affairs.[10] All the same, it does seem a little odd to read that, in Togliatti's view, Gramsci was the first Italian Marxist who understood and adopted both Lenin's and Stalin's positions,[11] or that, as recognition of his role in teaching the local workers to understand the Russian Revolution and love its leaders—Lenin and Stalin—he became chairman of the Turin chapter of the Italian Socialist Party in August 1917.[12] Certainly the formulaic juxtaposition of the names of the two Russian leaders was a tribute that Togliatti had to pay to the Soviet establishment; however, beneath the surface of this rhetorical homage, a more nuanced but also more consequential cultural move was been made. In his article, in fact, Togliatti lays the foundation for the image of Gramsci that will become "hegemonic" after the end of the war. At the heart of this image, we find the tragic biography of the Sardinian thinker: his upbringing; his encounter with the proletariat of a modern industrialized urban environment in Turin; his political activism, first in the Socialist Party, and then his crucial role in the birth of the Communist Party in 1921; his experience in Russia in direct contact with the Bolshevik leaders; and his long years in Fascist prisons, leading to his death as a martyr of the anti-fascist opposition. The exemplary moral character of Gramsci that such a biography conveys was intended as a model for the Communist militants fighting against the Fascist regime. The model was built around three basic discursive devices: the narrative of Gramsci as having disadvantaged social origins that resonated with the pauperism experienced by a large strata of the Italian population; the narrative of physical weakness turned into heroic resilience by a sheer act of will; and the tale of final martyrdom that elevated the story of Gramsci's existence both to the realms of history and into a state of secular sainthood.[13]

The perfect overlap of the biographical and political dimensions that characterize Togliatti's portrait of Gramsci was certainly motivated by the historical circumstances of the article, but it soon became a constant motif in the canonization of the Gramscian legacy. This was particularly the case after the collapse of the Fascist regime, when this narrative turned out to be a powerful instrument for the repositioning of the Communist Party in the changed political landscape. In 1944, when the end of World War II was already in sight, the leader of the PCI, with the so-called Svolta di Salerno, put forward a new strategy for the Communist Party that, by emphasizing the national and anti-fascist identity of the Italian workers' movement, ended up anesthetizing the revolutionary potential of the Resistance against the Nazi occupation and Mussolini's puppet republic (see Wright 2002, pp. 6–11; Magna 1978, pp. 301–305). Constrained within the borders established by the new geopolitical order sanctioned in Yalta, Togliatti's new party was forced to redefine both its role and political strategy. The leadership of the PCI then resorted to utilizing Gramsci as the catalyst that could ignite the palingenetic hopes of large masses of dispossessed people, inspire intellectuals to reposition themselves after the collapse of the Gentilian Moloch, and satisfy the need of militants and party cadres for an inspirational heroic model to follow.

The publication of Gramsci's *Letters* and the first thematic edition of the *Prison Notebooks* served as the springboard for this strategy of consensus building (see Vacca 1993; Daniele 2005). As Joseph Buttigieg points out in his introduction to the English translation of the Gerratana edition of the *Prison Notebooks*, "After Gramsci's death little was heard about him for quite a long while. . . . Between 1939 and 1943 only a handful of brief articles appeared on Gramsci, one of them . . . written by Mario Montagnana and published in *Lo Stato Operaio* (1942) . . . [which] contains the first public indication of the existence of Gramsci's prison notebooks" (Gramsci 1992–2007, vol. 1, p. 40). It was only in 1944, on the seventh anniversary of Gramsci's death, that Togliatti "provided the readers of the Communist daily *l'Unità* with a general description of 'Gramsci's literary legacy' and announced preparations for the publication of the notebooks were well under way" (Gramsci 1992–2007, vol. 1, p. 40). However, the first volume of the thematic edition of the notebooks—the famous Platone edition, which should in fact be called the Platone-Togliatti edition for the crucial role that the leader of the PCI had in that historic intellectual endeavor—was titled "Historical Materialism and the Philosophy of

Benedetto Croce" and was published only in 1948, a year after the publication of the prison letters. The order of publication and the choice of the theme of the first volume of the notebooks were not a coincidence.[14] While the letters provided the (auto-)biographical framework instrumental to supporting the martyrdom narrative and Gramsci's "credentials" as one of the fathers of liberated Italy, the first volume of the *Prison Notebooks* clearly targeted the Italian intellectual stratum by offering them a viable alternative to a return to the antebellum idealistic streak of liberalism, represented by the Crocean tradition. This image of Gramsci will gain a hegemonic status and, as Maria Antonietta Macciocchi posits, for the generation of militants active in those years, scarcely if at all acquainted with Gramsci's works, will represent the only point of access to the Sardinian thinker (Macciocchi 1974, pp. 36–44).[15] Yet, even this strong figure crafted with a mixture of sincere devotion and political deftness by Togliatti and the Communist leadership could not escape the constant revisionism of history.

The dramatic events that impacted the Eastern Bloc (Khrushchev's speech; the Polish October; the Hungarian uprising of 1956; the Prague Spring of 1968, to name a few), and the transformations of the social landscape brought about by economic recovery and the "Italian miracle,"[16] tested and eventually diverted the Gramscian strategy of the PCI. At the same time, intellectuals from both the radical left and the reformist "right" were adopting alternative interpretations of Gramsci's thought that openly questioned the official paradigm. It was this interplay of opposing readings of Gramsci that ultimately shaped the image(s) of the Marxist thinker that are still commonly accepted to this day, and it did so in a way that, while preserving the influence of Gramsci's work, limited and distorted its significance.

The dramatic events of 1956 radically changed the situation on both the international and national fronts. On the one hand, the process of de-Stalinization ushered in by Khrushchev's speech at the Twentieth Congress of the PCUS resonated all over Europe, shaking the stability of the Eastern Bloc as well as the conscience of many intellectuals and left-wing activists on the Western side of the Iron Curtain. On the other hand, the rampant growth of the Western European economies, combined with the American-ization of social and cultural norms, brought about a profound innovation in the mechanics of capitalism and an explosive reshaping of the social composition of the workforce. In Italy, the "economic miracle" of those years was made possible in large part by the constraints placed on the dynamic of the cost of labor. This repressive policy was also facilitated by the "conservative" approach that the Communist Party and the trade unions adopted in order to ensure economic recovery and achieve full employment. Moreover, this approach was more in keeping with the ethics of sacrifice that permeated both the Catholic and communist masses. The productivity imperative dictated by the unions was almost universally internalized by the majority of the population employed in agriculture as well as by the industrial workforce made up of cohorts of northern manual workers with relatively high levels of specialization. However, soon enough, the new organizational paradigms and technologies imported from the United States made possible radical changes in the system of production, which required the employment of masses of new workers. These workers, predominantly from southern Italy, constituted a new type of worker, less amenable to the factory's ideology and the discipline of the established workers' organizations. Under these conditions, the latent contradiction between the rhetoric used by political parties and trade unions focused on the nation's welfare and the reality of the class struggle finally exploded. The starting point of such a radical shift in the cultural and social profile of the workforce dates back to 1955, when the CGIL lost their majority in the elections for the new FIAT union representatives.[17] This historic defeat was the result of the growing distance between the new generation of workers and the outdated union organizations, as well as the increasingly aggressive attitude adopted by FIAT management (see Accornero 1978, pp. 32–35). Starting with Giuseppe Di Vittorio's famous "auto-critica,"[18] there was a renewed interest in the factory system. Italian workerism (*operaismo*) was, in part, the result of this newfound emphasis on the working conditions of factory workers: a new generation of socialist and communist intellectuals looked back at Marx in search of a paradigm that could both make sense of the radical changes affecting the country's economic structure and at the same time help conceptualize an alternative model of society. On the socialist side, this new wave of Marxian studies continued the long-lasting tradition of socialist "autonomy" that had in Rodolfo Morandi one of its most influential proponents.[19] It was under the guidance of Morandi that Raniero Panzieri, later to become one of the founding fathers of *operaismo*, began his political activism, and it was Morandi's focus on the role of manufacturing that inspired the line of inquiry of the first *operaisti*.[20] Morandi died in 1955, the same year CGIL was defeated at the FIAT elections for union representatives and the same year there was a heated international debate on the automatized factory that involved both union organizers (especially in the United Kingdom and the United States) and intellectuals.[21] In this climate, Panzieri set out to "'restore Marxism to its natural terrain, which is that of permanent critique, something which could only be accomplished by freeing it 'from the control of the party leaderships and party directions'" (Wright 2002, p. 16). The most consequential result of this intellectual endeavor will be the identification of technology as the main instrument of class despotism associated with capitalist production. In opposition to the well-established belief that technological and organizational systems had little to no effect on social order—a view adopted by the official labor movement—in his "Sull'uso capitalistico delle macchine nel neocapitalismo" and later in *Quaderni Rossi*, Panzieri argued that a codependency existed between social order and technological means of production. By referencing Marx's "Fragment on Machines" in the *Grundrisse* (a fundamental text for the Italian New Left), Panzieri put forward an intellectual and political agenda centered around the idea that worker control over the factory was a key political instrument for speeding up the revolutionary process (Vacca 1972, p. 74). This agenda put Panzieri and the group of socialist intellectuals around him in dialogue with the "young" Gramsci, the Gramsci of the factory councils and Ordine Nuovo at a time when, on the communist side, the Gramscian legacy, and with it the historicist hold on the cultural tenets of the party, was being questioned for the first time.

This anti-historicist perspective was shaped in large part by Galvano Della Volpe's scientific approach to Marxism. Della Volpe "converted" to Marxism after World War II and soon embarked on a mission to turn the hegemonic historicism of the official Italian Left into a scientific "Galilean" version of Marxist thought that he considered to be more faithful to the original. According to this reading, Marx rejected any moralistic approach to the critique of capitalism and instead formulated abstractions that were grounded in observations of a concrete and specific historical society, constantly submitted to rigorous verification (Wright 2002, p. 26). Della Volpe's Galilean Marxism involved only an epistemological shift at a philosophical level, but it paved the way for more aggressive attacks against the historicism of the PCI. These attacks came from Della Volpe's disciples and supporters, such as Lucio Colletti and Mario Tronti. Mario Tronti, in particular, will play a major role in the foundation and development of the Italian *operaismo*. Tronti's so-called Copernican revolution viewed labor, not capital, as the real "motor" of the development of capitalistic society. This perspective opened a new phase in the history of the Italian *operaismo*, marked by a split from the original *Quaderni Rossi* group and the birth of a new journal, *Classe Operaia*. A defining moment in the history of the radical Left in Italy, this Copernican revolution marked a fundamental shift in its relation with the Marxist/Marxian tradition. Moving away from dialectical materialism and any pretense of objectivity, the Trontian version of *operaismo* inaugurated a subjectivist and vitalist approach to working-class political theory. Eventually, this new strain of *operaismo* recognized the autonomy of politics as residing in its technical workings and therefore advocated a return to party politics within the ranks of the Communist Party. This was the choice made by Mario Tronti himself and Massimo Cacciari, among others, whose interpretation and appropriation of the tradition of "negative thought" that marked the eclipse of modernity will have a long-lasting impact on the Italian political and philosophical landscape. However, this was not the only option for the post–*Quaderni Rossi* generation of *operaisti*. Toni Negri, for instance, chose to turn his attention to the social dimension by singling out a new "ideal type" of worker, the *operaio sociale* (socialized worker). This new worker was the product of a "complete redefinition of the category of productive labour" (Wright 2002, p. 155), which, by extending the process of rationalization and exploitation of labor beyond the walls of factories and into society, brings about a homogeneity of conditions of exploitations across different categories of labor and ultimately a "new figure of a unified proletariat" (Wright 2002, p. 156).

All these different groups and intellectuals shared a controversial relationship with Gramsci. On the one hand, Gramsci represented the continuity of the PCI's reformist strategy of diluting the revolutionary potential of the Italian workers' movement; on the other hand, the appeal of the Togliattian narrative of Gramsci's biography and the recognition of his exceptional intellectual and moral status made it difficult (and politically costly) to abandon him completely. This contradictory relation with the Gramscian legacy emerged as early as 1958 in Mario Tronti's contribution to a conference on Gramsci organized by the Istituto Gramsci in Rome (Tronti 1969). There, Tronti makes two crucial points: first, that Gramsci's work must be considered essentially anti-Crocean and, more importantly, that it represents a definitive break from the Crocean idealistic legacy; and second, that precisely because of this, the Gramscian legacy can and must be overcome as well. However, overcoming such a legacy is not presented as a dismissal of or an attack on Gramsci; on the contrary, it is, in Tronti's view, already inscribed and anticipated in Gramsci's own interpretation of Marxism. It is, in fact, Gramsci's notion of Marxism as an open system, still at a stage of elaboration and discussion, which allows Tronti to argue that Gramsci's contribution to Marxism must be overcome, too. The specific aspect of Gramsci's thought that Tronti criticizes is the identification between philosophy and history, a trait that links the Gramscian legacy to the Crocean tradition, which Tronti believes should be replaced by the identification between science and history.

The continuity along the lines of the idealistic tradition of the Gramscian legacy and its lack of modernity becomes almost commonplace for most of the radical readings of Gramsci's thought. The target of such criticism was less Gramsci than it was the leadership of the Communist Party and a political and cultural strategy that was accused of quietism and populism. An example of such criticism is Alberto Asor Rosa's famous attack on *gramscianesimo* in his *Scrittori e popolo* (1965). In the context of his radical critique of populistic tendencies in Italian literature, Asor Rosa singles out *gramscianesimo* as one of the most prominent examples of that "provincial populism, and the petty bourgeois character of its culture that referred to a tradition created in the nineteenth and twentieth centuries that had its pillars in Gioberti, De Sanctis, Croce and Gramsci" (Capuzzo and Mezzadra 2012, p. 40). In his book, Asor Rosa openly distinguishes between Gramsci's intellectual rigor and the ambiguity of the Togliattian cultural politics that resulted in *gramscianesimo*. However, the possibility of the confusion between Gramsci's original contribution to Marxism and postwar *gramscianesimo* is ultimately based, according to him, on the connection between Gramsci's thought and the democratic tradition the author traces back to the Italian Risorgimento (Asor Rosa 1965, p. 210). It was this tradition that the Crocean system had attempted to bring to fruition within its all-encompassing bourgeois synthesis. Gramsci had eviscerated this synthesis by bringing to light its reactionary essence and, in doing so, managed to move beyond it, yet failed to displace it from its hegemonic position within the Italian political and cultural discourse. The reason for this shortcoming was, in Tronti's view, Gramsci's insistence on placing more emphasis on the "historical" than the "material" in "historical materialism" (Tronti 1969, p. 316). It is precisely Gramsci's absolute historicism that risks an interpretation of Marxism as a mere historicization of the idealistic tradition. Hence, Tronti advocates for a different appropriation of Gramsci, one that employs Gramsci's notion of the social nature of knowledge ("socialità del sapere")—a notion that played a major role in the development of the *operaisti*'s original methodology of worker inquiry—and opens the space for a radical autonomy of intellectual research and political action within the Marxist tradition. In those years and beyond, the debate on the real nature of Marxism, on its view of science and the tension between economic determinism and political voluntarism, lies at the very core of the Gramscian question. On the one hand, the higher level of rationalization imposed by this new stage in the development of the capitalistic mode of production and the new status acquired by the social sciences favored a scientific approach to Marxism within the workers' movement and the New Left. On the other hand, these new social movements were heavily influenced by voluntarist ideologies that were more concerned with the formation and agency of new subjectivities than with the analysis of objective conditions and power structures in a given society. Moreover, these groups increasingly saw the focus on the organizational needs for social and political change as obsolete political tools and conservative obstacles working against the revolution to come. As discussed, the workerist solution to this conundrum was the "subjectivation" of science. Science, like technology, far from being a neutral space of objectivity, was, according to the workerist intellectuals, a social construct that was to be used as a political weapon. The social essence of knowledge was certainly, as Tronti indicates, very clear to Gramsci, but along with that awareness there was a clear distinction between science, which dealt with facts, and philosophy, which uses facts to unveil possibilities that can only become reality as a product of human action—and therefore are historically determined (see Vacca 1993, p. 458). In Gramsci's analysis, the separation between the realm of science and that of history is what preserves the freedom of action and justifies the need for political organization and intellectual elaboration. The importance of the cultural dimension that marks the Gramscian legacy has this distinction at its root and, in turn, maintains validity for us today. Distinction, however, does not imply separation. The cultural and the economic, the political and the social, the ideological and the scientific maintain an inextricable dialectical relation with each other. The workerists were not alone in failing to understand the complexity of this relation. On the other side of the spectrum, Bobbio's reading of Gramsci and his emphasis on the cultural dimension of civil society fueled a series of long-lasting and impactful interpretations of Gramsci's thought.[22] In Bobbio's view, what characterizes Gramsci's Marxism (and sets it apart from the rest) is its notion of civil society as the place where hegemony is built, maintained, and challenged. Bobbio never questions the Marxist essence of Gramsci's thought (see Bobbio 1990, pp. 15–24), but in an attempt to highlight the originality of Gramsci's contribution to that tradition, he ends up isolating the moment of the superstructure and by doing so, legitimizes the cultural turn in the appropriation of Gramsci's work.

If it is true, as Romano Luperini stresses (in Bobbio 1990, p. 21), that when Bobbio's reading of Gramsci first appeared in 1967, it represented a remarkable contribution to liberating the Gramscian legacy from the chains of sectarian appropriations and immediate political goals, it is also true that it paved the way for a separation of such a legacy from the lineage of the Marxist tradition. This new approach had two major consequences for the uses of Gramsci. First, it supported, even from within the Communist Party, a more philologically accurate reading of Gramsci's work, which would culminate in Gerratana's 1975 edition of the *Prison Notebooks*. Second, it facilitated the evolution of the

Italian Communist Party into a Social Democratic Party by providing a strong ideological foundation for the political experiment of the so-called Eurocommunism. Regarding the first aspect, the Gerratana edition is considered a landmark in the field of Gramscian studies. For the first time, scholars and activists had access to a philologically accurate edition of the notebooks, one that respected the chronological order of the author's writings and allowed for readings autonomous from the political agenda of the party leadership. Ironically, the Gerratana edition also marked the beginning of a decade (the 1980s) of declining interest in Gramsci's work, and only in recent years has the Gerratana edition been put to use in the effort to build a new Gramscian political culture (see Thomas 2009b). This new and overdue "Gramscianism" faced the cultural turn that characterized the advent of late capitalism (Jameson 1998) and the development of the field of cultural studies in the United Kingdom, which induced a neutralization of Gramsci's revolutionary stance over time.[23]

In the meantime, in the political arena, a similar path was taken by the Western Communist leaders with their attempt to develop a new model of socialism independent from Moscow's directives and compatible with the tenets of liberal democracy. The birth of Eurocommunism entailed a historic shift in the geopolitical paradigm of postwar Europe, to the point that the then secretary of the Italian Communist Party, Enrico Berlinguer, stated during an interview with the Italian daily *Corriere della Sera* in June 1976 that he was feeling "safer" under NATO's protective shield.[24] At least according to Perry Anderson in *The Antinomies of Gramsci* (1976, p. 5), the theoretical foundation for such a shift was to be found in Gramsci's thought, specifically in his contradictory notion of hegemony and his take on the relations between state and civil society that characterize the capitalistic societies in the West vis-à-vis the East.

Anderson did not go so far as to accuse Gramsci of reformism or parliamentarism. In fact, he even quoted a note from the *Prison Notebooks* on a "Trotskyst solution" to the question of the "war of position" (that pertains to the level of civil society) versus "war of maneuver" (which pertains to the state) (Anderson 1976, p. 70). However, this solution appears only at the margins of a text that is marked by the persistency of profound and unresolved "antinomies." It is this contradictory nature that allows for the reformist distortions that, according to the British author, were at the core of the Eurocommunist involution of the Western workers' movement.[25]

But such involution was not to happen without opposition. Within the ranks of the Italian Communist Party, for instance, a left-wing minority was in the making in the late 1950s and early 1960s. During the 1960s in particular, these left-wing groups started coalescing around what would later become the

Manifesto group. In retracing the origin of this group, Lucio Magri singles out three main issues that constituted this new group's agenda: the "realization" that Italian capitalism had entered a new phase and that Italy had joined the club of the most advanced economies; the observation that this new stage in Italy's economic development brought about a complex societal stratification, including a multilayered articulation of the working class; and the impossibility of addressing the social and economic issues that originated in this new stage of capitalism through reformist policies.[26] Instead, the intellectuals of the Manifesto group, not unlike the *operaisti* of a decade before, were calling for a more sophisticated analysis of the new state of things, but unlike their predecessors, they were doing so from within the Gramscian tradition. It is, in fact, precisely in Gramsci's original elaboration of Leninism and his in-depth study of the specificity of Italian capitalism that Lucio Magri finds the roots of the Manifesto's heretic Marxism.[27]

However, if accepting the Gramscian legacy placed the Manifesto group within the Communist Party tradition, the conclusions they drew from this legacy gradually distanced the group from the leadership of the party and its attempt to articulate a hegemonic reading of Gramsci's thought. At the core of what eventually became an irreversible breach between the Manifesto group and the PCI was a shift in the focus of analysis from the realm of politics to that of social and economic dimensions. In this way, the Manifesto group was attempting to save the Gramscian legacy by separating it from Togliatti's appropriation, while at the same time building a bridge toward the new social movements emerging in those years in Italy (as in many other Western countries). The attention to the changes in the Italian social and economic landscape that characterized the Manifesto group was not intended as a dismissal of the cultural aspect of Gramsci's analysis. On the contrary, the cultural dimension and the role of intellectuals were central to the elaboration of the Manifesto, but it was a revolutionary strategy that was more in keeping with both the original objectives of Gramsci's work and those of the new social movements.

In a similar fashion, but with much more creative freedom and much less philological accuracy, Maria Antonietta Macciocchi, in her *Per Gramsci*, first published in 1975, tried to save Gramsci from the attacks coming from the New Left by proposing a Maoist reading of the *Prison Notebooks*. In Macciocchi's view, the Manifesto's reading of Gramsci was reductive because it focused primarily on the "consiliarist phase" of his production instead of privileging his more mature reflections contained in the *Prison Notebooks*.[28] According to Macciocchi, Gramsci articulates a strategy for a cultural revolution that lays the foundation for a new socialist society while avoiding the risk of a bureaucratic involution such as the one plaguing the Soviet Union. Macciocchi draws a daring comparison between the Chinese revolution and Gramsci's war of position.[29] In this sense, the role of culture becomes crucial, but only inasmuch as intellectuals succeed in building a connection between high and low culture. As per Macciocchi, the validity of Gramsci's thought in today's world is based on his understanding of the crucial importance of such a connection. Particularly in his reflections on the Reformation, Gramsci stresses the "national-popular" character of the Lutheran and Calvinist movements and contrasts this with the elitism of Erasmus's positions on the Catholic front. The appeal of the Reformation among the working class is, in Macciocchi's view, very similar to Mao's Cultural Revolution: "In Cina, solo dopo la lettura in massa del Libretto rosso, si è creata una forza culturale di massa, sulla quale può sorgere la lettura, da parte di decine di milioni di contadini e operai, del Manifesto, dell'Anti-Dühring, di Materialismo ed empiriocentrismo, di Stato e Rivoluzione. . . . Senza la rivoluzione culturale, non si sarebbero mai potute creare le condizioni politico-culturali per diffondere queste opere in 197 milioni di esemplari" (Macciocchi 1974, p. 23).[30] Today this comparison seems simply ludicrous, but at the time it was written, it did not seem so far-fetched, especially among militants and activists of the New Left. To understand the connection between interpretations of Gramsci's work such as Macciocchi's, one could think of Nobel laureate Dario Fo's representation of Gramsci in his plays. Of course, in Dario Fo's case we are dealing with an artistic creation that is not bound by any imperative to be either philologically or historically accurate. However, because of the popularity of Dario Fo and his political theater, such representation can give us a glimpse into the general images of Gramsci commonly accepted in those years.

This is especially true because the audience for Dario Fo's plays was constituted primarily of members of the radical movements. In *L'operaio conosce 300 parole, il padrone 1000, per questo è lui il padrone*, for instance, Gramsci makes his debut as a character, and in his first appearance on stage he is mistaken for a "cinese," a Maoist student: "a poor starving little student . . . half-scraggy . . . who used to go to the FIAT plant to annoy them and give them a piece of his mind" (Fo 1970, p. 290). Once again, today's readers cannot but be puzzled by such a comparison. In the context of those turbulent years, however, Fo's audience was ready to identify with this radical rendition of such an iconic figure of the history of the Italian Left.

Macciocchi and Fo are egregious examples of the progressive disarticulation of the hegemonic discourse on Gramsci established by Togliatti and the leadership of the Italian Communist Party after the end of the war. At the same time, they also mark the peak of that process. The 1975 Gerratana edition of the *Prison Notebooks*, in fact, changes the paradigm by forcing the Italian readers of Gramsci to confront the constraints of a philologically accurate version of the text. By the end of the 1970s, the conservative counterrevolution in the West and the irreversible crisis of the Soviet system in the East were seeking to make the Gramscian legacy less relevant in the political and intellectual arena. In Italy more particularly, the 1980s were characterized by a declining interest in Gramsci. The "weakness" that tainted the thought, politics, and ethics of that decade was ill-suited to engaging the complexity and stern intellectual integrity of Gramsci's work. It is precisely this "weakness" that Antonio Negri singles out as the defining trait of the Italian "philosophy": "Italian philosophy is not even provincial: it is just weak [*debole*], it has always been a weak philosophy, weak in the face of politics and bosses, dictators and popes. In the twentieth-century decline of ideas and debates, the vilest point was perhaps reached when some, with a certain pride, proclaimed their thought and their definition of contemporary philosophy as 'weak.' Others named it more properly 'limp thought' [*pensiero molle*]" (Negri 2009, p. 9). Even Negri, for whom Gramsci was never an author of choice, recognized the exceptional status of Gramsci and included him in his list of the three exceptions to the rule of "weakness" in the history of Italian philosophy.[31] Certainly, Negri's appreciation of Gramsci remains lukewarm, and his interpretation of Gramsci's thought as a materialist version of the Gentile's legacy remains problematic. However, this endorsement, coming from one of the most important intellectuals of the Italian New Left, testifies to the role of the Gramscian legacy in shaping the Italian philosophical landscape for the past sixty years. Moreover, it is also an indirect acknowledgment of the effectiveness of Togliatti's postwar strategy in establishing the cultural hegemony of the Italian Communist Party through Gramsci.

The country in which Negri writes at the beginning of the twenty-first century is very different from the one in which Togliatti's strategy was first conceived and implemented: a poor devastated country starting to rebuild itself after twenty years under the Fascist regime and a disastrous war. And yet, in the interconnected global fast-paced capitalism of which today's Italy is an integral part, and at the center of Negri's intellectual reflection and political activism, Gramsci's voice is still speaking to the contradictions of our times. The history of how his influence has survived thus far, despite the contrasting appropriations and the challenges to his authority coming from different sides of the political spectrum, is certainly fascinating in its own right, but it is also useful in determining the validity of Gramsci's thought in the context of today's world. In particular, as I have shown here, the debate on Gramsci in the 1960s and 1970s is particularly significant, because for the first time, the discourse on Gramsci was liberated from the hegemonic articulation set by the leadership of the Communist Party and was confronted with the emergence of a new stage in the development of the capitalistic system of production. In very general terms, the different approaches to the Gramscian legacy can be schematically grouped into two major tendencies. On the one hand, some intellectuals and political activists criticized Gramsci's emphasis on the cultural dimension, which they considered to be a product of an idealistic background, and instead called for a scientific approach to Marxism. This approach in Italy was represented by, among others, Della Volpe and his disciples, and in particular, although in a very distinct way, by Mario Tronti's streak of *operaismo*. An alternative tendency focused on the subjective, voluntarist dimension of Gramsci's thought. This approach was adopted from radical groups on the left of the Communist Party and also, with opposing goals, on the reformist right (e.g., Bobbio), which will end up constituting the cornerstone of the politics of Eurocommunism and the process of "social-democratization" of the PCI. Both tendencies brought important contributions to the preservation of the Gramscian legacy. It is, in fact, in the midst of the constant intellectual debates and political disputes that Gramsci's thought found a way to survive and maintain its significance to this day. Moreover, both tendencies challenged the hegemonic reading of Gramsci proposed by the leadership of the Italian Communist Party after the end of World War II, and in doing so, they helped liberate the Gramscian legacy from a specific political agenda (a process that was endorsed by Togliatti at the end of his life).[32]

However, both tendencies seemed to fail to fully understand the complex dialectical relation that Gramsci established between structure and superstructure, economics and politics, science and history, objective conditions and free will. It is, in fact, particularly in the way in which Gramsci envisioned the interplay between science and history that his thought continues to preserve all its revolutionary potential. Especially at a time when the status of the social sciences has been questioned for its inability to guarantee any predictive validity (i.e., economists failing to foresee the financial crisis of 2008), Gramsci's "absolute historicism" still offers a valid alternative that can help make sense of the complex dynamics of social interactions and power structures, while at the same time providing a compass for political action. In order to put to use this powerful intellectual apparatus, it is necessary to adopt an approach to the reading of his works that is less dependent on the hic et nunc of the political struggle or the cultural fads of the moment and that is, instead, more faithful to that system of accuracy and "active and conscious co-participation ... through compassionality" that Gramsci called "living philology" (Q11§25, p. 1430; Gramsci 1971, p. 429). In adopting this approach, a more balanced and historically accurate image of Gramsci emerges.

Since Togliatti's appropriation of Gramsci as part of his political and cultural strategy for a new party, there have been countless attempts at reinterpreting or bending, if not completely reinventing Gramsci in order to support different cultural and political perspectives. All these different appropriations were supported by contrasting narratives about and images of the Marxist thinker, from the secular saint at the core of the Resistance narratives to the brother-like persona imagined by Pier Paolo Pasolini in his civic poem to the father figure antagonized by certain radical intellectuals. Without suggesting any canonization of one true orthodox version of Gramsci, by applying Gramsci's own living philology, the reader would have a chance of drawing a different portrait of the author, one that would be more in tune with the self-portrait he proposes in his letter: "Some people think of me as a devil, others think of me as almost a saint. I don't want to be either a martyr or a hero. I believe that I am simply an average man who has his own deep convictions and will not trade them away for anything in the world" (Gramsci 1994, p. 140).

NOTES

1   The Cimitero Acattolico (Non-Catholic cemetery), often referred to as the Cimitero dei protestanti (Protestant cemetery) or Cimitero degli Inglesi (Englishmen's cemetery or English cemetery), is a public cemetery in Rome.
2   All quotations of "Le ceneri di Gramsci" are from Pasolini 1963, pp. 70–84.
3   For more on Pasolini's conflicted relationship with the leadership of the PCI at that time, see also Siciliano 2005, pp. 247–254.
4   This reference is to Pasolini's novel, *Il sogno di una cosa*, published in 1962.
5   As evidence of this ambivalence, we can think of "Poulantzas' engagement with Gramsci" (see Thomas 2012).
6   On this and, in particular, the much more troublesome history of Gramsci's influence in the field of literary studies, see Dainotto 2009a.
7   On the limits of the still fundamental Guido Liguori's *Gramsci conteso*, see Buttigieg 2009, p. 20.
8   On this approach on Gramsci, see Burgio 2014, pp. 91–97.
9   Letter to Tania, February 19, 1927 (Gramsci 1994, p. 74).
10 See Daniele 1999 for more on the heated epistolary exchange that took place in October 1926 between Gramsci and Togliatti on the division within the Soviet party.

11 "Comprende e si appropria le nuove posizioni conquistate dal marxismo nello sviluppo ulteriore datogli da Lenin e da Stalin" (Togliatti 1967, p. 11).

12 "Era il riconoscimento della parte che egli aveva avuto nel preparare gli operai torinesi a comprendere la rivoluzione russa, a comprendere e ad amare i suoi capi, Lenin e Stalin" (Togliatti 1967, p. 19).

13 This state of sainthood, however, does not protect him from criticism, as the few remarks on Gramsci's shortcomings in the fight against Bordiga's sectarianism testify (see, e.g., Togliatti 1967, pp. 28–29).

14 The thematic volumes appeared in the following chronological order: *Il materialismo storico e la filosofia di Benedetto Croce* (1948); *Gli intellettuali e l'organizzazione della cultura* (1948); *Il Risorgimento* (1949); *Note sul Machiavelli sulla politica e sullo stato moderno* (1949); *Letteratura e vita nazionale* (1950); *Passato e presente* (1951).

15 Significantly, Macciocchi takes notice of the editorial choices made by Togliatti, who decided not to publish Gramsci's work in the official publishing house of the party, choosing instead to use the independent Einaudi editions. In doing so, Macciocchi argues, Togliatti was not only protecting Gramsci's work and the Communist Party from Moscow's scrutiny but also allowing the leadership of the party more room to maneuver in the national political arena.

16 On the "Italian miracle" (i.e., the decade of fast economic expansion that characterized postwar Italy from the early 1950s to 1963), see Crainz 1996.

17 Confederazione Generale Italiana del Lavoro (CGIL) is the most important Italian trade union center. It was founded in 1944 by communist, socialist, and Catholic groups.

18 Giuseppe Di Vittorio, at that time the secretary of the CGIL, gave a famous speech in which he severely criticized himself after the 1955 defeat of the CGIL.

19 On this tradition and on the multifaceted and ambiguous meaning of the concept of "autonomy" in the socialist tradition, see Wright 2002, pp. 11–15.

20 On this, see his *Storia della grande industria in Italia*, and, for its influence on the development of the Italian *operaismo*, *Tesi sul controllo operaio*. On the role of Rodolfo Morandi in shaping the ideological framework of the radical New Left in Italy, see Giuseppe Vacca 1972, pp. 71–75.

21 In 1956, Friedrich Pollock's *Automation* was published.

22 "It is Norberto Bobbio who inadvertently sets the tone for the deconstruction of ideology, later attributed to Gramsci's influence that becomes the key leitmotif of postmodern politics" (Greaves 2009, p. 36). On this, see also Harris 1992.

23 The culmination of this tendency is the use of Gramsci by Ernesto Laclau and other discourse analysis theorists.

24 Interview with Giampaolo Pansa, *Corriere della Sera*, June 15, 1976.

25 As mentioned previously, this very same emphasis on the dimension of civil society in Italy had found its legitimation in Bobbio's reading of Gramsci and was gradually adopted by the post-Togliattian leadership of the Communist Party.

26 In "Le origini del Manifesto," 2012, http://www.luciomagri.com/saggirimini.

27 "Credo che da qui convenga partire se si vuol rintracciare soprattutto a livello di idee (nell'elaborazione di Gramsci) ma anche nella pratica politica del Partito comunista l'Italia, diciamo dal momento della crisi del bordighismo fino al 1928–29 (quando l'Internazionale impose nuovamente una ortodossia) l'origine lontana della sigla caratteristica dell'elaborazione del Manifesto, lo sforzo di riflettere sulla specificità della rivoluzione occidentale e su un modello di strategia rivoluzionaria che superasse creativamente quello dell'Ottobre del '17" (I believe that we should start from here [the period between the crisis of "bordighismo" and the years 1928–1929, when the Comintern imposed its orthodoxy again] if we want to trace back, both in Gramsci's thought and the Italian Communist Party's political strategy, the Manifesto group's original effort to reflect on the specificity of the western revolution and a model of revolutionary strategy that could creatively move beyond the precedent of the October 1917) ("Le origini del Manifesto," 2012; my translation).

28 "In Italia, la sinistra del 'Manifesto' ha privilegiato in Gramsci, per qualche tempo, solo la fase consigliare, operando in tal modo una riduzione di Gramsci e fissando come teorico della spontaneità" (In Italy, the left of the Manifesto group has, for some time, focused mostly on Gramsci's consiliarist phase. In so doing this group has reduced Gramsci to a theorist of voluntarism) (Macciocchi 1974, p. 26; my translation).

29 "Rileggendo Gramsci, nel corso del mio recentissimo viaggio in Cina, ho visto concretarsi le sue intuizioni teoriche nella prassi della rivoluzione culturale cinese" (In reading again Gramsci, during my recent trip to China, I saw his theoretical intuitions become praxis with the Chinese Revolution) (Macciocchi 1974, p. 19; my translation).

30 In China, only after the mass readings of the Red Book, we see the creation of a mass-culture force that made it possible for tens of millions of peasants and factory workers to read texts such as the *Manifesto*, the *Anti-Dühring*, *Materialism and Empiriocriticism*, *State and Revolution*. . . . Without the Cultural Revolution, there would have not been the political and cultural conditions to spread these works in 197 million copies (my translation).

31 "Let's move on to the exceptions: three, as we've said. The first one was Gramsci: the hunchback, the betrayer of Stalinism, the one whom the other political prisoners used to pelt with stones in jail. Gramsci re-established philosophy where it should have remained, in the life and struggles of ordinary people" (Negri 2009, p. 10).

32 In 1964, Togliatti, in reviewing Giansiro Ferrata's volume *Duemila pagine di Gramsci*, proposed a new image of Gramsci that aimed to reposition the Gramscian legacy outside the boundaries of the communist movement and into the larger framework of the European intellectual landscape (see Vacca 1993, pp. 451–452).

6

Subalterns in the World

Typologies and Nexus with Different Forms
of Religious Experience

COSIMO ZENE

In 1960, Vittorio Lanternari published the
book *Movimenti religiosi di libertà e salvezza
dei popoli oppressi*, later translated into
English and published in 1963 with the
title *The Religions of the Oppressed: A Study
of Modern Messianic Cults*. It is somewhat
surprising that Lanternari does not mention Gramsci at all in his book, although
he refers in its conclusion to Lazzaretti's
movement, abundantly discussed by
Gramsci. Moreover, while in the bibliogra-
phy he quotes Eric Hobsbawm's *Primitive Rebels* (1959), he does not cite Ernesto
de Martino, whom he knew rather well, since they both had been students of
Raffaele Petazzoni.[1]

The main asset of Lanternari's book is to have highlighted those characteristics common to various messianic movements during the postcolonial period—
hence from the 1950s onward—but included in his analysis also previous religious
movements, such as Judaism and Christianity, which later were recognized as
fully fledged "religions." The primary characteristics identified in these movements are freedom and salvation: "freedom from subjection and servitude to
the foreign powers as well as from adversity, and salvation from the possibility of having the traditional culture destroyed and the native society wiped
out as a historical entity" (Lanternari 1963, pp. 301-302). While for Lanternari

the "cultural conflict" produced by colonialism is not the sole power that propels messianic movements, it is the predominant motivation "because of its disconcerting effects upon native society, culture and religion" (Lanternari 1963, p. 310). There are, however, in various societies some "internal" (or endogenous) elements that have sparkled messianic movements, thus highlighting the "internal crisis" that is often resolved by escaping from society "in order to establish a society and world of their own beyond history, beyond reality, and beyond the necessity of fighting to bring about change and improvement" (Lanternari 1963, p. 314). This "escapism" motivates, according to Lanternari, the search for a "land where evil does not exist," the "new Jerusalem," or the "holy city" from which the "holy war against the forces of evil," both internal and external, often sets off. Ultimately, however, the intent of these movements is "to make a positive contribution to the regeneration of society as a whole, and the faithful may obtain a foretaste in terms of the sense of liberation experienced by these means" (Lanternari 1963, p. 315). Even the use of the Bible by Christians belonging to these "new movements" seems to promote escapism from reality and history, according to Lanternari, when he attributes to the Zulu a saying that has been more realistically attributed to Jomo Kenyatta, the autonomist leader of Kenya, and taken up later by Desmond Tutu, which says: "When the Missionaries arrived, the Africans had the Land and the Missionaries had the Bible. They taught us how to pray with our eyes closed. When we opened them, they had the land and we had the Bible" (Lanternari 1963, pp. 5, 316). Beyond mere escapism, or a peculiar use of the Bible by the Christian independent churches, these remarks reveal a clear consciousness of the inequality of exchange and the inherent complexities of the different aspects of colonialism. For instance, the reply given by Lanternari to Catholic missionaries in the preface to the English edition of his book (1963) is rather revealing. Because the missionaries had criticized him for not distinguishing between Protestants and Catholics, and for not explaining sufficiently that messianic movements originated mostly from Protestant evangelization, Lanternari provides a list of movements which developed within Catholicism, not least Lazzaretti's own movement.

Lanternari was not the only one to underline the presence of these movements as a direct consequence of the structural crisis provoked by colonialism, even though he, more than others, has emphasized the nexus religion-oppression, while the (mostly anthropological) research regarding various millenarianisms has a long history. Already in 1927, G. H. Pitt-Rivers made a clear reference to the "clash of cultures," which was destined to make a return in the famous work by S. Huntington (1996), *The Clash of Civilisations and the Remaking of the World*. Prior to this, Evans-Pritchard in *The Sanusi of Cyrenaica*

(1949) made this observation regarding "Islamic Orders": "Religious divisions in Islam have commonly been the expression of a sense of social and cultural exclusiveness.... [They] were all reactions against foreign domination as much as revolts against orthodoxy. The religious deviation was the expression of the intense desire of the people to live according to their own traditions and institutions" (Evans-Pritchard [1949] 1973, pp. 9–10). Here we find a strong combination of external and internal elements—not sufficiently underlined by Lanternari—which converge and motivate the development of religious movements as a response to situations of crisis.[2]

At this point, the question we must ask ourselves is what novel approach could be offered by a Gramscian reading of this reality—which could be summarized in the nexus "subalternity and religion"—as a historical reality that in fact could be defined not solely as colonial but also as pre- and postcolonial, and hence contemporary? I will return later to this central question. Prior to that, we must address a related issue, which is the limited and at times spurious use of Gramsci's thought by scholars of various disciplines interested in the "theoretical" perspective of subalternity.

Subalternity and Dalits in South Asia

The closest example I can quote with reference to the theory of subalternity and Dalits in India is a recent work by Clelia Bartoli, *La teoria della subalternità e il caso dei dalit in India* (2008). In the first chapter, Bartoli, supported by Bourdieu's and Moscovici's writings and expanding on the concept of *doxa*,[3] proposes a continuity—aided by the notion of *habitus*—between Bourdieu's "symbolic violence"[4] and Spivak's "epistemic violence," the latter defined as "a sweet violence with no bloodshed which ensues the violence of arms, is what gives legitimacy to usurpation and is exercised through symbols, thus providing continuity to the domination" (Bartoli 2008, p. 36). With this magnifying glass, Bartoli sets out in the first pages of her second chapter to tell us about the subaltern in Gramsci, quoting Joseph Buttigieg and Notebook 25 ("On the Margins of History"). After reporting the central passage in its entirety—"The subaltern classes, by definition, are not unified and cannot unite until they are able to become a 'State'" (Q25§5, p. 2288; trans. Gramsci 1971, p. 52)—Bartoli then reaffirms the main position supported by Spivak in "Can the Subaltern Speak?," but not without paying quick lip service to the initial Gramscian moment of the *Subaltern Studies* collective, which is soon followed, with the arrival of B. Cohn and Spivak in 1986, by a total abandonment of Gramsci. "These authors, by introducing a Foucauldian approach, deconstructionism and problems of gender, seem to wish to abandon the Gramscian slant *à la* Thomson [referring perhaps E. P. Thompson?] which had characterized their initial publications" (Bartoli 2008, p. 39n7). That seeming "wish to abandon"—in reality, rather pleonastic—becomes much clearer in the rest of the narrative in which, despite a meticulous reconstruction of the history of Dalits in India and its various phases,[5] we assist in a return to the concept of "subalternity as epistemic condition," which is focused on the sociocognitive approach. In reality, the historical trajectory offered by Bartoli does not provide any advancement on the initial hypothesis but simply becomes a thesis, which offers no space for alternatives: "It has been said that the subaltern subject is the one who has an authorial deficit, i.e. a scarce ability to elaborate representations of the self and others, who knows or better said recognizes what he meets in his path through representations already packaged, transmitted and disseminated, but he does not interact with the negotiation of meaning and with the conflict of classifications" (Bartoli 2008, p. 209).

Despite the fact that Bartoli defines as "tedious and inaccurate" the analysis "based entirely on the imaginary religious *à la* Dumont" (Bartoli 2008, p. 219), her final conclusions are not very dissimilar to what Dumont and others—in particular, anthropologists who worked in Tamil Nadu—sustain, reiterating the idea that "Untouchables" adhere to the caste system through their "total consensus" to the dominant ideology of the Brahmin caste (see Dumont 1966; Moffatt 1979; Deliège 1997). In other words, "The subaltern is the satisfied slave, the servant who idolizes his master, the woman who perpetuates the patriarchal model, the marginal who ends up hating himself: the one who has interiorized a dominant vision of the world and believes as legitimate his minority status" (Bartoli 2008, back cover). According to this view, the ex-Untouchables–Dalits would be proponents of their own situation, without even minimally opposing the status quo they occupy and, on the contrary, supporting the "ideological basis" on which the caste system rests, derived from the interpretation of sacred text and customary law. The fact that Bartoli uses the Dalit case to illustrate her own theory of subalternity is no small wonder, precisely because, in my view, Dalits offer an opposite, clear example of a subaltern group marching toward self-awareness and autonomy, thus offering a huge number of "traces of autonomous initiative" as proposed by Gramsci in Q25§2: "Every trace of independent initiative on the part of subaltern groups should . . . be of incalculable value for the integral historian. Consequently, this kind of history can only be dealt with monographically, and each monograph requires an immense quantity of material which is often hard to collect" (Gramsci 1971, p. 55). Later, in Q25§7, Gramsci provides us with a concrete example of these "traces" to be found as "indirect sources" present in the "utopias" and in the so-called philosophical novels. He writes: "These have been studied for the historical development of political critique, but one of its most relevant aspects is their unconscious reflection of the most elementary and profound aspirations of social subaltern groups, *even of the lowest among them*, albeit through the brain of intellectuals dominated by other concerns" (Q25§7, p. 2290, emphasis added; trans. Gramsci 1985, p. 238).

Herein lies the fundamental difference, which is not solely methodological, between the attitude that obliterates all "traces"—perhaps weak, but present—and the pursuit of those traces by the Gramscian "integral historian," who is able to track down these traces even in the writing of the absent-minded intellectual who writes of "utopias" as, for example, the history and the phenomenon of many millenarian movements.

It is no coincidence that Gramsci begins his discussion of Notebook 25 presenting the case of David Lazzaretti. What Gramsci writes with reference to the Italian intellectuals who evaluate Lazzaretti's case could be applied—without the presumption of offering an exhaustive parallel—to the way some scholars deal with the situation of the Dalits and their "subalternity." Not only are the Dalits divested of any ability for (however minimal) autonomy as thinkers, but every effort to overcome their present situation is annulled as "constitutive and innate impotence." Moreover, the same kind of impotence is attributed also to those intellectuals, or integral historians in a Gramscian sense, who, having chosen to side with the subalterns, would unwittingly fall into the "pitfalls of representing the subaltern."

The above discussion could be enlightened by the fact that in 2008, when Bartoli published her book, the National Commission for the Scheduled Castes, the official organ of the Indian state for the defense of the rights of ex-Untouchables and the promotion of their interests, sent all state departments a circular banning the use of the word *Dalit* in official acts, following a notification from the Ministry of Law and Justice. In short, the word *Dalit*, despite its current use and its political overtones, has no legal value (or "legal sanctity"), and only "Scheduled Caste," according to the state, is to be considered an official expression. This strong position, abundantly foretold, was no surprise, given that from the time of its initial usage, the word *Dalit* appeared in all its revolutionary character when Jyotirao Phule (1827–1890) during the nineteenth century adopted it to designate the so-called Untouchables as opposed to Brahmins all over South Asia. I will return later to the meaning and the importance of the word *Dalit*. Here, it suffices to point out the adjective *revolutionary* as defined by Mariátegui, when in a letter to the press after his arrest in 1927, he wrote: "The word 'revolution' has acquired a new meaning that is quite different from the traditional association with conspiracies" (cited in Basadre 1971, p. xxi). The long path of the revolution established by the use of the word *Dalit*, chosen by the former Untouchables for its alternative connotation, penetrates gradually into the state structures, thus disturbing them, and that is why it was abolished, at least from official documents. The adoption of the word *Dalit* cannot be motivated by the action of the "satisfied/ contented slave" but rather reveals the willingness of groups of "slaves" who strive consciously for an alternative in a move from self-pity to self-affirmation, or *consapevolezza* (self-awareness), in Gramscian terms. The path is still long and the obstacles are very numerous, but the Dalits have no wish to change their name; that is, they want to continue on the path of this slow revolution which—if we call it a revolution—can only be labeled a "permanent revolution."

I have already started to provide a partial answer to our initial question— that is, could Gramsci provide an authoritative answer to the question of subalternity, and in particular to the link "subalternity-religion"? But before getting into the heart of the question, I would like to propose a brief reflection on the importance of the "nexus" itself, starting from what has already been said, especially by G. Cospito about the *cautele* (cautions; Cospito 2015, pp. 28–42) in Gramsci's prison writing, so as not to betray the profound message of the author, "the rhythm of thought" (Cospito 2011a). When speaking of subalternity, and in my case, expanding the discussion to include the "world of subalterns," the risk of betrayal increases dramatically. Let me start by saying that I will not try to offer universal, essentialist answers, which do not really exist, but I intend to propose some concrete examples and details, in which one can also apply with rigor and intellectual honesty Gramscian methodological research. In putting together these incipient "monographs" of groups united by the experience of subalternity, we could find some itineraries of reflections on broader themes in which to include "subalterns in the world."

The Nexus "Religion-Subalternity"

I will use my own research to illustrate the religion-subalternity link, but I will also draw on various Gramscian scholars to support what I say in a more coherent manner. In particular, I will use Peter Thomas's *The Gramscian Moment* (2009b) and Fabio Frosini's *La religione dell'uomo moderno* (2010), together with other recent writings by Frosini, thus allowing us to maintain an open dialogue on the Gramscian texts.

Developing further the religion-subalternity nexus, I would like to propose, very briefly, this thesis: religion in its broadest sense—understood both as the study of religions and as religious practice—becomes a key factor to perceive in depth the existential, historical situation of "subaltern groups." Moreover, the "religious factor"—including the religious experience of subaltern groups—helps us to perceive both the acceptance of subordination on the part of subalterns, and their opposition to it. It is important to see the combination of these two components of religion together, even when they have contradictory characteristics. While some features of the religion of subalterns can be considered universal (in a very broad sense)—in that they tend to be present in different times and places—it is essential to highlight those characteristics derived from the historical and cultural experiences of individual groups. In other words, it is important to combine and reread diachronically both the universal moment and the particular one. In Gramscian terms, we know that there are historical "traces," but we also know that not all traces are the same.

The previous paragraph refers to another aspect of religion, emphasized by Gramsci (Q11§13, p. 1397; trans. Gramsci 1971, p. 420): the plurality of the concept of religion, or, if you will, the polysemy of the word *religion*, which is interpreted differently according to the social (historical, cultural, economic, etc.) background of the various groups (or interpreting subjects). Among these different interpretations I would also include that of the researcher-scholar or group of scholars who have a further concept of religion, emphasizing especially the "conceptual" element as the theoretical-reflective moment of religion, as well as the aspect of religion as a social fact-phenomenon.

This in turn triggers another important nexus that is typically Gramscian: the interplay between theory (as the study of religion) and the practice of religion, or "religious praxis" in a very broad sense, which includes a variety of actions, celebrations, rituals, beliefs, performances, common participation, and so on. In fact, the theory concerning the religious fact cannot, in the Gramscian sense, disregard the praxis, but refers to the practice and begins with the practice, so that the "theorizing" is not divorced from real life, from the history of subaltern groups. It is in this hermeneutic movement, in this osmosis between theory and practice, where I think that Gramsci's contribution becomes relevant and original, both for the reasons already given and those I have still to add.

The fact that subaltern groups operate "on the margins of history" means that they do not have the means by which they can express themselves and their history. Rather than narrating themselves, they are narrated and often defined by others. For this very reason, Gramsci invites the "integral historian" to find those traces that must be unearthed within the fragmentary history of these groups—as he says, "the most elementary and profound aspirations of even the lowest subaltern social group" (Q25§7; trans. Gramsci 1985, p. 238), thus implying the presence of different levels and/or phases of subalternity, and hence proposing a movement toward self-understanding and awareness of their subalternity.

"Religious language"—in its many forms, primarily as a metaphor—becomes the privileged locus through which Gramsci identifies the presence of these "traces." We also know how language itself occupies a prominent place in Gramsci's reflection, not so much or not only as a "means of communication," but as a genuine expression of an "integral conception of the world" ("concezione del mondo integrale"); that is, a philosophy (Q5§123, pp. 644–645; trans. Gramsci 1992–2007, vol. 2, p. 366; see also Q11§12). Although, for obvious reasons, subalterns were prevented from following the path of mainstream philosophy—being cut off from history and culture, and mostly from official religion—they are able to transmit and communicate their philosophy by other means. The question then remains, why does religious language seem to be a privileged language for the philosophy of the subalterns to narrate itself? A first, very immediate answer may be: for the same reason that Gramsci begins his reflections on subaltern groups with the story and the human vicissitude of a group/religious movement—that of Lazzaretti—within a precise moment in the history of Italy. It is the confluence of a number of historical, economic, cultural, and social factors that motivate the onset and development of these movements, as Lanternari, too, will later underline. To these explanations, Gramsci provides an additional dimension—namely, the reading of these events given by Italian intellectuals, thus highlighting the missing link between intellectuals—who fail to understand deeper historical reasons—and the popular masses. In Notebook 4, §33, Gramsci explains why intellectuals fail to understand: "The error of the intellectual consists in believing that one can *know* without understanding and, above all, without feeling and being impassioned . . . that is, without being emotionally tied to the people, understanding them, *without feeling the rudimentary passions of the people, understanding them and hence explaining [and justifying] them in the specific historical situation* and linking them dialectically to the laws of history, that is, to a scientifically elaborated superior conception of the world: namely 'knowledge'" (Q4§33, p. 452; trans. Gramsci 1992–2007, vol. 2, p. 173; emphasis added). Here Gramsci offers not only the methodology but also a theoretical framework for the content of the monograph concerning the history of subalterns.

Finally, returning to the initial question of the link between religion—as fact and religious experience—and subalternity, we must stress the methodology, at times complex but equally markedly dialogic, used by Gramsci. Part of the nexus, in fact, is brought to fruition by way of other links that explain the initial connection. In other words, the nexus religion-subalternity must be located within the wider context-nexus "religion, common sense, philosophy" (Q8§204, p. 1063; trans. Gramsci 1992–2007, vol. 3, p. 352). The latter, in turn, flows into the nexus "education-intellectual-the masses" (of which the subalterns are part), and hence flowing into the link "State = political society + civil society," but also the crucial triad "religion, politics, philosophy." In concrete terms, this would correspond to an accumulation of the many traces left in history by a particular group so as to bring together a "monograph" that will never be fully completed, since new traces are always being discovered.

Before proceeding with the presentation of some key examples I would like to propose in order to illustrate concretely the religion-subalternity link, let me clarify my immediate point of departure. As previously mentioned, I intend to use the work of two Gramscian scholars to support my point, although I will not be able to do this in a comprehensive way, only in outline. Peter Thomas, in *The Gramscian Moment* and "Gramsci and the Political," helps us to focus in a consistent and systematic manner on what I am trying to do, because he provides us with a broader overview and because he not only relocates Gramsci within Marxist philosophy but also proposes Gramsci as a privileged moment in this philosophy, beyond the multiple interpretations of Gramsci's work. Thomas does not intend to propose a new "Gramscianism," but, re-evaluating past critiques—in particular by Althusser and Perry Anderson—I think he intentionally makes us aware of that moment between 1931 and 1932 when Gramsci perceives intuitively in an almost existential manner the transition of the concept of hegemony from "metaphysical event" to "philosophical fact," thus bringing the philosophy of praxis to renew the entire philosophical apparatus, precisely because even those who thus far have always been excluded, finally become an integral part of it (Thomas 2009b, p. 39). Thomas then helps us to appreciate how, for Gramsci, the confluence of the intense activity of the intellectuals and the effort of the subaltern classes, expressed in their common sense, produces, through Marx, a new philosophy, a true revolution due to the "philosophy of praxis." The latter, writes Gramsci, "does not aim at the peaceful resolution of existing contradictions in history and society but is rather the very theory of these contradictions. It is not the instrument of government of the dominant groups in order to gain the consent of and exercise hegemony over the subaltern classes; it is the expression of these subaltern classes who want to educate themselves in the art of government and who have an interest in knowing all truths" (Q10ii§41xii, p. 1320; trans. Gramsci 1995a, pp. 395–396).

Rebuffing the path of the "history of philosophy," Gramsci proposes a solution in which history and philosophy are identified, but not without the irruption of a third element that is precisely politics, or the art of government, in which the subaltern classes are invited to play a part (Thomas 2009b, pp. 290–292). This overall view posited by Thomas promotes a more critical yet contemporary and thoughtful use of Gramsci, calling our attention to facile interpretations dictated by positions akin to postmodernism and poststructuralism, which can often be misleading.

Continuing on this theme, Frosini's *La religione dell'uomo moderno* allows us to combine the nexus religion-subalternity with other Gramscian links, as mentioned above. In particular, I would like to dwell on what Frosini argues in his article "Why Does Religion Matter to Politics?," in which the author provides a summary of a clear and eloquent exposition of the importance of religion in the *Notebooks* for politics, starting right from the nexus "religion, common-sense, philosophy," which opens up toward "language as a collective act" to then redefine the concept of universality and truth in linguistic terms. In other words: "The multiplicity of languages amounts to a multiplicity of truth productions, with different degrees of power. This difference is because different languages are traceable to different social classes, which are in conflict" (Frosini 2013b, p. 176). In this struggle to establish the supremacy of the universal language, the bourgeoisie tries to take possession of the common sense of subaltern groups and, in a sense, to "tame" it, thus trying to eliminate the barriers between "dominant and subaltern" so as to administer power. Hence the efforts by the dominant classes to achieve unification of political and civil society. For this to happen, it is essential for dominant politics to resort to "religious language," which is the only one capable of offering "*a form of total social praxis*" so that stable hegemony can be ensured (Frosini 2013b, p. 179; emphasis in original).

Just to be clear—even if the example might seem rather banal—"Cunservet Deus su Re" (God save the king, the Sardinian "national" anthem) and "God Save the Queen" are a part of religious language, but one within which politics needs to return to the universalizing and "founding myths" in which truth, politics, and religion meet. In this way, the dominant groups in different times and ways (Jacobinism, Bonapartism, Fascism, etc.) ensure the support of popular participation so as to obtain what Gramsci calls the "integral state" and the neutralization of conflicts, a situation that also reflects the separation between the intellectuals and the masses. During 1930 to 1933 Gramsci is reflecting on these realities in the European political scene that are a consequence of the postwar crisis and that result in what he calls "bureaucratic-democratic regimes," thus giving a different meaning to the concept of "war of position."

In other words, Frosini comments, this notion [war of position] does not consist in obtaining hegemony by separating the public from the private sphere any longer, but in unifying them in new and flexible forms. Thus, religion and politics form a new type of intertwining that turns religion into a fundamental element of aggregation and political ruling. This occurs in different ways from one country to another. Yet, these oscillations are symptomatic because they show how the intervention aimed at the transformation of common sense—given the structure of the national state—necessarily coincides with the de-politicization of conflicts, whereas the politicization of common sense necessarily assumes nationalistic ("religious") appearances that divert conflict from classes to nations (Frosini 2013b, p. 183).

This discourse deserves a more comprehensive discussion, but suffice it here to note, as a general idea, that "bourgeois universalism, devoid of any power content, absorbs the common sense of the subalterns and reorganizes its meaning. In this way bourgeois power incorporates the utopian energy of popular religious universalism, rendering it functional to its own expansion" (Frosini 2013b, p. 183)—namely, to the expansion of bourgeois power. Would this then be the end of all efforts, and the defeat of all aspirations for the subalterns? Apparently not, at least according to Frosini, who, rereading Gramsci, tells us more: "All the elements necessary to unify the signifiers 'people' and 'democracy' are already present in the religious representations that support the struggles of resistance by the subalterns. What the subalterns are lacking is not a class consciousness adequate to their practical function, but the *coherence* of those representations that already operate, fueling their resistance to domination and that for the moment do not find a concrete, political, mediation between local struggles and universal projection" (Frosini 2013b, p. 183; emphasis in the original).

Frosini concludes by proposing a reflection as a renewed challenge for the future of subalterns by resorting to the transformed figure of Machiavelli's Prince "as a creation of concrete fantasy which acts on a dispersed and *shattered people* to arouse and organise its collective will" (Q13§1, p. 1556; trans. Gramsci 1971, p. 126; emphasis added).[6] In addition, the utopia of the Prince is transmitted to the utopian representations of subalterns, so that the modern Prince becomes an "auto-reflection on the part of the people—an inner reasoning worked out in the popular consciousness, whose conclusion is a cry of passionate urgency" (Q13§1, p. 1556; trans. Gramsci 1971, pp. 126-127). For this very reason, the modern Prince "must be and cannot but be—as Gramsci says—the proclaimer and organiser of an intellectual and moral reform" (Q13§1, p. 1556; trans. Gramsci 1971, pp. 132-133).

Briefly, I would like to propose a concrete reflection of what has been said so far, providing a specific example that will hopefully help to further highlight a Gramscian understanding of subalternity by considering the nexus religion-subalternity.

On August 28, 2013, we celebrated the fiftieth anniversary of the civil rights March on Washington, made famous by Martin Luther King Jr.'s speech "I Have a Dream," which even now resonates highly of utopia. The main organizers of the march were the heads of various movements, including King himself. Of course, there was much apprehension, and police control was intense. The speakers, invited to be "moderate," manifested some reticence, though not all of them did so. Toward the end of King's speech, in which he quoted the Declaration of Independence and the Constitution to support his thesis, Mahalia Jackson, queen of gospel music, shouted, "Speak to them of the dream, Martin, tell them about the dream!" And King launched into an impromptu speech that made history.

On the commemoration of the fiftieth anniversary of the March on Washington, there was a division of opinion between those who pointed to the progress made in terms of civil rights and others who remembered how the 1963 demands for "freedom and work" were still a dream for many African Americans, especially in the southern states but also in cities affected by the economic crisis, such as Detroit and others. All this reminds us of the slow march in the history of liberation from slavery for these subalterns, but also the physical march into slavery that began much earlier, about which we often can read only at the margins of official history. The journey of the slaves, which began in West Africa and brought them to the United States (in very small numbers, because most of them ended up in the Caribbean and Latin America), and then continued after independence (1776) and after the official abolition in 1808 of the international slave trade, but also after the Civil War of 1861 to 1865. With the Thirteenth Amendment to the U.S. Constitution, in December 1865 slavery was formally abolished, but history tells us that this does not mark the end of their subalternity. On the contrary, this perhaps highlights still further the weakness of the state law and how subalternity was necessary to ensure unification. In all this, the role played by religion was not indifferent, neither for the ruling classes nor for the subalterns.

One aspect of this "religion of the slaves" was their conversion to Christianity and the syncretism that arose by combining African rituals and the new religion. This found expression in their music, especially gospel, blues, and jazz. Christianity played an ambiguous and contradictory role: while some Christian groups were abolitionists, others, especially in the southern states, preached resignation and obedience to authority. Among the different genres, blues is, for many reasons, best suited to analysis from a Gramscian perspective: the narrative that surrounds it, its oral history, the characteristics of "common sense" that it offers, and its proximity to popular religion, but also its reaction and subversion against certain religious tendencies and, in general, against the situation of continuous oppression.

Willie Dixon (1915-1992), bassist and blues composer for several big names (Muddy Waters, Howlin' Wolf, and the label Chess Records) declared in an interview, "Blues is about truth; if it is not true, it is not blues" (Burnett 2008). This approach remains constant in the history of the blues and the individual narratives of its protagonists. Derived from the spirituals of gospel music, blues was soon qualified as "the other music," and certainly as less sacred, even when performed by those who attended Christian churches. In fact, it came to be defined as "the devil's music," which became more apt with the myths about bluesmen such as Robert Johnson (1911-1938), who supposedly, like Faust, sold his soul to the devil, but in exchange for the art of playing the guitar. This new instrument for that blues represented not only novelty but also rebellion and dissent, and for this reason it was defined "an instrument of the devil." Between 1890 and 1906 in the southern states the African American Christian denominations were multiplying; the number of Baptist ministers rose from 5,500 to 17,000, and they were the first to "demonize the blues" because it interfered with their ministry.

However, many of the names associated with the blues were also close to the Christian churches, or were even children of ministers and "preachers" (Pearson 2005, p. 102), as in the cases of Big Joe Duskin (1921-2007) and John Lee Hooker (1917-2001). If, on the one hand, the guitar and the blues represented the other side of the "African soul" that was associated with the idolatry of sin and pleasure, on the other they also announced modernity, social change, and rejection of slavery. For Memphis guitarist Johnny Shines (1915-1992), the blues and gospel music were two sections of the same river. Muddy Waters (1913-1983) replied to those who accused him of deviating from the gospel: "The devil can quote scripture, they say, so I guess it's fair for good people to take the devil's tools and use them to live a good and decent life" (Gussow 2010, p. 90). The guitarist Jack Owens (1904-1997) defended himself with the same rhetoric, as did Mance Lipscomb (1895-1976). "I haven't played in church very often," Owens admitted, "See, they criticize me cause I'm a blues songster. You know what I am? Blues is in the church! I kin prove it ta you in one word: What is the blues? Blues is a feelin. If it's a feelin out in these nightclubs, it's a feelin in church. . . .

It's a sad feelin, and a worried feelin" (Alyn 1993, p. 57). Lipscomb confirmed the same idea, more vehemently: "I didn quit church: church quit me" (Alyn 1993, p. 52).[7] The "sadness and worries" of African Americans at that time—for a long time, indeed—were very real and existential concerns, as evidenced by the comments of a female guitarist (one of the few), Jessie Mae Hemphill (1923-2006): "People look at me, you know, when I go to church. They think it's so terrible for me to go to church because I sing the blues. . . . And I tell them, 'God knows everything. God knows why I'm doing this. He know I needs to pay my bills.' They say you can't serve the Devil and the Lord, too. But my belief about it is that God spared me and brought me this far" (Young 1997, p. 234).

Gussow rightly remarks on the commonality between different relationships in the experience of the blues: the father minister-preacher and the rebellious son, innovative and revolutionary, and the failed relationship between the blues singer and his wife, or "the imprisoning relationship between an addict and his fix," are all examples of the struggle taking place within the group (Gussow 2010, p. 93). However, there is also the relationship between the blues man and the white boss, especially after the Civil War, when all African Americans became freemen and no longer slaves. But in order to survive in the southern states many had to work as sharecroppers in the cotton fields. Their dream for some time, even though money could not be saved, was to escape to the north, the "promised land," like the people of Israel fleeing Egypt. And their music, both gospel and blues, became a message of hope but also a coded message for the fugitives so that they knew which way to go, whom to approach or trust on the long journey north. There are only scattered traces of this, and the historians of the "dominant groups" tend to downplay these events since there is no "definitive evidence"—the proof being left in songs and oral narratives. As in the Gramscian definition of "subaltern groups," this movement had no structure of real organization but was instead spontaneous and often disorganized. This movement, known as the Underground Railroad (spawning its own metaphorical terminology—train-station, the station-master, conductor, passengers, baggage, etc.) helped many to escape slavery, but many others remained, especially after the abolition of slavery, and, jobless, they were put in jail. Thus, wealthy individuals—usually plantation owners—paid the government and "rented" the inmates as cheap labor. Even here, in the prisons, the blues finds fertile ground, because it still resonates of sorrow and suffering and of a freedom that never comes, despite the new laws.

In 1949 John Lee Hooker, the "heretic" son of an evangelical minister, wrote the famous song "Burnin' Hell," taking inspiration from another older blues musician, Son House (1902-1988), who was also a Baptist preacher (often alternating between the two roles). In "Burnin' Hell" Hooker sings, "Well every-body's talking bout that . . . burnin' hell / Ain't no heaven or . . . ain't no burnin' hell / Where I die or where I go . . . nobody tell, I said." Hooker also talks about "Deacon Jones"—"the folkloric archetype of the black divine" (Murray 2000, p. 38)—who prays for the salvation of the musician. Jones is a fictitious, almost rhetorical figure that represents a kind of Manichean ideology (Gussow 2010, p. 96) but is nevertheless powerless against Hooker's strong desire to break free from his own ghosts through the blues; he concludes, "Yes, I done freed, I done sun / Did anything that a poor man sho could do / Ain't gonna pray no more."[8]

The march toward the North produced, in addition to the expansion of the Delta blues, new music and new blues (Motown, Chicago urban blues, etc.), to then explode into new waves of jazz but also rock and roll. All this became of considerable commercial importance, and while the work of the producers of blues and related music made progress in the 1960s, those who controlled the market, the so-called good American families, distributed leaflets that said, "Help Save the Youth of America. Do Not Buy Negro Records. . . . Don't Let Your Children Buy, or Listen to These Negro Records."[9] At the same time, King was delivering his famous speech at the March on Washington in 1963.

We would need to further discuss the Gramscian aspect of the history of blues, but we can already appreciate how the events of the African American experience, of both individuals and the group, highlight the characterization of subalternity and its strong connection to religion. In this history there is an overabundance of relevant "traces" concerning the nexus religion-subalternity that clearly constitute an incipient monograph destined to be expanded with the addition of other traces disseminated in multiple times and places. It is the task of the Gramscian integral historian to bring this fascinating history to fruition and to convey its profound and most original message to present-day "consumers" of this type of music, many of whom might be unaware of its deepest roots in life experience and human suffering.

The Ideal and Value of the "Work" in Sardinia— Experiences from the Fieldwork

On September 6 and 7, 2013, I was part of a group of scholars who met at Ghilarza, Gramsci's hometown, for the launch of the Ghilarza Summer School. When we arrived, the air still hung heavy with the smell of a forest fire that a month earlier had devastated this area of Sardinia. Not only did the fire threaten to enter the town, it also destroyed a whole year of work and the winter fodder for the animals. A farmer had died trying to save his herd. Trying to remedy this almost desperate situation of so much work "'gone up in smoke,'" ranchers and farmers of Gallura and Nurra—northern subregions of Sardinia—donated to Ghilarza and the surrounding villages a considerable amount of hay. This gesture of apparently spontaneous generosity has very deep roots in Sardinia and is known as *ponidura* in Gallura and *paradura* (literally, to repair) in other parts of Sardinia. This is a true social institution of solidarity through which shepherds and farmers form a partnership of mutual aid so as to provide "reparation" for incurred damage.[10]

In Sardinia, with a long history of colonization by successive invaders and the lack of a centralized government, people took it upon themselves to regulate communal living while trying to mitigate the fight for scarce resources. The generosity of the *paradura* and other systems of gift giving is contrasted with the implementation of the code of vendetta, particularly among the shepherds of the mountainous area of central Sardinia (see Pigliaru [1959] 1975). Given this background, people have learned to appreciate and also to respect the value of hard work, and at times to defend the results of labor with one's life. This is also reflected in the sense of "sacredness" with which villagers consider their activities, even the most common, within this predominantly agropastoral community. The sacredness of work is further accentuated during the celebration of certain festivities when daily activities become ritualized. I was able to verify this during extended periods of fieldwork in Nule, my native village, while conducting a research on the gift-giving system (*imbiatu*) and more recently during the making of an ethnographic film *S'impinnu* (The vow) about gift giving. The film recounts the celebrations that take place every year in Nule on the occasion of the feast of St. Anthony of Padua. The origin of these celebrations dates back to 1856, when a local shepherd (Antonio Manca) returned from the Crimean War after having made a vow: if he returned safe and sound from the war, he pledged to distribute on St. Anthony's feast day bread and melted cheese (*su bussiottu chin su casu furriadu*) to all children in the village.

The initial preparation of the festival is marked by the presence of the priest, who blesses those who take part in the work as well as the tons of flour that are used to make the bread. The person in charge, Antoniangela Manca—a direct descendant of Antonio, her great-grandfather—in turn "blesses" the first sack of flour, taking a fistful and sprinkling those present, as if it were holy water, saying, "Chi Deus b'appat parte, e vios e mortos s'ind'atthathene" (May God have his share and both the living and the dead be satiated). In other words, the work is blessed, coming to fruition when it satiates the whole community, including those who in the past were part of it.[11] At the conclusion of the work, when the last bread (*sa cozzula manna*) is removed from the oven and the fire extinguished, the success of the labors is conveyed though another expression, equally weighted with significance: "Pro chi 'nd'essada donz'amina dae pena, e donzi presoneri dae cadena" (So that every soul [of purgatory] is freed from punishment, and every prisoner from the chains [of prison]). The hardship of labor is thus offered for the "liberation" of those in the community who are in situations of greatest suffering: the souls in purgatory—as accentuated by the teaching of the Church—but also those who find themselves in prison, a constant preoccupation of the living community.

This same maxim is pronounced by the women of Nule, skilled artisans, when they finish weaving a rug and it is being removed from the loom. It is worth noting that the initial use of this saying needs to be situated historically: it dates from a time when the reality of prison—from the eighteenth to the early nineteenth century (1820, Editto delle Chiudende, or "Edict of the Enclosures")— involved many families of Nule and surroundings, including the subregions of Goceano and Barbagia (see Beccu 2000; Ruzzu 1999; Marongiu 2004). If, on the one hand, Catholic doctrine informed the mentality of the people in terms of popular religiosity such as the devotion to "the holy souls in purgatory," on the other hand, these souls were favored because they were, according to this belief, in a situation of suffering that could be alleviated by the contribution of the faithful, who offered for this purpose the sacrifice of their hard work. In addition, the popular piety extended this offer to a more concrete and visible "salvation," such as that of prisoners in jail. This sense of solidarity, which is widespread in the workplace and in everyday life, is reflected in the mutual help that the villagers did not fail to exercise, especially during periods of more intense work both in agriculture and herding: "giving a hand" (una 'ettada 'e manu) was a way of "being and acting" that characterized mutual generosity.

To this attitude of respect for work and mutual help, as part of common sense, a somewhat contradictory feature must be added: the reticence, or at least the failure, of the nulesi to promote cooperative enterprises. A massive dairy farm in Nule, built in the 1960s, has long been used as a slaughterhouse, and the Casa del Tappeto (carpet workshop), dating from the same period and managed until 1982 by the Istituto Sardo Organizzazione Lavoro Artigiano (ISOLA), was handed over to a local cooperative that has now ceased to exist. These two monuments to non-cooperativeness are in conflict, or at least in discontinuity, with the motto that the village has given to itself recently, and which is carved in large letters on a granite rock installed at the entrance of the village, where it is written "Nule, idda de manos bonas" (Nule, village of skilled hands), upholding the diligence and local talent of the artisans. Hence, talented hands, but not working in conjunction with other hands? Nevertheless, the feast of St. Anthony proves that the villagers are able to cooperate, and at least in that case, they can overcome the barrier of economic individualism. Why then this inability to turn the symbolic effort of the celebration into an effective shared economic activity of benefit for the local community? Why is this unity of purpose limited to the celebration of a feast and unable to be transferred into a long-lasting commitment, even a "vow," for the well-being of the community? Maybe the answer should be sought elsewhere, perhaps in the analysis of the way in which not only the *nulesi* but Sardinians in general have approached "modernity" and the shift that occurred when—from the period of the *Chiudende* (enclosures) onward—land, from a common good for all, has become the preserve of a few, especially some who simply grabbed it for themselves.[12]

What can we learn from the above notes on the value and even "sacralization" of human labor in relation to the Gramscian nexus subalternity-religion? One first lesson is perhaps that labor seems to remain inextricably linked to subalternity, be it in the case of slaves who were coerced into providing cheap labor or in the case of Sardinian villagers for whom labor remains caught between generosity and a fight for survival. In both cases, religion is invoked to provide a solution to shortcomings that originate elsewhere, thus preserving a structural ambiguity. Religion does, however, uncover those "traces" that indicate for both groups—slaves and villagers—an aspiration to the freedom of human dignity and an honorable job.

Now, many years down the line, we can appreciate that labor is still used—or rather misused—to bind people into new forms of "slavery" that signal new forms of subalternity. I am aware that the following might appear to be very sweeping statements, but they could signal the beginning of new "Gramscian monographs" vis-à-vis new subalterns. The cunning of transnational capital to provide work right where there is an abundance of (cheap) labor should help us reflect on the situation of the "world of labor," which, yesterday as today, remains the privileged place for the creation and re-creation of new forms of slavery and subalternity. For this very reason, yesterday as today, Gramsci's theoretical and methodological suggestions still remain valid if we wish to research in depth the situation of the "new subaltern," since "each monograph requires an immense quantity of material which is often hard to collect." Yesterday's slaves who picked cotton in the southern United States have been replaced by seasonal immigrant workers picking fruit, especially tomatoes, in Florida[13] but also in Italy and other countries in the Western world.[14] The cotton fields were relocated from the United States to Uzbekistan, where enforced child labor is imposed by the state (Kandiyoti 2009). The raw material, produced at a very low cost and then purchased by multinational corporations, is turned into fabric that will be used to "provide jobs" to millions of people—mostly women and children—in the infamous garment factories of South and Southeast Asia.[15] Perhaps for the Gramscian integral historian it would be worth the effort to shift the research interest from the much celebrated Silk Road to the study of the Cotton Road and the new subalterns. In all this, religion remains very prominent, even when it is in the background, as a pacifying instrument to keep subalterns content, as a tool for "development strategies" (see religiously motivated NGOs), or even as a means to gain self-consciousness by the subaltern.

José Carlos Mariátegui and the "Peruvian Reality"

The work of J. C. Mariátegui (1894-1930) is a privileged moment, in the Gramscian sense, for the rediscovery of "traces" within the history of Peru and Latin America in general, which become relevant for the integral historian devoted to the reconstruction of the history of "subaltern groups" left, to paraphrase Gramsci, on the margins of—a more or less official—history. It will be impossible in a few paragraphs to give a detailed account of his contribution, so I will concentrate on a few aspects that highlight our present discussion concerning the nexus religion-subalternity. I will do so by referring mainly to two of his major works: *Defensa del Marxismo* (Defense of Marxism; 1934) and *Seven Interpretative Essays on Peruvian Reality* (1929/1971).

We must take into account, first of all, that Mariátegui, despite dying at the early age of thirty-six, having suffered from many illnesses his whole life, managed to accomplish remarkable achievements, and he is still been considered one of the most important Latin American Marxists. Though Mariátegui has been called "Latin America's forgotten Marxist" (Gonzales 2007), his legacy has become crucial, from the 1990s onward, in assisting Indigenous resistance all over Latin America (see Becker 2006, pp. 450-479; Becker 2008). It must also be said that a number of experiences shaped his particular understanding of Marxism, which some would not refrain from defining as heterodox. Among these were his rise to prominence from humble origins, his becoming a skilled journalist, his starting work aged fourteen as typesetter for a newspaper in Lima (*La Prensa*), his efforts to educate himself through selected readings, and his travels to Europe and Italy:

> He was present at the founding conference of the Italian Communist Party at Livorno in 1921 and learned much of his Marxism during this period. Arriving after the Italian factory occupations, his articles and essays reflect his immersion in the debates around the issue of hegemony.

More importantly, Mariátegui saw first hand how the political weakness of the bourgeoisie and the vacillations of reformism could permit the emergence of fascism—and these would be the central themes in his lectures and classes on the world situation which he gave at the *Universidad Populares* after his return to Peru, and in a subsequent series of articles in various newspapers in 1923–4, published later under the title *Figures and Aspects of International Life*. (Gonzales 2007)

The Italian experience was very significant for Mariátegui. In addition to absorbing the ideas of Gramsci and the early Italian Communists, he met Benedetto Croce and was hence exposed to Sorel's work: "The combined influence of Crocean 'idealist Marxism' and Sorel's ideas on the role of myth gave Mariátegui's own thought a definite flavor. He writes at times about the socialist program as a 'myth' in the Sorelian sense; his works are softened with words such as 'faith,' 'agony,' 'mystique'; and he displays an openness to many non-Marxist currents of thought such as Freud" (O'Lincoln 1990, n.p.).

This line of thought is particularly evident in Mariátegui's refutation of the allegations of reductionism and economic determinism in Marxism, made by Henri de Man in his book *Beyond Marxism*.[16] Mariátegui insists in his *Defensa del Marxismo* that "Marxism, wherever it has shown itself to be revolutionary—that is, where it has been Marxist—has never obeyed a passive and rigid determinism" (Mariátegui 2011, p. 208). Moreover, he sustained that Marx "always understood the spiritual and intellectual capacity of the proletariat to create a new order through class struggle as a necessary condition" (Mariátegui 2011, p. 209). Indeed, for Mariátegui, "In the development of the proletarian movement every word, every Marxist act resounds with faith, will, heroic and creative conviction, whose impulse it would be absurd to seek in a mediocre and passive determinist sentiment" (Mariátegui 2011, p. 210).

Gramsci's influence is particularly noticeable in these passages that clearly resonate with the "intellectual and moral reformation" advocated by Gramsci, as well as by the latter's accusation made to Manzoni's "caste attitude" toward the so-called humble classes (*gli umili, i semplici*).[17] Drawing from Croce, but also from Unamuno, Sorel, Kautsky, and Gobetti, Mariátegui asserts the "ethical function" of socialism. While agreeing with Kautsky that "the ethic of the proletariat emanates from its revolutionary aspirations," Mariátegui insists that "the struggle for socialism elevates the workers, who with extreme energy and absolute conviction take part in it, to an asceticism, to which it is totally ridiculous to berate its materialism creed in the name of a morality of theorizers and philosophers. . . . The materialist, if he professes and serves his faith religiously, even if only for linguistic convention, can be opposed and distinguished from the idealist" (Mariátegui 2011, p. 203).

This becomes even more accentuated when Mariátegui discusses the specific situation of Peru in his *Seven Interpretative Essays on Peruvian Reality*, particularly in the fifth essay, "The Religious Factor," and the seventh, "Literature on Trial." In "The Religious Factor," Mariátegui, despite his harsh critique of the role of the Catholic Church as a colonizing power carrying out an ecclesiastic enterprise rather than a religious undertaking, is able to distinguish between institutional power and "religion" per se, as expressed also in popular religiosity. Contrary to the position of other Marxist thinkers, and certainly closer to a Gramscian understanding, he distances himself from "those fervent radicals who identified religion with 'obscurantism.'"[18] Contemporary commentators go even further by crediting Mariátegui with playing a prominent role in such a significant movement as Latin American liberation theology: "Though at variance with the usual interpretation of Marx's writings on religion, this section allows considerable insight into Mariátegui's focus on the religious fact in the development of human society and is quite clearly compatible with the Theology of Liberation movement that became so popular in Latin America in the early 1980s. It also suggests the extent to which his analysis was rooted in his own reality and life experience" (Vanden and Becker, in Mariátegui 2011, p. 43).

Perhaps, even more significant is the fact that Mariátegui has become relevant in supporting the philosophy of liberation precisely by providing one essential cornerstone to this philosophy. Enrique Dussel, one of the most prominent exponents of philosophy of liberation, has rightly pointed out that the "process of liberation" in Latin America concerns primarily the "American Indians" and their struggle for emancipation: "With Mariátegui I believe that the Indian problem is most closely linked with the future of South America" (Dussel 2003, p. 225; see also Gogol 2002).

In the second of his *Seven Essays* Mariátegui tackles "The Problem of the Indian." It falls between the first essay, "The Outline of Economic Evolution," and the third, "The Problem of the Land," and he links the three together as part of the one Peruvian reality: "Any treatment of the problems of the Indian that fails or refuses to recognize it as a socioeconomic problem is but a sterile, theoretical exercise destined to be completely discredited" (Mariátegui 2011, p. 40).

Mariátegui, like Gonzáles Prada before him,[19] believed that the economic condition of the Indians was essential to any understanding—or liberation. Indeed, Mariátegui remarked that "the socialist critic [the "integral historian" in Gramscian terms] defines the problem by looking for its causes in the country's economy. Indigenous impoverishment is a result of the land tenure system. One cannot talk of changing the lot of the Indian without changing the feudal landholding system. . . . Not surprisingly, Mariátegui believes that the solution must come from Indigenous peoples and not from any attempt to moralize or educate them by well meaning, but confused, liberal idealists or missionaries" (Vanden and Becker, in Mariátegui 2011, p. 40).

One would have expected that education of the Indian could have been an alternative solution to the problem, but Mariátegui is very clear on this: "The modern pedagogue knows perfectly well that education is not just a question of school and teaching methods. Economic and social circumstances necessarily condition the work of the teacher. *Gamonalismo* [latifundism] is fundamentally opposed to the education of the Indian; it has the same interest in keeping the Indian ignorant as it has in encouraging him to depend on alcohol. . . . We are not satisfied to assert the Indian's right to education, culture, progress, love and heaven. We begin by categorically asserting his right to land" (Mariátegui 1971, pp. 27–28, 31).

Mariátegui sustains that the solution to the Indian problem comes from recognizing and implementing those communitarian principles—called *ayllu*—that had survived for many centuries and were still present one hundred years into republican Peru, thus allowing Indigenous communities to administer land, agriculture, livestock, pasture lands, watering places, all for the benefit of the *ayllu*-community and not the individual as in a capitalist system: "The Indian, in spite of the one hundred years of republican legislation, has not become an individualist. And this is not because he resists progress, as is claimed by his detractors. Rather, it is because individualism under a feudal system does not find the necessary conditions to gain strength and develop. On the other hand, communism has continued to be the Indian's only defense. Individualism cannot flourish or even exist effectively outside a system of free competition. And the Indian has never felt less free than when he has felt alone" (Mariátegui 1971, pp. 57–58).

In the seventh and final essay, "Literature on Trial," Mariátegui dealt with the writings of Gonzáles Prada, whom he admired for being close to "the people," condemning colonialism, establishing a link between literature and politics, defending the cause of the Indians, and, although with some reservations, preaching an anti-religion:

> Today much more is known than in his time about many matters, including religion. We know that a revolution is always religious. The word 'religion' has a new value and it no longer serves to designate a ritual or a church. It is of little importance that the Soviets write on their propaganda posters that

"religion is the opium of the people." Communism is essentially religious, but not in the old sense of the word, which still misleads so many. Gonzáles Prada preached the passing of all religious beliefs without realizing that he himself was the bearer of a faith. This rationalism is to be most admired for his passion; this atheist, almost pagan, must be respected for his moral asceticism. His atheism is religious, especially when it appears to be most vehement, most absolute. Gonzáles Prada is found in his creed of justice, in his doctrine of love, and not in the rather vulgar anti-clericalism of some pages of *Horas de lucha*. (Vanden and Becker, in Mariátegui 2011, p. 212)

In 1926 Mariátegui published a new magazine, *Amauta* (Wise teacher, in Quechua) to signal once again the significance of the original cultural and historical presence in Peru and all over Latin America. *Amauta*, which he continued to publish until his death in 1930, was meant to "study all the great movements of political, artistic, literary and scientific renovation" (Mariátegui 1926, p. 1), featured writings by important names including the Spanish philosophers Miguel de Unamuno and Ortega y Gasset, and Mariátegui himself published his main works there—*Defensa del Marxismo* and *Seven Essays*. The journal became "a superb vehicle for disseminating ideas" (Vanden and Becker, in Mariátegui 2011, p. 36) and reaffirming its orientation *indigenista*, as Mariátegui pointed out when providing an evaluation of the work to date: "We certainly do not want socialism in Latin America to be a copy or imitation. It should be heroic creation. We have to give life to Indo-American socialism with our own reality, in our own language. Here is a mission worthy of a new generation" (Mariátegui 1928, p. 3).

This type of committed journalism as organizational forum, very close to Gramsci's experience in Turin with *Ordine Nuovo* and then *L'Unità*, can certainly become an opportunity to promote revolution and to favor a democratic pedagogical stance. At the same time, Mariátegui's life and work epitomizes the "integral historian" and the "collective thinker" who is able to discover those multiple traces left by subalterns on their long journey toward freedom and emancipation. Among these, we can clearly distinguish the "spiritual" and religious traces present in the lives of subalterns, though it is a rather secular and "immanent spirituality."

Some Partial Conclusions

In this essay I have sought to address a central concern in Gramsci's *Prison Notebooks*, in particular in Notebook 25, where he invites the "integral historian" to uncover and collect "traces of autonomous initiative" in the history of subaltern groups so as to produce an "alternative history" (monograph) that not only highlights "the most basic and profound aspirations" of even the lowest amongst subaltern groups but also points toward self-awareness and an overcoming of subalternity itself. The three examples I have provided demonstrate a clear presence of the religious nexus with the—necessarily limited—traces that have been recovered as part of an incipient monograph. This "religion of the subalterns"—often in opposition to official, institutional religion—is located in a very specific sociohistorical and geographical milieu, and it acquires enormous importance as a metaphor and a vehicle of traces pointing toward an experience of a lived reality that is ultimately beyond religion itself. The resulting broader picture allows us to value these traces and to reinterpret them as a partial and perhaps inarticulate response to overcoming subalternity. In Gramscian terms, it is the duty of the integral historian to "make sense" of this apparently incoherent nexus.

While in the case study of the subaltern history of the blues we have seen a greater group participation of individuals contributing to the same "monographic story," in the case of the work in central Sardinia the anthropologist is making efforts to uncover relevant traces following Gramscian suggestions but recognizing also that these traces belong both to him and to his community. The effort to become an integral historian or a collective thinker is not a given, but always in the making through the continuous dialogue between the people and the intellectual. This is quite evident in our third case study, in which we witness Mariátegui's role as totally immersed in the life of his own people and yet rising up as an *Amauta*-teacher to indicate to others—using their very insights, but with added impetus—the road to "liberation."

An obvious omission in our case studies is the discussion of Dalit subaltern groups, given that they figure so prominently in the first part of this essay. This would require, however, a fairly extensive analysis, especially if calling into the forum the combination of Gramsci's political philosophy with the very insightful experience of the Dalit leader B. R. Ambedkar. At present, I can only refer to some previous works of mine that deal precisely with their intellectual "encounter" and commitment toward subaltern groups (Zene 2013), the role of "religion and inner life" in the history of subaltern groups (Zene 2016), and the relevance of education for subalterns and Dalits as a means to achieve justice, freedom, and inclusion in democratic processes (Zene 2018).

1   Later, Lanternari recuperates de Martino in *La mia alleanza con Ernesto de Martino e altri saggi post-demartiniani* (1997), while Hobsbawm writes the postscript for the new edition of *Movimenti religiosi di libertà e salvezza* (2003). Hence, only indirectly did Gramsci land in Lanternari's book.

2   Recently, Kaczyński has sought to analyze the connection between "cultural contact" and "trauma," and more precisely, "sacral trauma," mostly for African religious movements. According to this line of thought, sacral trauma is provoked by the crisis of traditional African society as a result of "cultural shock," modernization, and the loss of sacred/religious values of these communities (see Kaczyński 2006, pp. 161-176). Franco Pignotti instead reconnects to the position taken by Lanternari and Hobsbawm, but passing through Latouche's hyper-occidentalisation, so as to rediscover in Italy new forms of religion "conveyed by a total of 189 nationalities present in our land" (Pignotti 2013, p. 1; see also Pace 2013).

3   "Doxa is a particular point of view, the point of view of the dominant, which presents and imposes itself as a universal point of view—the point of view of those who dominate by dominating the state and who have constituted their point of view as universal by constituting the state" (Bourdieu 1998, p. 57).

4   "Symbolic violence is the coercion which is set up only through the consent that the dominated cannot fail to give to the dominator" (Bourdieu 2000, p. 170).

5   These phases concentrate on the theme of "Untouchability" in both the colonial and postcolonial periods, the question of the name "Dalit" and the "official classification," and the results of the Mandal Commission (1980) instituted to safeguard the rights of underprivileged classes (reservation policy).

6   Frosini has rendered "popolo disperso e polverizzato" as "dispersed and shattered people." It is worth noting that the word *Dalit* means "squashed, crushed, shattered/pulverized."

7   As Adam Gassow comments: "Although a certain number of blues performers do indeed play up their putative proximity to the devil in a way that justifies the devil's-music charge, a far greater number echo Lipscomb, Owens, and Waters, disputing the charge and, when seeing no other option, indicting those who indict them in a way that exposes a painful social breach" (Gussow 2010, p. 91).

8   In the original 1949 recording of "Burnin' Hell," the harmonica was played by Eddie Burns (1928–2012), whose father was a deacon in the Baptist church as well as a blues guitarist himself and a supporter of his son Eddie as a blues musician.

9   The leaflet circulated by the Citizens' Council of Greater New Orleans in the 1960s can be viewed at the University of Mississippi Libraries Digital Collection: http://clio.lib.olemiss.edu/cdm/ref/collection/citizens/id/1631.

10 The mutual aid of the *paradura*, practiced mostly by shepherds, provided for the reconstruction of flocks by all shepherds in the village in favor of those who had suffered the loss of sheep through theft or fire. The same practice was in use when

a shepherd who had spent time in prison and returned to the village had his flock restored by fellow shepherds. In September 2009 Sardinian shepherds, resorting to the *paradura*, collected 2,500 sheep for the shepherds of Abruzzo, which had suffered an earthquake. Only 1,300 sheep were needed for Abruzzo; the rest were donated to the shepherds of Ittiri, Pozzomaggiore, and Torralba, affected by fire in July 2009.

11 The implications of this expression for the local "cosmology" are numerous. Here, it suffices to mention that the idea of community is supported by the memory of those who in the past have kept the community alive and active through their own work and their contribution; hence they are still invited to be part of it at times of celebration.

12 A proverb still in use in Nule is: "Deus sarvet dae poveru irricchidu" (God preserve us / save us from the poor become rich). It is unclear whether the proverb was coined by the wealthy who wanted to preserve their "caste" or by those who remained poor while others made their fortunes. The proverb certainly lends itself to describing what happened during this period in Sardinia when a minority enriched themselves by appropriating the common land, at the expense of the whole community.

13 Commenting on work by Barry Estabrook (2011), who says, "Workers who pick the food we eat cannot afford to feed themselves," Marc Gunther comments: "Children as young as 12 do farm work. Workers are paid, at least in part, by the number of containers of fruit they pick, a system that often leaves them with less than the minimum wage. They are on call daily, but work only when needed. They get no sick benefits, no vacation and if they are hurt on the job, they pay their own medical bills, assuming they can afford to see a doctor. Estabrook writes: 'This might explain why the life expectancy of a migrant worker in the United States is only 49 years . . . migrant workers typically make between $10,000 and $12,000 a year, a figure that is distorted because it includes the higher wages paid to field supervisors.'" Marc Gunther, "Why You Should Avoid Mass-Produced Tomatoes," GreenBiz, July 21, 2011, http://www.greenbiz.com/blog/2011/07/21/why -you-should-avoid-mass-produced-tomatoes.

14 In United States many university lecturers (adjunct faculty), although they constitute 76 percent of the workforce of the universities, have become "seasonal workers"—that is, precarious laborers, so the employer does not have to worry about paying for medical coverage or pensions, while these teachers receive starvation wages. An article giving a very indicative example equates the adjunct faculty to the Untouchables and university professors to Brahmins of the establishment; see Ivan Evans, "When Adjunct Faculty Are the Tenure-Track's Untouchables," Remaking the University, May 19, 2013, http://utotherescue.blogspot.co.uk/2013/05 /when-adjunct-faculty-are-tenure-tracks.html.

15 When I visited the garment factories in Dhaka in 1990, accompanying two French colleagues carrying out fieldwork in the garment industry, inside the enormous

sheds with very low tin roofs we could endure no more than ten minutes at a time, because the temperature inside was over 40 degrees Celsius. Only when tragedy strikes, such as the collapse of the Rana Plaza Building in April 2013, which killed 1,129 people and injured over 2,500, is the world made aware of what is happening. But for too many of these workers, tragedy is an everyday life experience.

16 This appeared first under the title *Zur Psychologie des Sozialismus* (1926) and was translated into French as *Au delà du marxisme* (1927).

17 "In the novel *The Betrothed*, there is not one common person who is not teased or laughed at. . . . They are depicted as wretched and narrow people with no inner life. Only the nobles have an inner life" (Q23§51, p. 2245; trans. Gramsci 1985, pp. 289–290).

18 "We have definitely left behind the days of anticlerical prejudice, when the 'free-thinking' critic happily discarded all dogmas and churches in favour of the dogma and church of the atheist's free-thinking orthodoxy. The concept of religion has become broader and deeper, going far beyond a church and a sacrament" (Mariátegui 1971, p. 124).

19 "The influence of Gonzáles Prada's 'Our Indians' is readily apparent in Mariátegui's writings" (Vanden and Becker, in Mariátegui 2011, p. 40). See Gonzáles (1924).

7

Some Reflections on Gramsci

The Southern Question in the Deprovincializing of Marx

HARRY HAROOTUNIAN

I would like to focus on three considerations that have prompted reflections
on situating Gramsci's *The Southern Question* in a larger process of deprovincializing
Marx that addresses the question of how
Marx was read in the interwar period. First,
the silhouette of this figure of a deprovin-
cialized and more worldly Marx, which
entailed taking into account a number of
thinkers from the world outside of Euro-
America, was probably inaugurated by Lenin in his early work *The History of
the Development of Capitalism in Russia* and driven by his conviction that Russia
was an Asiatic state. But it was forcefully conceptualized by Rosa Luxemburg
and, I believe, Antonio Gramsci, who especially has been claimed for Western
Marxism, with others, and whose thinking emphasized both an opening to
the colonial regions of the world, semicolonies, and latecomers on the industrial periphery and the singular importance of concentrating on the process
of production and labor in their regions of the world. I will then turn to a
brief accounting of Antonio Gramsci's *The Southern Question* as an inaugural
text announcing the presence of what has become known as the Global South,
which signified an early departure from those more dominant forms of Marxism as they were formulated in the interwar period to later authorize a cultural

unity of the West during the Cold War. I am referring especially to his effort to repair the division between north and south that had weakened Italian national unity and thus resolve the problem of unevenness it exemplified. Like so many, Gramsci ultimately called on the past to resolve the problems of his present and confront the present's classic problem of "coping with the past" (*Vergangenheitsbewältigung*). This task entails resituating Gramsci's text in a broader context preoccupied with the production process at the same time that the more immediate contemporaneity of Italian history and his reading of its past was brought into play to mediate his observations of the contemporary political situation. Finally, I'd like to consider the utility of the Gramscian conceptualization of what variously has been called "revolution without revolution," "revolution-restoration," and ultimately "passive revolution" in explaining the instance of large-scale historical transformations, which grew out of his historical analysis of Italian unification in the nineteenth century and the conditions attending the industrialization of the north and ultimately spurred his interest in assessing its applicability in the wider world of colonialism and capital, such as East Asia, the Middle East, and Latin America.

Deprovincialization

There have been few more important episodes in the history of Marxism than its provincialization in the figure of what the Soviets called "Western Marxism," to differentiate their own discussions from Georg Lukács's *History and Class Consciousness*. With this naming, it was clear that the intention was to show how Lukács represented a shift from preoccupations with labor and the production process, as such, to the force of the commodity form to exceed its capacity to structure social relationships by including thought and culture. While Lukács opened the way for a broader consideration of the role played by the commodity form in structuring social relationships and focusing particularly on the function of culture, mass consumption, and the commodification of pleasure, he remained faithful to his formulation of seeing the worker as both subject and object and how the dynamic of formal subsumption, the initial subordination of labor to capital, managed to harness past practices to capital's pursuit of value but never completely assimilate "living labor" (the historical past) to the regimen of "dead labor" (the historical present). Gramsci referred to this conservation and use of the past signified by formal subsumption as an "innovatory force," "immanent in the past," and, finally, "an element of the past, whatever of the past is alive and developing" (Gramsci 1995a, pp. 374–375). What he was referring to was the capacity to use some practice or institution from the past in a new present serving the demands of a different mode of production from the one in which it had originated. Yet, at the same time, what was subsumed, whether labor or practice or institution, was able to retain some trace of a prior identity. With labor, this meant that commodified labor still possessed the spark of an originating "living labor"—that is, history—that considerations of value, as such, could never fully extinguish.

In our time, this tendency to equate the structuring force of the commodity in culture has become so overwhelmingly hegemonic or accepted common sense that it has managed to mask its own culturally and politically specific origins and run the risk of making its claims complicit with capitalism's self-representation. This reflection undoubtedly derives from the presumption that the commodity relation has been finally achieved everywhere, signaling the realization of "real subsumption," the completion of the commodity relation, and capitalism's own self-image in the pursuit of progress. The apparent consequences in this changed perspective that assumes capital's completion has been the accompanying conviction that all of society has been subsumed and that capital itself has become both subject and object, deposing labor's claim to this identity. In this narrative, the importance of labor thus has been diminished to residual status, since, as Massimiliano Tomba explains, value is made to appear to proceed directly from the productive process and consumption is elastically expanded to fill every pore of society and inform all human activity. In this scenario, history virtually disappears and value appears to have triumphed over it—that is, labor once identified with producing commodities (Tomba 2013, pp. 60–91). This has been become a familiar trope that has captured cultural studies and is a familiar preoccupation in current accounts among Marxists and non-Marxists alike. In other words, I am proposing that what subsequently became a narrative of the forms of Western Marxism, based on the conviction of a realized completed capitalism disclosing what the West missed seeing, Marx had already grasped nearly a century before, and it was worked through by subsequent thinkers like Gramsci and others in the world beyond Euro-America and kept alive.

With the move to cultural critique and the progressive distancing from the economic for the cultural and the regime of consumption comes the risk of sacrificing historical capitalism, if not the historical itself, and overlooking the role played by precapitalist formations—what Marx called "historical presuppositions" in *Grundrisse*, which would show both the historicity of modes of production and how capitalism naturalized denatured relationships into a new individuality. But it also signaled a failure to take notice of the "distinct configurations, forms of the accumulation process, implying other combinations" for a commitment to one "unique configuration" (Banaji 2011,

p. 9). While Marx designated England as the "classic form" in explaining the process in *Capital*, vol. 1, he acknowledged that the model was limited to Western Europe at most, that changes occur according to particular spatial and temporal environments. By the same measure, he rejected any presumption regarding a "master key" of a "general historico-philosophical theory," which meant disavowing the generality of a replicable model and its principal categorial props like "transition." Instead of relying on the predictable schedule of a transition that would lead from feudalism to capitalism, Marx's category of primitive or original accumulation was historically more reliable and grounded and showed the production of plural temporalities that signified a sprawling "archaeological site of dialectic(s)" occupied by the coexisting "time levels" comprised of older practices and newer forms demanded by capitalism (Morfino and Thomas 2018, p. 8). Primitive accumulation was thus an indefinitely permanent transformational change of societies in which the accumulation of capital was coextensive with "political formations not yet capitalistic" (Federici 2009, p. 62). The process of swerving temporalities was driven by the logic of uneven developments brought together by combined temporally derived incommensurables with capitalist practices, which secured the social reproduction of presents that would continue to embody the multiversum of contemporaneous noncontemporaneity or, as Gramsci observed, its reverse, the "non-contemporaneity of the present" (Thomas 2018).

What Marx proposed, instead, was the "restructuring of the labor processes to generate surplus value" (Banaji 2011, p. 350), which could be reached through the analytic optic provided by identifying the operation of "formal subsumption." The operation of formal subsumption—which referred to the encounter of capitalism and received practices at hand, whereby the former subordinated and often combined with the latter in the creation of surplus value to produce the figure of uneven development yet permit a way to reinvest the historical text with the figure of contingency derived from specific historical circumstances that required recognizing the coexistence of different economic practices and relevant institutions found in certain places at different times. It also underscored the importance of the continuing persistence of practices from the past, now in combination with new capitalist procedures, not as remnants of a now discarded feudalism, as such, which would signify their uselessness, but as combinations of historical temporal forms capable of being put into the service of a new production agenda. Rather than look on surviving remnants of the past lingering in a present waiting to be either metabolized or fade away, the contemporaneity of capitalism redefined as noncontemporaneous these traces from a prior mode of production that were still capable of animating people to think and act. An account of the specific ways labor has been subordinated in a formal modality opened the way to considering the historical or epochal dimensions of the mode of production as it restructured the labor process, as well as its contingent direction. But it also widened the angle of vision to include the world beyond Western Europe and its difference in accounting for the encounter of labor and capital. Marx repeatedly explained that "formal subsumption is the general form of every capitalist process of production; at the same time it can be found as a *particular* form alongside the *specifically capitalist mode of production in its developed form*" (Marx 1977, vol. 1, p. 1019; author's own emphases). Moreover, he was proposing that formal subsumption was a form, not a stage taking its place in an inevitable transitional linear process, to be ultimately replaced by "real subsumption." Rather, the operation of formal subsumption sanctioned the production of the copresence of older practices, what was found near at hand, alongside the newer and advanced practices of capitalism. He clarified how this worked in his several draft letters to Russian progressive Vera Zasulich, when he envisioned in the existing Russian commune the promise of national economic development (looping back to his earlier valorization of premodern communes in the *Grundrisse*). Marx was convinced that the Russian commune could, by freeing itself from primitive fetters, be used to promote production on a national scale. Yet, "precisely because it is contemporaneous with capitalist production, the rural commune may appropriate achievement without undergoing its terrible vicissitudes. . . . We should not, then, be too frightened of the word archaic" (Shanin 1983, pp. 106–107). (This sense of the relationship between noncontemporaneous structures and practices and their utility for modern capitalism was also at the heart of economist Uno Kōzō's formulations later in Japan.)

In this way, the excluded societies on the periphery were no longer required to reproduce the singular narrative attributed to the "classic form" promoted by the colonial experience, even though the colonized could recognize in colonial expropriation a principal agent in the development of capitalism. It is in this respect, despite the specific context, that I would like to consider Gramsci's text, sharing a common ground with others like José Carlos Mariátegui, Wang Yanan, the early Mao Zedong, Amilcar Cabral, Uno Kōzō, and down to our present Jairus Banaji and a number of others from South Asia and South Korea. For, when Marx advised a fusion of the archaic Russian commune and capital, followed by Luxemburg's call for combining noncapitalism with capitalist accumulation, Gramsci's recommendation to join Italy's northern industry and southern semifeudal agriculture, Mariátegui's identification of Inca communalism, Spanish feudalism and modern capitalist elements as coexisting in Peru, and more, we have, I believe, instances of how these retained historical temporal forms from prior modes of production persisting in the present were positioned to perform in the new temporal environment once they encountered capitalism, how formal subsumption before the letter, so to speak, was virtually thought through and made manifest in different ways and circumstances. I should also add that all of those contemporary declarations attesting to an exceptionalist capitalism such as "Japanese-style" capitalism, "Confucian capitalism," "Indian capitalism," and so on, self-promoting and overstated expressions of national amour proper and the genius of an unchanging native culture, nevertheless reveal the faint trace of this process whereby the development of capitalist production encounters and appropriates what it finds nearest at hand. Moreover, we must not forget that in the development of capitalism in diverse regions of the world, capital itself often "re-created" and even reinvented these surviving residues.

Resituating *The Southern Question*

In this regard, Antonio Gramsci's call to combine northern industry, with its proletariat, and the archaic semifeudal rural communities of the south and islands was an early recommendation that appeared to merge different historical temporal forms as a solution to persisting unfulfilled national unity. His reading of Italian history concentrates on showing a heritage of failure in developing and creating a strong central state and how the final unification resulted in combining residual elements of the political and, I would assume, economic pasts with the desire to achieve a new, unified nation-state. Yet, at the same time, if his active involvement in the Comintern turned his attention to the wider world beyond Europe, his reading of Italy's history must have persuaded or provided him with the occasion to break discipline and bend a little in view of the recognition that the Comintern's policies often seemed arbitrary and uninformed by local conditions. In its history, the Comintern's program to impose policies on the world outside Europe frequently bypassed the specific conditions of the region. I would guess that this might have been true of Italy as well, but I have no real knowledge to support this contention. (This was certainly the case of areas like South Asia, Indonesia, China, Japan.) But what undoubtedly lay at the heart of Gramsci's analysis was the decision to seize on Marx's privileging of the present as the locus of history—as the momentous intersection of a contemporary capitalist present and its past, significantly glossed by Lenin's promotion of the "current situation" and made into a formal category by Uno Kōzō. Gramsci's conceptualization of revolution-restoration premised a distance from the French Revolution, which he saw as incomparable, and the Jacobin principle authorizing the overthrow and overcoming of the entire received sociopolitical endowment. As a result, the concept was able to provide for the forms of "conservation" and "innovation," which actually resembled Marx's rule of formal subsumption and possessed the capacity to combine the new with the useful old. The combination of incommensurables would be comparable commonality and differences whose need to be explained required appeals to specific historical times and places.

Analysis of the historical transformation announced by the Risorgimento revealed the conditions informing the failure to establish a strong central nation-state, which explained the circumstances that favored and promoted industrial development in the north and the unrealized offer of land to southern peasantry that remained only a "mirage," ultimately displaced to colonial acquisition overseas. It is interesting to note that Gramsci on several occasions situated this split between north and south within the category of the classic division between city and countryside as envisaged in *The German Ideology*, and the consequences of this separation once capitalism was introduced. In Japan, for example, during the 1920s, critics condemned the state for sacrificing the countryside, which they increasingly identified as a colony, in order to pour resources into the development of industrialized cities. Like Marx and Engels in *The German Ideology*, Gramsci was convinced that so much of the Italian present was still crowded with elements from a more distant past marking an uneven present that it was urgent to account for their persistence in any explanation of the current situation. His appeal to history was thus cast within the tensions generated by the city-countryside division, which, accordingly, the Risorgimento had apparently widened and preserved with the spreading domination of the Piedmont and northern capital (Adamson 1983, p. 188). In effect, the growing hegemonic domination of the north over the south reinforced the territorial relationships between city and countryside, making the south appear as a colony to northern colonization. It should be remembered that by Gramsci's time, the division had become "naturalized," inasmuch as a large mythography had replaced the explanations based on more objective conditions attending the division that held the south responsible for its own backwardness, attributing to it inherent laziness, barbarity, "biological inferiority," and "criminality" that weighs like "a ball and chain" on the nation. Despite performing the labor of bringing about the unification of the Italian peninsula (1861–1870), the Risorgimento fostered the very economic and political unevenness that would continue to haunt the modern nation-state and prevent it from fulfilling its initial goal. In this connection, Gramsci recognized that the split constituted a vital role in construing a new arrangement of authority that would, in time, elevate the southern question in the near future and raise again the necessity of resolving a past that had become something of an unyielding nemesis. By the time Gramsci began to address the question, its resolution was even more difficult, especially in view of embracing a strategy that sought to organize the proletarian subaltern classes for political mobilization, one that aimed at forging a bloc with southern peasants for whom they had the lowest regard.

It was the history of late eighteenth- and early nineteenth-century Italy that fixed the foundation for the subsequent historical move to unify the country, now "conscious of national unity," as a condition for expelling foreign rule and influence, as well as to introduce the reasons why Italy had failed to develop a hegemonic class capable of exercising power. In other words, the very ambiguity of the Risorgimento settlement, the "revolution-restoration," and the insufficiency of class leadership would affect the subsequent education and mobilization of the subaltern classes. What, therefore, the text of *The Southern Question* dramatizes is precisely the compelling imperative to make up for the historical deficit left by the uncompleted unification and overcome the economic and political asymmetries that had become the modern nation-state's unwanted legacy. In this way, *The Southern Question* recalls *The German Ideology*'s perceptive and relentless critique of contemporary German political and economic backwardness paralleling the juxtaposition of contemporaneity and modernity of philosophical reflection, a modernizing route followed by Japan in the 1920s and 1930s, which pointed to a shared sensitivity to the temporal discordance demanded by the lived noncontemporaneous. In addition, Gramsci's reckoning of the problem in Italy was to see it as a more complex issue that not only required attention to the economic deprivations inflicted on the south and the peasantry, but also recognized that because the south was subject to conditions of semifeudalism it was equally necessary to acknowledge how an oppressive political and cultural domination had organized life. The real reasons for southern underdevelopment stemmed in large part from the hegemony of northern industrial capital, a mode of economic development resembling colonial expropriation but also expansion of growth at the expense of sacrificing the countryside.

If the predominance of northern capital did not exactly create feudal remnants, as, say, it did in places with established industrial capital like Japan, its presence certainly reinforced their persistence within a capitalist nation-state. Gramsci observed that instead of developing the ground for subaltern participation, the Italian state had been marred by the formation of a ruling class that increasingly extended its reach after 1868—what he identified as "liberal politics" and "molecular" private enterprise that pooled their power to defeat any subsequent achievement and expectation of agrarian reform, thereby forfeiting the south to the expansive requirements of northern industrial growth. In fact, he wrote, "the dominant class inaugurated a new policy of class alliances, of political class blocs, a policy of bourgeois democracy." When confronted with a choice between aligning with the southern peasantry, promising a "free trade policy of universal suffrage," low prices for industrial products, and a decentralized administration or a "capitalist/worker bloc," without universal suffrage, with tariff barriers, and the preservation of a highly centralized state, they unsurprisingly chose the latter (Gramsci 1995b, p. 29). In response, Gramsci advised the formation of an alliance of northern proletarian and southern peasantry as the solution to unevenness and the condition for improving the productive capacities of southern agriculture. Yet, the obstacles to this strategy for realizing a new "revolutionary" formation entailed overcoming the hold of southern intellectuals and their mixed sympathies for peasant democracy on the one hand and reactionary politics of the large landowners and the state on the other. Here, he was convinced, the solution was in organizing a new political bloc he envisioned that could not only carry through a program dedicated to realizing a completed unification and exceed the class-based central authority but also work to alleviate the discrepant historical conditions that continued economic unevenness. Gramsci's call for an improbable alliance between northern industry and southern semifeudalism, between past and present, offered a credible possibility because he recognized that the present is never identical to itself and transparent as a fixed temporal perspective, but rather always an ensemble of fractured and heterogeneous combining of encounters between different times to create the figure of synchronous nonsynchronicities (Thomas 2009b, pp. 282–284).

Yet, the task may have been more daunting than imagined. Any reader of Carlo Levi's account of his year of political exile in in Basilicata, just north of Calabria, in *Christ Stopped at Eboli* in the mid-1930s, a little more than a decade after Gramsci had composed *The Southern Question*, will recognize that the south constituted not just backwardness but more importantly, an entirely different temporal register. "Christ never came this far (Eboli, where the railway terminated)," Levi's portrait begins, "nor did time, nor the individual soul, nor hope, nor the relation of cause to effect, nor reason nor history" (Levi 2008, pp. 1–3). But this was precisely the archaic south that Gramsci saw as vital to a unified Italy, which could only be realized by unifying with the modern and capitalist north, "since proletariat and peasant are the only two national forces and the bearers of the future" (Gramsci 1995b, p. 47). Here, too, was an audible echo of the kind of fusion of the archaic and modern (capital accumulation) Marx had recommended earlier to the Russian progressives and thus a shadowed appearance of the figure of formal subsumption, even though it was not named as such in the text. What differed was the intervention of time and place. Much of this Gramscian program was explicitly mirrored in the analysis and proposals of José Carlos Mariátegui, whose subalterns became the Indigenous native masses in a Peruvian state clearly divided by manufacturing and agrarian regions in a complex configuration consisting of Inca communalism, Spanish feudalism, and modern industrial capitalism. Others, elsewhere, would replicate the Gramscian program, not directly, but by working through the specific logic of capitalist development in conditions of their time and place to bring together the received with the new, the then with the now.

Passive Revolutions

Finally, it is necessary now to turn to the broader implications of the Gramscian assessment of modern Italy and the way the stalled transformation and persisting regional division provided the occasion for identifying the political form that produced an inventory of incomplete revolution—that is, the "passive revolution" that, now free from replicating the impossible model of the French Revolution, could identify most subsequent revolutionary moments. In this regard, the call to unify northern workers and southern peasants into a new, mass bloc, bringing together contemporary capital and the feudal past, and beyond that, the specific historical shape of the Risorgimento itself, prefigured his formulation of the larger explanatory category of passive revolution and its capacity to account for the occurrence of politically transformative events in diverse places and times. It was, he wrote, "precisely the brilliant solution of . . . (diverse) problems which made the Risorgimento possible, in the form in which it was achieved (and with its limitations)—as a 'revolution' without a revolution,' or as a 'passive revolution'" (Gramsci 1971, p. 59) or even a "revolution-restoration" (Gramsci 1992–2007, vol. 3, p. 257). In his explanation of Edgar Quinet's use of "revolution-restoration" and Vincenzo Cuoco's earlier idea of passive revolution, what appears to be missing from Italian history is the historical fact of popular initiative. Hence, "progress occurs as the reaction of the dominant class to the sporadic incoherent rebelliousness of the popular masses—a reaction consisting of 'restorations' that agree to some part of the popular demands and are therefore 'progressive restorations,' or 'revolutions-restorations,' or even 'passive revolutions.'" Gramsci could not have provided a better description of Japan's Meiji Restoration of 1868, in which a lower echelon of the ruling military elite overthrew a centralized feudal authority (the Tokugawa) partially in response to the countrywide disorder sparked by the "sporadic rebelliousness of the popular masses" (Gramsci 1992–2007, vol. 3, p. 252).

The importance of the form of the passive revolution refers to the retention of elements from the past that will be useful to newer components produced by capitalism. In its arrangement this is the meaning of restoration, the act of restoring and thus conserving some institution(s) or set of practices from the past that will function to mediate newer demands that will reflect more progressive and even revolutionary claims in a new emergent environment driven by capitalism. The figure of the passive revolution suggests that the past is still deeply rooted in the new present, and its continuity constitutes a necessary brake on the unconstrained claims of the new dominant capitalism. But its principal function seems to show that the new forces of capital appearing had not yet become sufficiently hegemonic. While it is tempting to call this combinatory as the sign of transition, as some have, such a conclusion misrecognizes the fundamental persistence of the character of unevenness that is repetitively and socially reproduced. The figure of combined unevenness would remain the common characteristic form of those societies that had realized a transformation to capitalism that would always be uncompleted, marked by the copresence of the past's visible traces produced by subsumptive appropriation to become, in some instances like Japan, bourgeois *after* the revolution-restoration. Gramsci saw such processes as gradualist rather than examples of the explosive convulsions classically dramatized by the French Revolution.

In this historical scenario, Gramsci bypassed the modularity of the French Revolution, which he saw as a classic paradigmatic example among bourgeois revolutions, unavailable as a workable model, to propose the candidacy of the passive revolution as the general form or "framework" of the kind of transformation Italy experienced, where neither bourgeois leadership was dominant nor the class numerically large. Just as the Risorgimento presumed leadership and sought to subsume the subaltern remainder, and capital personified by northern workers would assume leadership over peasant (feudal peasants), Gramsci was convinced that these coalitions comprised political acts utilizing what was at hand to further the interests of the hegemonic group or class by unifying the national political order. Under both circumstances, the leading class was able to formally subsume the subaltern groups by responding or giving formal expression to their aspirations. Neil Davidson, in this respect, has recently proposed that Gramsci saw the French example as an exception and as an event that functioned to explain why later revolutions assumed the particular form of ambiguity embodied in revolution-restorations

(Davidson 2012, p. 316). Davidson is the most recent in a line of interpreters who not only have seen parallel historical trajectories leading to revolutionary transformation in Italy and Japan but also have sought to expand the utility of the category of passive revolution to account for a range of revolutionary events that might be included as instances that correspond to its form. While many interpreters falter in their failure to recognize the category primarily as a form rather than a content or thematic, Davidson has avoided this trap to persuasively argue that the domination of the bourgeois in many so-called bourgeois revolutions closely corresponds to the political strategy that more often than not depended on recruiting and mobilizing what was near at hand, which would explain the passive form and ambiguous mix of different classes and political ambitions that signaled the occurrence of the "revolution." Gramsci had already entertained the possibility of extending the category to classify Japan's Meiji Restoration of 1868, which for him resembled both England and Germany. "Japan," he proposed, "comes to the English and German types of development—that is, an industrial civilization that develops within a semifeudal framework—but as far as I can tell, more like the English than the German type" (Gramsci 1992–2007, vol. 2, p. 207). India and China were not comparable cases. What Gramsci was interested in showing was not differences as much as the commonalities that qualified such national experiences as passive revolutions. Moreover, he was convinced that the concept of passive revolution would apply to "those countries that modernize the state through a series of national wars without undergoing a political revolution of a radical-Jacobin type" (Davidson 2012, p. 317; see Gramsci 1992–2007, vol. 2, p. 232), which meant the further possibility of broadening the form's compass to include other transformations in the world beyond Europe, like the Kemalist revolution in Turkey, the Iranian Islamic Revolution, the 1911 revolution in China, and others. I would like to further suggest that if we can accept Marx's definition of formal subsumption as the general form for all capitalist development, with its capacity to generate "hybrid" and other subforms that coexist with capitalist productive practices, then it is not too far afield to propose that the category of the passive revolution as an equivalent political form to a production process that privileged suborning what was near at hand—received from prior past practices—to serve capital's pursuit of surplus value and, along the way, to produce continuing economic unevenness modern nation-states are pledged to eliminate, but perhaps only in the last instance. Not a reflection of the economic structure, as such, but more like an analogue in the figure of a parallel political form representing the expansion of formal subsumption into the realm of politics, since passive revolutions embodied a similar combination of political practices and institutions, even though the involved dominant classes were invariably linked to capital accumulation, and their temporal associations belonged to received social configurations, fused with newer, contemporary political forms. In fact, Gramsci saw no differentiation between the political program of passive revolution and its economic goals.[1] In this connection, it is important to repeat what was earlier proposed, that Gramsci was committed to seeing how passive revolution worked historically to conserve useful parts of the past. Precisely because formal subsumption was form instead of a thematic and content, it contained the possibility of its future tradition within itself (Waite 1996, p. 83). Owing to the form's capacity, indeed, its compulsion for replication, its manifestation as passive revolution implied a conception of repetitious historical time (with difference) that sanctioned both singularity and comparability. Like the operation of formal subsumption in the realm of economic practices, moreover, there was clearly a hegemonic relationship informing the political configuration of political classes and participants that constituted the "passive revolution" or "revolution-restoration."

We know that revolutionary transformations under the domination of a class took on board both past political practices and personnel from prior regimes now yoked to serving a new kind of political order, environment, and purpose, the coming together of Benjamin's "then and now," in a flash, or a "tiger's leap," the new present's pasts. In this regard, the Meiji Restoration might have exceeded Gramsci's own expectation about its suitability as an instance of passive revolution, since its primary purpose, from the beginning, was to merge past and present, according to the Imperial Charter Oath of 1868, old customs and new knowledge, an archaic presence constructed out of a mythic no-time (*in illo tempore*—the moment of a realized origin and state foundation) capable of adjusting its narrative structure to provide a map for new presents. It is important to recognize that this archaic past was even more remote and different than Levi's Italian south situated in the capitalist present. Japan's passive revolution was carried out under the authority of a restored emperor claiming central authority as a divinely anointed manifest deity and the state's singular pursuit of capitalist development at the expense of either realizing social development or widening the enfranchisement of political participation. While the preceding Tokugawa regime constituted a form of centralized feudalism, the system began to heave and fall apart in the early nineteenth century with the serious withdrawal of certain regional and religious groups from the central authority, foreigners threatening colonization, and peasants accelerating the violence of their protests against market controls of rice. One of the paradoxes of this historical scene is that even though the older Tokugawa order represented a form of feudalism, it yielded to no transition leading to capitalism because it was brought down by imperial loyalists before it was possible. While the decades before the restoration witnessed what Japanese historians have invariably called economic developments attesting to the appearance of the "sprouts of capitalism" or "proto-capitalist social relations," the putative transition associated with the appearance of socioeconomic forces never happened. This task was left to Meiji Restorers, who opted for an advanced industrial capitalism offered by the model of contemporary England. In many ways, the restoration had to address and find a way to totalize the regional splintering, and the diverse temporal orders they were promoting, which meant that the momentum leading to it constituted an overdetermination that threatened to undermine both economic development and political stability. The first decade or so of the new regime (1870s, early 1880s) thus saw a good deal of popular disorder related to dissipating class struggle among the peasantry, who merely continued disturbances inaugurated in the Tokugawa system as if no political change had actually occurred, with an intensity covering a wider geographical area of activity. Peasant outbursts were joined by revolts brought about by members of the military class—the samurai—who saw in the new political arrangement the dissolution of their class privileges and stipends, announcing the prospect of social disappearance.

Where the Meiji transformation differed from the Italian experience was in its capacity to centralize the fragmented constituencies, the diverse secessions from the center and calls for restoration, even though much of Japan's modern history still echoes with the desire for a more complete social revolution. It is important to recognize that a Marxian accounting of this revolutionary makeover did not appear until late the 1920s and early 1930s with the formation of the great Marxian historiographical debate of the 1930s over the historical development of Japanese capitalism. Marxian historical practice and its consideration of the problems and aporetic status of capitalism actually highlighted the importance of modernity itself. This identification of modernity and capitalism was manifest in late-developing societies like Japan and China, where there appeared two major debates in the 1930s over how the historical was to be grasped,[2] and India, with its own experience with the Comintern and the efforts of local Marxian historians to unveil the economic consequences of British imperial policies on the stunting of native industries. The beginning of the Japanese debate (*ronsō*) was initiated at about the same moment Gramsci was formulating his views of the nature of passive revolution. Even though his random thoughts would have been useful to the debates' discussions, his views would not have been available to the Japanese until after World War II, at which time the different lines of controversy were virtually fixed in stone. The debate concentrated on understanding the structure of Japan's capitalism and how it had developed since the late Tokugawa period. Even though the debate stimulated the opening up of the study of Japan's modern history and its rapid progress, ultimately, differences of interpretation proliferated among the many participating historians that led to a violent fracturing into two principal groups. How the debate came down over the issue of determining the effects of the feudal elements persisting in contemporary Japan produced two opposing camps: those who considered the feudal remains in the present as only an inheritance and those who saw the feudal residues as the basis of Japanese capital's basic existence (Tōyama 2018, pp. 25–26). Whether the Meiji Restoration qualified as a genuine bourgeois revolution from the top down, as the agrarian-labor historians (rōnōha) believed, or resulted in an aborted one still engineered from the top, whereby the retention of feudal remnants blocked the way that would permanently stall the realization of a full and completed capitalism capable of leading only to refeudualization and political absolutism (zettaishugi), as envisaged by the Lecture Faction (kōzaha),[3] the two positions could still agree on the conjunctural forces confronting Japan and the capitalist world of the 1930s and the fact that the Restoration brought with its train immense unevenness and the possibility of new combinations capable of serving capitalism, denoted by the persistence of unwanted residues from the past, even as, Marx wrote in Grundrisse, "stunted" and "travestied" forms and as yet an incomplete revolution. The difference apparently was prompted by internal Communist Party disagreements among various camps over how best to envision a strategy capable of realizing a contemporary revolution (Tōyama 2018, p. 26).[4] What especially the kōzaha failed to recognize was a trajectory that condemned all revolutionary transformations, even the most classical examples, to incompletion and unfinished projects, but never necessarily destined to live in a permafrost social state of semifeudalism or semirevolution, as the Lecture Faction's principal theorist Yamada Moritarō reasoned.[5] The very feudal remnants Yamada considered as deforming the development of capitalism in Japan into a stunted figure he called "Japanese style" apparently had departed from some unexplained pure form the absolutist state had pursued with a "Japanese-style rationality." The problem with this analysis is the misrecognition of presuming the existence of a pure form.

The division between the two Japanese Marxian factions was more of a narcissism of small differences than a major, irreparable break. A closer look at the respective claims suggests that their shared commonalities outweighed differences. They could agree with the observation that the Meiji Restoration was a revolutionary transformation directed from the top and that Karl Kautsky's version of absolutism characterizing the Meiji new state was posited on the prior anticipation of some form of modern manufacturing capital as a necessary condition that, according to some historians, came after the opening of the ports in 1853 (Tōyama 2018, p. 51). Gramsci would not have known of this Japanese division marking the debate on Japanese capitalism which, ironically, was contemporary with his imprisonment in Italy. But he would have recognized in the Meiji settlement the persistence of uneven residues from a feudal past, the difficulty of removing them, and thus the necessity of accommodating these survivals in the construction of a political and economic edifice that would combine with newer forms of capitalist innovation to signify a kinship with other political transformations he had already recorded and classified as examples of passive revolution. Such new combinations of the old from prior modes of production and the new would be put into the service of capitalism's pursuit of surplus value. In Japan, the obvious example was the refiguration of the figure of a divine emperor now contemporary with modern capitalism positioned to compel the population to work and die for the emperor (as implied in the Meiji slogan *fukoku kyōhei*, "to enrich the nation, strengthen the military").

In fact, Gramsci was persuaded that that all "bourgeois revolutions involve a 'passive' element," which meant leadership and direction from the top, with little role accorded to the popular classes.[6] The transition was thus led to completion by the upper echelons by the "exercise of state power" positioned to accommodate capital rather than mass insurgency (Davidson 2012, p. 318). This was precisely the course taken by the Meiji reforms after the 1870s, principally recruited from lower class samurai (*kakyū shizoku*) from southwestern domains like Satsuma and Chōshū. Gramsci further observed that passive revolution came in the wake of the French Revolution and the search for a new form, involving a struggle for "superior forms," as he put it, to contain capitalism since a content had been already established. But the new form, as suggested, would not, like the French Revolution, immediately resort to "dramatic upheavals" by eliminating all feudal fetters, but rather utilize unevenness in new combinations (Davidson 2012, p. 318; Gramsci 1992–2007, vol. 3, pp. 381). The form Gramsci projected in the *The Southern Question* that sought to bring northern capitalist labor together with southern semifeudal agriculture resembled formal subsumption now serving the goal of political reorganization rather than merely economic practices. What passive revolution thus entailed was a gradualist program of reforms within a sufficiently elastic framework, enabling both to avoid the excesses of the apparatus of terror associated with the French experience (Davidson 2012, p. 319).

Accordingly, Gramsci appealed to Italian history as the lens through which to read other historical experiences that might conform to the category of passive revolution. In one observation, he proposed that success in organizing a state in Italy stemmed from its "victory over the feudal and semifeudal classes" and the good fortune of international circumstances, and was quoted by Davidson as suggesting that "the bourgeois State thus developed more slowly, and followed a process which had not been seen in many other countries" (Davidson 2012, p. 319; Gramsci 1992–2007, vol. 1, p. 231). But certainly it could be observed in Japan, where the bourgeoisie as a class began to develop only decades after the initial restoration, when a constitutional order was implemented. But this bourgeois state, according to Engels, is empowered to implement vast changes by "new classes or dominant fractions . . . with the old oligarchy." Because these changes in societies like Meiji Japan occur in the absence of "popular mobilization," "they remain partial, unfinished and incomplete."[7] Even though the Meiji state early announced its decision to "wash away old abuses" and customs, it actually was slow in doing so. In this regard, both *rōnōha* and *kōzaha* shared a common ground of agreement over the semirevolutionary state that appeared in the late nineteenth century. It was not as catastrophically extreme as Yamada Moritarō argued but rather closer to *rōnōha* economist Uno Kōzō's observation that the Meiji regime preserved or maintained the medieval village structure until there was sufficient industrial development to begin absorbing workers from the countryside in the early twentieth century, rather than releasing them (as in England three hundred years earlier) with no place to go and no adequate means to support themselves. As Michael Löwy wrote: "These 'semi-revolutions' or 'passive revolutions' (as Gramsci termed them)—together with certain limited 'bourgeois reforms . . . laid the basis for the European revolutions of the 20th century. Precisely because these reforms from above were incomplete—leaving considerably feudal detritus and or vestiges of the absolute state the bourgeois would or could not destroy— they created the explosive contradictions that would allow the proletariat to raise the banner of democracy in its own name" (Löwy 1981, p. 29).

While Japanese would have to wait until World War II and the American military occupation to see the momentary realization of their democratic aspiration, the Meiji transformation and transition to a capitalist order was accomplished by a small class who brought off the restoration-revolution, or passive revolution, not the peasant masses who were forced to pay for it, which embodied both retrograde elements of the past now serving a different economic system and capitalist modernization with its procession of never-ending new practices to create a society still navigating the temporalities of contemporary noncontemporaneity. In the end, it seems that one of the real consequences of passive revolution, whether in Italy or Japan or elsewhere, is that it actually defers indefinitely the difficult historical task of resolving the past and the demand to find ways to overcome the force of its barrier to the future. Clearly, what emerged from Gramsci's formulation of the passive revolution was the privilege accorded to the untimeliness of contemporary non-contemporaneity (expanded more fully by Mariátegui in Peru), the forging and fusing of different temporalities into a mixed and heterogeneous combinatory of past and present to produce its uneven countenance. This historical representation was, I believe, made explicit in *The Southern Question* as its ambiguous silhouette first appeared in the juxtaposition of northern industrial Italy to the semifeudalism of the south and the necessity of their unification.

NOTES

1 "Passive revolutions would be brought about through the fact of transforming the economic structure in a 'reformist' fashion from an individualistic to a planned economy" (Gramsci 1995b, p. 277).

2 For classic studies of the Chinese historical debate, see Dirlik 1979 and Walker 2016.

3 It is conceivable that Japanese theoreticians were following Marx's advice written in the wake of the Revolutions of 1848 ("The Bourgeoisie and the Counter-Revolution"), that "a purely *bourgeois revolution* . . . is impossible in Germany. What is possible is either feudal and absolutist counter-revolution of the *social-republican revolution*" (quoted in Löwy 1981, p. 13; Löwy's emphases). This is precisely the figure of counterrevolution the Lecture Faction attributed to the aborted Meiji Restoration. What is important in Marx's observation was that it made possible the conceptualization of broader alternative models like Gramsci's category of passive revolution.

4 But Tōyama, who represented the Lecture Faction after the war, was convinced that despite the differences produced by the historiographical debate on capital, its significance lay in starting out from the engagement of a practical theme and contemporary concerns of their immediate present.

5 See Walker 2016, 47–56; see also Harootunian 2015, pp. 174–184. It is hard not to conclude, perhaps somewhat cynically, that the divisions spawned by the debate served as a displacement for political action itself. If that is the case, the continuation of the "debate" into the postwar period was ultimately exceeded by the proliferation of numerous Left factional groups who seem to have been preoccupied with destroying their competitors.

6 See Löwy 1981, pp. 3–29, for an account of Marx and Engels's ambiguity toward the category of "bourgeois revolution," which they never really used.

7 Quoted from Friedrich Engels, "Klassenkampfen in Frankreich" (1895), in Löwy 1981, p. 28.

8

Why No Gramsci in the United States?

MICHAEL DENNING

It is now sixty-one years since the appearance of the first English translations of Gramsci's work: Louis Marks's translation, *The Modern Prince* (Gramsci 1957a), and Carl Marzani's translation, *The Open Marxism of Antonio Gramsci* (Gramsci 1957b) both appeared in 1957. Three decades later, in 1987, I wrote that everyone was now a Gramscian. It was an exaggeration, but one shared with others at the time; in 1984 Geoff Eley wrote that the "Gramsci reception in the English-speaking world" was "one of the more remarkable intellectual phenomena of the 1970s" (Eley 1984, p. 441).

So when I was asked to address the uses of Gramsci in the world, I thought I would return to that popular Gramscianism that seemed have been a fundamental part of the New Left and its turn to culture. However, after some reflection, I want to suggest that I and others made what Gramsci called a "common error in historico-political analysis," misreading "the correct relation between what is organic and what is conjunctural . . . in all types of situations." "One's own baser and more immediate desires and passions are the cause of the error," Gramsci noted, and it leads to "self-deception" (Q13§17, pp. 1580–1581; Gramsci 1971, pp. 178–179). Today, the question seems less why everyone was a Gramscian than why Gramsci's work had so little impact and influence in the United States and on the U.S. Left.

Why was the U.S. Left such inhospitable terrain for his work? Why was there nonetheless the appearance of a Gramsci renaissance, and why does it vanish on closer examination? Is a Gramscian turn still necessary for the U.S. Left?

The first point is that attention to the wide English-language reception of Gramsci obscures significant national unevenness. There is no question that Gramsci's work had a lasting impact on more than one generation of British radical thinkers, from Communist Party–linked historians like Eric Hobsbawm, E. P. Thompson, and Christopher Hill to the "cultural studies" figures like Raymond Williams, Stuart Hall, and Hazel V. Carby; even those who eventually took their distance from Gramsci—one thinks of Perry Anderson— did it through detailed engagement with his texts. Similarly, it was the English-language Gramsci that was so important to the subaltern studies group of South Asia. But it is much less clear that Gramsci's work had much of an impact on the U.S. Left. As an experiment, I asked our long-standing Marxism reading group at Yale—graduate students and faculty from a number of disciplines—to brainstorm a list of the most influential U.S. Left thinkers of the last decade or so. A dozen or more names quickly emerged as uncontroversial; for better or worse, these were U.S. Left intellectuals that one finds in Left journals, on publishing lists, and at Left forums. I won't go through the specific names; our conversation turned to the question of who had been left out and what that said about our own interests as well as forms of Left celebrity. Nonetheless, when I then asked which of them had been significantly influenced by the work of Gramsci, the answer was virtually none. Marcuse, Fanon, Foucault, C. L. R. James, the anarchist tradition: there are plenty of powerful influences and engagements, but not Gramsci. When I turned the question around, people were able to name a few figures who were not Gramsci scholars but had been deeply influenced by Gramsci's work, but it did not change the overall pattern.

So I looked back at the remarkably catholic *Encyclopedia of the American Left*, edited by the Buhles and Dan Georgakas in 1990; it had only a couple of passing references to Gramsci. For the U.S. Left, the prison notebooks of Gramsci have long been overshadowed by the prison letters of his Italian emigrant contemporaries, Nicola Sacco and Bartolomeo Vanzetti, executed in the United States the year after Gramsci was incarcerated in Italy (there does not seem to be a study that thinks Gramsci together with Sacco and Vanzetti). I did a quick search of major Left journals: *Science and Society* did publish an essay on Croce constructed from Gramsci's prison letters as early as 1946, but *Monthly Review* never engaged Gramsci. Of the journals of the U.S. New Left, *Studies on the Left* had only one, albeit well-known article on Gramsci (a review of John Cammett's pioneering book by Eugene Genovese); *Radical America* published only one essay on Gramsci, by Carl Boggs (later there was an essay on Gramsci and Steve Biko); and *Socialist Revolution*, which became *Socialist Review*, also had only one essay, again by Carl Boggs.

Perhaps there is a good reason why the two concepts that have been adopted into the vernacular of U.S. Leftism and that signify Gramsci—hegemony and organic intellectuals—are used in ways that suggest more the temper of American populist radicalism than any understanding of Gramsci's work.

Why this missed connection? And why did it seem so different three decades ago? Let me suggest three reasons. First, in many places, and particularly in Britain, the reception of Gramsci was part of a communist reformation; the 1957 English translations (the better known one by a member of British Communist Party Historians' Group [Marks], the lesser known by U.S. communist writer and publisher [Marzani]) marked an attempt to set out a post-Stalinist trajectory in the wake of the crisis of 1956. Both editions began by emphasizing Gramsci's reimagining of Marxism as a conception of the world. In addition, the Marks collection emphasized Gramsci's rethinking of the party, titling his selection "The Modern Prince." Gramsci's "open Marxism" and the relative success of the PCI in Italian politics and culture was a powerful beacon for a disoriented communist movement, and remained so through the moment of Eurocommunism in the 1970s.

However, Italian communism—and Gramsci—was less important to the U.S. communist movement, even though the first references to Gramsci in the United States were in the Communist Party's Italian-language journal *L'Unità Operaia* in the mid-1930s, and there was a Gramsci club in the party in the early 1940s. However, insofar as U.S. communism revived in the 1960s and 1970s, it did so through the reworking of its historic link with the black liberation movement: one thinks not only of Angela Davis's prominent role in the Communist Party but of the various dissident black Communists—Harry Haywood, Nelson Peery, Amiri Baraka. The heated debate over African Americans and the U.S. Communist Party generated major historical studies of the party in Harlem and Bronzeville, powerful controversies over cultural figures like Paul Robeson, Richard Wright, and W. E. B. Du Bois, as well as black radical political formations like the Black Panthers and the League of Revolutionary Black Workers. None of this political-intellectual work invoked Gramsci (again, there does not seem to be a study that thinks Gramsci together with Du Bois).

Second, in other places the Gramsci revival spoke to the students and teachers of the 1968 student uprisings: this explains the peculiar starting point of the Hoare and Nowell-Smith *Selections*: "The Intellectuals" and "On Education" (Gramsci 1971, pp. 1–43). But here again, the U.S. student Left was influenced more by figures who opened up the world of mass culture, not only Marcuse writing in the midst of the struggles but also the forgotten and now recovered works like Adorno and Horkheimer's *Dialectic of Enlightenment* and Benjamin's "Work of Art" essay, and by figures who opened up the logics of race and imperialism, like Fanon. In the face of this, Carl Boggs's efforts to bring Gramsci to the U.S. New Left through his articles in *Radical America* and *Socialist Revolution* (leading to the widely circulated little book *Gramsci's Marxism*, 1976), and his work in the New American Movement are testimony to how rarely the U.S. New Left engaged Gramsci's work (even Anne Showstack Sassoon admits that there was no significant feminist engagement with Gramsci). I am not sure why Boggs's insistence on the Gramsci of the factory councils did not resonate, but it may be that the electrifying workplace occupations in Britain and France—Clydeside and Lip in the early 1970s—that led to films by Ken Loach and Jean-Luc Godard, among others, did not have a U.S. equivalent, even though there was a major upsurge in wildcat strikes and young worker militancy.

There are, of course, two exceptions to this picture; together, they deceived me and others in 1987: one might call them Eugene Genovese's Gramsci and Stuart Hall's Gramsci. Genovese's fine 1967 essay, "On Antonio Gramsci, in *Studies on the Left* and his direct invocation of Gramsci in his classic study of "the world the slaves made" (Genovese 1974) linked Gramsci's thought to the emerging social history, history from below, in a way that even E. P. Thompson had not (there is no reference to Gramsci in *The Making of English Working Class*). So it is true that by the mid-1980s, Gramsci and the concept of "hegemony," often recast as "cultural hegemony," was being invoked and debated in the *American Historical Review* (Haskell 1987; Davis 1987; Ashworth 1987; Lears 1985) and the *Journal of American History* (Lipsitz 1988; Fink 1988; Lears 1988), albeit largely as a new and improved version of postwar "consensus" historiography. But it was often Genovese's formulations on Gramsci that were invoked; few if any of these historians engaged the formulations in Gramsci himself.

The other exception was Stuart Hall's Gramsci. Again, in a series of powerful and lucid essays from 1978 to 1987 (Hall 1986, 1987; Lumley, McLennan, and Hall 1977), culminating in his *The Hard Road to Renewal* (1988), Hall not only crafted Gramsci's notes into a powerful and plausible synthesis but also used it to analyze the contemporary Bonaparte: Margaret Thatcher and the authoritarian populism of Britain's New Right. Hall's mobilization of Gramsci's concepts to understand both the relations of force in a particular conjuncture and the competing social and cultural projects to form a new conception of the world, a new common sense, still seems to me the high point of a Gramscian political project; and the concurrent rise of Ronald Reagan and the U.S. New Right meant that the U.S. Left resonated with Hall's analysis.

If Genovese's impact on social history and Hall's on cultural studies gave the impression of a vital U.S. Gramscianism in the late 1980s, it was a moment that evaporated quickly. Ironically, just as a new era in English-language Gramsci scholarship opened with the publication of the first volume of the translated critical edition in 1992, the conjuncture in which the New Lefts emerged—the age of three worlds—came to an end. The cluster of concerns that had so moved the New Lefts to which Gramsci's notes spoke—the role of culture and ideology, the state apparatuses of education and mass communication, the peculiarities of the national-popular—seemed to vanish into thin air, as globalization, the movements of capital and the fundamentalisms of the market, the intricacies of debt, finance, and the international division of labor took center stage. The very specificity of Hall's conjunctural analysis came to seem a limitation.

Reagan and Thatcher looked less like Bonapartist authoritarian populist solutions to police the crisis than like the vanguard of a new epoch, not a new deal but a new world order, a neoliberalism. A political and economic doctrine adopted by a historical bloc of conservatives and capitalists had created a hegemonic apparatus, conforming the superstructure to the structure, and becoming a new common sense. It never won consent of the subalterns—the age of Reagan was, after all, also the age of hip-hop—and it triggered a new cycle of struggles, struggles against neoliberalism, against "globalization." A new cluster of radical thinkers emerged, but this global justice Left has not been a Gramscian one. With the collapse of the cultures of European communism—including the Italian Communist Party and the *Marxism Today* tendency in Britain—Gramsci's role as a sign of innovation and reform within Marxism was no longer vital. Paradoxically, as Gramsci suffered from the evaporation of Marxism, Marx's own work—particularly *Capital*—re-emerged less for its place in a long Marxist tradition than for its understanding of a globe-straddling circuit of capital.

Does that matter? Do we need a Gramscian Left? On the one hand, I think not. A vital Left needs new vocabularies, and new revivals. I teach the *Prison Notebooks* every year but find the latest crop of students less excited than any earlier cohorts. Gramsci—by which I mean those of us who keep his ideas alive, in print, and circulating—is now the old mole, burrowing underground, ready to emerge in another moment, perhaps as new readings produce new ways of seeing him, not unlike what David Harvey's dense and originally little-noticed *The Limits to Capital* (1982, reprinted in 2007) did for the Marx of *Capital*.

But in another sense, the U.S. Left does need a new version of the "art and science of politics" that Gramsci pioneered, particularly the "two basic points" that, Gramsci wrote, "should structure the entire work" (Q13§1, p. 1561; Gramsci 1971, p.133): the question of the formation of a national-popular collective will; and the "question of intellectual and moral reform."

The first project is the analysis of situations, of relations of force, pitched at the level of the conjuncture rather than the epoch, the dialectic of crisis and settlement (both political and economic, but not necessarily in sync), the relations of parties and social movements, the relation between the organization of work and the self-organization of workers, without fetishizing any particular form of organization, whether party, union, or council. "It may be said that to write the history of a party means nothing less than to write the general history of the country from a monographic viewpoint" (Q13§33, p. 1630; Gramsci 1971, p. 151). In the United States we don't even really have a Marxist analysis of the Democratic Party, which I think would have to be on the lines of Gramsci's work. We need a "Notes on American History."

The second project is the understanding and transformation of popular conceptions of the world, the question of how conceptions of the world are adopted and are changed: "It would be interesting," Gramsci writes, "to study concretely the forms of cultural organization which keep the ideological world in movement within a given country, and to examine how they function in practice" (Q11§12, p. 1394; Gramsci 1971, p. 343). Do we really understand the forms of faith and common sense in the United States: the weird mixture of philosophy and common sense that makes "pragmatism" a genuine conception of the world; the extraordinary varieties of charismatic American gospels; the populist radicalisms of Left and Right that would occupy Wall Street and reclaim the Tea Party; the vernacular transcendentalisms to which Emerson stands as the American Croce; the cults of the Constitution and the Founding Fathers, with fundamentalists of the first and second amendments; the commitment to the freedom "on the road" and the fantasy of being self-movers— auto-mobile? And can a Left engage and transform these conceptions of the world without reaching for the easy answer: Who profits? Your dissent is commodified, Occupy is just a media event, there is something wrong with Kansas, the Tea Party is an illusion created by master manipulators like the Karl Roves and the Koch brothers? "This sort of infallibility," Gramsci writes in his brilliant account of how one should analyze a populist movement in Q13, "comes very cheap. It not only has no theoretical significance,—it has only minimal political implications or practical efficiency. . . . It thus appears as a moralistic accusation of duplicity and bad faith, or (in the case of the movement's followers), of naivety and stupidity. Thus the political struggle is reduced to a series of personal affairs between on the one hand those with the genie in the lamp who know everything and on the other those who are fooled by their own leaders but are so incurably thick that they refuse to believe it" (Q13§18, pp. 1596-1597; Gramsci 1971, pp. 166-167).

Gramsci as method: what is vital is less his vocabulary—integral state and historical bloc, hegemony and common sense—than his starting points—"a study might be made . . . it must first be shown, it is necessary to study"—his, to use a favorite phrase, "methodological criteria" (Q14§5, p. 1659; Gramsci 1995a, pp. 284-285).

9

Gramsci on
la questione dei negri

Gli intellettuali and the Poesis of Americanization

R. A. JUDY

**Preliminary Consideration:
The Black Radical Tradition**

The late Cedric Robinson described the black radical tradition in 1983 as a "specifically African response to an oppression emergent from the immediate determinants of European development in the modern era and framed by orders of human exploitation woven into the interstices of European social life from the inception of Western civilization" (Robinson 1983, p. 73). This was not an essentialist description but rather was one rooted in the historical encounter between Europe and Africa that began with Portuguese incursions into Angola. The violent generative process of that encounter created different historical processes of conquest, racialization, alienation, and human exploitation, but also what Aimé Césaire called the process of "thingification" (Césaire 2000, p. 42). That process produced a new set of questions about the nature of the human species and constituted a distinctive intellectual, political, and aesthetic tradition of thought and practices, which we might well call the black radical intellectual tradition. One of the earliest discursive formulations in this tradition was the writings of Ottobah Cugoano, whose 1787 *Thoughts and Sentiments on the Evil and Wicked Traffick of the Slavery and Commerce of the Human Species* is arguably the first slave narrative to explicitly call for absolute abolition of slavery worldwide, indicting it as a perverted economic and political order at the very foundation of European modernity. The basis of Cugoano's indictment is the inviolable rights of all humans, which the existing political economy of modernity continues to fundamentally violate. His including in evidence of that violation the parable of Pizarro's massacre of the Inca underscores the indissoluble connection between slavery and colonialism in his critique, which is indicative of the distinctive contours of the tradition. Another instance of this is president Jean-Jacques Dessalines's declaring the establishment of the Republic of "Hayti" in January 1804, naming the new country by the assumed Taino term for the island of Hispaniola—the very first place to see the arrival of Iberian colonists and the emergence of Europeans, as such, on the world stage. Those contours outline a form of radicalism distinct from that associated with the British movement that emerged in the aftermath of the American Revolution—the Radical Whig movement, generally traced from the democratic egalitarian principles of the English Civil War Levellers—as well as Jacobinism, and Utilitarian radical philosophy, in which racialization was subordinated to the dynamics of class. Given the broad scope of Cugoano's critique, which focuses in tandem on two distinct non-European historical experiences of modernity as oppression without losing perspective on their particularities, the phrase "black radicalism" suggests a tradition of resistance to capitalist modernity that develops a dialectic of liberation out of the material historical conditions of racialized oppression. It is a tradition of resistance, rehumanization, and revolution as well as one that reframes radical questions in ways that challenge the more predominant forms of Marxism because the subject of revolutionary change is neither bourgeoisie or proletariat but rather the dehumanized subject—the figure created by the historical force of "thingification"—that, rejecting the anthropology of modernity, presents an alternative understanding and practice of sociality and individuation. Bringing the imperatives of the black radical tradition into generative communication and collaboration with Marxism has been a vexing problematic in the context of the long international struggle for revolutionary transformation. Taking it up again today is all the more necessary in light of the challenges faced by the diverse movements for revolutionary social transformation, from Movimento Negro to the so-called Arab Spring and Black Lives Matter. At issue are the fundamental conceptions of the human, of the material processes of *hominization* in an indisputably capitalist global order. In that vein, it is crucial to map an itinerary of the resonances as well as the direct associations of various radicalisms of the twentieth-century striving for what Fanon called a new humanism. An important incident in that itinerary is the Third International's official policy on the Negro question, "Theses on the Negro Question," the relevance of which is not the Soviet attempt to define the terms of what would come to be Third Worldism, but rather that its attempt is illustrative of the still pressing need to shift the conceptual basis for understanding the relation between race and class in order to achieve something like a viable radicalism of the human.

The text of the "Theses on the Negro Question," first drafted at the Fourth Congress in 1922, bears a complex genealogy. Its direct relationship to the earlier 1920 Lenin-Roy "Theses on the National and Colonial Questions" is explicitly testified to in the charge given near the end of the document: "Therefore the Fourth Congress gives Communists the special responsibility of closely applying the 'Theses on the Colonial Question' to the situation of the Negro" (Comintern 2005, p. 11). But the overall language of the "Theses on the Negro Question," particularly the historiography underlying its depiction of the centrality of the Negro to American political economy and social formation, is an iteration of the remarks made by Claude McKay to the congress in his "Report on the Negro Question." Although not an official representative to the congress, McKay's prominence as a principal figure of the Harlem-based New Negro movement, and his Marxist, indeed Bolshevik, bona fides as a long-standing contributor to Cyril Briggs's *Crusader*, positioned him as the purveyor of radical New Negro political theory, influencing the Comintern's understanding of the constitutive role raciology plays in global capitalist formation. This is evidenced in the Soviet state publishing house's decision to have McKay elaborate his report into a monograph, published in 1923 as *негры в Америке* (*Negry v Amerike*) and in 1979 as *The Negroes in America*. McKay's influence in the drafting of the Comintern policy is further attested in the introduction to *The Negroes*, which reproduces a letter to him from Trotsky that appeared in *Pravda Izvestia* on March 13, 1923, concurring with the assessment that supporting the revolutionary consciousness of the Negro was an essential element in ending worldwide capitalist domination.[1] A personal letter McKay received in May of that year from Zinoviev shows that the Comintern's embrace of New Negro radicalism through McKay extended beyond the left-wing faction to include the triumvirate. After Trotsky's expulsion, Stalin would subsequently fix the Comintern policy, according to his acutely reductive notion of nation, in the 1928 Sixth Congress "Black Belt Nation Thesis," which was coauthored by another Briggs-associated New Negro, Harry Haywood. The influence of Harlem New Negro Bolsheviks on the Third International's formulation of its Negro question policy notwithstanding, the relationship between them was one of political opportunism rather than doctrinaire.

Even on a cursory reading, McKay's *The Negroes in America* departs significantly from the 1922 "Theses on the Negro Question." McKay does not go as far as the then Trotskyite C. L. R. James's assertion in his 1948 "Revolutionary Answer to the Negro Problem in the U.S.A." that independent Negro struggle is the sine qua non for a truly revolutionary proletariat in America. But he does insist on the productive force of autonomous Negro labor organization in the specific American context, in which the dynamics of racism articulate a material situation not readily reducible to simple class struggle. The challenge McKay puts to the Comintern, or rather the challenge he posits for America, is to understand racism, and the attendant modalities of social being and consciousness it engenders, as a constitutive element in capitalism's development and deployment in the world, but one that is not sufficiently analyzable according to the paradigm of European class formation. The Negro offers a special case of emergent historical consciousness consequent to capitalism's development in a way resonant with the emergence of the proletariat, but whose particular formation and agency cannot be subsumed under the latter's historical experience. What was called for, and what McKay had hoped to achieve through the "Theses on the Negro Question," was a theorization of race that better folded it into the historiography and ultimately the epistemology of Marxist revolutionary change. The Comintern never fulfills that ambition. Nor, arguably, does it ever quite share them. Rather, the Comintern's focus was on arriving at the most effective propaganda instrument for attracting and organizing Negroes into its ranks, in full accord with its pronouncedly centralist historiography and praxis. This is abundantly clear in the language of Trotsky's February 1923 letter to McKay, with its insistence that "the training of black propagandists is the most imperative and extremely important revolutionary task of the present time" (McKay 1979, p. 8). It is even more forcefully driven home in Zinoviev's personal letter to McKay, where he admonishes him to bear in mind that it is through his agency that the Comintern expects "the Negro-workers to organize their own circles, to enter in the Trade Unions, and in every way to strive immediately to create their own mass organization and to link up with other divisions of the fighting proletariat" (quoted in Maxwell 1999, p. 90). Even the document of the 1922 "Theses on the Negro Question" suggests as much, with its invocation of the Lenin-Roy "Theses on the National and Colonial Questions." In retrospect, given what we now know about the failure of the Comintern to bring the CPUSA in line on the Negro question, it seems that the great insight into the complexities of the American situation evident in the 1922 "Theses on the Negro Question" was a residual effect of McKay's thinking and never well enough digested by the Comintern Presidium. In the end, America was as unfathomable to the Third International as it was to the fascists and the various national bourgeoisie intelligentsias of Europe. As a result, the Comintern never seriously bought into the thesis that the capitalist raciology developed and implemented in the United States during the last quarter of the nineteenth century modeled the organizing principle of capitalist imperialism. And so, it never took seriously the proposition that understanding the history of that formation would provide greater insight into the prospects for a truly global revolutionary change. Such analysis would have to come from the margins of Marxist thought—that is to say, marginal thinking equally as firmly grounded in understanding the material circumstances and histories of particular historical formations from a Marxist perspective as were the Harlem New Negro Bolsheviks, and so just as equally problematical for the Third International.

Gramsci's *la questione dei negri*

Antonio Gramsci's active engagement in the proceedings of the Fourth Congress of the Third International as one of the delegates from the Italian Communist Party suggests that he was aware of the McKay report—how could he not have been, given the spectacle the Presidium made of McKay's presence? Although he does not make explicit reference to the McKay report in his correspondence, he does offer some rather significant assessments of the Negro question scattered throughout his letters and *Prison Notebooks*, which not only seem to take up the McKay line but anticipatorily resonate with the more careful elaborations of C. L. R. James. Gramsci's most significant remark on the Negro question occurs in the course of a well-known extended reflection in Q4 on the historical question of the intellectual along the lines of national situations, whose rubric is "Notes on Philosophy. Materialism and Idealism. First series." More precisely, the remark occurs in Q4§49, under the heading "Gli intellettuali" (The intellectuals). In its entirety, the Q4 reflection elaborates Gramsci's critique of the relationship between nation formation and historical change, a relationship in which the question of the exact nature of human agency in change is of paramount importance for understanding the relationship between particular and general intelligence. In giving an account of the formation of national intellectuals, Gramsci traces a history of the material manifestation of intelligence, embodied in human institutions, in the course of which he delineates the famous distinction between traditional and organic intellectuals as a function of the transition from feudal estates to nation-states in Europe. When he gets to the United States, however, he discerns a complete absence of traditional intellectuals, suggesting a development of intelligence altogether distinct from that in Europe. This is the gist of the first paragraph on America in Q4§49, standing in stark contrast to the elaborate country-by-country analysis of class formation that precedes it. The second paragraph on America, the one about the Negro, contradicts the first; it is more like the rest of the note, offering the suggestion at least of a historical analysis of a class formation:

> There is another interesting symptom in America that still has to be examined: the formation of a surprising number of Negro intellectuals who absorb American culture and technical knowledge. One might look into the indirect influence that these [American] Negro intellectuals could exercise on the backward masses in Africa, and even the direct influence they could exercise if either of the following hypotheses were verified: (1) if American expansionism used American Negroes as agents to take hold of the African market (something of this sort has already happened, but I do not know to what extent); (2) if racial conflicts in America became exacerbated to such a degree as to cause the exodus and return to Africa of those Negro intellectual elements who are the most spiritually independent and active and therefore the ones least likely to submit to some possible legislation even more humiliating than the current widespread customs. This rises the questions: (1) of language—since the language of American Negroes is English, whereas in Africa there are myriad dialects; (2) of whether national sentiment can replace racial sentiment, raising the African continent to the function of common fatherland of all negroes (it would be the first case of an entire continent being regarded as a single nation). American Negroes, it seems to me, are bound to have more of a negative than a positive national and racial spirit; a spirit, in other words, born out of the struggle waged by the whites in order to isolate and dishearten them. But was not this the case with the Jews until the end of the eighteenth century? *Liberia*, already Americanized and with English as its official language, could become the Zion of American Negroes, aiming to become all of Africa, to be the Piedmont of Africa. (Q4§49; trans. Gramsci 1992–2007, vol. 2, pp. 206–207; Gramsci's emphasis)

There are a number of reasons this is an extraordinary passage. Although Gramsci has numerous notes on America scattered throughout different notebooks, most of which he later incorporated into Q22, composed in 1934 under the rubric "Americanism and Fordism," there are only two paragraphs dealing with the United States in the "Intellectuals" note of Q4, and this passage is the longer and more critically careful of the two. It is repeated with very slight modifications along with the rest of note 49 in note 1 of Q12, which was written in 1932. This is significant because Q12 was the first to be organized by Gramsci in a thematically coherent way; and it is clear by how it carries forward straightaway the themes of Q4, without any organizational changes, that its exposition of the intellectuals question was a fully thought through and careful presentation.[2]

Two obvious points are to be made here, I think. The first is that Gramsci is thinking about the nature of intelligence and human agency in change in terms of the history of thought as a function of the history of class formation. But he approaches America as a complex of historical events that are unexplainable according to the history of thought that explains Europe. The second point is that when Gramsci does attempt to approach America in terms of the history of thought as an aspect of a historical analysis of a class formation, he does so through the Negro. We must be careful regarding this second point to keep an eye on the fact that Gramsci is not discussing slavery, which is to say, he is not equating the type of individuation and socialities constitutive of the Negro as slave with that of the proletariat. A critique could be made that Gramsci's apparent inattentiveness to the socioeconomics of slavery is a serious flaw in his understanding of America. But then we should bear in mind that he is careful to remark elsewhere, in Q22§2, "Rationalization of the Demographic Composition of Europe," that the nonintegration of the Negro element—indeed, the complete preclusion of broader societal consolidation in the face of the Negro presence—is a chief factor contributing to the particularities of American societal creativity. More on this later; for the moment, I want to underscore that the Negro Gramsci is referencing is the same postbellum figuration W. E. B. Du Bois so thoroughly elaborated as a type of human subjectivity achieved in relation to U.S.-centered international capitalism. Du Bois recognized the Negro as an articulation of the forces of an emergent transformation of capitalism from a system based on the evaluation of material property identified with management of labor value (measured by the ratio of energy expended over time against cost of consumption) into one where evaluation was wholly symbolic, undermining the isomorphic relationship between money and labor—a transformation he neatly describes in an exposition of Andrew Johnson's drawing an explicit symmetry of evaluation between the $3 million in Negro labor lost in futures because of Emancipation and the $2.5 million in national debt.[3] Du Bois's exposition shows a way to better understand what is at stake in Gramsci's remarks on the Negro in Q4§49.

Bearing this in mind, we see that in Gramsci's note, the Negro is the limit-concept of America in two respects. First, it is a limit-concept with respect to the perception of America as a "new civilization." As a category of historical analysis, the Negro poses a challenge to that concept by functioning as a verifiable instance of the historical processes by which humans are civilized. The Negro is made in America, is the decisive expression of the historical social situation of America. What the Negro expresses, then, is the very complex of historical events that are unexplainable by historicism. The Negro differs from America as a limit-concept in another respect, however—as the concept of America's task, which is to elaborate a new type of human suited to the new type of work and productive processes of capitalism. This task can be construed as the history of the perceptual and intellectual functional unity of America in the world. Gramsci approaches that history through the Negro. This is abundantly clear in the slight refinements he makes to his observations subsequently in Q12. Two of these modifications are particularly significant. The first is the change made to the principal hypothesis, which Gramsci rewrites as: "that American expansionism should use American negroes as its agents in the conquest of the African market and the extention of American civilisation" (Q12§1, p. 1528; trans. Gramsci 1971, p. 21). This addition of "civiltà Americana" indexes the first reference to Americanism in the *Prison Notebooks*, which occurs in Q3§11, also written in 1930. That note is a critical engagement with some remarks made by Pirandello in an interview conducted by Corrado Alvaro, which appeared in *L'Italia Letteraria* in April 1929.

Pirandello asserts that "Americanism is overwhelming Europe" with what he calls "a new beacon of civilization" (un nuovo faro di civiltà), based on the establishment of a global financial network, which carriers a new way of life and culture (in Alvaro 1929, p. 1). Gramsci critiques this assessment for failing to grasp the significance of material historical change. The issue is not whether Americanism is indicative of a new *civiltà*. It is not. "The problem is," Gramsci writes,

> whether America, with the implacable preponderance of its economic production, will force or is already forcing Europe to undergo an upheaval of its socioeconomic alignment, which would have happened anyway, but at a slow pace—whereas now it looms as a repercussion of American "overbearingness" [*prepotenza*] In other words, whether a transformation of the material bases of civilization [*trasformazione delle basi materiali della civiltà*] is taking place. . . . The elements of life that are now being dissemi-

nated under the American label are just the first, groping efforts, and they are due not to the "order" born out of this new alignment, which has yet to take shape, but to initiatives of those who have been déclassés by the earliest operations of this new alignment. (Q3§11, p. 196; trans. Gramsci 1992–2007, vol. 2, p. 17)

What Pirandello imagines as a new and somewhat barbaric order emerging out of the New World to conquer Europe, Gramsci recognizes as symptomatic of a transformation in social history, and not the establishment of a new order. In fact, Americanism is not about a new *civiltà* "because it does not change the character of the fundamental classes; it is about the extension and intensification of European civilization [*della civiltà europea*], which, however, has assumed certain peculiarities in the American climate" (Q3§11, p. 196; trans. Gramsci 1992–2007, vol. 2, p. 18). What does Gramsci mean, then, when subsequently in Q12 he explicitly identifies American market expansion in Africa with *civiltà americana*? How does he account for the apparent contradiction, and why does it occur around the figure of the Negro?

The key is in understanding precisely what is meant by the term *civiltà*. There are two distinct, perhaps even contradictory senses of it at play in Gramsci's reading of Americanism. In the first sense, the one he cites from Pirandello, *civiltà* is something like the condition of a people having achieved a certain degree of technological and spiritual progress through the totality of the humanistic control over the political, industrial, and social spheres of activity. This sense, prevalent among Italian intellectuals at the time, echoes the conservative notions expressed by Mathew Arnold or John Ruskin, for whom industrialization carried the threat of destroying civilization. It is in this sense that *civiltà* might be understood to mean the customs of civil life characterized by the genteel and urban persona of elevated sentiment, achieved through an elevated cultural education, which may be why Hoare and Nowell-Smith, as well as Buttigieg, were inclined to translate it as "civilization," which carries the nineteenth-century European sense of culture as the instrument with which civilized man was formed. And if the problem is formulated in this way, Gramsci states, then "all they do in America is remasticate the old European culture" (Q3§11, p. 296; trans. Gramsci 1992–2007, vol. 2, p. 17). But, as he also states, that is not the problem; the problem is "whether a transformation of the material bases of *civiltà* is taking place." The focus on transformations in material basis suggests *civiltà* in the sense of the relationship between changes in the modalities of material production, technology—industrialism, in this instance—social institutions, and the expressions of intelligence—both institutional and particular—fostered in that relationship. A good deal of the work of Q4§49 is to elaborate the history of this relationship with the exposition of how the history of class formation informed contemporary intellectual practices in Europe so that European intellectuals across the full spectrum, from conservative to liberal and radical responses to industrialism, were incapable of thinking beyond the ideological horizons of their common class. That is, they could not think about transformation in material modalities except in terms of a struggle over continuity or rupture, which is why America presented such a conundrum. They could only think about the intellectual expression of transformation in terms of culture. Their sense of Americanism, then, is symptomatic of a failure to engage the difficult question of the historical relationship between materiality and intelligence.

For Gramsci, the complexity that fell under the designation "America" was significant because of how it foregrounded this question as an event of transformation in *civiltà* that may yield a rupture but is not yet the expression of that rupture. In fact, he insists that understanding what Americanism is requires recognizing it as an aspect of a transformation in European *civiltà*—a point he explicitly makes in Q22§2, where he observes, "America does not have great 'historical and cultural traditions'; but neither does it have [to support the leaden burden of classes that are purely parasitic] that characterizes *la 'civiltà' europea*" (Q22§2, p. 2145; trans. Gramsci 1971, pp. 285, 281). America's lacking the history of class formation explains Gramsci's assertion that there is a complete absence of traditional intellectuals in America. The absence of traditional intellectuals is not a function of a historical rupture, of an epiphenomenal American exceptionalism. Rather, it is a function of events in the realignment of European class formation that are coincidental with the material transformations associated with the emergence of mercantilism, exploration, the nation-state, and early capital accumulation. To the extent that we are to understand *civiltà* as the history of that process and its institutions, America is a transformation in *civiltà* that may be symptomatic of its end, but not a heterogeneous cause of it. The transformation is in the reduction of all intellectual energy to the solving of practical problems.

This line of interpretation finds support in note Q3§41, titled "Father Bresciani's Progeny," where Gramsci remarks because the tendency in America is that "all human energies [*tutte le forze umane*] become focused on structural work, and one cannot yet talk of superstructures . . . the only kind of poiesis [*poesia*]—that is, 'creation' [*creazione*]—would be the economical-practical" (Q3§41, p. 318; trans. Gramsci 1992–2007, vol. 2, p. 40, translation modified). Citing Victor Cambon's translator's preface to the French edition of Henry

Ford's autobiography *My Life and My Work*, Gramsci adds that "the Americans have even created a theory out of this," stressing that this is a poesis and a theory of poesis, rousing "the vital forces, energies, wills and enthusiasms" (Q3§41, p. 318; trans. Gramsci 1992–2007, vol. 2, p. 40). Ford is quite explicit about the problems confronting him in his effort to achieve nearly absolute efficiency in creative production. Chief among these was a desperate, one might say, vulgar population exhibiting a tendency to waste or lose energy in forms of thinking and acting that distracted from the economical-practical problems. Ford chose to address those distractions as moral problems presented by the seamless identification of industrialism with the city, with an accelerated process of urbanization. As moral problems, they formed a legitimate basis for capital's intervention into the full spectrum of the workers' lives in order to achieve an absolutely governable labor population. In this sense, Gramsci was correct; Americanism does not equal a new *civiltà*, but rather a transformation in the procedures of *civiltà* as governance. Although the notion of *civiltà* as a form of civil government is archaic, it has some bearing on Gramsci's account of the dynamic of thinking articulated in the relationship between modalities of materialization, social institutions, and intelligence—so much so that *civiltà* is arguably best translated as "civility," in contradiction to the current dominant Anglophone preference for "civilization," which has consequences for how we think about civil society.[4] In any event, translating *civiltà* as "civility" underscores how Gramsci's use of *civiltà Americana* entails his recognition that the object of American power is the subjection of life itself to governable labor.

What Gramsci finds in Americanism, then, is a rationalism that has determined the need to elaborate a new type of human, suited to the new type of work and productive process. He postulates that the predominance of this rationalist tendency in America stems from the absence of the class formation found in Europe, concordant with "the absence of a national homogeneity, the mixture of race-cultures, the negro question" (Q22§2, p. 2147; trans. Gramsci 1971, p. 287). This leads to a paradox in Gramsci's analysis because these absences have impeded adequate formulation of "the fundamental question of hegemony" (Q22§2, p. 2146; trans. Gramsci 1971, p. 286). The paradox is exacerbated by his referring to the Negro as the agent for extending American civility to a supposedly prenational Africa through market expansion, which goes to the heart of the nature of the relationship Gramsci presumed between the Negro and civility; that is, how the supposed backwardness of the "masses of Africa" is contrasted to the American Negro intellectual.

This brings us to the second significant modification to the "Intellectuals" note as it appears in Q12. There is a change to the two subordinate hypotheses which are rewritten so that, in the first instance, the question of language suggests the possibility of English as the lingua franca of a coherent continental intellectual class—"since the language of American Negroes is English, whether it could become the educated language of Africa bringing unity in the place of the existing myriad of dialects" (Q12§1, p. 1528). The second question is then revised accordingly to suggest that "this intellectual stratum could have sufficient assimilating and organising capacity to give a 'national' character to the present primitive sentiment of being a despised race, thus giving the African continent a mythic function as the common fatherland of all the negro peoples" (Q12§1, p. 1528; trans. Gramsci 1971, p. 21). Particularly noteworthy is how this modification elaborates and emphasizes the interrelationship between the two subordinate hypotheses. Language is interrelated to the potential for the expression of a constituting mythology of nation. Given Gramsci's reflections throughout the *Notebooks* on the necessity of a national language literature for national formation, this is not at all surprising. What's more, in keeping with his recognition of the centrality of the economical-practical in Americanism, it is logical that, in the instance of the American Negro, this formation should be a function of market expansion.

There is, however, a portion of the note that occurs in Q12 exactly as it did in Q4, without modification. I refer to Gramsci's remark about American Negroes having "more of a negative than a positive national and racial spirit; a spirit, in other words, born out of the struggle waged by the whites in order to isolate and dishearten them" (Q4§49, p. 481; Q12§1, p. 1528; trans. Gramsci 1992–2007, vol. 2, pp. 206–207). It is not a farfetch to read this passage as indicating Gramsci's understanding the Negro's orientation toward *civiltà* along lines quite similar to W. E. B. Du Bois's. In other words, to the extent that *civiltà* is understood as the history of the process of material transformations associated with the emergence of mercantilism, exploration, the nation-state, capitalism, and its institutions—that is, as civilization—Negro national consciousness is a negative function of that history. And to the extent that *civiltà* is understood as the intelligence of that system unfolding in law—that is, as civility—the same consciousness is a reactionary response rather than a positive articulation of law. It is an articulation *from* the law but not *of* the law. Fully aware that the Negro, per se, is a figure of positive law—the hypothesis is that the force of continual racial legislation would drive out active Negro intelligence—Gramsci discerns in that very intelligence a force that while indexed by the legal category Negro, exceeds the law's capacity of categorization. Recognizing this excess as the limit of law, and so symptomatic of a resistant counterforce to the power of civility, he discovers the Negro intellectual to be a product of the struggle between intelligence and power.

In Gramsci's account, the struggle is dialectical, of course, so that the Negro intellectual is a synthesis of the American conflict between power and intelligence, realized in the global expansion of markets. The Negro intellectual is a transformative function of American civility, a figure of creative destruction, which is the basis for the speculation that the Negro could Americanize "the backward masses in Africa." The backwardness is precisely in the sense of the African masses being outside of the *civiltà* of the market, because they lack the language of American civility as economic force. The American Negro is the bearer of that civility through the necessary deployment of the English language as the vehicle of both conceptual and economic unification.

Gramsci's speculation turns on the recognition of a profound difference between the American Negro and the African masses, having to do with the historicality of the Negro as an articulation of American power formation, indicative of how it preempts social formation's functioning as a counter to political-economic forces. Moreover, this is an endemic aspect of its globalization. The Negro is an institution of American power that will "Americanize" Africa through market expansion. It is a particular sort of Americanization, however. The Negro will, as it were, "Negroize" Africa. It should be clear at this point that this is not an issue of biological or ethnographic race; instead, it is about how such knowledges, functioning as instruments of power, deploy a persona (in this case, the Negro) as a way of consolidating intelligence into fixed manageable modes of existence. Although wanting in more detailed careful analysis, Gramsci's preliminary thinking about the historicality of the Negro question clearly discovered it to be symptomatic of America as a perpetual and violent pattern of globalizing, coercive transformative power; one whose modalities, however varied in space and time, always move toward the consolidation of intelligence into practical political-economic thought. The implication is that the Negro is energy converted to capital through absolute coercive force, a conversion that makes irrelevant the old, still humanist problem of how to definitively determine the difference between authentic and inauthentic life.

NOTES

This piece is dedicated to Joe Buttigieg, who fueled its conceptualizations during the semester-long seminar on Gramsci we conducted together at Notre Dame and the University of Pittsburgh in spring 2006. It is a small testament to the enduring importance of his thinking.

1   McKay reproduces the letter, along with his reply, in the introduction to *The Negroes in America*. He does not date the Trotsky letter, but gives the date of February 20, 1922 to his reply. This is clearly erroneous, perhaps simply a typographical error, because the Comintern was in November and December of that year. Maxwell Williams gives the date of Trotsky's letter as February 23, 1923, and states that it had been previously published in *Izvestia*. While the letter may very well have been composed by Trotsky on that date, it did not appear in *Izvestia* until the following month. Confusion of dates notwithstanding, the exchange records the Comintern's active engagement with McKay's thought.

2   The thematic structure of Notebook 12 is reflected in Gramsci's title for it: "Appunti e note sparse gruppo di saggi sulla storia degli intellettuali." Antonio Santucci accounts for the title as indicating how Gramsci gradually broadens the horizon of his history of intellectuals. See Santucci 2010, p. 33.

3   Du Bois remarks in chapter 9 of *Black Reconstruction*, "The Price of Disaster," apropos President Andrew Johnson's struggle with the emergent power of international finance capitalism: "Monopoly profits from investments were increasing, and destined to increase, and their increase depended upon a high protective tariff, the validity of the public debt, and the control of the national banks and currency. All of these things were threatened by the South and by Andrew Johnson as leader of the South. On the other hand, humanitarian radicalism, so far as the Negro was concerned, was not only completely harnessed to capital and property in the North, but its program for votes for Negroes more and more became manifestly the only protection upon which Northern industry could depend. The Abolitionists were not enemies of capital" (Du Bois 1935, p. 327). Driving this point home, he then quotes labor historian William Herberg: "The American Abolitionists were typical bourgeois-democratic revolutionists under specific American Conditions. They felt their movement linked up with the great humanitarian causes of the day (the 'labor question,' the 'peace question,' the emancipation of women, temperance, philanthropy) and with the bourgeois revolutionary movement in Europe" (p. 327).

4   I thank Wlad Godzich for pointing the way toward this reading of *civiltà* in Gramsci.

10

Reverse Hegemony?

MARIA ELISA CEVASCO

This piece, which tries to mobilize Gramscian categories in order to understand Brazilian political reversals, was written in 2013. The road to much-needed social change seemed to be a bit more open in those days when Dilma Rousseff, the president who succeeded Lula after his second term, was still sending contradictory signs, sometimes veering toward keeping up Lula's reforms and sometimes maintaining his efforts to keep rentier capitalists happy. As it happened, the president was impeached in the middle of her second term, amid great economic recession. The way to change seemed to be blocked again as neoliberal policies reasserted themselves. The Workers' Party itself is now in ruins, enmeshed in endless corruptions charges. I could have modulated the hope for a new hegemony that pervades my piece. I preferred to leave it as it was, as a document of what we thought and hoped then. History may yet turn again, and what we think of now as error of analysis may turn out to be the seeds that will grow in a better future.

As Raymond Williams says, "We begin to think where we live" (Williams 1989, p. 32). I would like to add—I think Williams would be pleased—that we also begin to think according to what time it is in the historical clock that shapes our thoughts. I teach cultural studies and cultural theory at the University of São Paulo, Brazil. This location on the periphery of global capitalism, where the contradictions of this iniquitous system appear in their most unequivocal materialization, demands a peculiar engagement from intellectual work. The famous Eleventh Thesis on Feuerbach makes immediate sense to peripheral intellectuals, as it is so glaringly clear that the world around us needs change. I came of age intellectually in the early 1980s, during the military dictatorship that from 1964 to 1984 curtailed any hopes for a just future. As my life and work continued, I witnessed how this hope was endlessly postponed as the recurrent structural movement of Brazilian society—that is, the repositioning of the old order of inequality at every movement of progress toward social change—reasserted itself. We saw the past happening over and over again, from the first directly elected president in 1989 through the neoliberal adjustments to the global market in the 1990s, a movement we all thought would end with the election of the first working-class president in Brazilian history, Luiz Inácio Lula da Silva, in 2002.

This is the frame of reference from which I propose to examine my theme, Antonio Gramsci and Raymond Williams—from Brazil and of course from my own sore perspective, that of a functionary of the superstructure. I will begin by telling you something about Gramsci's reception in Brazil. His work first circulated among Italian migrants and anti-fascist exiles. In what was perhaps the first printed mention of Gramsci in the country, his name was on a list of prisoners of the Fascist regime in a 1927 edition of *La Difesa*, a newspaper of the Italian socialists in Brazil. The first article dedicated to him was published as early as 1933, and the translation of Romain Rolland's "For Those Dying in Mussolini's Prisons: Antonio Gramsci" made his name and trajectory better known. The second phases of this reception, from the 1940s to the mid-1960s, was the Communist Party's version of Gramsci, as an anti-Trotskyite and an enemy of liberal thought, a follower of comrade Stalin's directions. In the 1960s, the Communist Party lost its hegemony in the Brazilian Left and the door was open to another Gramsci. Carlos Nelson Coutinho, who himself had been a member of the Communist Party, was to start his lifelong dedication to traslating Gramsci, publishing some of Togliatti's version of the *Cuaderni*. To give you an idea of what it was like to translate Gramsci in those years of military dictatorship, *Il materialismo storico e la filosofia di Benedetto Croce* was published as *A concepção dialética da história* (The dialectic conception of history). In the mid-1970s, with the progressive opening of the strictures of the dictatorship, there was a flowering of translations that were to turn Gramsci into a major figure in the Brazilian Left. From the beginning of the democratization process in the mid-1980s, his notions of hegemony, passive revolution, and war of position became current in discussions of Brazilian conservative modernization and new political organization. Lula's Workers' Party has a number of Gramscians in its membership. The First Congress of the Workers' Party in 1991 stated its official policy to achieve socialism in clearly Gramscian terms as "the constitution of the workers as a hegemonic and dominant class in State Power, eliminating the distinction between cadres and mass party, and associating the construction of power in daily struggle with the strategic moment of taking over political power" (for the reception of Gramsci in Brazil, see Secco 2002). In 1999 Carlos Nelson Coutinho, Marco Aurélio Nogueira, and Luiz Sergio Henriques started the ten-volume project of the translation of Gramsci's complete *Cuaderni*. He is present in many discussions in leftist movements. At my university, his academic influence is greater in education and social services, history, and sociology departments.

In departments of literature, where I teach, Gramsci is very often read through the lens of cultural studies and more particularly through Raymond Williams's acknowledgment of the centrality of his contribution to Marxist cultural theory. In an article published in *The Listener* in 1977, Williams highlights the signposts of what he calls an alternative tradition of Marxism that was going to be fundamental to him: Lukács's *History and Class Consciousness*, Sartre's works from the 1950s and 1960s, and the *Prison Notebooks*. For Williams's work, the most significant feature of this alternative Marxist tradition is its account of consciousness: a social analysis that seems to him "radically different from what most people understood as Marxism in Britain" (Williams 1972, p. 375).

Williams seems to have found in Gramsci two related central interests: his capacity for categorical invention and the setting up of strategies to counteract the patterns of domination and submission that secures the functioning of capitalist societies in the industrialized West, where universal suffrage prevails.

Let me begin with the categorical invention. In Williams's most strenuously theoretical book, *Marxism and Literature*, he revises the fundamental categories to think about culture through materialist lenses. As the examination of categories unfolds, it becomes clear that he is writing to found a new position, which he would call cultural materialism. In order to do so, he needs to reject the orthodoxies of the two most influential traditions in his social formation: idealist cultural criticism and the Marxism of the Communist Party. He concedes that any modern approach to a Marxist theory of culture must begin by considering the proposition of a determining base and a determined superstructure. He then adds that, theoretically, "it would be in many ways preferable if we could begin from the proposition which was originally equally central, equally authentic: namely the proposition that social being determines consciousness" (Williams 1977, p. 75). It is this proposition that opens up his understanding of Gramscian hegemony:

> Hegemony is then not only the articulate upper level of "ideology," nor are its forms of control only those ordinarily seen as "manipulation" or "indoctrination." It is a whole body of practices and expectations, over the whole of living: our senses and assignments of energy, our shaping perceptions of ourselves and our world. It is a lived system of meanings and values—constitutive and constituting—which as they are experienced as practices appear as reciprocally confirming. It thus constitutes a sense of reality for most people in the society, a sense of absolute because experienced reality beyond which it is very difficult for most people in the society to move, in most areas of their lives. It is, that is to say, in the strongest sense a "culture," but a culture which has also to be seen as the lived dominance and subordination of particular classes. (Williams 1977, p. 110)

The notion of hegemony allowed Williams to go beyond the founding metaphor of a determining base and a determined superstructure. As John Higgins points out in his study of Williams, "Hegemony is always and essentially an active and ongoing process. It is determination at work and in process and as such, it is a volatile, heterogeneous and mobile system, an economy of experience governed by the interplay of what are referred to as dominant, emergent, and residual forces and social meanings" (Higgins 1999, p. 113). As such, it can become a fundamental resource for social struggle:

> What we saw emerging in the 1960s was a new form of corporate state; and the emphasis on culture, which was often taken as identifying our position, was an emphasis, at least in my own case, on the process of social and cultural incorporation according to which it is something more than simply property or power which maintains the structures of capitalist society. Indeed, in seeking to define this, it was possible to look again at certain important parts of the Marxist tradition, notably the work of Gramsci with his emphasis on hegemony. We could then say that the essential dominance of a particular class in society is maintained not only, although if necessary, by power, and not only, though always, by property. It is maintained also and inevitably by a lived culture: that saturation of habit, of experience, of outlook, from a very early age and continually renewed at so many stages of life, under definite pressures and within definite limits, so that what people come to think and feel is in a large measure

Maria Elisa Cevasco

a reproduction of the deeply based social order which they may even in some respects think they oppose and indeed actually oppose. (Williams 1989, p. 74)

Hence the political strategy open for organic intellectuals:

I know there is a profoundly necessary job to do in relation to the processes of cultural hegemony itself. I believe that the system of meanings and values which a capitalist society has generated has to be defeated in general and in detail by the most sustained kinds of intellectual and educational work. This is a cultural process I called the "long revolution" and in calling it "the long revolution" I meant that it was a genuine struggle which was part of the necessary battles of democracy and of economic victory for the organized working class. . . . The task of a successful socialist movement will be one of feeling and imagination quite as much as one of fact and organization. Not imagination or feelings in their weak senses— "imagining the future" (which is a waste of time) or the "emotional side of things." On the contrary we have to learn and teach each other the connections between a political and economic formation, and, perhaps hardest of all, the formations of feelings and relationships which are our immediate resources in any struggle. (Williams 1989, pp. 75–76)

Cultural revolution? A successful socialist movement? Victory for the organized working class? All those terms do not seem to compute in our time of the domination of the commodity form all over the world on an unprecedented scale, which is so thoroughly and persuasively described by Fredric Jameson as the time in which the future itself has been colonized by the sameness of the present (see Jameson 2005). And yet, as Galileo would say, *Eppur si muove*, and in the era of inevitabilities, in the country of repetition, after two terms of a neoliberal president who tried hard to make Brazil catch up with globalization without balancing out our appalling social inequality, lo and behold, after having been defeated three times, Lula was elected. As is well known, he rose to prominence as a union leader and then as the leader of the greatest political novelty in the Americas in late twentieth century, an organized Workers' Party with a socialist project for a big country. When he became president, hopes on the left flew high, as it was the first time in Brazilian history that "one of us" had won a democratic election and received a mandate to change. And yet, even before the election, Lula was appeasing the financial sector, and in his first term in office, pace some gestures toward social assistance, he adopted very conservative economic policies, balancing the budget at the expense of increasing unemployment—from 10.5 percent in the last year of Fernando Henrique's neoliberal rule to 10.9 percent in Lula's first year, and decreasing the average wage at a rate of 12 percent, thus inaugurating an era of, at worst, neoliberal repositioning of Brazilian social inequality, and at best, a politics of very gradual reformism. That is how two sociologists on the left put it: "Instead of launching an alternative mode of doing politics the program of the Workers' Party affirmed a state logic with a view to gradually updating the economic structure of Brazilian capitalism by means of successive transitions directed by the state, avoiding the active intervention of the subaltern classes in this process. In this logic are inscribed fiscal discipline, social security reform, and giving value to private pension funds. Such funds established a bridge that makes viable the organic alliance of a union bureaucracy, now the managers of those funds, and globalized financial capital" (Bianchi and Braga 2005, p. 1745).

Whatever happened to the desire for change of the millions who had voted for him? This incongruous situation prompted an intense intellectual debate among the Brazilian Left, whose terms prompted one of the participants to call it a Gramscian odyssey. For Ruy Braga and Alvaro Bianchi, Lula conducted a passive revolution Brazilian-style, in which popular consent was secured through meeting some of the long-repressed demands of a number of social movements while reproducing the logic of rentier capitalism. The fact that former union leaders managed the pension funds would be a paramount example of *transformismo* as it paved the way for a new unionism that would not defend the interests of the subaltern classes. Carlos Nelson Coutinho, our foremost Gramscian, argued in favor of a specific kind of hegemony, the hegemony of small politics as it becomes common sense that politics is nothing but a dispute over power among the elites who all agree that whatever exists is "natural" and cannot be changed.

Francisco de Oliveira, whom Perry Anderson considers the "most original sociological mind in Latin America" (Anderson 2011, p. 9), soon gave his own account of the new situation. Chico, as we call him, had been one of the most well-known organic intellectuals of the Workers' Party but had left the party soon after Lula's first election, as it became clear to him that there would be no radical changes. In an article written in January 2007, the month of Lula's second inauguration, he took recourse to a formulation that would, as most of his formulations do, provoke a lot of controversy:

> The re-election of Luiz Inácio da Silva in October 2006 allows us to decipher the ways in which Brazil's political landscape has been reconstituted under the Workers' Party government. The whirlwind of deregulation,

privatization and restructuring under Fernando Henrique Cardoso in the 1990s—and with it, the dissolution of the industrial working class created during the developmentalist era—had torn up all established relations between economy and politics, classes and representation. The result was a period of indeterminacy, the context of Lula's first presidential victory in 2002. Since then, a novel combination of neo-populism and party statification, shored up by social-liberal handouts, on the one hand, and government graft, on the other, has helped to forge a new form of class rule in Brazil that could be characterized as "hegemony in reverse." (de Oliveira 2006, p. 5)

What would the characteristics of this "hegemony in reverse" be? During what de Oliveira calls "the age of invention," the Workers' Party, and the social movements linked to it, came closest to providing a potentially hegemonic moral direction, in the Gramscian sense. Its watchwords expanded from the generalization of social conflicts to the demand for civil rights, extending the notion of citizenship; from condemnation of patrimonialism to popular control over public spending and oversight of the affairs of state. In sum, the party provided a republican renewal without parallel in the history of Brazil. When they seized state power, or, in de Oliveira's assessment, when "the party was dissolved into the state," they renounced their pre-election moral direction. The result was an indefinite prolongation of the Brazilian "passive way," with the possibilities for social transformation once more endlessly deferred. And yet:

> This set of appearances conceals something for which we do not yet have a name. The dominated realize the 'moral revolution'—defeat of apartheid in South Africa, election of the Workers Party in Brazil—which is then transformed and deformed through capitulation to unfettered exploitation. The terms of the Gramscian equation "force + consent = hegemony" have been turned upside down: "force" has disappeared, and the direction of consent has been reversed. For it is no longer the dominated who consent to their own subordination; now it is the dominant who consent to being ostensibly "led" by representatives of the dominated—on condition that they do not question the forms of capitalist relations. This new paradigm may prove to be a functional one for globalized capitalism. It is an epistemological revolution before which all existing theories of politics pale. (de Olivera 2006, p. 22)

Provocation aside, Chico de Oliveira was giving an assessment of the current situation that presented an inversion of other situations of change we know from history, where revolutions sometimes transform the base but not the superstructure. He is arguing the opposite: for him, we witnessed in Lula's Brazil a transformation of the superstructure that left the base untouched. An intellectual response to de Oliveira's assessment of the country soon emerged. André Singer, who had been de Oliveira's student and also worked as the president's press secretary during Lula's first term in office, offered a challenge to de Oliveira's picture. For Singer, it was expected that once in power, the Workers' Party would implement an intensively reformist program, which would probably have led to a radical split between the different interests of the bourgeoisie and the proletariat. In practice, he says, what really occurred was a semi-transformism; the members of the party in power became agents of a weak reformism that took great care not to cause the radicalization that they had originally defended. Singer's argument is that reformism under Lula was slow and demobilizing, but it was still a reformism that had a detectable material base: the program of Bolsa Familia, which gives a monthly allowance to families under the poverty line, the increase in the minimum salary, and the expansion of credit. Lula's policies, which were followed by his successor Dilma Rousseff, indicate a different politics, less dependent on international ties as it focuses on the expansion of the internal market as one of the means of attaining economic stability. Above all, government policies have to take into account the newly conquered political base of the Workers' Party. Analyzing the social profile of those who voted for Lula in the second term, Singer comes up with a political novelty that he says may be interpreted as the Brazilian solution to the southern question as described by Gramsci. In the case of Brazil, until 2005, the "backward" sector of Brazilian society, the rural and semirural mass of workers from the largely agrarian northeast, had traditionally supported right-wing candidates. In 1989 they voted for Collor against Lula. Their lot did not improve in the next governments, and it worsened during the neoliberal period. Singer's research shows that a whole class faction changed its traditional support for right-wing candidates to vote for Lula in the second term. Borrowing a term coined by his father, the economist Paul Singer, he calls them the "subproletariat"—that is, the underpaid workers who do not achieve the minimum conditions that would allow them to take part in class struggle. The subproletariat includes not only the rural workers but also those who do not find formal jobs and who populate the slums that can be found in any Brazilian city. They represent almost half of the Brazilian workforce. Taking his inspiration from Marx's *Eighteenth Brumaire*, Singer sees this subproletariat as isolated and unable to organize. Like the peasant smallholders studied by Marx, this class faction projects its aspirations onto a leader in power, hence their support for Lula. They are both progressive and conservative: they do not support social conflict—they are mostly against strikes, for instance—and are in favor of state intervention to ameliorate social conditions. One of the many results of this change in the political basis of the government has been to dislocate the positions in the political debate: now they have a voice that must be heard. This, says Singer, is the radical novelty of what we have to call Lulism to differentiate the current form of politics from the one associated with the Workers' Party. For Singer, Chico de Oliveira is right when he states that there is a new phenomenon underway in Brazil, which is different from any of the practices of domination that existed in Brazilian history. It is not, he maintains, any kind of "reverse hegemony," but the effective representation of the interests of the subproletariat (see Singer 2012). Once Lula conquered this sizeable political support, Lulism conquered an autonomy that allowed him to be both progressive—in the sense of creating a state that protects workers independent of the wishes of capital—and conservative, as it does so without disrupting the economic order: as an example, the family allowance, which benefits over thirteen million families, represents less than 0.5 percent of the GNP, prompting Lula, always a great phrase maker and not always a tactful one, to say, "It is cheap to take care of the poor."

Has Brazil changed, as Singer maintains, or are we witnessing the "vanguard of backwardness and the backwardness of the vanguard," as Chico de Oliveira puts it in his afterword to a 2010 collective volume of essays, titled "Reverse Hegemony"?

I myself am a member of a research team led by both Singer and Chico de Oliveira. Our aim is precisely to study Brazil after Lulism. Both present very persuasive accounts, and it is difficult to decide who is right. Chico de Oliveira appeals to the ideals shared by generations of the Brazilian Left, the formation most of us have come from. André Singer shows what has been possible. Where do I stand? Do I support a position that favors the politics of hope, or one that favors the politics of the possible? Can the possible be radicalized?

By way of an answer I cannot give and in place of a conclusion I cannot reach, I propose to go back to Williams and offer a very brief comment on the ways current cultural hegemony constituted by the interplay of residual, dominant, and emergent are represented in contemporary Brazilian culture. I want to focus on a documentary that won first prize at the 2011 It's All True film festival. The film is called *A Família Braz: Dois Tempos* [The Braz family in two times], and it depicts the ascension of a family from the subproletariat to the ranks of an incipient middle class often referred to in Brazil as the "C class." This elevation, as we have seen, is considered one of the most creditable achievements of Lulism. As the title suggests, the film depicts two visits made by the film directors to interview the family, one in year 2000, and another ten years later. They still live in the same house on the periphery of São Paulo, but their lives have changed a lot for the better. They have enlarged the house many times, an incongruous architectural project shown on film as space is added wherever possible. All four of the children have managed to study and find better jobs than their father has had. Seu Tonico, the father, who had been a plumber working for whoever wanted his services, now has two people working for him. One of the most impressive things in the interviews that comprise the film is the pleasure they all share in being able to join consumer society: they now have no less than four cars and can aspire to vacations. A recurrent aspiration is to be able to go on a four-day cruise of the Brazilian coast. It is clear that the model of a happy life is the typical life of the middle classes, which is confirmed as the hegemonic model. There is not a hint of a critique of consumerism, which is accepted by all of them as the best thing in the world. As the very engaging members of the family are interviewed, the camera travels over their neighborhood and shows that prosperity has been very restricted. Seu Tonico's sister, who lives next door, is still in the very shabby house she had ten years before. Yet there is not a single hint of concern for the ones whose lives have not improved. It is as if the Braz family, together with consumerism, have acquired the lack of class consciousness that characterizes the middle class, for whom social improvement is linked exclusively to individual merit. The director of the film, Dorrit Harazim, calls our attention to the alienation that accompanies the Brazes' social ascension. She comments in an interview on their lack of interest in political matters: "If politics did not arise in their conversations, this means a very important thing, that politics is not important for them."

That would be the disquieting dominant aspect. The hopefully residual one is the rest of their neighborhood whose lot has not improved. What about the emergent? I think we can catch a glimpse of the positive emergent precisely in the contradiction between the cars, the owners, and their social environment. Rather than contented, the family seems to be defiant, as if saying, now that we got here, we are ready to take possession of everything this society has to offer. The coupling of the defiance and the setting forms a revealing contradiction. The development of capitalism in the last two hundred years has proved Marx right, and shown that it can never produce equality. Is it unreasonable to think that material integration amid the ruins of the periphery of a global city like São Paulo may lead to promising political effects? It is true that nowadays the Brazes do not fully perceive the structural limitations of capitalism, because their lot did improve but those limitations are sure to reassert themselves. This may either lead to further alienation or, given their past, it could allow them to perceive that the system requires inequality and that they are the ones who pay, and have for generations paid, its human costs. It might then be the case that Perry Anderson is right in his assessment of Lula's Brazil when he says, "Should passive improvement ever become active intervention, the story would have another ending" (Anderson 2011, p. 12). And I add, perhaps we will then be able to consider Lulism among the conditions of possibility for a much needed change.

11

Thinking Andean Abya Yala with and against Gramsci

Notes on State, Nature, and *Buen Vivir*

CATHERINE E. WALSH

By Way of Introduction

This text breaks the mold. It is not a study about Antonio Gramsci, his conceptual tenets, or his paths of thought. It is also not a treatise about how to think and use Gramsci in the world today, although there are certainly elements here that could open such consideration.

Instead, the pages that follow represent my urge to speak directly to him, to tell him of my walkings and askings in a Zapatista sense, of my shifts and movements in thinking both with and against him, first in the context of the United States and then, since the mid-1990s, in South America and the Andes, or as I refer to it here, Andean *Abya Yala*. The text is conceived and written as open notes to and for Antonio Gramsci, and to and for others who wish to read them.

Notes that Recall Times Past

More than a quarter of a century has passed since our last communication, Antonio. That was in a different epoch, space, and place. It was hegemony that concerned me then, Marxism and linguistics, dialogic opposition and its human agency, and war(s) of positions. Resistance and struggle, pedagogy, language, and voice were, if you recall, my central interests, most specifically the particularized nature of the lived colonial relation of power for Boricua (Puerto Rican) communities and youth in the United States.

My communication to you then was frequent and fluid as we—our several-person Gramsci study group in Western Massachusetts[1]—seriously grappled with both the significance of confronting hegemony in activist and intellectual terms and the lived meaning of organic intellectuals and political praxis. We grappled as well with the question of how to confront the "subaltern" blindness of Marxism within much of the then radical Left, in which the singular vision of class struggle shrouded the struggles of race, gender, and heteropatriarchy perpetuating, more often than not, patterns of colonial power. You were also never far during the years of that same decade—the 1980s—which I spent working alongside Paulo Freire, and in the related discussions and debates engendered in the sphere of what we then termed critical pedagogy, debates in which Stanley Aronowitz, Maxine Green, Henry Giroux, Peter McLaren, Roger I. Simon,[2] and Myles Horton from the Highlander School, among others, also took part. Indeed, my copy of the *Selections from the Prison Notebooks* began to show use's wear and tear. The annotations and side notes evidenced my effort to "think with you"—that is, and following Stuart Hall, to "think" the problems that concerned me in a Gramscian way (Hall 1987). I never thought of you as a prophet or theoretician to be universalized or generalized, but as a sort of intellectual ancestral combatant from whom there was much to think and learn.

Those notebooks of yours—along with the texts of Freire but also of Frantz Fanon—traveled with me to Ecuador in the mid-1990s, to that "other" America that Indigenous peoples collectively prefer to call *Abya Yala*, roughly translated as a land in full maturity or a land of vital blood. While I did not forget you, your presence and maybe even your relevance for me waned as I sought *to be in* and *think from* this radically different place, living its becoming home. Certainly you yourself would probably not have wanted it any other way. Localization for you was always fundamental.

Notes in, from, and with Abya Yala

"Latin" American Travel Notes

The travel of your thought to Latin America dates back to your pre-prison years. The strong Italian presence in Argentina first enabled your movement between what Juan Carlos Portantiero referred to as "Occidental or Western peripheries": Sardinia and Argentina. Portantiero, of course, was recalling your differentiation of two types of Western societies: a center West and a West of the periphery (see Portantiero 1980, 1981). The fluid contact between the Italian and Argentinian socialist presses in the early 1900s facilitated the circulation and translation of your essays by Italian immigrants who saw the commonalities of histories. With the massive immigration of anti-fascists, you had an increasing presence in Argentina's class struggle, causing serious divisions at times with Stalinist and Trotskyist ideologues and in the Communist Party itself. Their refusal to seriously engage your thought led to splits, including the formation in the 1960s of the group Pasado y Presente (Past and Present) and the magazine by the same name led up by the Argentinian Gramscians José Aricó and Héctor Agosti. The primary aim of both the magazine and the group was the *translatability* (a term you explored in Notebook 11) of your thought to Latin America. The possible similarities of historical-cultural contexts and the potential relevance of your critical analytic categories in the transformation of leftist thought, including with respect to the radical interrelation between culture and politics, were themes of constant debate and discussion (see Portantiero 1981; Aricó 2005; Infranca 2009). However, and as Antonino Infranca contends, the group's gaze—typical of most of Argentinian society—remained focused on Europe and European modernity; the differential realities and internal colonialism of the Americas were outside the gaze and lens.

In the 1960s you appeared in Mexico, in large part the result of the growing presence of exiled Argentinians. After the Argentinian military coup of 1976, Pasado y Presente was exiled to Mexico as well; there they opened an editorial press dedicated to the diffusion of your work.[3] In Brazil your thought also began to circulate among intellectuals in the 1960s. For many, your relevance was in the thinking of Brazilian civil society, a society that some Brazilian Gramscians thought was Eastern-like, following your thought and, as such, a "gelatinous civil society" (Infranca 2009). You were read by liberation theology intellectuals and by intellectuals associated with the São Paulo working class, many of whom validated your concept of the subaltern. Bit by bit, your work traveled to other Latin American nations. Yet in all of these contexts, you became an interlocutor in the political and ideological debates of a Left that, while positioning itself from the "periphery of the West," continued to be primarily white, male, and Euro-centered.[4] Many tried to see in you their own reflections.

The Ordvinovist—and Not Just Gramsci—Connection

The case of the Peruvian José Carlos Mariátegui was different. Numerous authors have alluded to your relation. Some say you briefly met in passing in Turin in 1921. Others suggest that you were more ephemerally tied by the times, your journalistic pursuits, socialist projects, and your "Ordinovism" brand of Marxism particularly strong in Italy in the 1920s. These were your pre-prison years, the years in which you were actively involved in building the party and directing, with Terracini and Togliatti, the newspaper *L'Ordine Nuovo* in Turin (see Spriano 1965; Gramsci 1987). As you remember, *L'Ordine Nuovo* was a central organ in the formulation of the project of a new communist order that articulated the workers' struggle with the Communist International in a particularly Italian-brand of socialism, and that endeavored to think with and from unionism and its popular bases (Beigel 2005, pp. 23–49). These were also the years that Mariátegui lived and studied in Italy (1919–1922); the years when he developed his own socialist political thought, thinking with and learning from the historical moment of the Italian-Ordinovist process but never losing his Peruvian place of enunciation and his Andean perspective.

Fernanda Beigel reminds us that the Gramsci that Mariátegui could have known through references or possibly in the offices of *L'Ordine Nuovo* during these years was an important militant, but of course not the Gramsci that the world came to know through the publication of the *Prison Notebooks* well after Mariátegui's death. Thus, while some continue to see you in Mariátegui's Marxism, Beigel's argument that it was Ordinovism and not you that influenced Mariátegui seems more true. Mariátegui's reading of Ordinovism in *L'Ordine Nuovo* while in Italy probably contributed to his own thinking about Marxism and socialism with regard to Peru. Ordinovism was an Italian construction, thought from the particularity of Italy and of that geopolitical, geocultural, and historical moment. It opened Marxism, localized its frames of thought, praxis, and struggle, and gave credence and force to both the local production of knowledge and the production of local knowledge. Ordinovism, as you too helped to construct it, was not a dogma or theory to be universalized and applied; it was a way of thinking and being in struggle that gave centrality to the idea and possibility of a "new order."

Peasants, the "Indigenous Question," and Andean Abya Yala

The "Cartas de Italia" (Letters from Italy) that Mariátegui wrote for the Peruvian press while in Rome and Turin suggest his interest was not with following the Communist International or with the building of a socialist hegemony per se. Neither was it with reifying and universalizing Italian political thought and thinkers, including you. Instead, it was thinking with the localized experience of Italy and Europe from his own particular geopolitical and epistemic localization. The concern of Mariátegui, unlike fellow members of the South

American Left—and particularly after he returned to Peru—was the "indigenous question" (see Mignolo 2012, pp. 191–217). His hope, vision, and project: the dismantling of colonial legacies and the positioning of an agrarian-based struggle from the particular reality of Indigenous peasants. This was to the exclusion—I must add—of black peoples, whom he conceived as primitive, superstitious, and servile to colonialism, and without ties to culture, agriculture, or land; black peoples were, as such, outside his conception of peasants.

For Mariátegui, as for you, revolutionary hope was in the culture, practices, beliefs, and the political potential of the peasantry (see Chatterjee 2012, pp. 119–136). Neither of you were particularly interested in their thinking, thought, or knowledge. The difference, of course, was that Mariátegui's "peasants"—he himself naming them as such—were native Indigenous peoples, marked not just by class but more complexly by coloniality, its designs of racialization and dehumanization, and its control over labor, authority, knowledge, and subjectivity. This colonial model or matrix of power that began in the Americas with the so-called conquest (read: invasion) initiated what Enrique Dussel calls the first modernity, giving form—from 1492 on—to "modern Europe" as the center of world history, thus challenging the idea—also present in a certain sense in your thought—of modernity as an intra-European phenomena (see Dussel 2000, pp. 465–478). Of course, important to consider here as well is how the Left throughout the world has most often been blind to its own perpetuation of the modern/colonial matrix of power. The insistence on class difference and struggle (to the exclusion of race, ethnicity, and gender), including the construction of the classificatory nomenclature of "peasants," is one clear example.

By the time I moved to South America, Indigenous peoples, with the exception of those in the highlands of Peru, had rejected the non-Indigenous Left-imposed category of peasant or campesino. They were defining themselves and their struggles on their own terms. The counter-celebrations of 1992 organized and conceived as five hundred years of resistance, marked the beginning of a new era—Abya Yala—interrupting and displacing not only the hegemonic project of "Latin" America but also the hegemony of the white-mestizo Left, further fractured then by the fall of the Soviet Union and the Berlin Wall but also by the rise of so-called South American democracies. While the Spanish translations from Mexico of your notebooks were circulating from 1975 on (with the last notebook finally published in 2000), and translations of some of your letters decades before in Argentina, serious engagement with your thought, particularly in the Andes, was in all practicality absent by the 1990s, including in academic circles.

Notes of Decolonial Distance: On State, Nature, and *Buen Vivir*

The Ecuador of the 1990s took me, and probably others, away from you, and at times even against you. Your concepts and ideas that I had grappled with and held on to so dearly a decade before did not seem of much relevance in this historical context and moment of struggle that went beyond, transgressed, and interrupted Marxism and the "Left."

On and about State

The mobilization and demands of Ecuadorian Indigenous organizations against capitalism, free trade, and neoliberal designs, and for a radically distinct project of a plurinational and intercultural society and state, rallied the masses, bringing together sectors across racial/ethnic, gender, and class lines in a way that the Left had never been able to do. Much of the Left joined this insurgence, changing T-shirts and putting Marx and Althusser, as well as you, at least for a time, on the back shelf. For the first time in history, ancestral peoples—those historically marked as the "subaltern" (to use your word, a term seldom used in Abya Yala–Latin America outside academic circles)— were leading and shaping a coalition-struggle (not a "multitude" or a "bloc"). It was their social, political, and epistemic insurgency and agency—surpassing by far a mere "reactive" resistance—that gave orientation, substance, and focus to the vision of a new shared social project and vision of state. This project and vision targeted the historical problem of what the *kichwa* leader, intellectual, and lawyer Luis Macas calls the "colonial tare," in which Marxist modernity (or Marxism in/as modernity) is included (see Walsh 2008, pp. 506–518).

Does all this not counter and put into question the "subalterns" that need to be brought into consciousness, but also the very notions you had of civil society and of political society as the state (see Gramsci 1971, esp. pp. 12, 52–53)? The struggle here was not necessarily for subaltern classes to become a state; this was understood by you as a necessary condition of their unification (Gramsci 1971, p. 52). Instead (and in both Ecuador and Bolivia), it was to rethink state itself—that is, to refound its idea and project. Here the reflections of the Bolivian Raúl Prada are revealing and useful: "The plurinational State is not now a State in the strict sense of the word; the plural 'event' dislodges the unitary character of the State. The State is now not the political synthesis of the society, nor is it comprehensible now the separation of State, political society, and civil society, particularly since the forms and practices of social organization now absorb the functions that correspond to the field of State" (Prada 2010, p. 88; my translation).

For Prada, the idea of a plurinational state, differentially present in both Bolivia's and Ecuador's constitutional debates and subsequent charters (2008 in Ecuador and 2009 in Bolivia), recognized the limits of an economy subsumed by capitalist accumulation. You of course wrote about the relation of state and capitalism in your *Prison Notebooks*. There you argued: "The State finds itself invested with a primordial function in the capitalist system." Moreover and as you went on to say: "in theory the State appears to have its socio-political base among the ordinary folk and the intellectuals, while in reality its structure remains plutocratic and it is impossible for it to break its links with big finance capital" (Gramsci 1971, pp. 314-315). The proposals in Bolivia and Ecuador suggested the possibility of something radically different.

In Ecuador, Indigenous-led insurgency enabled the participatory making in 2008 of a new constitution, deemed the most radical in the world, an historic process I had the privilege to participate in, never once thinking, I have to admit, of you. This political charter begins, in its preamble, by recognizing millennial roots and celebrating Nature as *Pachamama* (roughly translated as Mother Nature or Mother Earth). It calls forth the wisdom of the country's diverse cultures and positions the populace as inheritors of the social struggles of liberation against all forms of domination and colonialism. It goes on to refound the state as plurinational and intercultural, to make Nature the subject of rights, and to establish *buen vivir*—life in plentitude or collective well-being—as the transversal axis of the charter and its social project of society and state. While capitalism did not disappear, the intention was to take distance from neoliberalism (what President Rafael Correa then called "the long neoliberal night") and move the economy from the model of accumulation to one grounded on and in the concept of *buen vivir*.

In the years hence, and particularly since 2010, I have often asked if the contradictions of government policy do not outweigh and displace the social, political, epistemic, economic, and structural transformations laid out in the political charter, including its other-project of capital and state. During the Correa regime (2007-2017), neo-extractivism became the central economic base of a centralized authoritarian state in which there was no effective separation of powers. While extractivism was and still is state controlled, the concessions for oil, mining, and hydroelectric plants are overwhelmingly in the hands of China.[5] In March 2016, Ecuador's debt to China was more than $6 billion, nine hundred times more than in 2007 (before the present constitution).[6] Big finance capital has not disappeared; it just has a new geopolitical project, place, and face. At the end of 2016, as I write this letter, Indigenous leaders and social activists are criminalized for defending Nature's rights and named as terrorists of the state—the plurinational state that they initially helped posture and conceive. Moreover, *buen vivir* in both government policy and discourse is an instrument of capitalism and development (see Walsh 2010). The "state" has not been refounded; under Correa it was re-engineered as a tripartite unified and unifying power: president-state-government. Here your notion of civil society is subsumed within—co-opted, redefined, and mandated from the top down—as state. The plurinational and intercultural as signifiers of an otherwise conceived from "below" are emptied of their transformational significance.

I have also queried about the return, renewal, and recreation of the Left or Lefts, wondering at times if the government labels in the region (Venezuela, Bolivia, and Ecuador) of "twenty-first-century socialism" or, in the specific case of Ecuador, the "Citizens' Revolution," do not somehow recall the socialist hegemony for which you once fought, of course now in a distinct time, place, and circumstance. In fact, among the younger generations in public universities, there seems to be a curiosity about such connections. The international Gramsci seminars held in Bogota, Colombia, in 2008 and in Quito, Ecuador, in 2009, organized by public university collectives and presented in the context of local and regional integration as counters to neoliberalism's practice and project, are an example (see Herrerra Zgaib 2009; Herrerra Zgaib and Ortiz 2010).

Yet I also ponder the fact that "socialism" and "revolution" remain as terms of the Left, not of Indigenous and Afro-descendant organizations and social movements concerned instead with re-existence in societies still marked by the colonial tare and its perpetuation of racism, patriarchy, and dehumanization. As such, I muse about what all this suggests in terms of the decolonial, particularly the shifts in nature, being, and living reflected in the Ecuadorian constitution but more broadly in process—from the bottom up—in many places of the Global South. It is this "otherwise" that challenges the hegemony of capitalism and/as Western "civilization," defies modernity/coloniality's hold, and opens decolonial cracks or fissures in the dominant world order.

These ruminations are the reason of my notes to you here. With these notes I do not pretend to renew the relationship I had with you in the 1980s, to start up where it left off, or to think once again in a "Gramscian way." Instead, I portend to move forward in serpentinian (rather than lineal) fashion,[7] to simultaneously think with and against you in an Abya-Yalean way. Here what interests me most (and what I have only recently begun to explore) is your thinking on the praxical relation of nature, society, and conceptions of being in the world.

In your Notebook 11 (Q11§27), you describe praxis as reflective of an "absolute earthliness of thought," tied to the organic practices and struggles of existing reality and the conditions, including of contradiction, in which new conceptions of possibility, consciousness, and historical action can emerge (Gramsci 1971, p. 465; see also Thomas 2009b). Praxis, in this sense, simultaneously builds on and transforms worldviews and life visions, something clearly evidenced in the Ecuadorian constitution. Here it is interesting to delve a bit more into your thoughts—not clearly elaborated but scattered throughout the *Notebooks*—on nature in relationship to your philosophy of praxis.

My interest is not to position you within the realm of geography and political ecology, as some authors are presently attempting to do. Alex Loftus's claim that "Gramsci may well be considered *the* preeminent theorist of 'political ecology' within the Marxist tradition" (Loftus 2013, p. 194) is not mine. For me, political ecology's concept and project remain framed, for the most part, within the confines of Western modernity and Western thinking and their simplification and instrumentalization of "nature." Arturo Escobar argues, and in conversation with the Mexican environmental sociologist Enrique Leff and the Brazilian liberation theologian Leonardo Boff, that political ecology (in its emergent Latin American framework) affords a geopolitical perspective that underscores the civilizational character of the current environmental crisis, in essence a crisis of modernity, of instrumental rationality, and of logocentric thought (Escobar 2010, p. 51). This is true. Feminists similarly argue for and recognize the presence in many regions of the world, most especially the Global South, of lived political ecologies, of feminist engagements in creating connections and knowledge in, on, and with the environment that consider "the everyday, embodied and the emotional relations to resources and 'natures'" (Harris 2015, p. 158).

Despite these visions and projects of an alternative hegemony, "ecology" (the term *Ökologie* was coined in 1866 by the German scientist Ernst Haeckel) and "environment" remain essentially modern Western inventions and terms grounded in "science," in human-centered understandings, interactions, problems, and solutions to the (human-dominated) natural world. Historically prior and still present ancestral—collective—relational cosmologies, epistemologies, and worldviews of nature, including *Pachamama*, *Gaia*, and *Ubuntu*, among others, are most often overlooked, negated, and suppressed. Nature, more integrally understood as Mother Nature or Mother Earth, is the base of a philosophy and praxis in which being (human and nonhuman), knowledge, land/territory, spirituality, and existence are inseparable from and constitutive of life itself. Certainly, this is different from Marx's idea, recently summarized by Terry Eagleton (but also referenced in your *Notebooks*), that "human beings are part of Nature yet able to stand over against it; and this partial separation from Nature is itself part of their nature" (Eagleton 2012, p. 223). The assertion that nature is there to be dominated and controlled by "man," and the accompanying presumption that nature is synonymous with natural resources, are component parts of the coloniality of power in general, and most especially of what I have termed the coloniality of Mother Nature or Mother Earth. As I have explained elsewhere: "By this I refer to the coloniality that finds root and ground in the intertwined projects of civilization, scientific exploration, Christianity and evangelization, development, and education. A coloniality that works at the intersection of the cultural, ontological, existential, epistemic, territorial, cosmological, and socio-spiritual, imposing a notion of a singular world governed by the central dichotomous binary of humans over nature" (Walsh 2015, p. 103).

Your thinking on nature is what interests me here; I am interested most especially in how you postured the relation, not the separation, of humans and nature, of the human and nonhuman worlds. In your Q11§34 and in critique of Lukács, you point out the problem of dualism and the "conception of nature proper to religion and to the Graeco-Christian philosophy, and also to idealism which does not in reality succeed in unifying and relating man [sic] and nature to each other except verbally." You then go on to ask: "But if human history should be conceived also as the history of nature (also by means of the history of science), how can the dialectic be separated from nature?" (Gramsci 1971, p. 448).

In the recent book *Gramsci: Space, Nature, and Politics*, Benedetto Fontana describes your perspective as, on the one hand, attacking all forms of dualism. Gramsci's "critique of a nature and of a reality independent of human action and human history is based on his view that nature and man are intimately linked, indeed inseparable," Fontana says, "and since man to Gramsci is always rooted ineradicably in history, nature is first and always a becoming, embedded within the historical process whose actor and subject is humanity. Nature and man, subject and object, both mutually interwoven, assume form and meaning only in history" (Fontana 2013, p. 125; see Gramsci 1971, pp. 445–446). On the other hand, Fontana argues that it is in and through humanity and history (humanity as "both the creator and the creature, the subject and object, of history") that your understanding of nature takes on a more material form, and that your understanding of humans becomes that of not-nature. He suggests, as such, that your understanding of the relation between nature and society is also one of domination (Fontana 2013, pp. 127–133).

You yourself said:

One must conceive of man as a series of active relationships (a process) in which individuality, though perhaps the most important, is not, however, the only element to be taken into account. The humanity which is reflected in each individuality is composed of various elements: 1. the individual; 2. other men; 3. the natural world. . . . Man does not enter into relations with the natural world just by being himself part of the natural world, but actively, by means of work and technique. . . . In this sense the real philosopher is, and cannot be other than, the politician, the active man who modifies the environment, understanding by environment the *ensemble* of relations which each of us enters to take part in. (Gramsci 1971, p. 352; emphasis in original)

How are we to read you? Some interpret here the re-enactment of Marx's view of humans over nature. Others see in your perspective a nondualistic, practical, and relational conception to "being-in-the-world" (Wainwright 2013, p. 162) and a "dialectical approach to the mutual co-production of human and nonhuman others" (Loftus 2013, p. 181). Joel Wainwright, for example, argues that for you, nature, humanity, and society are inseparable active relations joined through the struggles of distinct social groups and related to the problem of forging critical conceptions of the world (Wainwright 2013, p. 170). In Wainwright's reading of your notebooks (which are not so distinct from mine), such conceptions are not mechanical but relational, tied to the distinct realities, histories, geographies and ways of being in the world of particular social groups. For you, Wainwright says, "political transformation requires grasping how particular conceptions of the world become effective" (Wainwright 2013, p. 164).

Key here is your questioning of conceptions of the world—including your own—and your reflections on the relation of these conceptions with collective life, self-determination, and the possibilities and problematic of integration. Such questionings and reflections point to issues of hegemony, social struggle, and "an historical, dialectical conception of the world, which understands movement and change, which appreciates the sum of effort and sacrifice which the present has cost the past and which the future is costing the present" (Gramsci 1971, pp. 34–35). Here, and more broadly, we might highlight your attention—sometimes explicit and other times implicit—to the practical activity of struggle of subalternized groups, and to a philosophy of praxis that engages the relation of nature, society, action, and the "earthliness" of thought.

In this, I consider your posture as inextricably grounded in and tied to humanity and humanization. By this I am not just referring to what Marx in *Capital* called the human element of socionatural processes. More critically and broadly, I am referring to the praxical character, action, and necessity of humanity itself. That is, on the one hand, the human process of reflecting on, being in, and transforming the world, and on the other hand, the ongoing process and struggle that subalternized peoples and groups know well—that is, rehumanization against dehumanization. This process and struggle defined much of your life, from the years after your fall as a young child and the subsequent struggles to feel and be accepted as "human" to the dehumanizing prison years reflected most poignantly in your letters to your children, your wife Giulia, and your sister-in-law Tania.

Still, your perspective, context, time, and world conception are not the same as mine. While on the one hand I can still think some things with you, on the other hand I have to think against. Against not so much as "opposition," but as "alongside"; from the possibilities afforded by the plural rather than the singular, and the challenges and horizons opened and enabled by contradictions, difference, and inter-versal (rather than uni-versal) connections. My "against" here is postured not in the frame of modernity and Western civilization, or the Occidental peripheries that Portantiero referred to with relation to Sardinia and Argentina, frames that inevitably situated you, your life, and your thought. It is postured instead from and with the decolonial processes, political pedagogies, and horizons of Abya Yala, where Nature is understood as life itself, as the integral relationality of beings (human and nonhuman, living and dead), knowledges, cosmologies, land and territorialities, and ways of being in and with the world; of coexistence or existence *with*. This moves us away from your attention to the human as modern individual.

The concept of *buen vivir* as initially postured in the Ecuador constitution (*vivir bien* in Bolivia) also finds base in this integral relationality, in a distancing from capitalism, the logics of development, and the imbalances propagated by Western civilization and its perspective of the good life (as *polis*). Neither Nature or *buen vivir* are suggestive of identity-based essentialisms, nor do they call for a return to an idealized indigenous past. They are orientations, inter-versals in the path toward a radical transformation of the social, political, economic, epistemic, and existence-based orders, transformations that continue "from below" and in and from the cracks or fissures of the system, transformations despite and regardless of the state, and despite and regardless of so-called—and top-down—revolutions.[8]

Notes Asking and in Closing

For you, Antonio, changing the world required transforming our conceptions of the world. That was your project, in your time, and in your context, first in Sardinia and later in Turin and more broadly in Italy. I wonder if you could have conceived then, or could conceive from the other world in which you are now, conceptions not just outside the Marxist tradition, but in its otherwise. I also ask about the Gramscians still left—and more generally for the Left(s) of the Global North and West—is it possible for them to learn from and think with the political, epistemic, and existence-based transformational insurgencies of the South, and most especially Abya Yala? Does this not turn the notions of the subaltern, and maybe even of hegemony—at least in the ways you initially understood them—on their heads?

With the emotion of this first re-encounter, I leave these questions with you until the next time. And one thing more in closing: despite all I have said, you remain, and probably forever will be—to use the expression of the Colombian thinker Manuel Zapata Olivella—one of my intellectual "ancestral combatants" (Zapata Olivella 2010).

NOTES

1   Composed primarily of Deborah Britzman, Juan Aulestia, and myself.
2   I am referring here to the late Canadian critical educator and not the British Gramscian scholar.
3   With the rise to power in the early 1980s of the leftist party and government of Raúl Alfonsin, the Pasado y Presente group returned to Argentina. However, the protagonism of the group's members declined in the subsequent years, as did the arguments (particularly of Portantiero) of the usefulness of your thought for the Argentinian Left and the democratic transitions.
4   In his arguments on why Gramsci in Latin America, Aricó argues: "The delimitation of Gramsci as a thinker of the 'West' makes sense only in the condition of not converting him into a 'lettered' Euro-communist and admitting that his reflections are applicable for situations not typically western." The problem, however, is that for Aricó (as well as for many other Latin American Gramscian intellectuals), the particularities of class struggle are what mark the particularity of "situations," a particularity that the Latin American Left has not always understood. "The misadventures of the Latin American Left derive from the fact that its narrow ideological paradigms have impeded the comprehension of the singularity of a

Catherine E. Walsh   **202** continent inhabited by profound and violent class struggles, but in which these [struggles] have not been principal actors of their history" (Aricó 2005, pp. 116–117). Here the interrelation of class with race, ethnicity, territoriality, and gender are once again left by the wayside.

5   Under the government of Lenín Moreno (2017–), there is a noted shift to re-establish ties with the United States, although China still controls a large portion of the extractive industry.

6   See "La dueda con China suma USD 6 395 milones," *El Comercio*, March 24, 2016, http://www.elcomercio.com/actualidad/deuda-ecuador-china-suma-millones.html.

7   Isaac Carrillo, presentation of *Danzas de la noche*, Duke University, February 2013.

8   Of course, one of the key problems today with respect to *buen vivir* is its cooptation by state in ways that empty it of its critical significance and make it synonymous with "development." See Walsh 2010.

12

Gramsci and the Chinese Left

Reappraising a Missed Encounter

PU WANG

Gramsci as a "Chinese Comrade": Time Lag and Contemporaneity

Can we examine the Chinese Left, its history and its present fate, through the lens of a Gramsci-China parallel or dialogue, a dialogue that actually did not happen *on time*? Ever since the late 1990s, Antonio Gramsci (1891–1937) has indeed gradually become a noticeable presence in the critical discourse in China and a source for frequent invocations or appeals among contemporary Chinese intellectuals. Many have drawn attention to the parallel between Gramsci and the Chinese Left. Such a parallel, however, has to be defined as a missed encounter. Gramsci's intellectual endeavors and China's protracted revolution (from the 1920s through the Maoist Cultural Revolution) were developed in isolation from each other; more precisely, they were "imprisoned" in their own uneven developments and therefore were "exceptional" in their own ways.[1] Yet on the other hand, as I shall demonstrate in detail, Gramsci and the Chinese Left were responding to some similar cultural, political, and social situations that characterized a shared moment of what I call the international interwar period. Liu Kang, for example, famously called Gramsci and Chinese leftists *wei xianghui de zhanyou* (Liu Kang 2002, p. 86), meaning "comrades-in-arm who never met with each other."

This chapter is not interested in providing a study of the Gramsci reception in mainland China, yet it has to start with the time lag in China's encounter with the Italian Marxist thinker and revolutionary. When Gramsci's lifework was first introduced to China, it was already eight years after the founding of the People's Republic of China. In 1957 the first Chinese biography of Gramsci appeared amid the high waves of the socialist transformation and construction. A forgotten yet highly suggestive historical detail is worth mentioning here. In fact, it was also in the 1950s that Gramsci's works were introduced into the English-speaking world. George Derwent Thomson, a British Marxist scholar and activist who later became a sympathizer of Maoism, proposed in his 1957 review of *The Modern Prince and Other Writings* a comparison between Gramsci and Mao Zedong: "Just as Mao Tse-tung set himself the task of applying the general truths of Marxism to the Chinese revolution, so Gramsci applied those truths to the Italian revolution" (Thomson 1957, p. 61).

But in Maoist China's celebration of an international solidarity of communism, Gramsci was primarily portrayed as a revolutionary martyr rather than a political thinker. The potential relevance of Gramsci's strategic thinking to China's revolutionary path never really entered the theoretical consciousness of Mao's party, which became, in the 1960s and 1970s, preoccupied with both the antirevisionist debate about the "historical experiences of proletarian dictatorship" and the ultileftist alternative of "continued revolution." Despite the appearance of two more biographies of Gramsci in socialist China, the Chinese reception of what Thomson deemed the "first Italian Marxist" remained minimal—until the translation of Perry Anderson's *Consideration on Western Marxism* in 1981, which was made possible by the end of the Cultural Revolution and the ensuing initiation of the reforms. As Xin Liu has shown in his study of Gramsci's presence in China, Anderson's book "reintroduced Chinese intellectuals to this leading figure of the Western Communist movement who had been forgotten for almost twenty years" (Liu 2011, p. 71). It is then necessary to bear in mind that this post-Maoist interest in Gramsci's work was inextricably intertwined with the introduction of Western Marxism, an alternative discourse to which Chinese leftist intellectuals turned in the wake of their disillusionment with the Leninist party-state and the Maoist social experiments.

In other words, Gramsci's entry into Chinese intellectual discourses was, perhaps ironically, coincidental with China's "farewell to revolution." In 1992, the Central Bureau of Translation of Marx, Engel, Lenin, and Stalin, China's official institution responsible for the publication of international communist movement materials, published its own translation of Gramsci's *Selected*

Works in Chinese. One could hardly find a more unwelcoming atmosphere for Gramsci's work: in the same year, Deng Xiaoping (1904–1997) made his final push for economic reforms during the southern tour, arguing that the socialist state and the market economy could coexist perfectly. The whole country, still recovering from the trauma of the 1989 social movements and the Tian'anmen Square incident, showed an impetuous tendency to embrace the systematic marketization and capitalization in a post–Cold War brave new world. In the meanwhile, official Marxism—that is, the ideology of the Marx-Lenin-Mao synthesis—lost the last bit of theoretical luster in China; even the attraction to Western Marxism waned, whereas postmodernism started to be celebrated in response to the rapid commercialization and commodification of social relationships in a promarket party-state. Due to this widespread weariness with leftist discourses, Chinese scholars' initial responses to the *Prison Notebooks* were "either lukewarm or totally indifferent" (Liu 2011, p. 72).

It was only when the shocking consequences and social costs of China's economic boom started to be widely felt and the debates broke out against the neoliberal-developmentalist complex of market fetishism toward the end of the 1990s that Gramsci's work emerged as an important point of reference in the intellectual world of contemporary China. The discourse critical of the dominant global and local consensuses of neoliberalism was to be labeled—initially pejoratively—as China's "New Left" (*xin zuo pai*). Against this background of the New Left versus liberalism, Gramsci gained new currency and was associated with the scholarly trends of cultural studies, postcolonialism, and subaltern studies in the first decade of this century in China. Gramsci's concept of hegemony, in particular, has been widely and often freely used. It is now translated as *baquan* in Chinese, with a strong connotation of cultural hegemony, and as a result, the concept's link with the Leninist-Maoist emphasis on *lingdao quan* (leadership) is more or less blurred—an issue that has recently triggered new discussions and will be addressed later on here.

Commenting on the belated renown of Gramsci in parts of Europe other than Italy, Perry Anderson ended his 1976 essay with the following statement: "We have yet to be sufficiently contemporary with our past" (Anderson 1976, p. 78). What I find most meaningful in the equally interesting time lag of China's reception of Gramsci is that in postrevolutionary contemporary hindsight, we can finally start to be contemporary with the past represented by Gramsci's thought, and also the past of the Chinese Left. More precisely, it is after the Leninist-Maoist party politics exhausted its revolutionary potential and the socialist institutions were dismantled both in China and globally that leftists had to confront the contemporaneity of the two legacies—one of Gramsci's thought, the other of the Chinese Revolution. In contrast to the time lag, in my view, any serious engagement with Gramsci's work in the discussions about *contemporary* China must be built on a critical return to the parallel—a missed encounter, a forgotten *contemporaneity*—between Gramsci and the Chinese leftist movement from the 1920s onward as a radical process of strategic reorientations and experiments. With a series of variations of time lag and contemporaneity, my aim is, first, to engage critically the pre-existing comparisons between Gramsci's theory and Chinese Marxism; second, to deprovincialize Gramsci from the context of "Western Europe" and show in the interwar period a shared international moment when strategies for revolutionary "hegemony" (translated by Qu Qiubai as *lingxiuquan*) were articulated, imagined, practiced, and debated in different national situations; third, to apply Gramsci's theory to a re-examination of the uneven yet dialectical combination of the politicization of armed struggle and the military art of the cultural "war of position" (represented in the work of Lu Xun) in revolutionary China; and finally, to unveil the relationship of Gramsci's conceptualization of the "national-popular" with China's leftist politics of "the people"(*renmin*) and conclude with speculations on the relevance of the *Prison Notebooks* to today's China.

Gramsci and Mao: Arif Dirlik's Comparison

In 1983 Arif Dirlik, an important scholarly voice defending China's leftist legacies in the post-Mao era, offered a Gramsci-Mao comparison to the English-speaking world by publishing "The Predicament of Marxist Revolutionary Consciousness: Mao Zedong, Antonio Gramsci, and the Reformulation of Marxist Revolutionary Theory." At the outset, Dirlik's observation assumes Gramsci as the theory and Mao as the practice:

> At the risk of sounding outrageous, it is possible to observe, I think, that Mao did what Gramsci thought. Mao was not given to theoretical speculation for its own sake. The considerations underlying his revolutionary practice remain imbedded in his revolutionary activity and writings, which were invariably practical in purpose. Gramsci, equally practice oriented, was nevertheless forced into speculation by the tragic circumstances of his life. The concept of hegemony, which he elaborated in his prison cell to cope with the problems of Italian politics, very often reads, at least for a novice in Gramsci's thought, as a description of Mao's activities. (Dirlik 1983, p. 184)

Dirlik was concerned with a central question in the evaluation of Maoism: why did the Chinese Revolution obsess over the issue of consciousness, culture, and cultural revolution? He turned to Gramsci's idea of hegemony for an answer. Mao's agenda of New Democracy (a Chinese version of a popular united front that led to the building of the "people's democratic dictatorship" codified in the constitution) "appears as a drama enacted under the direction of the idea of hegemony" (Dirlik 1983, p. 203). Due to the protracted nature of Chinese revolution, the Chinese Communist Party (CCP) emphasized the importance of leadership suffusing across social classes. Mao's Sinification of Marxism also bears a close resemblance to Gramsci's idea of a national-popular culture. In a way, one may see Dirlik's efforts as finding new ways to articulate or theorize an international relevance of Maoism when it was denounced both domestically and globally. He went as far as to say "Gramsci might have been Mao announcing the Cultural Revolution" (Dirlik 1983, p. 203). But of course, Dirlik was aware of the divergences between Gramsci and Mao; he reminded the reader that for Gramsci, hegemony was an issue related to bourgeois civil society. In Gramsci's work, "civil society" often means the economic working of society. The socioeconomic formation of modern China takes its particular form in contrast to the history of European bourgeois societies. In the meanwhile, the conceptual applicability of "civil society"—translated into Chinese as *shimin shehui* or *gongmin shehui*—in the studies of Chinese society and history has long been a trigger of controversy and debate among both Marxist revolutionaries and academic scholars.

The most important conclusion of Dirlik's comparison pertains to the issue of revolutionary consciousness as a central predicament for twentieth-century Marxism. Gramsci and Mao reached the very limit, in both theory and practice, of Leninist ideal of the party as the vanguard of class consciousness: "This parallel recognition of the problem of culture and consciousness by Mao and Gramsci adds a new dimension to the understanding of Marxist revolutionary theory, and in particular to the relationship between revolutionary consciousness and the consciousness of the culture that revolutionaries find at hand" (Dirlik 1983, p. 204). Both the Italian and Chinese Marxists refused to see class identity in an abstract and purely deterministic fashion, and they argued to define class consciousness on the basis of a dynamic of social experience and a process of constant becoming. "A truly hegemonic class . . . 'articulated other interests to its own.' . . . A class that seeks to establish its hegemony must likewise come to terms with its culture and society" (Dirlik 1983, pp. 204–205). Mao and Gramsci held onto the model of the Leninist party, but in struggles against the alienation of the party from the masses they "realized the need to integrate the party closely with the working classes the party sought to represent" (Dirlik 1983, p. 206). Resonating with Gramsci's theory, "Mao's idea of the mass line, which was intended to achieve leadership rather than the domination of the masses, may be the closest approximation to a political solution of the problems of class consciousness and identity" (Dirlik 1983, p. 207). However, Dirlik immediately added that "it is, at best, only an approximation," as it fails to "abolish the separation from people" (Dirlik 1983, p. 207).

At least to a certain degree, Dirlik's observation echoed the widespread feeling that twentieth-century communist practice had failed. While Perry Anderson (1979) traced the roots of Western Marxism in a profound sense of the historical defeat of revolutionary Marxism in the West (advanced capitalist countries), in the early 1980s Dirlik was writing against the downfall of radical leftism in China in particular, and the twilight of socialism in the East and Third World in general. His implicit assignment of Gramsci to thought and Mao to activity seems to have also confirmed the deeper issue of the split or uneven development between theory and practice, an issue that Gramsci and Mao had actually tried painstakingly to overcome. Dirlik concluded by stating: "And the line between leadership and domination is easily confused as long as power is concentrated in the hands of the party organization—as the Chinese experience past and present has shown. Socialists must still face the challenge of discovering a political strategy that is at once democratic and loyal to the vision of social and economic equality" (Dirlik 1983, p. 207). This critique of Leninist party politics was to be radically developed in Ernesto Laclau and Chantal Mouffe's reformulation of the Gramscian idea of hegemony, in which the two theorists attempted to carry Gramsci's thought beyond the Leninist rigidity and to provide the logic of "articulation" as a new basis for radical democracy. According to Laclau and Mouffe, Gramsci's conception of the "democratic practice of hegemony" is still "unable fully to overcome the dualism of classical Marxism. For Gramsci, even though the diverse social elements have a merely relational identity—achieved through articulatory practice—there must always be a single unifying principle in every hegemonic formation" (Laclau and Mouffe 2014, p. 59). Laclau and Mouffe's diagnosis of this "essentialist core" in Gramsci pertains in a crucial sense to the historical experience of Chinese Marxism, but can also be seen as yet a leftist version of bidding farewell to socialist revolution.

Qu Qiubai and the Concept of Hegemony

Another tangible and more concrete point of comparison between Gramsci's thought and Chinese leftism was brought up in Liu Kang's work in the mid-1990s. Faced with a new reality of the post–Cold War capitalist globalization,

Kang Liu pointed out that the academic Left of the West appropriated Gramsci's work as an anti-essentialist discourse regarding "contemporary cultural issues that have little to do with social revolution" (Liu 1997, p. 69). Discontented with the farewell to revolution, Liu proposed a return to the contemporaneity of Gramsci and Chinese Marxists in terms of their shared focus on hegemony and cultural revolution. He drew particular attention to another Marxist thinker and activist, Qu Qiubai.

Qu Qiubai (1899–1935) was an important modern Chinese literary critic and intellectual who championed the turn to Marxism following the May Fourth new culture movement (1917–1925)—which has long been considered as China's own enlightenment movement. Like Gramsci, Qu Qiubai went to Moscow and participated in the Third Congress of the Communist International in 1921. Just as Gramsci raised the "southern question" in the Italian context, so Qu was the first to introduce to the whole party Mao's report on peasants' movements during the final days of the 1925 to 1927 National Revolution, the first non-Western revolution in which the Communist Party played a vital role. In 1927, the right-wing sect of the Guomindang (also known as the Kuomintang or the Nationalist Party; GMD hereafter) severed the coalition with the CCP, a coalition that had been the core of a national bourgeois-democratic revolution, leading to what was to be known as the "tragedy of the Chinese Revolution."[2] Amid the collapse of the united front and the nationwide massacre of communists in 1927, Qu became the interim general secretary of CCP for a short and chaotic period of time. In the final decade of his life, as Liu has argued, "Qu Qiubai's thought overlapped and intersected in many areas with Gramsci's." In particular, "his critique of the Western hegemony of modernity in May Fourth thought and his theory and practice of rural cultural revolution contributed centrally to the establishment of a Chinese Marxism" (Liu 1997, p. 73). In the wake of the failure of the first revolutionary united front, Qu mounted powerful attacks on the "Europeanization" of the bourgeois national literature and culture created by the May Fourth enlightenment, and called for—and eventually experimented on—a new cultural reform based on "the language of the masses" (dazhong yu). Similar to Gramsci's interest in the national-popular culture, Qu Qiubai proposed the culture of the masses, argued for the vulgar language as a potential literary language, and experimented with the romanization of the Chinese written system in order to fight against illiteracy among workers and peasants and disseminate the revolutionary culture. His characterization of the May Fourth generation of urban Chinese intellectuals as "wondering bohemians" (Qu 1985, p. 113), alienated from traditional China but politically rootless or sentimental, is also reminiscent of Gramsci's relentless diagnosis of the modern Italian intellectuals' social-political weaknesses. Qu participated in both the CCP-led urban cultural warfare and the military struggles in the countryside (the latter of which resulted in the birth of Maoism). When the Chinese Red Army was forced by the GMD's military campaigns to start the Long March—a strategic retreat from southern to northwestern China, with a high human cost—Qu was left behind in the chaos and soon arrested by the GMD. Whereas Gramsci suffered a long sentence under the Fascist rule, Qu was executed by the GMD in 1935, only months after his arrest.

However, for Lik-Kwan Cheung, a scholar based in Hong Kong, Liu's illuminating account remains unsatisfactory, as it does not go beyond the realm of Marxist cultural theory despite its intention to bring to the fore the issue of revolutionary practice. In contrast to the attention Liu once drew to Qu's critique of the Europeanization of modern Chinese culture and his proposal of a national-popular culture, Cheung's 2010 essay—in my view, one of the most important articles published on Gramsci in Chinese since the turn of this century—emphasizes the role of both Gramsci and Qu as strategic thinkers of communist revolutionary practice. In particular, Cheung's essay, titled "The Modern Prince and the Organic Intellectual: On Qu Qiubai, Gramsci, and the Formation of the Hegemony Theory," unearths the shared ground of the uses of the concept of hegemony in both Gramsci's work and the Chinese leftist tradition.

First, Cheung turns to Perry Anderson's account of the metamorphosis of hegemony as a concept in communist movements from the Russian social-democratic tradition to the Third International and the case of Gramsci. Cheung suggest that the genealogy Anderson offers is more "concrete and reliable" than that provided by Laclau and Mouffe (Cheung 2010, p. 38). Anderson's 1976 study stresses that the concept of hegemony was not Gramsci's creation; rather, this notion "had a long prior history" (Anderson 1976, p. 15), especially in the Russian revolutionary practice from the late nineteenth century all the way to the October Revolution. In the Leninist or Bolshevist political discourse, hegemony (*gegemoniya*) meant a theoretical debate on the leadership of "the working class in a bourgeois revolution" (Anderson 1976, p. 20), whereas Gramsci had to confront the reality of socialist revolution's ebbing and the "mechanisms of bourgeois rule over the working class in a stabilized capitalist society" (Anderson 1976, p. 20). At the Fourth Congress in 1922, the Comintern "for the first time internationalized Russian usages of the slogan of hegemony," calling for the proletariat's "hegemony over the other exploited groups that were its class allies in the struggle against capitalism" (Anderson 1976,

p. 18). Gramsci participated in that congress, and his treatment of the term *hegemony* (*egemonia*) in the later *Prison Notebooks* in fact directly derived from the Comintern's definitions. Yet, he not only extended or generalized this concept but also reoriented it "toward the advanced capitalist countries of Western Europe" (Anderson 1976, p. 22), where the bourgeois civil society was an almost impenetrable bloc and the capitalist rule was based not only on coercion but also on consent. "This was a new and decisive step" (Anderson 1976, p. 20).

While Anderson is primarily concerned with the questions that Gramsci's ambiguous treatment of hegemony raised (and failed to answer, according to Anderson's conclusion) about the difficulties of socialist revolution in the advanced capitalist West, Cheung attempts to trace the "travel of a theory" into the protracted Chinese Revolution (Cheung 2010, p. 37), an "Eastern" case that was qualitatively different from both the Western-European situation and the Russian-Bolshevik experience. Qu also attended the Comintern's Fourth Congress (though we have no evidence that he and Gramsci met in Moscow), and by then he was already an excellent Chinese translator of Russian sources. As Cheung has reminded us, Qu must have been familiar with Lenin's debates on *gegemoniya*, and he is by consensus considered to be one of the first Chinese leftists to raise the Leninist issue of the working class's leadership in China's democratic revolution in the 1920s. The Chinese term Qu employed was *lingxiuquan* (leadership, or more literally, the leader's power), which later lost its currency to another more commonly used word, *lingdaoquan* (literally, the leading power, or the right to lead). As Cheung has convincingly indicated, it was during the crisis of the CCP's first alliance with the GMD that Qu explicitly confirmed that the English equivalent of his term *lingxiuquan* was "hegemony." In a long 1927 article titled "The Polemical Issues in the Chinese Revolution," Qu emphasized the question about which class is the "class-hegemony" in the united front, and tried to elaborate on the struggle for "hegemony" between the proletariat and bourgeoisie (Qu 1989, p. 435). By providing the two keywords both in Chinese and English, Qu coined *lingxiuquan* as hegemony. As a result, Cheung parallels Qu's focus on *lingxiuquan* (hegemony and leadership) and Gramsci's ambiguous employment of *egemonia* and *direzione*, and argues that they at least shared the "same political-theoretical source" of Leninism and the Third International (Cheung 2010, p. 41).

The major breakthrough of Cheung's theoretical scrutiny not only concerns the itinerary of a revolutionary terminology. More important, it shifts the current focus of the Gramscian discourse in China and reconnects it to China's own tradition of strategic thinking and practice of class hegemony/ leadership in a situation where the national democratic revolution was yet to be accomplished. In contemporary China, Gramsci's notion of hegemony, as I mentioned earlier, is translated as *baquan*. Following the anti-essentialist and anti-Leninist fashion of Laclau and Mouffe, this theoretical term is now understood primarily in the sense of "cultural hegemony" (*wenhua baquan*). Resisting this overemphasis on culture in current interpretations of Gramsci's notebooks, Cheung urges us to translate Gramsci's *egemonia/direzione* back into Qu's term *lingxiuquan*, and to see Gramsci's work as a discourse on the revolutionary strategy that was in deep dialogue with the Chinese Left.

In my view, Cheung's account can best help us revisit the international interwar period as a shared moment of global revolutionary debates that were not necessarily divided into "West," Russia ("East"), and "non-West," as one may initially assume. Anderson has indicated that the disputes that involved Gramsci and many other European Marxists "represent the last great strategic debate in the European workers' movement" in the twentieth century; but actually, Gramsci's thought also speaks volumes to the non-Western Marxists' search for a solution to how to adopt the Leninist line to their own national situations. Precisely because Gramsci and Qu, among many others, based their own reflections on the vastly different *national* realities and experiences, their interventions into the Leninist tradition formed an *international* contemporaneity of revolutionary intensity.

With this act of "de-provincializing" Marxism (Harootunian 2015, pp. 1–20), we can see more historically and politically why Gramsci and Qu are "comrades in arms." As Cheung notes, the world-historic significance of the sudden October Revolution as the true beginning of the twentieth century played a key role in the two's subjective formation as revolutionaries (Cheung 2010, pp. 51–56). Liu Kang also suggests that "the many parallels between Qu Qiubai and Gramsci are not surprising once the historical contexts in which they formulated their concepts are compared" (Liu 1997, p. 74). In their efforts to become a new type of intellectual for the modern Leninist-Jacobin party/prince, the defeats suffered by post–October Revolution leftist movements conditioned their theoretical and strategic reflections. Gramsci's reorientation had its roots in the response to the failure of the "war of manoeuver" in the March Action in Germany and the great blow struck at the young Italian party by the Fascist ascendancy. He offered a note about the fight for hegemony: "The politico-historical criterion on which our own inquiries must be grounded is this: that a class is dominant in two ways, namely it is 'leading' [*dirigente*] and 'dominant' [*dominante*]. It leads the allied classes, it dominates the opposing classes" (Q2§70; trans. Gramsci 1992–2007, vol. 1, p. 136). In 1927, the catastrophe of the White Terror following the downfall of the united front and the rise of the nationalist right wing also dealt an almost fatal blow to the young CCP. According to Qu, during that unsuccessful national revolution orchestrated by the Third International, the CCP failed to keep its own leadership in the alliance with the national bourgeoisie, and on the other hand, failed to build on the political energy of the peasants. Qu's insistence on *lingxiuquan* (as Cheung has shown) and his proposal of cultural reforms (as is emphasized in Liu's account) for the masses were both based on a critique of the incompleteness of the bourgeois enlightenment and revolution in China and a search for the new subjectivity of class alliance. This condition predetermined the Chinese Left's protracted experience of the military art of both political and cultural struggles.

Lu Xun and the Military Art

As is well known, Quintin Hoare and Geoffrey Nowell Smith, in an attempt to clarify and specify Gramsci's theory of hegemony, translated *dirigente* in the above-cited passage as "intellectual and moral leadership," in contrast to the "domination" or "liquidation" by (potentially and ultimately military) force: "The supremacy of a social group manifests itself in two ways, as 'domination' and as 'intellectual and moral leadership.' A social group dominates antagonistic groups, which it tends to 'liquidate,' or 'subjugate' perhaps even by armed force; it leads kindred and allied groups" (Gramsci 1971, p. 57).

A lot of critical attention has been paid to the Chinese Left's long march toward a political hegemony, or a liquidation of both internal and external enemies. Following the traumatic experience of the 1925 to 1927 National Revolution, the issue of political leadership and military struggle developed into a vital preoccupation of the CCP's consciousness, eventually giving rise to a Maoist military science, with Mao as the supreme artist of warfare, summarized in the famous mantra: "Political power grows out of the barrel of a gun."[3] The Chinese Revolution then has long been interpreted as a historical encyclopedia of (both positive and negative) military experiences, encompassing urban putsches, peasants' uprisings, the military base in the countryside (the starting point of Mao's line) and guerilla warfare, the tragic-heroic Long March (a strategic retreat), the "protracted war" against the Japanese invasion, the post-1945 negotiations and the all-out civil war (something similar to a "war of position"), the takeover of mainland China (a decisive seizure of power and "war of manoeuver"), the internationalist warfare in Korea, the brutal repression of antirevolutionary forces (militarizing tactics of social reforms), the chaotic fights among ultra-leftist rebellious groups, and eventually the "palace coup" against ultra-leftism.

Corresponding to this richness of military struggles was the militarization of the Maoist discourse itself—a discourse characterized by a "philosophy of struggle" (*douzheng zhexue*) in the first place—so much so that political leadership always also meant military leadership and any struggle followed the military command in a warfare for such a political leadership. As Chen Yue, a leading contemporary Chinese interpreter of Gramsci's work, has stated, this case was an epitome of the widespread dissemination of the military terminology and science (predominantly deriving from the work of Clausewitz) in the leftist political language, running from Engels to Kautsky, Luxemburg, Lenin, Trotsky, and Mao. Mao's discourse of "people's war" (*renmin zhanzheng*) is then the ultimate "return of military antagonism to the political," whereas for Gramsci, "war is the hidden code of the civil society."[4] This observation can be traced back to Laclau and Mouffe's critique of the Marxist-Leninist tradition: "From Kautsky to Lenin, the Marxist conception of politics rested upon an imaginary owing a great deal to Clausewitz." Re-examining this militarization of politics, Laclau and Mouffe remark, "From Kautsky's 'war of attribution' to the extreme militarism of the Bolshevization drive and 'class against class,' the establishment of a strict dividing line was considered the very condition of politics—'politics' being conceived simply as one of the terrains of *class* struggle." Emphasizing Gramsci's concept of "intellectual and moral leadership," their philosophy of radical democracy argues that "war of position" represents a more fluid and in effect demilitarizing approach to the political within the civil society that resists the pre-fixed class identities: "Indeed, the military metaphor is here metaphorized in the opposite direction: if in Leninism there was a militarization of politics, in Gramsci there is a demilitarization of war" (Laclau and Mouffe 2014, p. 60).

What has been overshadowed by the legacy of Mao's military-political encirclement of the cities by the countryside is the critical importance of the cultural, intellectual, and moral arena (or in the CCP's own parlance, the work of the cultural front and the united front) in the GMD-controlled urban region where direct class warfare was all but impossible. Liu Kang has argued that "in light of Gramsci's theory, a main feature of the Chinese revolutionary legacy can be seen as the construction and consolidation of a revolutionary hegemony through cultural revolution" (Liu 1997, p. 71). I would further contend here that in the Leninist-Maoist practice there was in fact no "strict dividing line" between the military-political struggle (based in the countryside to the extent that the CCP was seen as a party of the peasants) and the cultural revolution (whose existence in the urban region is easily forgotten); rather, what defined the experience of the Chinese Revolution as a whole was an overdetermined (and therefore uneven yet sometimes highly productive) complementariness and interpenetration of the two "fronts." It is in my view necessary to confront this dialectical entanglement of the politicization of military domination and the militarization of cultural-intellectual-moral leadership at every historical conjuncture and moment.

In order to reach a Gramscian military reading of cultural hegemony, one needs to inquire into the role of Lu Xun in the history of the Chinese Left. Lu Xun (1881–1936) is considered by consensus to be the most important twentieth-century Chinese writer and intellectual, famous for his critical vigor, modernist depth, and spiritual militancy. Here we need to focus on the last and perhaps most controversial decade of his life, during which he became a leading figure in China's left-wing literary, cultural, and artistic movements. In his 1933 introduction to Lu Xun's works, Qu iconized Lu Xun by analyzing the latter's intellectual-political trajectory from "evolution theory to class theory," "from a rebel against the feudal gentry to a true friend of the proletariat and working class, and even to a fighter" (Qu 1985, p. 115). For Qu, Lu Xun eventually moved his position to the new "entrenchment" (*haoqian*) of the Chinese Left. When proposing the agenda of "New Democracy" (Mao's version of a national-popular front with the CCP hegemony, see later discussion) in 1940, Mao looked back at the formation of the Chinese Left and famously enshrined Lu Xun as the "chief commander of China's cultural revolution" (Mao [1940] 1965, p. 372).

This militarized language existed not only as a metaphorical framework in the revolutionary idolization of Lu Xun. The militarization of literature was a major creative trait and productive mode of Lu Xun's leftist writings and activities. During the years on the Left from 1928 to 1936, he contributed a newly invented genre of *zawen* to China's revolutionary literature. *Zawen*, usually translated as "miscellaneous essay," was a polemical form of essay writing, representing the most impure (and therefore politically productive) status of Chinese literary modernity. Just as Mao's strategy found in the heartland countryside the weak link of the semifeudal, semicolonial society of China, so Lu Xun's creation of *zawen* was able to find a weak link of "print capitalism" within what today's scholars call "Shanghai modern." He managed to do so by becoming a "military tactician" of essay writing: he constantly changed his pen names, shifted the positions of literary barracks among different publishing venues, played "hide and seek" with the GMD censorship by using all kinds of typographical tricks, and, above all, constantly strived to open up a polemic space, by confrontation, in the ever-shrinking literary sphere. That does not mean, however, that Lu Xun transformed a literary sphere into a political tribunal for revolution. On the contrary, it was a matter of incorporating all these practical "tactics" into his aesthetical and stylistic "decision making" of *zawen* writing as a minor literature, and creating a frontier of true revolutionary literature in which the revolutionary politics could unfold itself in concrete terms rather than degenerating into an empty ideal or pure slogan chanting. By doing so, he pushed literature into a zero degree of "literariness," in which writing had to take the risk of being nonliterary in order to fulfill its role in a revolutionary crisis. Hence, *zawen* meant grammatological guerilla. In Lu Xun's own words: "The essays that live on must be daggers and javelins" (Lu 1980, vol. 3, p. 343). Within every polemical piece of *zawen*, one can witness a literary "war of maneuver" on a miniature scale.

But taken together, the numerous *zawen* outputs constituted a tireless, laborious, and patient "war of position" for cultural, intellectual, and moral leadership. Collecting his *zawen* pieces into a book in 1932, Lu Xun envisioned a volume that would also include all the attacks he received from both reactionaries and ultra-leftists, a volume he would call *Weijiao ji* (Encirclement campaign; Lu 1980, vol. 3, p. 173). In other words, the counterattacks he mounted in his *zawen* works formed a seemingly impossible and yet constant campaign of antiencirclement and counteroffensive at the urban center of the GMD's rule in semifeudal, semicolonial China during the dark times that revisionist historians would later call the golden age of Chinese bourgeoisie. *Zawen* writing was given its avant-gardist definition by Qu: "fighting feuilleton" (Qu 1985, p. 86). Qu also perceptively characterized Lu Xun's war of position as "resilient fighting" and, in a Gramscian spirit, "a war of entrenchment" under the White Terror (Qu 1985, p. 118). This combination of "war of maneuver" and "war of position" was prefigured in a prose poem Lu Xun composed in 1925. In that poem's existentialist language, literature is on the one hand the "shield," meaning a stoic resistance against illusion, emptiness, and despair, and on the other hand, writing is an audacious act of "flinging," of throwing away one's remaining life (Lu 1980, vol. 1, pp. 326–327).

Lu Xun's military rhetoric of antiencirclement calls to mind the CCP's military struggles against the GMD's offensives of "encirclement" in the same period of time. After the CCP found its new base region in Yan'an, Mao, who had started to gain the central leadership in the party, declared the survival of the Red Army through all the GMD's offensives. Lu Xun's activities were geographically and tactically isolated from these armed struggles. But in Mao's retrospective characterization of the years 1927–1937—which were also Gramsci's ten years in prison—as the period of first revolutionary civil war, Lu Xun's work figured prominently and was put on equal footing with the beginning of the CCP's long armed struggle. The importance of Mao's summary warrants a lengthy quote:

The third period was the new revolutionary period of 1927–37. As a change had taken place within the revolutionary camp towards the end of the second period, with the big bourgeoisie going over to the counter-revolutionary camp of the imperialist and feudal forces and the national bourgeoisie trailing after it, only three of the four classes formerly within the revolutionary camp remained; that is, the proletariat, the peasantry and the other sections of the petty bourgeoisie (including the revolutionary intellectuals), and consequently the Chinese revolution inevitably entered a new period in which the Chinese Communist Party alone gave leadership to the masses. This period was one of counter-revolutionary campaigns of "encirclement and suppression," on the one hand, and of the deepening of the revolution, on the other. There were two kinds of counter-revolutionary campaigns of "encirclement and suppression," the military and the cultural. The deepening of the revolution was of two kinds; both the agrarian and the cultural revolutions were deepened. At the instigation of the imperialists, the counter-revolutionary forces of the whole country and of the whole world were mobilized for both kinds of campaigns of "encirclement and suppression," which lasted no less than ten years and were unparalleled in their ruthlessness; hundreds of thousands of Communists and young students were slaughtered and millions of workers and peasants suffered cruel persecution. The people responsible for all this apparently had no doubt that communism and the Communist Party could be "exterminated once and for all." However, the outcome was different; both kinds of "encirclement and suppression" campaigns failed miserably. The military campaign resulted in the northern march of the Red Army to resist the Japanese, and the cultural campaign resulted in the outbreak of the December 8th Movement of the revolutionary youth in 1935. . . . The most amazing thing of all was that the Kuomintang's cultural "encirclement and suppression" campaign failed completely in the Kuomintang areas as well, although the Communist Party was in an utterly defenceless position in all the cultural and educational institutions there. Why did this happen? . . . It was in the very midst of such campaigns of "encirclement and suppression" that Lu Hsun, who believed in communism, became the giant of China's cultural revolution. (Mao [1940] 1965, p. 376)

According to this account, there were two battle fronts in the revolutionary civil war; Mao was the leader of the military struggle in the base region, whereas Lu Xun, a nonparty writer, a communist sympathizer, championed the cultural warfare in the urban region. More important, Mao emphasized that these two fronts were unevenly developed but at the same time inseparable and even integral to each other. Lu Xun was living in a China segmented by the Japanese invasion, imperialism, semicolonialism, and the country/city divide. Like Gramsci in prison, he was isolated in his Shanghai study, cut off from any direct links to the revolutionary struggles in the countryside. But his militarization of literature showed the possibility of a strategy in the nonmilitary struggle for hegemony under a highly counterrevolutionary regime, and his lonely labor of *zawen* writing bore a distant yet powerful correspondence to the military-political front. For example, toward the end of his life, in resistance to widespread fatalism, Lu Xun wrote:

> Since ancient times we have had men and women who worked doggedly in silence, who worked stubbornly at the risk of their lives, who strove to save others, who braved death to seek the truth. . . . Even now there are many such men and women. They have firm convictions and do not deceive themselves. When one in front falls others behind fight on. It is only because they are trampled on, kept out of the news, smothered in darkness, that most people have no means of knowing of them. . . . Whether self-confidence exists or not cannot be seen from the writings of scholars and minsters—to find it we have to look underground. (Lu 1980, vol. 4, p. 130)

This passage contains an implicit and unmistakable reference to the CCP and its army—the invisible and "underground" fighters for Lu Xun—surviving the long retreat in the remote parts of China. Another link between Lu Xun's stoic "warfare" and the CCP's survival comes from a piece written on his deathbed: "While outside night took its course, and all that infinite space, those innumerable people, were linked in some way with me. I breathed, I lived, I should live on. I began to feel more substantial and experienced an urge to action" (vol. 4, p. 307). Within this "infinite" united front in a dark Shanghai night for a sick lonely fighter, the Chinese Revolution emerged as a "substantial" whole, at least poetically.

My purpose here, again, is not only to draw attention to the terrain of cultural revolution that has been less studied with regard to the long Chinese Revolution, but also to demonstrate that there was a dialectical entanglement of war of maneuver and war of position, the fight for military domination and the labor for cultural-intellectual leadership. The unevenness and remote correspondence between Mao and Lu Xun, two faces of the military art of the Chinese Left, amounts to an actual and contemporaneous correlative of the problems raised in Gramsci's notebooks.

From the "National-Popular" Bloc to Contemporary China

We have seen how both Gramsci and the Chinese Left represented the intensity and complexity of the interwar debates on revolutionary strategies. To conclude, we may turn to another issue of Gramsci's theory that corresponded to the later development of China's leftist movements. That is the issue of the "national-popular" culture and the social "bloc."

Chen Yue devotes one of his recent interpretations of Gramsci's notebooks in Chinese to the concept of the "national-popular." What looms large in Chen's reading is a related notion that was of great importance to the Chinese Revolution: the people (*renmin*). How to conceptualize/politicize "the people"? From Rousseau's ideal of the people's sovereignty as the collective will to the French Revolution, from the nineteenth-century traditions of socialist movements to the Russian and Chinese communist practices, this question haunted modern emancipatory politics. Furthermore: how to develop the political organization (the party) and the "high culture" (and a new type of intellectuals) of "the people"? As the Chinese translator of Gramsci's *Modern Prince*, Chen goes so far as to assert that the "popular nature of the modern prince" (that is, the Jacobin vanguard party) is nothing but the "revolutionary potential of the people" (Chen, "Ruhe").

On this note, I wound scrutinize some less cited passages in the *Prison Notebooks*, showing that Gramsci's formulation of the national-popular was in fact associated with his reading of modern China. In an entry devoted to "the national-popular" in the fifth notebook, Gramsci directly compares the "more restricted meaning" of the "national" and "popular" in Italian with the Chinese case in the "three principles of Sun Yat-sen's national-popular politics" (Q5§122; trans. Gramsci 1992–2007, vol. 2, p. 362). The pioneering Chinese revolutionary Sun Yat-Sen's doctrine San Min Chu I—sometimes rendered as the Three People's Principles—is almost untranslatable into European languages, as Gramsci observes. It is largely due to the fact that all three principles—nation, democracy, and welfare—refer back to the same Chinese character, *min* (the people). In addition to having a deep interest in this combination of "nation" and "people" in Chinese revolutionary discourses, Gramsci is also concerned with a similar disengagement of the intellectuals and the "people" in both Italy and China. He mentions in passing in the same entry: "In China, too, the intellectuals are far removed from the people" (Q5§122; trans. Gramsci 1992–2007, vol. 2, p. 362). This line leads us back to his earlier "brief notes on Chinese culture" in the same notebook. Due to the division between a universal written system of traditional high culture and the various spoken dialects of the masses, "China cannot have a very widespread popular culture." Gramsci's remark was strikingly similar to Qu Qiubai's demand for a new national-popular language that is different from the traditional classical Chinese and the Europeanized modern written language. Gramsci continued: "At a certain point it will become necessary to introduce the syllabic alphabet" (Q5§23; trans. Gramsci 1992–2007, vol. 2, p. 285). He even speculated whether "Russian or the English alphabet" would be better for Chinese. What Gramsci perhaps did not know was that Qu, among many other Chinese intellectuals, also proposed the romanization of Chinese, and even experimented it in the mountainous rural regions of the Chinese Soviet.

As is well known, toward the end of his legendary life, Sun Yat-sen reformed the GMD according to the Leninist model of party organization, formed the GMD's coalition with the young CCP, and collaborated with the Third International. As a result, both the GMD and CCP worshiped Sun as a revolutionary saint, cherishing his dogma of *min* (the people/nation). After the GMD's rightist turn and its massacre of the communists, Gramsci analyzed the "politics of the right-wing successors of Sun Yat-sen" (Q5§23; trans. Gramsci 1992–2007, vol. 2, p. 286) and observed that they continued to propagate the Three Principles of the People in the education system (one suspects that Gramsci must have had the rise of fascism in Europe in mind as a point of comparison). His fifth notebook thus demonstrates that he carefully read a splendid variety of documents, books, and articles on Chinese culture and politics. Unfortunately, he did not live long enough to see that the protracted revolution of the CCP eventually led to the triumphal founding of a new China that carries the term *renmin* in its official title: *renmin gongheguo* (the People's Republic).

According to Gramsci, "[the] structure and the superstructures form a 'historical bloc'"; "only a comprehensive system of ideologies rationally reflects the contradictions of the structure and represents the existence of the objective conditions for revolutionizing praxis" (Q8§182; trans. Gramsci 1992–2007, vol. 3, p. 340). Within "the necessary reciprocity between structure and superstructures"—that is, "the real dialectical process"—a political alliance may take shape. What lay behind the CCP's long armed struggles was a continuous, painstaking building of a new class alliance of "national-popular" nature, a bloc of *renmin* composed of the working class, peasants, the petit bourgeoisie (including modern intellectuals), and the national bourgeoisie. Mao summarized this coming hegemony as a project of "New Democracy," or "people's democratic dictatorship." This agenda should not be oversimplified either as a straightforward imitation of the popular front in the West or as a simpleminded adaptation of the Stalinist postwar prescription of people's democracy in the East. The CCP's project was based on the positive and negative experiences of an uninterrupted process of revolution and Sinification of Marxism. The formation of the CCP's leadership in this bloc was accompanied by the elimination of what Gramsci saw as the alienation of the intellectual from the people, and by the creation of the people's "high culture," which led to numerous debates (the debate of the "national form" in cultural productions was one of them, in a way predicted already in Gramsci's fifth notebook). Mao's search for China's own socialist path in the post-1949 era could be seen as a series of attempts to overcome the contradiction between united front and dictatorship, between domination and leadership within this people's democracy as a historical bloc. His final yet unsuccessful solution was the continued revolution under the proletariat's dictatorship, which meant the disintegration of this national-popular bloc.

The post-Mao reforms of marketization and the transformation of the party-state as the guarantor/arbiter of stability and development (a historical process of "passive counterrevolution" of capital?) has given rise to a unique existence of what is officially called "socialist market economy" within the system of global capitalism. Yet even today, the politics of the people or *renmin* remains as the key legacy, mandate, and legitimacy for the CCP's current developmentalist (and arguably class-neutral) rule. Can the "national-popular" be reactivated and a bloc of the people be rebuilt under certain circumstances within the depoliticized space of the party-state? In other words, can the CCP be repoliticized as a "prince" of the people, thereby giving new emancipatory content to the empty name of "the people"? Is there any space for the emergence of the critical intellectuals and their cultural agenda within the party? These are the questions lurking behind Chen Yue's reading of Gramsci in today's China. He has to arrive at a highly philosophical and poetical conclusion: "Gramsci and solitude." Gramsci's solitude in prison becomes the solitude of the absent Jacobin of prince-party-intellectual in contemporary cultural politics. Chen urges us to work within this solitude ("Gelanxi").

Outside the space of the party-state, Wang Hui, an important critical Chinese intellectual and scholar who has been seen as a representative of China's New Left, once called Lu Xun a model of the "organic intellectual" (Wang Hui 2000, p. 429). Wang was not only concerned with how to evaluate Lu Xun. His use of Gramsci's notion was intended to revive a cultural war of position amid the new institutionalization of global capital, national power, mass media, and knowledge production, as he championed an intellectual resistance that was denigrated as "New Left" at the turn of this century. Even though the battle of neoliberals versus New Left has lost much of its momentum in the current cultural landscape, China's New Left amounts to a critical sparkle that is not confined to the party-state framework as the new structure of encirclement and entrenchment is taking shape in this rapidly changing postsocialist country and globally. What will be the new forms of popular socialist politics for the remaking of the Chinese "people" in this brave new world, of course, remains to be seen.[5] Chen concludes his study of Gramsci by citing a famous line about the war of position: "This is concentrated, difficult, and requires exceptional qualities of patience and inventiveness" (Gramsci 1971, p. 238). In the spirit of Chen's minimalist yet defiant optimism, I do not want to end this essay with a pessimistic answer. We have to be patient and inventive in any forms of solitude, in order to be contemporary not only with Gramsci but also with Mao, Qu Qiubai, and Lu Xun. The Gramscian seeds are still in the Chinese sociopolitical soil.[6]

NOTES

1   Perry Anderson, for example, sees "the case of Gramsci" as an "exception" in the rise of Western Marxism (Anderson 1979, p. 54).

2   Harold R. Isaacs, a Trotskyist sympathizer, was one of the first historians to narrate the national revolution as a "tragedy" (see Isaacs 1938). It should be noted that Moscow was deeply involved, and the direction of the Chinese Revolution became one of the topics in the disagreements between Stalin and Trotsky.

3   This line is originally from Mao Zedong's speech at an emergency meeting of the CCP in mid-1927.

4   Chen Yue, "Zhendi" (unpublished work). I am very grateful to Professor Chen for sharing his unpublished work on Gramsci with me and helping shape the argument of this chapter.

5   This chapter was originally written in 2013 to 2014. In this revised version, I want to further suggest that the more recent developments of Chinese culture and society—and especially the significant shifts within the party-state over the past few years—demand, with heightened urgency, a Gramscian analysis, which unfortunately cannot be fully pursued here.

6   I would like to thank the anonymous reviewers for their insightful comments, which played an important role in the reshaping of this chapter.

13

Antonio Gramsci in the Arab World

The Ongoing Debate

PATRIZIA MANDUCHI

An Intellectual Paradigm in Crisis

What was going on in the Arab world as Gramsci was living through such extraordinary and tragic personal and political experiences while writing his *Prison Notebooks*? Several events that are anything but insignificant coincidences immediately spring to mind. On May 9, 1916, when France and Great Britain signed the secret Sykes-Picot agreements defining their respective spheres of influence in the Near East, the young Gramsci was living through a difficult period in Turin. His name, however, was starting to become known and the initials "A. G." regularly appeared in all the publications of the Italian Left. In April 1919, Gramsci, along with Togliatti, Terracini, and Tasca, launched *L'Ordine Nuovo*, a socialist weekly paper devoted to socialist culture. Its founding practically coincided with Egypt's massive popular uprising against the British, which marked the beginning of a lengthy and troubled process of independence. In March 1928, the primary school teacher Hasan al-Banna founded the Muslim Brotherhood (Jamā'at al-ikhwān al-muslimīn), whose "political slogan" can be summarized in five points: "God is our goal, the Prophet our leader, the Qur'an our Constitution, the *jihād* our way, the *shahāda* our desire." Just a few months later, on July 19, Antonio Gramsci, by then founder of the Italian Communist Party and a prominent figure in international Marxism, walked through the gates of the Turi prison to start serving his long sentence of twenty years, four months, and five days. This signaled the start of one of the most striking intellectual adventures in the history of twentieth-century political and philosophical thinking, which, many years later, led to the publication of the *Prison Notebooks*. Gramsci died at dawn on April 27, 1937, in Rome's Quisisana Clinic. This was just one month after a crowning moment in the colonial pomposity of Fascist Italy, when Mussolini made his celebrated propaganda trip to Libya, unsheathing the "sword of Islam" and proclaiming himself protector of the Muslim world.

Although these distant and unrelated events mainly serve as the starting point for our reflection, it is certainly not mere chance that the 1970s were the period when Gramsci's thought first came to be known in the Arab world. This is the time when leftist, socialist, and Marxist Arab thinking enters into an irreversible phase of decline. In fact, the secular and progressive ideologies that had dominated the Arab political debate for at least two decades have reached a moment of deadlock. In particular, the Third Worldism, pan-Arabism, and Nasserism[1] of the 1950s and 1960s are now perceived as failures, as exogenous, and as somehow "imported" from the West. Muslim Brotherhood ideology, summed up in their serendipitous slogan "al-qur'ān huwa'l-haqq" (the Qur'an is the solution), now invades the political debate. This was flanked by the promises of Wahhabism,[2] a consequence of the "petro-Islam" so liberally propagated by the Gulf petro-monarchies at the beginning of the 1970s and especially after 1973 (see Kepel 2001). The decade ends with the Iranian Revolution of 1979, an epochal and traumatic event in Middle Eastern history. The political and cultural debate that takes place within the Muslim world (in particular the Arab one) especially in the 1980s and 1990s seems to be limited to the question of the "modernization of Islam" or of the "Islamization of modernity"—in other words, it revolves around the theme of the rebirth of Islam, its role in recovering an awareness of identity and in overcoming the crisis.

Gramsci's thinking comes into play in this cultural context of confusion and transition, even though it clearly does so in a rather fragmentary and discontinuous manner and not in an immediate way. Our starting hypothesis is that this is no mere coincidence. On the contrary, the new interest in Gramsci's reflections stems from the common roots that gave rise to both his theorizations and to "political Islam"—namely, the crisis of a previously commonly shared cultural and political paradigm. Such a crisis stems from a series of concomitant causes that can only be briefly mentioned here: the dysfunction and instability deriving from the painful and persistent legacy of the colonial experience, starting from the creation of "postcolonial" states that were anything but independent, with borders often drawn by foreign powers (see Campanini 2016); the fragile fabric of these young nations when facing the economic but also cultural imperatives of the great world powers; the generally authoritarian and monolithic regimes that arose after the struggles for freedom, whose fierce censorship abolished every form of free speech and all intellectual production; the perception of Islam as the only group of belonging from a cultural point of view (see Manduchi 2017). Moroccan historian Abdesselam Cheddadi recalls: "By showing an interest in Islamic culture and its history as one of the sources of the modern world, Gramsci is one of the first thinkers of the twentieth century to give up the idea that modernity is solely or essentially a European phenomenon" (in L'Abbate 2007, p. 18).

It appears then that both the formation process of the Arab nations and the most recent events call for a Gramscian reading. For many scholars, the use of Gramscian categories becomes pertinent to examining the parallel between the formation of the Italian state and the Arab states that emerged from decolonization in a subaltern position as the manifestation of colonial and postcolonial relationships (Marchi 2017, pp. 50–51).

The Usefulness of Gramsci

In the 1970s, just as in other parts of the extra-European world, and particularly in South America and India, a great number of publications focusing on Gramsci and his thought began to circulate in the Arab world, albeit with varying analytical perspectives:

> Gramsci enjoyed a new period of success abroad between the late 1960s and the first half of the 1970s. . . . Among the publications of this period, there are also six volumes in Arabic: five anthologies and the translation of Jean-Marc Piotte's work on Gramsci's political thought. To be noted, the works in Arabic are exclusively about Gramsci's political thought and to date there is still no translation of his *Lettere*. After this "Lebanese" period (in fact, all the books, except for a volume issued by the Syrian Ministry of Culture, were published by Beirut's *Dar al-Talia* publishing house), the only anthology of Gramsci's writings to appear afterwards in Arabic is the translation of the anthology by Hoare and Nowell Smith, translated by Tahsin al-Chaykh Ali in 1994, ten years after the translation of Cammett's biography. (Giasi and Righi 2009, p. 95)

One might expect that Gramsci's thought was recuperated, studied, and circulated among political militants mainly by leftist parties and movements. But in fact, this was not the case. The orthodox, conservative, and hence pro-Soviet approach of Arab socialism and communism meant that Gramsci was little known at the political level, or if he was known, no one dared to cite him openly for fear of being accused of heterodoxy.[3] The earliest references to Gramsci's thought come from the reflections of Arab Marxist intellectuals living in Europe or the United States, who—thanks to the circulation of the first English and French translations of Gramsci's works and works about him (Texier 1966; Cammett 1967; Piotte 1970; Gramsci 1971)—come into contact with his conceptual categories and begin to make use of them for their own reflections. What is relevant for Arab intellectuals in Gramsci's writings is the importance he gives to cultural discourse, particularly on topics such as the role of the intellectual (*muthaqqaf*), hegemony (*haymana*), and subalternity (*taba'iyya*).

It thus comes as no surprise to find these specific themes highlighted in contexts seeking cultural identity after the colonial experience and after the evident failure of the economic and cultural policies of the postindependence regimes. Until then, the Arab intellectual elite had considered religion and popular culture as obstacles in the race to modernity, almost a "nonculture" to be overcome without too many regrets; in so doing, they had embraced seemingly successful exogenous models, remaining completely detached from the Arab masses. The inevitable outcome was that their intellectual commitment lacked social impact and their disconnection from real society created a gap for fundamentalists to step into: "In the Arab cultural context, where even leftist intellectuals see themselves as part of the elite, this Gramscian 'ethic' of militant, of 'organic intellectual' is a real revolution. It will be well received and bring many of these intellectuals to a sort of deconstruction of their relationship with the people, with society" (El-Kenz, 1994, p. 56).

Gramsci's distinction between organic and traditional intellectual is thus a key concept in the first period of diffusion of Gramsci's thought in the Arab world. As we know, Gramsci dedicated ample space to the subject of intellectuals in more than one passage in his *Quaderni*; Q12 is titled "Appunti e note sparse per un gruppo di saggi sulla storia degli intellettuali" ("Scattered Notes and Comments for a Group of Essays on the History of Intellectuals"). One of the first draft passages which then is reworked in Q12 reads:

> First question: are intellectuals an autonomous social group, or does every social group have its own category of intellectuals? . . . 1) Every social group coming into existence on the primal basis of an essential function

in the world of economic production, creates together with itself, organically, a rank or several ranks of intellectuals who give it homogeneity and
a consciousness of its own function in the economic sphere. . . . 2) But
every social group emerging into history out of the economic structure
finds or has found—at least in all of past history—preexisting categories
of intellectuals that moreover seemed to represent a historical continuity
uninterrupted even by the most complicated changes in social and political forms. . . . The intellectuals have a function in the "hegemony" that is
exercised throughout society by the dominant group and in the "domination" over society that is embodied by the state, and their function is precisely "organizational" or connective. The intellectuals have the function
of organizing the social hegemony of a group and that group's domination
of the state; in other words, they have the function of organizing the consent that comes from the prestige attached to the function in the world of
production. (Q4§49, pp. 474-476; trans. Gramsci 1992-2007, vol. 2, p. 199)

This food for analytical thought inspires a number of great contemporary
Arab thinkers, such as the Egyptian historian Anouar Abdel-Malek (1924-
2012), a Marxist professor at the Sorbonne in Paris. He was certainly one of
the first, in the 1970s, to quote Gramsci directly and to consider his insights
on intellectuals as being perfectly matched to what was happening to the Arab
intelligentsia of that period. Abdel-Malek insists that it is the intellectuals' task
to "set in motion again history, historical becoming, rather than just being the
greatest scholars of thought" (Abdel-Malek 1970, p. xxxii). Another forerun-
ner in Gramscian studies in the Arab world is the Moroccan historian Abdallah Laroui (b. 1933), whose main works—*L'idéologie arabe contemporaine* (1973),
La crise des intellectuels arabes (1974), and *Islam et modernité* (1987)—once again
address the theme of the role of the intellectual. He initially focuses on the
background to the 1967 crisis; that is to say, after the Third Arab-Israeli War,[4] a
defeat that marks not only an unprecedented political crisis in the Arab world
but also a time of intellectual trauma for the entire Arab intelligentsia.

In the United States, another Gramsci scholar was Hisham Sharabi (1927-
2005), a Palestinian professor at Georgetown University. Among the first to
introduce Gramscian studies in the United States, he also founded the prestigious Center for Contemporary Arabic Studies in 1975; the Jerusalem Fund
for Education and Community Development in Washington in 1977; and in
1991, the Center for Policy Analysis on Palestine. In his *Arab Intellectuals and
the West (1970)*, Sharabi, from the particular perspective of the Palestinian
cause, deals with the role of the intellectual: Arab intellectuals, unhampered

by the legacies of tradition (for instance, he was a tireless campaigner for gender equality), must first of all engage in a dialogue with civil society rather than with the political powers. As Tahar Labib—another Gramscian intellectual from Tunisia—recalls (Labib 1994, p. 21), Sharabi uses the famous quote from Gramsci (indeed, a reuse of Romain Rolland's phrase), "pessimism of the intelligence, optimism of the will," as the opening and closing words of his celebrated *Neopatriarchy* (first published in Arabic in 1987).

Finally, who can forget Edward Said (1935–2003)? He too questioned the relationship between intellectuals and power by adopting Gramsci's perspective to read the Arab world. Best known for having elaborated the concept of "Orientalism," which provided the title for his fundamental book in cultural and postcolonial studies (the topic of a still raging debate), Said broadens the discourse and gets to grips with purely cultural arguments. This brings him to explore the dynamics of domination and subordination between the northern and southern world and hence the Gramscian theme of hegemony. One of the cues for his reflections is the difference between a dominant and a subaltern culture:

> In the *Prison Notebooks* Gramsci says: "The starting-point of critical elaboration is the consciousness of what one really is, and is 'knowing thyself' as a product of the historical process to date, which has deposited in you an infinity of traces, without leaving an inventory." The only available English translation inexplicably leaves Gramsci's comment at that, whereas in fact Gramsci's Italian text concludes by adding, "therefore it is imperative at the outset to compile such an inventory." . . . In many ways my study of Orientalism has been an attempt to inventory the traces upon me, the Oriental subject, of the culture whose domination has been so powerful a factor in the life of all Orientals. (Said 1979, p. 25)

The 1970s, therefore, are the time when the theme of the recovery of a cultural identity silenced by a hegemonic and foreign culture forcefully resurfaces among Arab intellectuals. The failure of the grand ideologies that had ushered in the early years of independence had led to a disillusionment that coincided with a moment of reflection on the concept of culture in general; the role of the intellectual; the significant shortcomings of the corrupt, inefficient, and authoritarian state institutions; and the need for freedom of thought and speech. On the one hand, this forced the Left to take a long hard look at itself, and on the other hand, a matrix of conservative Islamic thought was restored and seen as the means of "providing the solution."

For the leftist Arab intelligentsia, Gramsci's concept of the organic intellectual, close to popular sentiments, offered a helping hand in fully rethinking their role in society. All the same, as the Tunisian sociologist Tahar Labib so aptly pointed out:

> It is clear that the generous munificence of Gramsci's presence does not necessarily mean that an epistemic consolidation exists within Gramscian theory, in the sense of an integral and organic intellectual method. In other words, this generous presence focuses on certain priorities: civil society (in the sense of a political-social space in the struggle for democracy) and the critical role of intellectuals are, at least for the time being, the two essential issues, and—together with all that goes with them—they draw attention to Gramsci. This Gramsci is an "intellectual" Gramsci to a fault. (Labib 1991, p. 177)

Translations and Translatability

One of the issues that immediately stands out is the question of "translatability," a problem that is common to each and every context where Gramsci's thought is disseminated. I consider the term *translatability* as having two senses here. First of all, it refers to the difficult task of making a true translation from one language to another (and then often to another, seeing that Gramsci is often translated from Italian into French or English, and from those languages into Arabic). Second, it regards the problems involved in translating Gramscian concepts from one context to another, since their widespread diffusion has led to an excessive freedom of use, to a certain nonchalance of utilization (even though at times these new "uses" actually prove to be valuable and fresh interpretative keys).

Gramsci himself speaks about the concept of translatability in both senses in a letter to his wife Giulia of September 5, 1932: "A qualified translator should not only be able to translate literally, but also to translate conceptual terms of a specific national culture into the terms of another national culture" (Gramsci 2014, p. 414). Then again in the *Notebooks*: "If it is true that every language contains the elements of a conception of the world and of a culture, it could also be true that from anyone's language one can assess the greater or lesser complexity of his conception of the world. . . . A great culture can be translated into the language of another great culture, that is to say a great national language with historic richness and complexity, and it can translate any other great culture and can be a world-wide means of expression" (QII§12, p. 1377; trans. Gramsci 1971, p. 325).

As far as the first point is concerned, we must remember that Arab writers rarely read Gramsci in Italian and that there are no good complete translations in Arabic. Generally speaking, they are able to read the French or English translations of works *by* and *on* Gramsci, available throughout the Arab world. A number of Arabic translations do however exist and there is still some work in progress, even though, to date, the *Quaderni del carcere* and Gramsci's other major works have yet to be fully translated.

A brief overview of the translated editions of Gramsci's works gives us an idea of how Gramsci's thought has gradually been made available to Arab-speaking readers. Lebanon, with the Dār al-talī'a publishing house, was the key player in the diffusion of Gramscian thinking.

After *Al-amīr al-hadīth* (*Il Principe moderno* [*The Modern Prince*]) in 1970,[5] *Qadāyā al-māddiya al-tārīkhiyya* (*Questioni di materialismo storico* [*Matters of Historical Materialism*])[6] and *Al-majālis al-'ummāliyya* (*I Consigli dei lavoratori* [*Workers' Councils*])[7] were published in Beirut by Dār al-talī'a in 1971 and 1975, respectively. Then there is also *Ghārāmshī: Dirāsāt mukhtāra* (*Gramsci: Scritti scelti* [*Selected Writings*])[8] published in Damascus by the Ministry of Culture in 1972; *Fikr Ghārāmshī—Mukhtārāt* (*Il pensiero di Gramsci—Brani scelti* [Gramsci's thought—selected passages])[9] in Beirut, Dār al-Farābi, 1976 (vol. 1) and 1978 (vol. 2); and more recently *Kurrāsāt al-sijn* (*Quaderni dal carcere* [*Prison Notebooks*])[10] in Cairo in 1994, by the Dār al-mustaqbal al-'arabī publishing house.

The first two essays *on* Gramsci to be translated into Arabic were both published in Beirut, in 1975 and 1984, respectively, based on the French and English translations of two classic volumes that had placed the work of the Sardinian politician on the world stage: *La pensée politique de Gramsci*, by J. M. Piotte (1970), translated by Georges Tarabichi for Dār al-talī'a with the title *Fikr Ghāramshī al-siyāsī*; and *Gramsci and the Origin of Italian Communism*, by J. M. Cammett (1967), translated by Afif al-Razzaz and titled *Ghāramshī, hayātuhu wa 'amāluhu* (Beirut, Mu'assasat al-abhāth al-'arabiyya li'l-dirāsāt wa'l-nashr).

It should be said that even though these Arabic translations enjoyed a discreet success, scholars continued to use the English and French originals. The two most-cited direct references to Gramsci in these years come from *Selections from the Notebooks* and *Gramsci dans le texte*, an anthology published by Éditions sociales. Arab readers continue to use the English and French versions first, then refer directly to the Italian ones, and finally to translations in Arabic.

As far as the other sense of the term "*translatability*" is concerned, I feel that it indicates the difficulty in correctly grasping Gramsci's thinking. Obviously, this problem is not limited to the Arab context alone, but arises from the enormous diffusion of his thought and the innumerable elaborations to which it has been subjected, especially within the multitude of different geographical, political, social, cultural, and linguistic contexts. For example, let us consider the concept of *società civile* (civil society), which does not easily lend itself to the complex sociocultural contexts of the contemporary Arab world and which also defies clear and unequivocal definition (see Zghal 1991); or again, the distinction between organic intellectuals and traditional intellectuals, which may somehow be "upside-down" in the Arab context, since the organic intellectual could be identified with the Islamic militant, the one from the secular Left with the traditional intellectual (see Jaghloul 1982).

The conclusion reached by many Arab authors is that we are in danger of depriving Gramsci of his "Gramscianism," of his specific political value, by using such and such a conceptual category that has been blindly and superficially detached from any political and militant value. Some decades ago, Tahar Labib warned about the danger of "'Orientalizing' Gramsci, a mistake he would never have made. This is the goal behind this insistence on Gramsci's specificity. Gramsci teaches an idea and a praxis. This could be a useful source of inspiration for what our visions and analyses have become inured to, in response to the disregard for certain aspects of the present situation in the Arab world. It could give us new inspiration to understand the causes behind our inability to implement any real change of reality" (Labib 1981, p. 121).

A New Political Vision

The first true "Gramscian moment" (to use Peter Thomas's opportune expression) in the Arab world appears around the turn of the 1990s within the reconstruction of a new Marxist political vision following the collapse of the Soviet model. A new awareness, not only of the failure of the various forms of socialism in the Arab countries but also of the intrinsic strength of the conservative-Islamist ideological currents, makes of Gramsci "the gateway for [Arab] socialists to rethink their position in the debate on civil society" (Browers 2007, pp. 86–87). Gramsci begins to be studied at the universities in Beirut, Cairo, and Tunis; the first international conferences are held in Tunis and in Cairo in 1989 and 1990.

Unsurprisingly, the range of Gramscian categories used by Arab intellectuals is broadened: no longer just the intellectual, but also *società civile* (civil society, *al-mujtama'a al-madaniyya*), *egemonia* (hegemony; *haymana*), *subalternità* and *subalterni* (subalternity and subalterns, *taba'iyya, al-tābi'ūn*), the *blocco storico* (historic bloc; *al-kutla al-tārikhiyya*), the *rivoluzione passiva* (passive revolution; *al-thawra al-salbiyya*), the *filosofia della praxis* (philosophy of praxis; *falsafat al-brāksīs*), the *spirito di scissione* (spirit of cleavage; *naz'a al-infisāliyya*), and the *questione meridionale* (southern question; *al-qadiyya al-janūbiyya*) appear in Arab discourse. Such concepts have proven to be exceptional keys to understanding the various Arab sociocultural contexts and have been implemented in reflections that cover many analytical fields. For the sake of brevity, I single out only some of Gramsci's most popular key terms, paying particular attention to the direction taken by the categories of civil society (al-mujtama'a al-madaniyya) and hegemony (haymana).

For Gramsci, civil society, as opposed to political society, is made up of a group of private associations and organizations (trade unions, political parties, publishers, newspapers, churches, etc.) that are independent from the public sphere. Unlike political society, they are based on voluntary membership rather than on coercion and legal control. Gramsci writes, "In the West there was a proper relation between state and civil society, and when the state tottered, a sturdy structure of civil society was immediately revealed. The state was just a forward trench, behind it stood a succession of sturdy fortresses and emplacements" (Q7§16, p. 866; trans. Gramsci 1992–2007, vol. 3, p. 169). Rarely does the concept of civil society appear in intellectual and political Arab debate prior to the early 1980s, because before then, independence had inspired total confidence in the new national regimes and their choices. The intelligentsia almost always approved and sometimes blindly supported the modernization theory carried forward by state policies, which left little room for debate and dissenting opinions. Against this background, the rejection of tradition and everything that had to do with the public sphere led to the passive acceptance of a politics that was only expressed in terms of domination. Civil society practically did not exist.

But around the turn of the 1990s, the powerful regimes of the Arab world are in crisis, the IMF has imposed ironclad financial and economic regulations, and the spread of Islamic fundamentalism is at its peak. Religious terrorism begins with the attacks in Egypt, the civil war in Algeria, and the proliferation of jihadist movements, particularly after the withdrawal of the Soviet Army from Afghanistan (1989). The increasingly frequent use of the concept of *civil society* in the Arab debate reflects this moment of raging disappointment with the *state* category and all those forgotten promises and failed objectives. A new reading of Gramsci coincides with the discovery that a civil society does exist in Arab countries—a civil society that is incarnated by lively opposition movements (students, journalists, magistrates, women, etc.) whose members begin to show their dissenting views in an increasingly obvious way.

As a matter of fact, this encounter was like an act of liberation, and after a few years, Gramsci will become one of the most widely read authors amongst leftist groups in the Arab world. It must be said that reading him is "useful": it helps to analyze the world around us, the society that exists in its various forms, and the collective "praxis" in which we are immersed and which the avant-garde trends of the previous periods had transformed into "uniform and undifferentiated masses." The discovery of Gramscian thought thus coincides—and this is no mere coincidence—with the concomitant discovery of the importance of the social experience. Because the latter, aided by the drift of the states, has come to be recognized as something that is "worthy" of reflection, and also as a key social actor, the basis of every action (El-Kenz 1994, pp. 54-55).

The other Gramscian idea we shall consider here is the concept of hegemony (*haymana*), which, in a nutshell, is supremacy that is not achieved by domination alone, but also through consensus: "A class is dominant in two ways, namely it is 'leading' and 'dominant.' It leads the allied classes, it dominates the opposing classes. Therefore, a class can (and must) 'lead' even before assuming power; when it is in power it becomes dominant, but it also continues to 'lead'" (Q1§44, p. 41; trans. Gramsci 1992-2007, vol. 1, pp. 136-137). Gramsci's reflections on hegemony allow Arab intellectuals to analyze the theme of "state failure" in the Arab world in terms of a lack of hegemony. It also explains the rise of radical Islamic groups as a hegemonic conquest of power, thanks to their authoritative political discourse revolving around the "utopia of the Islamic state."

The Palestinian literary critic Faysal Darraj, one of the greatest Gramsci scholars in the Arab world, neatly sums up the first point: "Hegemony, in the Gramscian sense, does not exist in our countries. The local State relies on repression, and the capitalist system of the big cities approves and only supports repressive governments capable of maintaining some form of division of labor. This kind of double-edged coercion makes the national struggle for liberation a class struggle and the class struggle a national one" (Darraj 1994, p. 48). The Egyptian Nazih Ayubi, in his *Over-stating the Arab State* (1995), tackles the issue of the fragility of the Arab regimes. Despite their proven ability in developing tools to suppress any form of dissent on the one hand, they completely underestimated the need to create consensus on the other. They thus only managed to create a dimension of domination lacking in any moral or intellectual leadership—in other words, a true hegemony in the Gramscian sense of the term. The resulting void was filled by the Muslim Brotherhood, against whom, for example, the Mubarak regime engaged in a Gramscian "passive revolution," supporting the process of Islamization from behind the scenes in the hope that it would prove useful in avoiding any change in the status quo.

As far as the second point is concerned, the rise of radical Islamic groups is a key issue that is central to the debate currently raging in the Arab world: the relationship between intellectuals and popular culture, and consequently, between intellectuals and Islam. Although Gramsci is talking about Italy and the Catholic Church, he helps us to understand "the place and the role of the mosque in the imagination of the Arab working classes, allowing us to make a peaceful analysis of the Islamist movement without any 'Meridionalism'" (El-Kenz 1994, p. 59).

Indeed, already around the defeat of June 1967, a new form of political action materialized in Arab societies. This action was concurrent and parallel to that of the Left but closely bound to the widespread religious culture, and it was undertaken in successive phases, in a diachronic development that can be compared to Gramscian dynamics. Turning its back on the state apparatus from which nothing was expected, the action focused on society and its mobilization. Privileging the long term over the short term, cultural hegemony at the immediate seizure of power, it managed to organize the social movement through a dense network of charitable and cultural, economic, and social associations and ended up "encircling" the state and political society in a "counter-society" that is autonomous at the economic, cultural, and political levels. A typical example of this is the Egyptian case of the Muslim Brotherhood, but this strictly Gramscian strategy of political action can be found in varying forms and degrees in the modern Islamic movements of all the other Arab countries. Of course, the universalism of the philosophy of praxis has little to do with the claim for Islamic identity, but the dynamics of its expansion are completely comparable to the Gramscian approach to political action and to hegemony in particular (El-Kenz 1994, p. 59). In fact, Islamist strategy closely resembles what Gramsci called a "war of position":

> Yet the most striking exponents of this reading of Gramsci were Islamist movements. Around the same time when Gramsci was penning down his Prison Notebooks (late 1920s and early 1930s), Hassan al-Banna, founder of al-Ikhwān al-Muslimīn (Muslim Brothers), the world's first and largest Islamist movement, expressed the need to change *al-rouh al-'am alazi uhai-min* (the hegemonic public spirit) in Muslim countries before Islamists can target power. . . . From that time on, with the obvious differences between Islamists and leftists notwithstanding, strategies of cultural transformation have become central to most Islamist movements around the world. . . . Islamists drew on religious symbols and practices to alienate the masses from their secular rulers and turn them into political dissidents. . . . Islamists shared Gramsci's belief that replacing the rulers' hegemony with their own is a necessary first step to winning the political struggle. (Kandil 2011, pp. 38–39)

In short, the 1980s and 1990s are, above all, a period that saw the discovery and use of the concepts of civil society and hegemony in the Arab world. Such concepts had an antistate function and served as a reflection, from a Gramscian perspective, on the new social actors (activists, students, politicians, human rights advocates, movements against gender discrimination, journalists, etc.) and on the most useful strategies to conquer political power.

Not irrelevant to our analysis is the general backward slide on the path to Arab democratization, which came about especially in the early 1990s, and the hardened attitude caused (officially) by the rise of radical Islamism and its lunatic fringe, with its increasing propensity for acts of violence and terrorism. The process of approaching Gramsci coincides with the feelings of detachment, disaffection, and *disenchantment* with the state and its theoretical construction, and with an interest in society, its protagonists, and its various activities and struggles. It therefore opens a new chapter in the secular Arab political debate, mainly because it coincides with the discovery of the importance of the social experience in the aftermath of the sense of disillusionment caused by the collapse of all the statist-developmentalist ideologies so prominent in the Arab countries after independence. This encounter is an "act of liberation"; indeed, Gramsci will shortly become the most widely cited author in the leftist movements of (not only) the Arab world.

Out with the Old, but Not in with the New

The end of the century and of the millennium opens up a new phase: the attacks of September 11, 2001, and their terrible consequences altered the West's perception of the Arab and Muslim world, but above all, they changed the very course of history in the entire Middle East. And even more so, the explosion of the so-called Arab Spring—the incredible wave of mass protests whose domino effect brought about the fall of three of the strongest and longest-lasting Arab regimes (Tunisia, Egypt, Libya)—led to substantial changes in other states and, in fact, to a remodeling of the entire Mediterranean area.

However, once the initial enthusiasm had died down, the "spring" was soon replaced by disillusionment, painful counterrevolutions, dramatic civil wars, and even more repressive and authoritarian regimes that seem to have crushed every form of democratic ferment in almost every place. Once again, Gramsci's perspective proves useful in reading the events that preceded, accompanied, and followed the Arab revolutions, especially as regards the themes of hegemonic conquest and the concepts of revolution (*al-thawra*) and passive revolution (*al- thawra al-salbiyya*).

Whilst the debate that broke out after the uprisings has yet to define the importance of such revolutionary events (revolutions? passive revolutions? counterrevolutions?), Gramsci himself provides us with illuminating food for thought: "The crisis consists precisely in the fact that the old is dying and the new cannot be born: in this interregnum morbid phenomena of the most varied kind come to pass" (Q3§34, p. 311; trans. Gramsci 1992–2007, vol. 2, p. 33). The interpretative key that Gramsci offers us can be applied to all the states involved: in Tunisia, where a stony path to democratization was underway; in Egypt, where a tragic counterrevolution brought to power a military regime that was far more authoritarian and ruthless than Mubarak's had ever been; and in a chaotic Libya, or Syria entrenched in a bloody civil war tainted by foreign intervention. The Arab world is in the grip of "morbid phenomena" that are unmistakable signs of the transition from old to new. The latest generations of scholars have engaged in a lively debate in which Gramsci is very present.

In their critical reflections on revolutionary situations in their countries, these scholars have come to use the Gramscian categories that had already entered common language and often, political practice. They participate in different ways in the struggle in their home countries, analyzing the hegemonic and counterhegemonic dynamics of the ruling classes, or the role of intellectuals, whose condemnation of a perennial crisis is useful in deconstructing and reflecting on the near future. As a result, more than philological analyses of Gramscian texts, what emerges are reflections on some of the key concepts useful for interpreting Arab countries—for understanding a present moment through "Gramscian" themes and concepts (see Marchi 2017).

Among the many examples of the use of Gramsci in the most recent historical phase of the Arab world, two recent publications should be mentioned. The Tunisian Baccar Gherib (whose *Repenser la transition avec Gramsci: Tunisie, 2011–2014* opens with the above-cited passage from Gramsci on the concept of crisis) tries to reread the phases of Tunisia's recent history in light of the Gramscian paradigms of *questione meridionale*, *rivoluzione passiva*, and *blocco storico* to "clarify the mechanisms, the scope and challenges of the Tunisian transition," reflecting on "their problems in a Gramscian manner" (Gherib 2017, p. 23).

Gramsci's morbid phenomena reappear in the title of the latest volume by the Franco-Lebanese scholar Gilbert Achcar (*Morbid Symptoms: Relapse in the Arab Uprising*, 2016) to assess the tragic historical phase of the postrevolutionary situation in the region, with particular focus on Egypt and Syria. In the various states that the author defines as practically being "owned" and run by the ruling families and clans, the wave of popular protest that broke out in 2011 has been transformed from "spring" into "winter" on account of intrinsic difficulties and devastating foreign interference. Gramsci is also recalled in the statement that these failures or, in any case, difficulties, are related to the spontaneity of the Arab revolts and the absence of a "modern Prince" capable of leading the postrevolutionary phase.

Many of the youth of Tahrir Square are suffering from the superficial cosmopolitanism Gramsci talks about when describing the intellectuals of the Italian Risorgimento. This has rendered them incapable of being an authentic "national-popular" movement. These young people have often studied at prestigious universities, such as the American University in Cairo, they are comfortable with social media, but they have little to do with the subproletariat that lives in the poor *ashawiyyāt* (slums) of Cairo or with the rural population. The Islamization of the subproletariat has also been made possible in the last few decades by the gap between the secular intellectual elites, be they liberal, socialist, or communist, and the disinherited masses. Instead, in Gramsci's opinion, the simultaneous entrance of the masses into political life, under the intellectual and moral leadership of the Modern Prince, was fundamental for the creation of a genuine national-popular will. A Gramscian analysis therefore exposes not only the hegemonic crisis that has hit the regimes and the Islamist movement, but also the difficulty in organizing new projects.

In conclusion, Gramsci has continued to be the most influential European thinker in the Arab world at least since the 1980s. This is because his Marxism seems to be less dogmatic and more open; because he has a unique perception of the strictly cultural context and because he is a courageous activist; because his categories can be applied relatively easily to contexts other than the Italy of his time; because Arab scholars take heart from the universality of his reflections but also from his origins and life story, from his "specificity." It is also true that using Gramsci calls for a certain amount of caution. The challenge lies in understanding the limits and expediency of his categories for reading the "great and terrible" world in a process that is, and always has been, dialectical between empiricism and universality (perhaps the greatest lesson the Sardinian thinker imparted to human thought). Nevertheless, let us end with the feeling of pleasant surprise offered by the reading of another of Gramsci's writings that so aptly reflects the present-day reality of the Arab world:

> Ignoring and even worse despising so-called "spontaneous" movements—
> that is, declining to give them a conscious leadership, and raise them to a
> higher level by inserting them into politics—may often have very bad and

serious consequences. It is almost always the case that a "spontaneous" movement of the subaltern classes is matched by a reactionary movement of the right wing of the dominant class, for concomitant reasons: an economic crisis, for example, produces, on the one hand, discontent among the subaltern classes and spontaneous mass movements and, on the other, conspiracies by reactionary groups, who take advantage of the objective enfeeblement of the government to attempt coups d'état. (Q3§48, p. 331; trans. Gramsci 1992–2007, vol. 2, p. 51)

NOTES

1   Most of the Arab regimes of the time more or less explicitly claimed to be socialist.
2   *Wahhabism* is the name given to the puritan and conservative ideological trend founded in the Arabian Peninsula in the eighteenth century. It has been the official version of Islam in Saudi Arabia ever since the nation's constitution in 1932.
3   Hassem Hamdan is the best-known example of a Gramsci thinker who never makes explicit references to Gramsci. Better known as Mahdi 'Amil, this prestigious intellectual and member of the Lebanese Communist Party was assassinated by Shiite militia in 1987. Nicknamed the "Arab Gramsci," his *L'État confessionnel* (Beirut 1996), the book considered his political testament, reiterates the need to undertake a tough struggle against the confessional regime to realize a socialist transformation of his country.
4   During which Israel defeated the Egyptian, Syrian, and Jordanian armies and conquered the Gaza Strip, Sinai, the West Bank (with East Jerusalem) and the Golan Heights in just six days (June 5–10).
5   Translated by Zahi Charfan and Qays Chami (pseudonyms of Waddah Charara and Fawwaz Trabulsi).
6   Translated by Fawwaz Trabulsi.
7   Translated from the Italian by Afif al-Razzaz.
8   Translation of Texier 1966 (by Mikhail Ibrahim Makhawwal).
9   Translation of Salinari and Spinella 1977 (by Tahsin al-Shaykh 'Ali).
10 Translation of Gramsci 1971 (by 'Adil Ghunaym).

Abdel Malek, Annouar. 1970. *La pensée politique arabe contemporaine*. Paris: Seuil.

Accornero, Aris. 1978. "Operaismo e sindacato." In *Operaismo e centralità operaia*, edited by Fabrizio D'Agostini, 27–43. Rome: Editori Riuniti.

Achcar, Gilbert. 2016. *Morbid Symptoms: Relapse in the Arab Uprising*. Palo Alto, CA: Stanford University Press.

Adamson, Walter. 1983. *Hegemony and Revolution: A Study of Antonio Gramsci's Political and Cultural Theory*. Berkeley: University of California Press.

Agosti, Héctor Pablo. 1959. *El mito liberal*. Buenos Aires: Ediciones Procyón,

Aloisi, Massimo. 1950. "Gramsci, la scienza e la natura come storia." *Società* 3:106–110.

Althusser, Louis. 1999. *Machiavelli and Us*. Translated by Gregory Elliott. London: Verso.

Althusser, Louis, et al. 2015. *Reading Capital: The Complete Edition*. Edited by Ben Brewster. London: Verso.

Alvaro, Corrado. 1929. "Pirandello parla della Germania, del cinema sonoro, e di altre cose." *L'Italia Letteraria* 5 (15): 1–2.

Alyn, Glen, ed. 1993. *I Say Me for a Parable: The Oral Autobiography of Mance Lipscomb, Texas Bluesman*. New York: W. W Norton.

Anderson, Perry. 1976. "The Antinomies of Antonio Gramsci." *New Left Review* I (100): 5–78.

Anderson, Perry. 1979. *Considerations on Western Marxism*. New York: Verso.

Anderson, Perry. 2011. "Lula's Brazil." *London Review of Books* 33 (7): 3–12.

Anderson, Perry. 2016. "The Heirs of Gramsci." *New Left Review* 100:71–97.

Antonini, Francesca. 2016. "'Il vecchio muore e il nuovo non può nascere': Cesarismo ed egemonia nel contesto della crisi organica." *International Gramsci Journal* 2 (1): 167–184.

Aricó, José M. 2005. *La cola del diablo: Itinerario de Gramsci en América Latina*. Mexico City: Siglo XXI.

Aristotle. 1984. *Poetics*. In *The Complete Works of Aristotle*. Edited by Jonathan Barnes. Princeton, NJ: Princeton University Press.

Ashworth, John. 1987. "The Relationship between Capitalism and Humanitarianism." *American Historical Review* 92 (4): 813–828.

Asor Rosa, Alberto. 1965. *Scrittori e popolo: Il populismo nella letteratura italiana contemporanea*. Rome: Edizioni Samona e Savelli.

Ayubi, Nazih. 1995. *Over-stating the Arab State: Politics and Society in the Middle East*. London: Tauris.

Badaloni, Nicola. 1972. *Per il comunismo: Questioni di teoria*. Turin: Einaudi.

Banaji, Jairus. 2011. *Theory as History: Essays on Modes of Production and Exploitation*. Chicago: Haymarket.

Bandinelli, Ranuccio Bianchi. 1962. *Dal diario di un borghese e altri scritti*. Milan: Il Saggiatore.

Baratta, Giorgio. 1993. "Il ritmo del pensiero nei Quaderni del Carcere." *Paradigmi* 11 (32): 397–423.

Barthas, Jérémie. 2011. *L'argent n'est pas le nerf de la guerre: Essai sur une prétendue erreur de Machiavel*. Rome: École française de Rome.

Bartoli, Clelia. 2008. *La teoria della subalternità e il caso dei dalit in India*. Soveria Mannelli, Italy: Rubbettino.

Basadre, Jorge. 1971. Introduction to *Seven Interpretive Essays on Peruvian Reality*, by José Carlos Mariátegui, ix–xxxiv. Edited by Jorge Basadre. Austin: University of Texas Press.

Beasley-Murray, Jon. 2010. *Posthegemony: Political Theory and Latin America*. Minneapolis: University of Minnesota Press.

Beccu, Enea. 2000. *Tra cronaca e storia\; Le vicende del patrimonio boschivo della Sardegna*. Sassari: Carlo Delfino Editore.

Becker, Marc. 2006. "Mariátegui, the Comintern, and the Indigenous Question in Latin America." *Science and Society* 70 (4): 450–479.

Becker, Marc. 2008. *Indians and Leftists in the Making of Ecuador's Modern Indigenous Movements*. Durham, NC: Duke University Press.

Beigel, Fernanda. 2005. "Una mirada sobre otra: El Gramsci que conoció Mariátegui." *Estudos de Sociologia, Araraquara* 18 (19): 23–49.

Bergson, Henri. 1944. *Creative Evolution*. Translated by Arthur Mitchell. New York: Modern Library.

Bergson, Henri. 1946. *The Creative Mind*. Translated by Mabelle L. Andison. Westport, CT: Greenwood Press.

Bianchi, Alvaro, and Ruy Braga. 2005. "Brazil: The Lula Government and Financial Globalization." *Social Forces* 83 (4): 1745–1762.

Bianchi, Alvaro, and Daniela Mussi. 2013. "Il Principe e seus contratempos: De Sanctis, Croce e Gramsci." *Revista Brasileira de Ciência Política* 12:11–42.

Bobbio, Norberto. 1968. Introduction to *Umanismo di Marx: Studi filosofici 1908-1966*, xi–xlviii. Turin: Einaudi.

Bobbio, Norberto. 1990. *Saggi su Gramsci*. Milan: Feltrinelli,

Bobbio, Norberto. 2014. "Gramsci and the Conception of Civil Society." In *Gramsci and Marxist Theory*, edited by Chantal Mouffe, 21–47. New York: Routledge.

Boggs, Carl. 1976. *Gramsci's Marxism*. London: Pluto Press.

Bollettino, Vincenzo. 2010. "Gramsci's Reception in Latin America." *Italian Quarterly* 47:31–39.

Boothman, Derek. 2008. "The Sources for Gramsci's Concept of Hegemony." *Rethinking Marxism* 20 (2): 201–215.

Bourdieu, Pierre. 1998. *Practical Reason: On the Theory of Action*. Stanford, CA: Stanford University Press.

Bourdieu, Pierre. 2000. *Pascalian Meditations*. Stanford, CA: Stanford University Press.

Brissa, Ettore. 1970. "Note sulla ricezione di Gramsci in Germania." In *Gramsci e la cultura europea: Atti del Convegno internazionale di studi gramsciani tenuto a Cagliari il 23-27 aprile 1967*, edited by Pietro Rossi, 389–395. Rome: Editori Riuniti.

Broadie, Alexander. 2003. Introduction to *The Cambridge Companion to the Scottish Enlightenment*, 1–7. Cambridge: Cambridge University Press.

Browers, Michaelle. 2007. "Il dibattito sul concetto di società civile nel mondo arabo." In *Studi gramsciani nel mondo 2000-2005*, edited by Giuseppe Vacca and Giancarlo Schirru, 79–117. Bologna: Il Mulino.

Buchan, James. 1995. "Presto!" Review of the *Life of Adam Smith* by Ian Simpson Ross. *London Review of Books* 17 (24): 13.

Buhle, Mari Jo, Paul Buhle, and Dan Georgakas, eds. 1990. *Encyclopedia of the American Left*. New York: Oxford University Press.

Burgio, Alberto. 2003. *Gramsci storico: Una lettura dei "Quaderni del carcere."* Rome: Laterza.

Burgio, Alberto. 2014. *Gramsci: Il sistema in movimento*. Rome: DeriveApprodi.

Burgio, Alberto. 2018. *Il sogno di una cosa: Per Marx*. Rome: DeriveApprodi.

Burnett, Charles. 2008. "Warming by the Devil's Fire." *Martin Scorsese Presents the Blues.* Snapper Music.

Buttigieg, Joseph A. 1992. Introduction to *Antonio Gramsci: Prison Notebooks*, vol. 1, edited by Joseph A. Buttigieg, 1–64. New York: Columbia University Press.

Buttigieg, Joseph A. 2009. "Reading Gramsci Now." In *Perspectives on Gramsci: Politics, Culture and Social Theory*, edited by Joseph Francese, 20–32. London: Routledge.

Buttigieg, Joseph A. 2013. "Subaltern Social Groups in Antonio Gramsci's *Prison Notebooks*." In *The Political Philosophies of Antonio Gramsci and B. R. Ambedkar: Itineraries of Dalits and subalterns*, edited by Cosimo Zene, 35–42. London: Routledge.

Cacciari, Massimo. 1978. "Problemi teorici e politici dell'operaismo nei nuovi gruppi dal 1960 A.D. oggi." In *Operaismo e centralità operaia*, edited by Fabrizio D'Agostini, 45–79. Rome: Editori Riuniti.

Callinicos, Alex. 2010. "The Limits of Passive Revolution." *Capital and Class* 34 (3): 491–507.

Cammett, John McKay. 1967. *Antonio Gramsci and the Origins of Italian Communism*. Stanford, CA: Stanford University Press.

Campanini, Massimo. 2016. *Storia del Medio Oriente contemporaneo*. Bologna: Il Mulino.

Campbell, R. H., and A. S. Skinner. 1976. General introduction to *An Inquiry into the Nature and Causes of the Wealth of Nations*, edited by R. H. Campbell and A. S. Skinner, 1–60. Oxford: Clarendon Press.

Canfora, Luciano. 2012. *Spie, URSS, antifascismo: Gramsci, 1926–1937*. Rome: Salerno Editrice.

Capuzzo, Paolo, and Sandro Mezzadra. 2012. "Provincializing the Italian Reading of Gramsci." In *The Postcolonial Gramsci*, edited by Neelam Francesca Rashmi Srivastava and Baidik Bhattacharya, 34–54. New York: Routledge.

Casarino, Cesare. 2011. "Marx before Spinoza: Notes toward an Investigation." In *Spinoza Now*, edited by Dimitris Vardoulakis, 179–234. Minneapolis: University of Minnesota Press.

Césaire, Aimé. 2000. *Discourse on Colonialism*. Translated by Joan Pinkham. New York: Monthly Review Press.

Chartier, Roger. 1997. "Du livre au lire." *Réseaux: Communication-Technologie-Société* 1:271–290.

Chatterjee, Partha. 2012. "Gramsci in the Twenty-First Century." In *The Postcolonial Gramsci*, edited by Neelam Francesca Rashmi Srivastava and Baidik Bhattacharya, 119–136. New York: Routledge.

Chen Yue. 2015. "Ruhe sikao renmin: Lun Gelanxi de minzu-renmin de gainian" [How to contemplate on the people: On Gramsci's concept of the "national-popular"]. *Baoma* [For Marx], July 2. http://chuansong.me/n/645622451279.

Chen Yue. 2017. "Gelanxi he gudu" [Gramsci and solitude]. *Shaonian zhongguo* [Young China], January 22. https://m.chuansongme.com/n/1504751251214.

Chen Yue. Unpublished. "Zhendi zhan de yishu: Cong Gelanxi yuhui de sikao, tigang" [The art of war of position: A detour via Gramsci, a draft].

Cheung, Lik-Kwan. 2010. "Xiandai junzhu yu youji zhishifenzi: Lun Qu Qiubai, Gelanxi yu 'lingxiuquan' lilun de xingcheng" [The modern Prince and the organic intellectual: On Qu Qiubai, Gramsci, and the formation of the hegemony theory]. *Xiandai zhuwen xuekan* [Journal of modern Chinese studies] 4:35–60.

Coben, Diana. 2005. *Gramsci y Freire*. Buenos Aires: Mino y Davila.

Comintern. 2005. "The Negro Question: Resolution from the Fourth Congress of the Comintern, 30 November 1922." *The Communist International and Black Liberation: Internationalist Group Class Readings*, September, 10–11.

Cospito, Giuseppe. 2011a. *Il ritmo del pensiero: Per una lettura diacronica dei "Quaderni del carcere" di Gramsci*. Naples: Bibliopolis.

Cospito, Giuseppe. 2011b. "Verso l'edizione critica e integrale dei *Quaderni del carcere*." *Studi Storici* 52 (4): 896–904.

Cospito, Giuseppe. 2015. "Le 'cautele' nella scrittura carceraria di Gramsci." *International Gramsci Journal* 1 (4): 28–42.

Cospito, Giuseppe, and Gianni Francioni. 2009. "Nota introduttiva a Quaderno 13 (1932–1933)." In *Quaderni del carcere: Edizione anastatica dei manoscritti*, vol. 14, edited by Gianni Francioni, 1–7. Rome: Biblioteca Treccani.

Couturier, Maurice. 1991. *Textual Communication: A Print-Based Theory of the Novel.* London: Routledge.

Crainz, Guido. 1996. *Storia del miracolo italiano: Culture, identità, trasformazioni fra anni cinquanta e sessanta.* Rome: Donzelli.

Croce, Benedetto. 1921. *La poesia di Dante.* Bari: Laterza.

Croce, Benedetto. 1963. *Scritti e discorsi politici (1943-1947).* 2 vols. Bari: Laterza.

Cuoco, Vincenzo. (1799) 1998. *Saggio storico sulla rivoluzione di Napoli.* Edited by Antonino De Francesco. Bari: Lacaita.

Dainotto, Roberto. 2009a. "Consenso, letterature e retorica: Gramsci e i *literary studies.*" In *Americanismi: Sulla ricezione del pensiero di Gramsci negli Stati Uniti,* edited by Mauro Pala, 29-45. Cagliari, Italy: CUEC.

Dainotto, Roberto. 2009b. "Gramsci and Labriola: Philology, Philosophy of Praxis." In *Perspectives on Gramsci: Politics, Culture and Social Theory,* edited by Joseph Francese, 50-68. London: Routledge.

Dainotto, Roberto. 2013. "Notes on Q6§32: Gramsci and the Dalits." In *The Political Philosophies of Antonio Gramsci and B. R. Ambedkar: Itineraries of Dalits and Subalterns,* edited by Cosimo Zene, 75-86. London: Routledge.

Daniele, Chiara, ed. 1999. *Gramsci a Roma, Togliatti a Mosca: Il carteggio del 1926.* Turin: Einaudi.

Daniele, Chiara, ed. 2005. *Togliatti editore di Gramsci.* Rome: Carocci.

Darraj, Faysal. 1994. "Autonomia, Egemonia, Democrazia." In *Omaggio a Gramsci,* edited by Tommaso Sanna et al., 46-48. Cagliari, Italy: Tema.

Davidson, Alastair. 2008. "The Uses and Abuses of Gramsci." *Thesis Eleven* 95 (1): 68-94.

Davidson, Neil. 2012. *How Bourgeois Were the Bourgeois Revolutions?* Chicago: Haymarket.

Davis, David Brion. 1987. "Reflections on Abolitionism and Ideological Hegemony." *American Historical Review* 92 (4): 797-812.

Day, Richard J. F. 2005. *Gramsci Is Dead: Anarchist Currents in the Newest Social Movements.* London: Pluto Press.

Deleuze, Gilles. 1991. *Bergsonism.* Translated by Hugh Tomlinson and Barbara Habberjam. New York: Zone Books.

Deliège, Robert. 1997. *The World of the Untouchables: The Paraiyars of South India.* Delhi: Oxford University Press.

Del Lucchese, Filippo. 2004. *Tumulti e indignatio: Conflitto, diritto e moltitudine in Machiavelli e Spinoza.* Milan: Ghibli.

de Oliveira, Francisco. 2006. "Lula in the Labyrinth." *New Left Review.* 42:5-22.

De Smet, Brecht. 2016. *Gramsci on Tahrir: Revolution and Counter-Revolution in Egypt.* New York: Pluto Press.

Diggins, John P. 1988. "The Misuses of Gramsci." *Journal of American History* 75 (1): 141-145.

Dirlik, Arif. 1979. *Revolution and History: Origins of Marxist Historiography, 1919-1939.* Berkeley: University of California Press.

Dirlik, Arif. 1983. "The Predicament of Marxist Revolutionary Consciousness: Mao Zedong, Antonio Gramsci, and the Reformulation of Marxist Revolutionary Theory." *Modern China* 9 (2): 182–211.

Du Bois, W. E. B. 1935. *Black Reconstruction*. New York: Harcourt Brace.

Dumont, Louis. 1966. *Homo Hierarchicus: Essai sur le système des castes*. Paris: Gallimard.

Dussel, Enrique. 2000. "Europe, Modernity, and Eurocentrism." *Nepantla: Views from South* 1 (3): 465–478.

Dussel, Enrique. 2003. *Beyond Philosophy: Ethics, History, Marxism, and Liberation Theology*. Edited by Eduardo Mendieta. Lanham, MD: Rowman and Littlefield.

Eagleton, Terry. 2012. *Why Marx Was Right*. New Haven, CT: Yale University Press.

Eley, Geoff. 1984. "Reading Gramsci in English: Observations on the Reception of Antonio Gramsci in the English-Speaking World, 1957–1982." *European History Quarterly* 14:441–477.

El-Kenz, Ali. 1994. "Gramsci et les Arabes: Une rencontre tardive?" In *Gramsci dans le monde arabe*, edited by Michele Brondino and Tahar Labib, 51–60. Tunis: Alif–Les Editions de la Méditerranée.

Emerson, Roger. 2003. "The Contexts of the Scottish Enlightenment." In *The Cambridge Companion to the Scottish Enlightenment*, edited by Alexander Broadie, 9–30. Cambridge: Cambridge University Press.

Escobar, Arturo. 2010. "Worlds and Knowledges Otherwise: The Latin American Modernity/Coloniality Research Program." In *Globalization and the Decolonial Option*, edited by Walter Mignolo and Arturo Escobar, 33–64. Durham, NC: Duke University Press.

Estabrook, Barry. 2011. *Tomatoland: How Modern Industrial Agriculture Destroyed Our Most Alluring Fruit*. Kansas City, MO: Andrews McMeel Publishing.

Evans-Pritchard, Edward Evan. (1949) 1973. *The Sanusi of Cyrenaica*. Oxford: Clarendon Press.

Farris, Sara R. 2013. *Max Weber's Theory of Personality: Individuation, Politics and Orientalism in the Sociology of Religion*. Leiden: Brill.

Federici, Sylvia. 2009. *Caliban and the Witch*. Brooklyn, NY: Autonomedia.

Ferrata, Giansiro. 1964. "Prefazione." In *2000 Pagine di Gramsci*, edited by Giansiro Ferrata and Niccolò Gallo, 10–45. Milan: Il Saggiatore.

Filippini, Michele. 2016. *Using Gramsci: A New Approach*. Reprint. London: Pluto Press.

Finelli, Roberto. 2014. *Un parricidio compiuto: Il confronto finale di Marx con Hegel*. Milan: Jaca Book.

Fink, Leon. 1988. "The New Labor History and the Powers of Historical Pessimism: Consensus, Hegemony, and the Case of the Knights of Labor." *Journal of American History* 75 (1): 115–136.

Fiorillo, Michele. 2008. "Dalla machiavellistica 'elitista' al moderno Principe 'democratico.'" In *Gramsci nel suo tempo*, edited by Francesco Giasi, 839–859. Rome: Carocci.

Fo, Dario. 1970. *Compagni senza censura: Teatro politico di Dario Fo*. Milan: Mazzotta editore.

Fontana, Benedetto. 1993. *Hegemony and Power: On the Relation between Gramsci and Machiavelli*. Minneapolis: University of Minnesota Press.

Fontana, Benedetto. 2013. "The Concept of Nature in Gramsci." In *Gramsci: Space, Nature, Politics*, edited by Michael Ekers, Gillian Hart, Stephan Kipfer, and Alex Loftus, 123-141. Malden, MA: Wiley-Blackwell.

Forgacs, David. 1989. "Gramsci and Marxism in Britain." *New Left Review* 1 (176): 70-88.

Francioni, Gianni. 1984. *L'officina gramsciana: Ipotesi sulla struttura dei "Quaderni del carcere."* Naples: Bibliopolis.

Francioni, Gianni. 2009. "Come lavorava Gramsci." In *Quaderni del carcere: Edizione anastatica dei manoscritti*, vol. 1, edited by Gianni Francioni, 21-60. Rome: Biblioteca Treccani.

Francioni, Gianni. 2016. "Un labirinto di carta (Introduzione alla filologia gramsciana)." *International Gramsci Journal* 2 (1): 7-48.

Frosini, Fabio. 2010. *La religione dell'uomo moderno: Politica e verità nei "Quaderni del carcere" di Antonio Gramsci*. Rome: Carocci.

Frosini, Fabio. 2013a. "Luigi Russo e Georges Sorel: Sulla genesi del 'moderno Principe' nei *Quaderni del carcere* di Antonio Gramsci." *Studi Storici* 54 (3): 545-589.

Frosini, Fabio. 2013b. "Why Does Religion Matter to Politics?" In *The Political Philosophies of Antonio Gramsci and B. R. Ambedkar: Itineraries of Dalits and Subalterns*, edited by Cosimo Zene, 173-184. London: Routledge.

Frosini, Fabio. 2014. "Storicismo e storia nei *Quaderni del carcere* di Antonio Gramsci." *Bollettino Filosofico* 27:351-367.

Gatto, Marco. 2016. *Nonostante Gramsci: Marxismo e critica letteraria nell'Italia del Novecento*. Macerata, Italy: Quodlibet.

Genovese, Eugene. 1967. Review of *On Antonio Gramsci*, by John Cammett. *Studies on the Left* 7 (2): 83-107.

Genovese, Eugene. 1974. *Roll, Jordan, Roll: The World the Slaves Made*. New York: Pantheon Books.

Gerratana, Valentino. 1997. *Gramsci: Problemi di metodo*. Rome: Editori Riuniti.

Gherib, Baccar. 2017. *Penser la transition avec Gramsci: Tunisie, 2011-2014*. Tunis: Diwen.

Giasi, Francesco, and Maria Luisa Righi. 2009. "La bibliografia gramsciana on line e gli studi in Asia e in Africa." *Gramsci in Asia e in Africa*. Eds. Annamaria Baldussi and Patrizia Manduchi, 93-105. Cagliari, Italy: Aipsa.

Gogol, Eugene. 2002. *The Concept of Other in Latin America Liberation: Fusing Emancipatory Philosophic Thought and Social Revolt*. Lanham, MD: Lexington Books.

Gonzales, Mike. 2007. "José Carlos Mariátegui: Latin America's Forgotten Marxist." *International Socialism* 115 (July 2). http://isj.org.uk/jose-carlos-mariategui-latin -americas-forgotten-marxist/.

Gonzáles Prada, Manuel. 1924. "Nuestros Indios." *Horas de lucha*. Callao, Peru: Tip. Lux.

Gramsci, Antonio. 1949. *Note sul Machiavelli, sulla politica e sullo stato moderno*. Torino: Einaudi.

Gramsci, Antonio. 1957a. *The Modern Prince and Other Writings*. Translated by Louis Marks. London: Lawrence and Wishart.

Gramsci, Antonio. 1957b. *The Open Marxism of Antonio Gramsci*. Translated by Carl Marzani. New York: Cameron Associates.

Gramsci, Antonio. 1971. *Selections from the Prison Notebooks*. Edited by Quintin Hoare and Geoffrey Nowell Smith. London: Lawrence and Wishart.

Gramsci, Antonio. 1972. *Lettere dal carcere*. Edited by Paolo Spriano. Torino: Einaudi.

Gramsci, Antonio. 1975. *Quaderni del carcere*. Edited by Valentino Gerratana. Turin: Einaudi.

Gramsci, Antonio. 1985. *Selections from Cultural Writings*. Edited by David Forgacs and Geoffrey Nowell-Smith. Cambridge, MA: Harvard University Press.

Gramsci, Antonio. 1987. *L'Ordine Nuovo*. Edited by Valentino Gerratana and Antonio A. Santucci. Turin: Einaudi.

Gramsci, Antonio. 1992–2007. *Prison Notebooks*. 3 vols. Translated by Joseph A. Buttigieg. New York: Columbia University Press.

Gramsci, Antonio. 1994. *Letters from Prison*. Edited by Frank Rosengarten. Translated by Raymond Rosenthal. New York: Columbia University Press.

Gramsci, Antonio. 1995a. *Further Selections from the Prison Notebooks*. Translated by Derek Boothman. Minneapolis: University of Minnesota Press.

Gramsci, Antonio. 1995b. *The Southern Question*. Translated by Pasquale Verdicchio. West Lafayette, IN: Bordighera.

Gramsci, Antonio. 1996. *Lettere dal carcere 1926-1937*. Edited by Antonio Santucci. Palermo: Sellerio.

Gramsci, Antonio. 2009. *Quaderni del carcere. Edizione anastatica dei manoscritti*, 18 volumes. Edited by Gianni Francioni. Rome-Cagliari: Biblioteca Treccani-L'Unione sarda.

Gramsci, Antonio. 2010. *Cronache teatrali 1915-1920*. Edited by Guido Davico Bonino. Turin: Nino Aragno Editore.

Gramsci, Antonio. 2014. *Lettere dal carcere*. Edited by Antonio Santucci. Palermo: Sellerio.

Greaves, Nigel M. 2009. *Gramsci's Marxism: Reclaiming a Philosophy of History and Politics*. Leicester, UK: Matador/Troubador.

Green, Marcus E. 2011a. "Gramsci Cannot Speak: Presentations and Interpretations of Gramsci's Concept of the Subaltern." In *Rethinking Gramsci*, edited by Marcus E. Green, 68-89. London: Taylor and Francis.

Green, Marcus E. 2011b. "Rethinking the Subaltern and the Question of Censorship in Gramsci's *Prison Notebooks*." *Postcolonial Studies* 14 (4): 387-404.

Guha, Ranajit. 1997a. *Dominance without Hegemony: History and Power in Colonial India*. Cambridge, MA: Harvard University Press.

Guha, Ranajit. 1997b. *A Subaltern Studies Reader, 1986-1995*. Minneapolis: University of Minnesota Press.

Gussow, Adam. 2010. "Ain't No Burnin' Hell: Southern Religion and the Devil's Music." *Arkansas Review: A Journal of Delta Studies* 41 (2): 83-98.

Hall, Stuart. 1986. "Gramsci's Relevance for the Study of Race and Ethnicity." *Journal of Communication Inquiry* 10 (2): 5–27.

Hall, Stuart. 1987. "Gramsci and Us." *Marxism Today*, June, 16–21.

Harootunian, Harry. 2015. *Marx after Marx: History and Time in the Expansion of Capitalism.* Columbia University Press.

Harris, David. 1992. *From Class Struggle to the Politics of Pleasure: The Effects of Gramscianism on Cultural Studies.* London: Routledge.

Harris, Leila M. 2015. "Hegemonic Waters and Rethinking Natures Otherwise." In *Practising Feminist Political Ecologies: Moving beyond the "Green Economy,"* edited by Wendy Harcourt and Ingrid Nelson, 157–181. London: Zed Books.

Harvey, David. 2007. *Limits to Capital.* London: Verso.

Haskell, Thomas L. 1987. "Convention and Hegemonic Interest in the Debate over Antislavery: A Reply to Davis and Ashworth." *American Historical Review* 92 (4): 829–878.

Haug, Wolfgang Fritz. 1999. "Rethinking Gramsci's Philosophy of Praxis from One Century to the Next." *boundary 2* 26 (2): 101–117.

Haug, Wolfgang Fritz. 2000. "Gramsci's "Philosophy of Praxis: Camouflage or Refoundation of Marxist Thought?" *Socialism and Democracy* 14 (1): 1–19.

Herrerra Zgaib, Miguel Angel, ed. 2009. *Hegemonías y Contra-Hegemonías en la Subregión Andino-Amazónico: Primer Seminario Internacional Antonio Gramsci.* Bogota: Universidad Nacional de Colombia.

Herrerra Zgaib, Miguel Angel, and Julieta Ortiz, eds. 2010. *Liberémos de la Guerra: Pasado, presente y futuro de las clases y grupos subalternos: Segundo Seminario Internacional Antonio Gramsci.* Bogota: Universidad Nacional de Colombia.

Hewitt, Nicholas, and Sarah Wasserman. 1989. Introduction to *The Culture of Reconstruction: European Literature, Thought and Film, 1945–50,* edited by Nicholas Hewitt, and Sarah Wasserman, 1–11. New York: Palgrave Macmillan.

Higgins, John. 1999. *Raymond Williams, Literature, Marxism and Cultural Materialism.* London: Routledge.

Hoare, Quintin, and Geoffrey Nowell Smith, eds. (1971) 1992. *Selections from the Prison Notebooks of Antonio Gramsci.* London: Lawrence and Wishart.

Hobsbawm, Eric J. 1959. *Primitive Rebels: Studies in Archaic Forms of Social Movement in the 19th and 20th Centuries.* Manchester, UK: University of Manchester.

Hobsbawm, Eric J. 1987. "Per capire le classi subalterne." *Rinascita-Il contemporaneo* 8:15–34.

Hobsbawm, Eric J. 2010. Preface to *Antonio Gramsci*, by Antonio Santucci. New York: Monthly Review Press.

Holub, Renate. 1992. *Antonio Gramsci: Beyond Marxism and Postmodernism.* London: Routledge.

Hooker, John Lee. 1949. "Burnin' Hell." *Sensation 21.*

Infranca, Antonino. 2009. "Los usos de Gramsci en América Latina." *Herramienta: Revista de Debate y Crítica Marxista,* Buenos Aires. Accessed February 18, 2020. https://herramienta.com.ar/articulo.php?id=977.

Isaacs, Harold R. 1938. *The Tragedy of the Chinese Revolution*. London: Secker and Warburg.

Jaghloul, Abdelkader. 1982. Interview, *Algérie Actualité* 846, January, Algiers.

Jameson, Fredric. 1998. *The Cultural Turn: Selected Writings on the Postmodern, 1983-1998*. London: Verso.

Jameson, Fredric. 2005. *Archaeologies of the Future: The Desire Called Utopia and Other Science Fictions*. London: Verso.

Judt, Tony. 2005. *Postwar: A History of Europe since 1945*. New York: Penguin.

Kaczyński, Grzegorz J. 2006. "Contatto culturale come trauma: Glossa socio-antropologica." *Annali della Facoltà di Scienze della Formazione* 5:161-176.

Kalyvas, Andreas. 2000. "Hegemonic Sovereignty: Carl Schmitt, Antonio Gramsci, and the Constituent Prince." *Journal of Political Ideologies* 5 (3): 343-376.

Kamenev, Lev. 1962. "Preface to Machiavelli." *New Left Review* 1 (15): 39-42.

Kandil, Hamze. 2011. "Islamizing Egypt? Testing the Limits of Gramscian Counterege-monic Strategies." *Theory and Society* 40:37-62.

Kandiyoti, Deniz, ed. 2009. *Invisible to the World? The Dynamics of Forced Child Labour in the Cotton Sector of Uzbekistan*. London: University of London. http://www.soas.ac.uk/cccac/events/cotton-sector-in-central-asia-2005/file49842.pdf.

Kepel, Gilles. 2001. *Jihad: Ascesa e declino del fondamentalismo islamico*. Rome: Carocci.

Kidd, Colin. 2010. "Maiden Aunt." Review of *Adam Smith: An Enlightened Life* by Nicholas Phillipson and *Adam Smith and the Circles of Sympathy: Cosmopolitanism and Moral Theory* by Fonna Forman-Barzili. *London Review of Books* 32 (19): 21-23.

Krätke, Michael. 2011. "Antonio Gramsci"s Contribution to a Critical Economics." *Historical Materialism* 19 (3): 63-105.

Kuleshov, Lev Vladimirovich. 1974. *Kuleshov on Film: Writings*. Edited by Ronald Levaco. Berkeley: University of California Press.

L'Abbate, Arianna, ed. 2007. "Gramsci, gli Arabi e l'appropriazione della storia. Intervista a Abdesselam Cheddadi." *Critica Marxista* 1:17-23.

Labib, Tahar. 1981. "Dars Ghramshi" [Gramsci's lesson]. In *Al-Karmal* 2:115-121.

Labib, Tahar. 1991. "Ghrāmshī fi al-fikr al-'arabī" [Gramsci in the Arab thought]. In *Qadāyā al-mujtama' al-madānī al-'arabī fī daw' utrūhat Ghrāmshī*, edited by Amina Rashid, 164-180. Cairo: Center for Arab Studies.

Labib, Tahar. 1994. "Gramsci dans le discours des intellectuels arabes." *Gramsci dans le monde arabe*. Eds. Michele Brondino and Tahar Labib, 13-39. Tunis: Alif-Les Editions de la Méditerranée.

Labriola, Antonio. 1902. *Del materialismo storico: Dilucidazione preliminare*. Rome: Ermanno Loescher and Company.

Labriola, Antonio. 1973. *Scritti filosofici e politici*. Edited by Franco Sbarberi. Turin: Einaudi.

Laclau, Ernesto. 2005. *On Populist Reason*. London: Verso.

Laclau, Ernesto, and Chantal Mouffe. 2014. *Hegemony and Socialist Strategy: Towards a Radical Democratic Politics*. London: Verso.

Lahtinen, Mikko. 2009. *Politics and Philosophy: Niccolò Machiavelli and Louis Althusser's Aleatory Materialism*. Leiden: Brill.

Lanternari, Vittorio. 1963. *The Religions of the Oppressed: A Study of Modern Messianic Cults*. Translated by Lisa Sergio. London: MacGibbon and Kee.

Laroui, Abdallah. 1973. *L'idéologie arabe contemporaine*. Paris: Maspero.

Laroui, Abdallah. 1974. *La crise des intellectuels arabes*. Paris: Maspero.

Laroui, Abdallah. 1987. *Islam et modernité*. Paris: La Découverte.

Lears, Jackson. 1985. "The Concept of Cultural Hegemony." *American Historical Review* 90 (3): 567–593.

Lears, Jackson. 1988. "Power, Culture, and Memory." *Journal of American History* 75 (1): 137–140.

Lefort, Claude. (1972) 1986. *Le travail de l'oeuvre Machiavel*. Paris: Gallimard.

Lenin, Vladimir Ilych. 1964. *Collected Works*. Moscow: Progress Publishers.

Lenin, Vladimir Ilych. 2010. *Imperialism: The Highest Stage of Capitalism*. Sydney: Resistance Books.

Levi, Carlo. 2008. *Christ Stopped at Eboli*. Translated by Frances Frenaye. New York: Farrar, Straus and Giroux.

Liguori, Guido. 1991. "La prima recezione di Gramsci in Italia (1944–1953)." *Studi Storici* 32 (3): 663–700.

Liguori, Guido. 2006. *Sentieri gramsciani*. Rome: Carocci.

Liguori, Guido. 2012. *Gramsci conteso: Storia di un dibattito, 1922-1996*. Rome: Editori Riuniti.

Lipsitz, George. 1988. "The Struggle for Hegemony." *Journal of American History* 75 (1): 146–150.

Lisa, Athos. 1973. *Memorie: In carcere con Gramsci*. Milan: Feltrinelli.

Liu, Kang. 1997. "Hegemony and Cultural Revolution." *New Literary History* 28 (1): 69–86.

Liu, Kang. 2002. *Quanqiuhua/minzuhua* [Globalization/nationalization]. Tianjin, China: Tianjin renmin.

Liu, Xin. 2011. "Gramsci's Presence in China." *Carte Italiane* 2 (7): 69–80.

Lloyd, Genevieve. 1996. *Spinoza and the Ethics*. New York: Routledge.

Loftus, Alex. 2013. "Gramsci, Nature, and the Philosophy of Praxis." In *Gramsci: Space, Nature, Politics*, edited by Michael Ekers, Gillian Hart, Stephan Kipfer and Alex Loftus, 178–196. Malden, MA: Wiley-Blackwell.

Löwy, Michael. 1981. *The Politics of Combined and Uneven Development*. London: Verso.

Lumley, Robert, Gregor McLennan, and Stuart Hall. 1977. "Politics and Ideology: Gramsci." *Working Papers in Cultural Studies* 10:45–76.

Luperini, Romano. 1971. *Gli intellettuali di sinistra e l'ideologia della ricostruzione nel dopoguerra*. Rome: Edizioni di Ideologie.

Lussana, Fiamma. 1997. "L'edizione critica, le traduzioni e la diffusione di Gramsci nel mondo." *Studi Storici* 38 (4): 1051–1086.

Lu Xun. 1980. *Selected Works*. 4 vols. Translated by Yang Xianyi and Gladys Yang. Beijing: Foreign Languages Press.

Macciocchi, Maria Antonietta. 1974. *Per Gramsci*. Bologna: Il Mulino.

Macherey, Pierre. 2011. *Hegel or Spinoza*. Translated by Susan M. Ruddick. Minneapolis: University of Minnesota Press.

Machiavelli, Niccolò. 1961. *The Prince*. Translated by George Bull. London: Penguin.

Magna, Nino. 1978. "Per una storia dell'operaismo in Italia. Il trentennio postbellico." In *Operaismo e centralità operaia*, edited by Fabrizio D'Agostini, 295–345. Rome: Editori Riuniti.

Mahdi, 'Amil (Hassem Hamdan). 1996. *L'État confessionnel: Le cas libanaise*. Montreuil, France: La Bréche.

Maine, Henry Sumner. (1861) 1986. *Ancient Law: Its Connection with the Early History of Society and its Relation to Modern Ideas*. Dorchester, UK: Dorset Press.

Manduchi, Patrizia. 2017. "Intellettuali, società civile, egemonia nel mondo arabo: La lezione di Gramsci." In *Gramsci nel mondo arabo*, edited by Patrizia Manduchi, Alessandra Marchi, and Giuseppe Vacca, 23–47. Bologna: Il Mulino.

Mao Zedong. (1940) 1965. "On New Democracy." In *Selected Works*, vol. 2, 339–384. Beijing: Foreign Languages Press.

Marchi, Alessandra. 2017. "Nuove letture gramsciane del mondo arabo: Continuità ed evoluzione del pensiero critico." In *Gramsci nel mondo arabo*, edited by Patrizia Manduchi, Alessandra Marchi, and Giuseppe Vacca, 49–70. Bologna: Il Mulino.

Mariátegui, José Carlos. 1926. "Presentación de *Amauta*." *Amauta* I (I): I.

Mariátegui, José Carlos. 1928. "Aniversario y balance." *Amauta* 3 (17): 2–3.

Mariátegui, José Carlos. 1971. *Seven Interpretative Essays on Peruvian Reality*. Translated by M. Urquidi. Austin: University of Texas Press.

Mariátegui, José Carlos. 2011. *An Anthology*. Edited by Harry E. Vanden and Marc Becker. New York: Monthly Review Press.

Marks, Louis. 1957. *The Modern Prince and Other Writings*. New York, London: Lawrence and Wishart.

Marongiu Pietro, ed. 2004. *Criminalità e banditismo in Sardegna: Fra tradizione e innovazione*. Rome: Carocci.

Marx, Karl. 1977. *Capital: A Critique of Political Economy*. 3 vols. Translated by Ben Fowkes. New York: Penguin.

Marx, Karl, and Friedrich Engels. 1976. *Collected Works*. 50 vols. Edited by Jack Cohen. London: Lawrence and Wishart.

Marx, Karl, and Friedrich Engels. 1978. *The Marx-Engels Reader*. Edited by Robert C. Tucker. New York: Norton.

Massardo, Jaime. 1999. "Gramsci in America Latina: Questioni di ordine teorico e politico." In *Gramsci e la rivoluzione in Occidente*, edited by Alberto Burgio, and Antonio A. Santucci, 324–355. Rome: Editori Riuniti.

Matteucci, Nicola. 1951. *Antonio Gramsci e la filosofia della prassi*. Milan: Giuffré.

Maxwell, William J. 1999. *New Negro, Old Left: African-American Writing and Communism between the Wars*. New York: Columbia University Press.

McKay, Claude. 1979. *The Negroes in America*. Translated by Robert J. Winter. Port Washington, NY: Kennikat Press.

Merleau-Ponty, Maurice. 1955. *Les aventures de la dialetique*. Paris: Gallimard.

Mignolo, Walter. 2012. "Mariátegui and Gramsci in 'Latin' America: Between Revolution and Decoloniality." In *The Postcolonial Gramsci*, edited by Neelam Francesca Rashmi Srivastava and Baidik Bhattacharya, 191–217. New York: Routledge.

Moe, Nelson. 2011. "Production and Its Others: Gramsci's 'Sexual Question.'" In *Rethinking Gramsci*, edited by Marcus E. Green, 131–146. London: Taylor and Francis.

Moffatt, Michael. 1979. *An Untouchable Community in South India: Structure and Consensus*. Princeton, NJ: Princeton University Press.

Mommsen, Wolfgang J. 1989. *The Political and Social Theory of Max Weber*. London: Polity Press.

Monasta, Attilio. 2002. "Antonio Gramsci: The Message and the Images." In *Gramsci and Education*, edited by Carmel Borg, Joseph Buttigieg, and Peter Mayo, 67–85. Lanham, MD: Rowman and Littlefield.

Mordenti, Raul. 2011. *Gramsci e la rivoluzione necessaria*. Rome: Editori Riuniti University Press.

Morfino, Vittorio. 2002. *Il tempo e l'occasione: L'incontro Spinoza-Machiavelli*. Milan: LED Edizioni Universitarie.

Morfino, Vittorio. 2009. *Spinoza e il non contemporaneo*. Verona: Ombre Corte.

Mossner, Ernest Campbell. 1980. *The Life of David Hume*. Oxford: Oxford University Press.

Morfino, Vittorio, and Peter D. Thomas, eds. 2018. *The Government of Time*. Chicago: Haymarket.

Murray, C. S. 2000. *Boogie Man: The Adventures of John Lee Hooker in the American Twentieth Century*. New York: St. Martin's.

Mussolini, Benito. (1924) 1979. "Preludio al Machiavelli." In *Scritti politici*, edited by Enzo Santarelli. Milan: Feltrinelli.

Negri, Antonio. 1999. *Insurgencies: Constituent Power and the Modern State*. Translated by Maurizia Boscagli. Minneapolis: University of Minnesota Press.

Negri, Antonio. 2009. "The Italian Difference." *Cosmos and History* 5 (1): 8–12.

O'Lincoln, Tom. 1990. "A South American Revolutionary: José Carlos Mariátegui and Peruvian Socialism." Marxists Internet Archive. http://www.marxists.org/archive/mariateg/biography/biography.htm.

Pace, Enzo, ed. 2013. *Le Religioni nell'Italia che cambia: Mappe e bussole*. Rome: Carocci.

Paggi, Leonardo. 1969. "Machiavelli e Gramsci." *Studi Storici* 10 (4): 833–876.

Paggi, Leonardo. 1970. *Antonio Gramsci e il moderno principe*. Rome: Editori Riuniti.

Paggi, Leonardo. 1984. *Le strategie del potere in Gramsci: Tra fascismo e socialismo in un solo paese, 1923-1926*. Rome: Editori Riuniti.

Paris, Robert. 1979. "Gramsci en France." *Revue française de science politique* 1:5–18.

Pasolini, Pier Paolo. 1963. *Le ceneri di Gramsci: Poemetti*. Milan: Garzanti.

Pasolini, Pier Paolo. 1999. "Scritti corsari." In *Saggi sulla politica e la società*, 267–540. Milan: Mondadori.

Pearson, Barry Lee. 2005. *Book Right On: Blues Stories and Blues Storytellers*. Knoxville: University of Tennessee Press.

Phillipson, Nicholas. 1981. "The Scottish Enlightenment." In *The Enlightenment in National Context*, edited by Roy Porter and Mikuláš Teich, 19–40. Cambridge: Cambridge University Press.

Phillipson, Nicholas. 2010. *Adam Smith: An Enlightened Life*. New Haven, CT: Yale University Press.

Pigliaru, Antonio. (1959) 1975. *Il banditismo in Sardegna: La vendetta barbaricina come ordinamento giuridico*. Milan: Giuffrè.

Pignotti, Franco. 2013. "Dai movimenti profectico-religiosi alle Chiese Indipendenti Africane tra le popolazioni dello Zambesi." *Cultura e Prospettive* 20:63–86.

Piotte, Jean-Marc. 1970. *La pénsee politique de Gramsci*. Paris: Anthropos.

Pitt-Rivers, George Henry Lane. 1927. *The Clash of Cultures and the Contact of Races*. London: Routledge.

Pons, Silvio. 2004. "L'*Affare Gramsci-Togliatti* a Mosca (1938–1941)." *Studi Storici* 45 (1): 83–117.

Portantiero, Juan Carlos. 1980. "Gramsci para latinoamericanos." In *Gramsci y la política*, edited by Carlos Sirvent, 29–51. Mexico City: UNAM.

Portantiero, Juan Carlos. 1981. *Los usos de Gramsci*. Mexico City: Folios.

Prada, Raúl. 2010. "Umbrales y horizontes de la descolonización." In *El Estado: Campo de lucha*, edited by Alvaro García Linera, Raúl Prada, Luis Tapia, and Oscar Vega Camacho, 43–96. La Paz: Muela de Diablo and CLASCO.

Qu Qiubai. 1985. "Lu Xun zagan xuan ji xuyan" [Preface to *A Selection of Lu Xun's Essays*]. In *Qu Qiubai wenji: Wenxuebian* [Selected works of Qu Qiubai: Literature], vol. 3, 95–123. Beijing: Renmin wenxue.

Qu Qiubai. 1989. "Zhongguo geming zhong zhi zhengyi wenti" [The Polemical issues in the Chinese revolution, 1927]. *Qu Qiubai wenji: Zhengzhi lilun bian* [Selected works of Qu Qiubai: Volumes in political theory], vol. 4, 434–559. Beijing: Renmin.

Riechers, Christian. 1970. *Antonio Gramsci: Marxismus in Italien*. Frankfurt am Main: Europäische Verlagsanst alt.

Robinson, Cedric J. 1983. *Black Marxism: The Making of the Black Radical Tradition*. Chapel Hill: University of North Carolina Press.

Rosengarten, Frank. 1986. "Gramsci"s "Little Discovery": Gramsci"s Interpretation of Canto X of Dante's *Inferno*." *boundary 2* 14 (3): 71–90.

Rossi, Angelo, and Giuseppe Vacca. 2007. *Gramsci tra Mussolini e Stalin*. Rome: Fazi.

Rothschild, Emma. 2001. *Economic Sentiments: Adam Smith, Condorcet and the Enlightenment*. Cambridge, MA: Harvard University Press.

Russo, Luigi. 1931. *Prolegomeni a Machiavelli*. Florence: Le Monnier.

Ruzzu, Antonello. 1999. *La casacca del re: Archivio penale e strategie di potere nella Sardegna contadina e pastorale di fine Ottocento fra Stato di diritto e Stato sociale*. Milan: Mondadori.

Said, Edward W. 1979. *Orientalism*. New York: Vintage Books.

Salinari, Carlo, and Mario Spinella, eds. 1977. *Il pensiero di Gramsci*. Rome: Editori Riuniti.

Santucci, Antonio A. 2001. *Senza comunismo: Labriola, Gramsci, Marx*. Rome: Editori Riuniti.

Santucci, Antonio A. 2010. *Antonio Gramsci*. Translated by Graziella Dimauro and Salvatore Engel-Dimauro. New York: Monthly Review Press.

Sartorello, Luca. 2009. *Machiavelli nella storiografia post-risorgimentale: Tra metodo storico e usi politici*. Padua: CLEUP.

Sassoon, Anne Showstack. 1987. *Gramsci"s Politics*. Minneapolis: University of Minnesota Press.

Secco, Lincoln. 2002. *Gramsci e o Brasil*. São Paulo: Iluminuras.

Shanin, Theodore. 1983. *Late Marx and the Russian Road: Marx and the Peripheries of Capitalism*. New York: Monthly Review Press.

Sharabi, Hisham. 1970. *Arab Intellectuals and the West*. Baltimore: Johns Hopkins Press.

Siciliano, Enzo. 2005. *Vita di Pasolini*. Milan: Mondadori.

Singer, André. 2012. *Os sentidos do Lulismo*. São Paulo: Cia das Letras.

Smith, Adam. 1976. *An Inquiry into the Nature and Causes of the Wealth of Nations*. Edited by R. H. Campbell and A. S. Skinner. Oxford: Clarendon Press.

Soriano, Marc. 1993. "In Francia con Gramsci." *Belfagor: Ressegna di Varia Umanità* 48:465–474.

Spinoza, Benedict de. 1951. *A Theologico-Political Treatise and a Political Treatise*. Translated by R. H. M. Elwes. New York: Dover.

Spinoza, Benedict de. 2000. *Ethics*. Edited by G. H. R. Parkinson. Oxford: Oxford University Press.

Spriano, Paolo. 1965. *Gramsci e l'Ordine Nuovo*. Rome: Editori Riuniti.

Spriano, Paolo. 1977. *Gramsci e Gobetti: Introduzione alla vita e alle opere*. Vol. 298. Turin: Einaudi.

Spriano, Paolo, Carlo Ricchini, and Luisa Melograni. 1988. *Gramsci in carcere e il partito*. Rome: L'Unità.

Stewart, Dugald. (1794) 1980. "Account of the Life and Writings of Adam Smith." In *Adam Smith: Essays on Philosophical Subjects*, edited by W. P. D. Wightman and J. C. Bryce, 269–351. Oxford: Clarendon Press.

Texier, Jacques. 1966. *Gramsci: Présentation, choix de texts, biographie, bibliographie*. Paris: Seghers.

Texier, Jacques. 2014. "Gramsci, the Theoretician of Superstructures: On the Concept of Civil Society." In *Gramsci and Marxist Theory*, edited by Chantal Mouffe, 48–79. New York: Routledge.

Thomas, Peter D. 2009. *The Gramscian Moment: Philosophy, Hegemony and Marxism*. Leiden: Brill.

Thomas, Peter D. 2012. "Conjunctures of the Integral State? Poulantzas's Reading of Gramsci." In *Reading Poulantzas*, edited by Alexander Gallas, 277–292. London: Merlin Press.

Thomas, Peter D. 2018. "Gramsci's Plural Temporalities." In *The Government of Time*, edited by Vittorio Morfino and Peter D. Thomas, 185–187. Chicago: Haymarket.

Thomson, George Derwent. 1957. "Gramsci, the First Italian Marxist." *Marxism Today* 1:61–62.

Togliatti, Palmiro. 1967. *Gramsci*. Rome: Editori Riuniti.

Togliatti, Palmiro. 2014. *La politica nel pensiero e nell'azione: Scritti e discorsi 1917–1964*. Edited by Michele Ciliberto and Giuseppe Vacca. Milan: Bompiani.

Tomba, Massimiliano. 2013. *Marx's Temporalities*. Translated by Peter D. Thomas and Sara R. Ferris. Leiden: Brill.

Tosel, André. 1995. "I malintesi dell'egemonia. Gramsci in Francia (1965–1989)." In *Gramsci nel mondo: Atti del convegno internazionale di studi gramsciani. Formia, 25-28 ottobre 1989*, edited by Maria Luisa Righi, 55–60. Rome: Fondazione Istituto Gramsci.

Tōyama Shigeki 2018. *Meiji ishin* (The Meiji Restoration). Tokyo: Iwanami bunko.

Tronti, Mario. 1969. "Alcune questioni intorno al marxismo di Gramsci." In *Studi Gramsciani: Atti del convegno tenuto a Roma nei giorni 11-13 gennaio 1958*, edited by Istituto Antonio Gramsci, 305–321. Rome: Editori Riuniti.

Tronti, Mario. 1976. "Tra materialismo storico e filosofia della prassi: Gramsci e Labriola." In *La città futura: Saggi sulla figura e il pensiero di Antonio Gramsci*, edited by Alberto Caracciolo and Gianni Scalia, 71–91. Milan: Feltrinelli.

Vacca, Giuseppe. 1972. "Politica e teoria del marxismo italiano negli anni sessanta." In *Il marxismo italiano degli anni sessanta e la formazione teorica delle nuove generazioni*, edited by Fondazione Istituto Gramsci, 71–157. Rome: Editori Riuniti.

Vacca, Giuseppe. 1990. "La politica di unità nazionale dei comunisti (1945–1949)." *Studi Storici* 31 (1): 9–25.

Vacca, Giuseppe. 1993. "l'interpretazione di Gramsci nel secondo dopoguerra." *Studi Storici* 34 (2–3): 443–462.

Vacca, Giuseppe. 2012. *Vita e pensieri di Antonio Gramsci 1926–1937*. Turin: Einaudi.

Viroli, Maurizio. 2010. *Machiavelli's God*. Translated by Antony Shugaar. Princeton, NJ: Princeton University Press.

Viroli, Maurizio. 2014. *Redeeming "The Prince": The Meaning of Machiavelli's Masterpiece*. Princeton, NJ: Princeton University Press.

Voza, Pasquale. 2004. "Rivoluzione passiva." In *Le parole di Gramsci: Per un lessico dei "Quaderni del carcere*," edited by Fabio Frosini and Guido Liguori, 189–207. Rome: Carocci.

Wainwright, Joel. 2013. "On the Nature of Gramsci's Conceptions of the World." In *Gramsci: Space, Nature, Politics*, edited by Michael Ekers, Gillian Hart, Stephan Kipfer and Alex Loftus, 161–177. Malden, MA: Wiley-Blackwell.

Waite, Geoff. 1996. *Nietzsche's Corps/e: Aesthetics, Politics, Prophecy, or the Spectacular Technoculture of Everyday Life*. Durham, NC: Duke University Press.

Walker, Gavin. 2016. *The Sublime Perversion of Capital: Marxist Theory and the Politics of Modern Japan*. Durham, NC: Duke University Press.

Walsh, Catherine E. 2008. "(Post)Coloniality in Ecuador: The Indigenous Movement's Practices and Politics of (Re)Signification and Decolonization." In *Coloniality at Large: Latin America and the Postcolonial Debate*, edited by Mabel Moraña, Enrique Dussel, and Carlos Jáuregui, 506–518. Durham, NC: Duke University Press.

Walsh, Catherine E. 2010. "Development as Buen Vivir: Institutional Arrangements and (De)colonial Entanglements." *Development* 53 (1): 15–21.

Walsh, Catherine E. 2015. "Life and Nature 'Otherwise': Challenges from the Abya-Yalean Andes." In *The Anomie of the Earth: Philosophy, Politics, and Autonomy in Europe and the Americas*, edited by Federico Luisetti, John Pickles, and Wilson Kaiser, 93–118. Durham, NC: Duke University Press.

Wang Hui. 2000. *Si huo chongwen* [A dead fire rekindled]. Beijing: Renmin wenxue.

Weber, Max. 1994. *Political Writings*. Edited by Peter Lassman and Ronald Speirs. Cambridge: Cambridge University Press.

Wenzel, Gisela. 1995. "Sulle tracce di Gramsci nella RFT." In *Gramsci nel mondo: Atti del Convegno internazionale di studi gramsciani, Formia, 25–28 ottobre 1989*, edited by Maria Luisa Righi, 87–95. Rome: Fondazione Istituto Gramsci.

White, Jonathan, and Lea Ypi. 2010. "Rethinking the Modern Prince: Partisanship and the Democratic Ethos." *Political Studies* 58:809–828.

Williams, Raymond. 1972. "Lucien Goldmann and Marxism's Alternative Tradition." *The Listener* 87:375–376.

Williams, Raymond. 1977. *Marxism and Literature*. Oxford: Oxford University Press.

Williams, Raymond. 1989. *Resources of Hope: Culture, Democracy, Socialism*. London: Verso.

Wood, Paul. 2003. "Science in the Scottish Enlightenment." In *The Cambridge Companion to the Scottish Enlightenment*, edited by Alexander Broadie, 94–116. Cambridge: Cambridge University Press.

Wright, Steve. 2002. *Storming Heaven: Class Composition and Struggle in Italian Autonomist Marxism*. London: Pluto Press.

Young, Alan. 1997. *Woke Me Up This Morning: Black Gospel Singers and the Gospel Life*. Jackson: University Press of Mississippi.

Zapata Olivella, Manuel. 2010. *Changó, the Biggest Badass*. Translated by Jonathan Tittler. Lubbock: Texas Tech University Press.

Zene, Cosimo. 2013. "Subalterns and Dalits in Gramsci and Ambedkar: Prologue to a 'Posthumous' Dialogue." In *The Political Philosophies of Antonio Gramsci and B. R. Ambedkar: Itineraries of Dalits and Subalterns*, edited by Cosimo Zene, 1–32. London: Routledge.

Zene, Cosimo. 2016. "Inner Life, Politics, and the Secular: Is There a 'Spirituality' of Subalterns and Dalits? Notes on Gramsci and Ambedkar." *Rethinking Marxism* 28 (3–4): 540–562.

Zene, Cosimo. 2018. "Justice for the Excluded and Education for Democracy in B. R. Ambedkar and A. Gramsci." *Rethinking Marxism* 30 (4): 494–524.

Zghal 'Abd al-Qader. 1991. "Mafhūm al-mujtama' al-madanī wa al-taḥawwul naḥwà al-ta'addudiyya al-ḥizbiyya" [The concept of civil society and the transition to multiparty system]. In *Qadāyā al-mujtama' al-madānī al-'arabī fī daw' utrūhat Ghrāmshī*, edited by Amina Rashid, 136–163. Cairo: Center for Arab Studies.

Alberto Burgio is professor of history of philosophy at the University of Bologna. His publications on Gramsci include *Gramsci storico* (2003), *Per Gramsci: Crisi e potenza del moderno* (2007), *Gramsci: Il sistema in movimento* (2014), and "On the Transition to Communism," in *A Companion to Antonio Gramsci: Essays on History and Theories of History, Politics and Historiography*, edited by Davide Cadeddu (2020).

Cesare Casarino is professor of cultural studies and comparative literature at the University of Minnesota. He is the author of *Modernity at Sea: Melville, Marx, Conrad in Crisis* (2002), coauthor of *In Praise of the Common: A Conversation on Philosophy and Politics* (2008) with Antonio Negri, coeditor of *Marxism beyond Marxism* (1996) with Saree Makdisi and Rebecca Karl, and cotranslator with Vincenzo Binetti of Giorgio Agamben's *Means without End* (2000). His essays on literature, cinema, and philosophy have appeared in *boundary 2, October, Raritan, Strategies, Paragraph, Social Text*, and *Arizona Quarterly*.

Maria Elisa Cevasco is professor of cultural studies and literature in English at the Universidade de São Paulo. She has published several articles and books in Brazil and abroad, including *Para ler Raymond Williams* (2001) and the coedited *O espírito de Porto Alegre* (2003).

Kate Crehan is professor emerita, College of Staten Island and the Graduate Center, City University of New York. Her publications include *The Fractured Community: Landscapes of Power and Gender in Rural Zambia* (1997), *Gramsci, Culture and Anthropology* (2002), *Community Art: An Anthropological Perspective* (2011), and *Gramsci's Common Sense: Inequality and Its Narratives* (Duke University Press, 2016).

Roberto Dainotto is professor of Italian and literature at Duke University, where he teaches courses on modern and contemporary Italian culture. His publications include *Place in Literature: Regions, Cultures, Communities* (2000), *Europe (in Theory)* (Duke University Press, 2007, winner of the 2010 Shannon Prize in Contemporary European Studies), and *Mafia: A Cultural History* (2015). He has also edited *Racconti Americani del '900* (1999) and a monographic issue of *Italian Culture* on Giambattista Vico (2017).

Michael Denning is William R. Kenan Jr. Professor of American Studies and English at Yale University. He is the author of *Mechanic Accents: Dime Novels and Working-Class Culture in America* (1987), *Cover Stories: Narrative and Ideology in the British Spy Thriller* (1987), and *The Cultural Front: The Laboring of American Culture in the Twentieth Century* (1997).

Harry Harootunian is an American historian of early modern and modern Japan with an interest in historical theory. He is professor emeritus of East Asian studies, New York University, and Max Palevsky Professor of History and Civilizations, Emeritus, University of Chicago. His publications include *Marx after Marx: History and Time in the Expansion of Capitalism* (2015), *History's Disquiet: Modernity, Cultural Practice and the Question of the Everyday Life* (2000), *Overcome by Modernity: History, Culture and Commodity in Interwar Japan* (2010), and *Uneven Moments: Reflections on Japan's Modern History* (2019).

Fredric Jameson is Distinguished Professor of Comparative Literature at Duke University. The author of numerous books, he has, over the last three decades, developed a richly nuanced vision of Western culture's relation to political economy. He was a recipient of the 2008 Holberg International Memorial Prize. Among his publications are *Postmodernism: Or, The Cultural Logic of Late Capitalism; The Cultural Turn; A Singular Modernity; The Modernist Papers; Archaeologies of the Future; Brecht and Method; Ideologies of Theory; Valences of the Dialectic; The Hegel Variations;* and *Representing Capital*.

R. A. Judy is professor of critical and cultural studies in the Department of English at the University of Pittsburgh and a member of the editorial collective of *boundary 2, an international journal of literature and culture*. Professor Judy is the author of *(Dis)forming the American Canon: The Vernacular of African Arabic American Slave Narrative* (1992) and has edited numerous special issues and dossiers for *boundary 2*, including *Tunisia Dossier* (2012), *Ralph Ellison: The Next Fifty Years* (2003), *Sociology Hesitant: W. E. B. Du Bois's Dynamic Thinking* (2001), *Reasoning and the Logic of Things Global* (1999), and *Scattered Speculations on Value: Exchange between Etienne Balibar, Antonio Negri, and Gayatri Spivak* (1999).

Patrizia Manduchi is professor of history of Islamic countries at the University of Cagliari. She is the president of GramsciLab, the Interdepartmental Centre for International Gramscian Studies. Her publications, which include several contributions on both Gramsci and Islamic politics, include *Università e movimenti studenteschi nell'Egitto* *contemporaneo (1908-1981)* (2015), *Questo mondo non è un luogo per ricompense: Vita e opere di Sayyid Qutb, martire dei Fratelli Musulmani* (2009), and the coedited volumes *Gramsci in Asia e in Africa* (2010), *Gramsci nel mondo arabo* (2017), and *A lezione da Gramsci: Democrazia, partecipazione politica, società civile in Tunisia* (2019).

Andrea Scapolo is assistant professor of Italian at Kennesaw State University. His work on Gramsci in the cultural production of the Italian youth movements has been published in *Annali d'italianistica* and *Italica*.

Peter D. Thomas is a historian of political thought, philosophy, and a political theory at Brunel University. He has previously studied and worked at the Universities of Queensland, Naples, Berlin, and Amsterdam. He has published widely on Marxist political theory and philosophy, the history of political thought, and the history of philosophy, and is an editor of the journal *Historical Materialism: Research in Critical Marxist Theory* and author of *The Gramscian Moment*, winner of the Premio internazionale Giuseppe Sormani 2011, awarded by the Fondazione Istituto Piemontese Antonio Gramsci in Turin for the best book or article on Gramsci in the period 2007 to 2011 internationally.

Catherine E. Walsh is a senior professor and director of the Latin American Cultural Studies Doctoral Program at the Universidad Andina Simon Bolivar in Quito, Ecuador, where she also coordinates the Afro-Andean Collective Memory Archive. She has been an invited professor and lecturer all around the world. Her recent publications include *On Decoloniality: Concepts, Analytics, Praxis*, cowritten with Walter D. Mignolo (Duke University Press, 2018), *Entretejiendo lo pedagógico y lo decolonial: Luchas, caminos y siembras de reflexión-acción para resistir, (re)existir y (re)vivir* (2018), "Lewis Gordon: Existential Incantations that Cross Borders and Move Us Forward," in *Black Existentialism: Essays on the Transformative Thought of Lewis R. Gordon* (2019), and "Decolonial Notes to Paulo Freire Walking and Asking," in *Educational Alternatives in Latin America: New Modes of Counter Hegemonic Learning* (2019).

Pu Wang is assistant professor of Chinese and the Helaine and Alvin Allen Chair in Literature at Brandeis University. Having produced a book, two conference seminars, and a number of articles, the major component of his research of the past few years focuses on translation, revolution, and historical imagination in modern Chinese culture. His book *The Translatability of Revolution: Guo Moruo and Twentieth-Century Chinese Culture* (2018) is the first comprehensive study in English of the lifework of Guo Moruo (1892-1978), a towering—and highly controversial—figure of China's revolutionary century who worked as a Romantic writer, Marxist historian, and prolific translator.

Cosimo Zene is professor emeritus of religions and world philosophies at the School of Oriental and African Studies in London. Since his historical-anthropological research among a group of Dalits in Bengal and Bangladesh, Zene has published extensively on Dalit religions and on the ways Gramsci's thought can establish meaningful associations with the thought of the Dalit leader B. R. Ambedkar in highlighting the Dalits' human, social, and religious experiences. On Gramsci and Dalit thought, he has published several essays in the *International Gramsci Journal, felsefelogos, Rethinking Marxism: A Journal of Economics, Culture and Society*, and *LARES—Quadrimestrale di Studi Demoetnoantropologici*, and edited the volume *The Political Philosophies of Antonio Gramsci and B. R. Ambedkar* (2013).